Generative AI
for Effective
Software
Development

Anh Nguyen-Duc • Pekka Abrahamsson •
Foutse Khomh
Editors

Generative AI
for Effective
Software
Development

 Springer

Editors
Anh Nguyen-Duc (iD)
Department of Business and IT
University of South-Eastern Norway
Bø I Telemark, Norway

Pekka Abrahamsson
Tampere University
Tampere, Finland

Foutse Khomh
Polytechnique Montréal
Montréal, QC, Canada

ISBN 978-3-031-55641-8   ISBN 978-3-031-55642-5   (eBook)
https://doi.org/10.1007/978-3-031-55642-5

This Springer imprint is published by the registered company Springer Nature Switzerland AG
The registered company address is: Gewerbestrasse 11, 6330 Cham, Switzerland

If disposing of this product, please recycle the paper.

Preface

1 The Rise of Generative AI in Software Engineering

This era marks a significant advancement and application of generative artificial intelligence (Generative AI). At the time of writing this section (December 2023), the significance of Generative AI is unquestionable with a prevailing consensus that the technology will bring about a transformative effect across all sectors of society and industry. Generative AI is most referred to as a technology that (i) leverages deep learning models to (ii) generate humanlike content (e.g., images, words) in response to (iii) complex and varied prompts (e.g., languages, instructions, questions). A McKinsey report highlights the immense potential of Generative AI, estimating its capability to add a value of $2.6 to $4.4 trillion across diverse industries. Its impact on software engineering productivity alone could lead to a 20–45% reduction in current annual spending, primarily by streamlining activities such as drafting initial code, code correction, refactoring, root-cause analysis, and system design generation.

Generative AI tools are increasingly becoming a staple in software development, aiding in both managerial and technical project facets. Prominent models like Meta's LLaMA, OpenAI's ChatGPT, GitHub Copilot, and Amazon CodeWhisperer are reshaping traditional concerns about productivity and quality in technology adoption. These tools, with their advanced code generation capabilities and AI-assisted environments, are transforming the software development process by automating routine tasks, enhancing code, and even writing significant code segments. Beyond coding, generative AI aids in areas like requirements engineering and project management. However, generative AI isn't just about task automation; it signifies a fundamental shift in problem-solving within software development. This paradigm shift transcends process automation, redefining human roles, teamwork dynamics, and decision-making in software development. Software developers are transitioning from code-centric roles to AI collaborators, focusing on high-level architecture, setting AI goals, and interpreting AI-generated solutions. This shift enables developers to concentrate on more complex, creative aspects, fostering an interdisciplinary approach with teams comprising domain experts, data scientists, and ethicists to maximize generative AI's potential.

2   Vision of Generative AI in Future Software Development

The advanced machine learning that powers generative AI-enabled products has been decades in the making. But since ChatGPT came off the starting block in late 2022, new iterations of generative AI technology have been released several times a month. In March 2023 alone, there were six major steps forward, introducing significant improvement for software engineering-related innovation.

The future of software engineering holds exciting promises with the integration of generative AI. As technology continues to advance, AI-driven systems are poised to revolutionize the way software is designed, developed, and maintained. One of the most compelling visions is the concept of collaboration between AI agents and software engineers. In this vision, generative AI will work alongside human developers, assisting them in various aspects of the software development lifecycle. These AI collaborators will have the capability to understand natural language requirements, generate code based on high-level descriptions, and even help in debugging and optimizing code. This collaborative partnership between human developers and AI is expected to significantly accelerate the software development process, reduce errors, and open up new possibilities for innovation.

Another key aspect of the future of software engineering is the potential for AI to automate routine and time-consuming tasks. Generative AI models can generate code snippets, templates, and even entire modules based on patterns and best practices learned from vast repositories of code. This automation will allow developers to focus on more creative and complex aspects of software development, such as requirement elicitation, crafting user-centric interfaces, high-level architectural decisions, and ethical considerations and compliance. In 2022, GitHub reported on the impact of Copilot on developer productivity and happiness. Eighty-eight percent of survey respondents replied that they feel more productive with Copilot. Moreover, 74% say they are faster with repetitive tasks and can focus on more satisfying work. We envision that the positive impact of tools like Copilot will expand, benefiting various types of projects and adapting to diverse organizational environments.

Furthermore, generative AI in software engineering will enable the creation of highly personalized and adaptive software systems. These AI-driven applications will be capable of learning from user interactions and preferences, continuously evolving to meet the changing needs of their users. For instance, in the realm of user interface design, AI can generate user interfaces that are tailored to individual preferences and accessibility requirements. This level of personalization will lead to more engaging and user-friendly software experiences, ultimately enhancing user satisfaction and the overall quality of software products. In essence, the future of software engineering with generative AI holds the promise of increased productivity, improved software quality, and the creation of highly customized and adaptive software solutions.

Another significant impact of generative AI in software engineering will be in the realm of personalized software solutions. AI will enable the creation of highly customized software that can adapt to the specific needs and preferences of individual users or businesses. This will be made possible by AI's ability to learn from user interactions and evolve over time. The software will become more intuitive and user-friendly, as it will be able to anticipate user needs and offer solutions proactively. This level of personalization will not only enhance user experience but also open up new avenues for innovation in software design and functionality.

To provide a complete perspective, it's essential to acknowledge the existing challenges of generative AI technologies, which currently stand as key areas of focus for research and development among software engineering scholars and professionals. In general, large language models (LLMs) are still easy to produce hallucination, misleading, inconsistent, or unverifiable information. Models built on top of historically biased data pose problems of fairness and trustworthiness, and when incidents happen, issues about safety and responsibility can arise. LLMs may fall short of mastering generation tasks that require domain-specific knowledge or generating structured data. It is nontrivial to inject specialized knowledge into LLMs. Techniques like prompting, augmenting, fine-tuning, and the use of smaller AI models present potential solutions, yet applying them to specific problems is nontrivial. For software engineering tasks, the current evaluation of generative AI focuses more on code generation tasks, with less emphasis on evaluating or researching other tasks such as requirement generation, code fixes, and vulnerability repair. It is anticipated that exploring these areas will be a significant and influential line of research for the software engineering community.

Finally, generative AI will also play a crucial role in democratizing software development. With AI-assisted coding, individuals who may not have formal training in programming will be able to create and modify software. This will break down barriers to entry in the field of software development and foster a more inclusive and diverse community of software creators. It will empower a wider range of people to bring their unique ideas to life, leading to a more vibrant and innovative software landscape. This democratization will not only spur creativity but also lead to the development of solutions that cater to a broader spectrum of needs and challenges in various industries.

3 Purpose of the Book

The purpose of this book—Generative AI for Effective Software Development—is to provide a comprehensive, empirically grounded exploration of how generative AI is reshaping the landscape of software development across diverse environments and geographies. This book emphasizes the empirical evaluation of generative AI tools in real-world scenarios, offering insights into their practical efficacy, limitations, and impact on various aspects of software engineering. It focuses on the human aspect, examining how generative AI influences the roles, collaborations, and decision-making processes of developers from different countries and cultures. By presenting case studies, surveys, and interviews from various software development contexts, the book aims to offer a global perspective on the integration of generative AI, highlighting how these advanced tools are adapted to and influence diverse cultural, organizational, and technological environments. This multifaceted approach not only showcases the technological advancements in generative AI but also deeply considers the human element, ensuring that the narrative remains grounded in the practical realities of software developers worldwide. While generative AI technologies encompass a wide range of data types, our cases focus mainly on LLMs with text and code generation. The evaluation is done with current models, such as Llama 2 or ChatGPT-4, acknowledging the current limitations associated with them.

4   Structure and Topics

This book is structured to provide a comprehensive understanding of generative AI and its transformative impact on the field of software engineering. The book is divided into four main parts, each focusing on different aspects of generative AI in software development. Below is a detailed outline of the book's structure and the topics covered in each section.

Part I presents the fundamentals of generative AI adoption. The introductory chapter offers a brief overview of generative AI and its growing relevance in the field of software engineering. It also provides a roadmap of the book's structure and chapters.

Part II is a collection of empirical studies on patterns and tools for the adoption of generative AI in software engineering. This section delves into the practical aspects of integrating generative AI tools in software engineering, with a focus on patterns, methodologies, and comparative analyses. In this part, Dae-Kyoo Kim presents a comparative analysis of ChatGPT and Bard, highlighting their complementary strengths for effective utilization in software development (Chap. 2). Jorge Melegati and Eduardo Guerra introduce DAnTE, a taxonomy designed to categorize the automation degree of software engineering tasks (Chap. 3). Jules White and colleagues discuss ChatGPT prompt patterns for enhancing code quality, refactoring, requirements elicitation, and software design (Chap. 4). Krishna Ronanki and co-authors explore the use of generative AI in requirements engineering, focusing on prompts and prompting patterns (Chap. 5). Also on requirements engineering, Chetan Arora, John Grundy, and Mohamed Abdelrazek assess the role of large language models (LLMs) in advancing requirements engineering (Chap. 6).

Part III presents case studies that showcase the application and impact of generative AI in various software development contexts. Particularly, Arghavan Moradi Dakhel and colleagues provide a family of case studies on generative AI's application in code generation tasks (Chap. 7). Dang Nguyen Ngoc Hai et al. explore the CodeBERT approach for automatic program repair of security vulnerabilities (Chap. 8). Väinö Liukko and colleagues present a case study of ChatGPT as a full-stack Web developer (Chap. 9).

Part IV examines how generative AI is reshaping software engineering processes, from collaboration and workflow to management and agile development. To start with, Rasmus Ulfsnes and co-authors provide empirical insights on how generative AI is transforming collaboration and workflow in software development (Chap. 10). Beatriz Cabrero-Daniel, Yasamin Fazelidehkordi, and Ali Nouri discuss the enhancement of software management with generative AI (Chap. 11). Dron Khanna and Anh Nguyen Duc conduct a survey study on the value-based adoption of ChatGPT in Agile software development among Nordic software experts (Chap. 12). Guilherme Pereira and colleagues share early results from a study of generative AI adoption in a large Brazilian company, focusing on the case of Globo (Chap. 13).

Part V is about future directions and education. The final section of the book looks toward the future, exploring emerging trends, future directions, and the role of education in the context of generative AI. Shunichiro Tomura and Hoa Dam discuss generating explanations for AI-powered delay prediction in software projects (Chap. 14). Mohammad Idris Attal and team present a prompt book for turning a large language model into a start-up digital assistant (Chap. 15). Mika Saari and colleagues explore effective approaches to utilize AI tools in programming courses, guiding students in this new era of AI-assisted software development (Chap. 16).

5   What This Book Is and Isn't

This book is not a technical manual on how to code with generative AI tools. The book is also not about customizing or developing generative AI models but rather their application in software engineering. The book offers a strategic, managerial, and process-centric viewpoint, highlighting how generative AI can be a potentially in different software development activities, irrespective of the programming language, software technologies, or development framework.

While this book presents various empirical applications of generative AI in software development, it is not an exhaustive guide on all aspects of software engineering. It is, however, a crucial read for anyone interested in understanding how generative AI is revolutionizing software development and what it means for the future of this field.

The book offers diverse perspectives as it compiles research and experiences from various countries and software development environments, reflecting a global view of generative AI's impact. The book offers non-technical discussions about generative AI in management, teamwork, business, and education.

Advanced generative AI technologies with powerful capacities can come with severe risks to public safety, be it via misuse or accident; hence, safety-ensured mechanisms, i.e., enforcing safety and security standard for development and deployment of generative AI models, processes, and practices for developing responsible generative AI models, are relevant topics. These topics, however, fall outside the scope of this publication. Instead, our focus remains on the current state and capabilities of generative AI technologies, exploring their existing applications and immediate impacts. For a comprehensive understanding of the broader implications and future potential of these technologies, including safety and ethical considerations, readers may need to consult additional specialized resources.

6 Acknowledgments

This book would not have been possible without the massive collaborative effort of our reviewers, authors, and editors. The insights encapsulated within these pages are a product of the knowledge and experiences shared by many software engineering researchers and practitioners. Although the authors and editors are specifically acknowledged in each chapter or callout, we'd like to take time to recognize those who contributed to each chapter by providing thoughtful input, discussion, and review. We extend our gratitude to Khlood Ahmad, Christian Berger, Beatriz Cabero-Daniel, Ruzanna Chitchyan, John Grundy, Eduardo Guerra, Helena Holstrom Olsson, Zoe Hoy, Ronald Jabangwe, Marius Rohde Johannessen, Dron Khanna, Foutse Khomh, Dae-Kyoo Kim, Johan Linåker, Jorge Melegati, Anh Nguyen Duc, Amin Nikanjam, Dimitris Polychronopoulos, Tho Quan, Usman Rafiq, Viktoria Stray, Ingrid Sunbø, Rasmus Ulfsnes, Hironori Washizaki, and Jules White.

This book represents a collaborative effort that extends beyond the boundaries of any single institution or discipline. We are profoundly grateful to the numerous contributors whose expertise, insights, and unwavering dedication have been instrumental in bringing this project to fruition:

- Norwegian University of Science and Technology, Norway
- University of Oslo, Norway
- University of South Eastern, Norway
- SINTEF, Norway
- Chalmers University of Technology, Sweden
- University of Gothenburg, Sweden
- Volvo Cars, Sweden
- Solita Ltd., Finland
- Tampere University, Finland
- Free University of Bozen-Bolzano, Italy
- University of California Irvine, USA
- Vanderbilt University, USA

- Oakland University, USA
- Polytechnique Montreal, Canada
- Pontificia Universidade Catolica do Rio Grande do Sul, Brazil
- Globo, Brazil
- Deakin University, Australia
- Monash University, Australia
- University of Wollongong, Australia
- Waseda University, Japan
- Ho Chi Minh City University of Technology (HCMUT), VNU-HCM, Vietnam

Hanoi, Vietnam   Anh Nguyen-Duc
Tampere, Finland   Pekka Abrahamsson
Montreal, QC, Canada   Foutse Khomh
December 31, 2023

Contents

Part III   Generative AI in Software Development: Case Studies

Part IV   Generative AI in Software Engineering Processes

Part V   Future Directions and Education

Part I
Fundamentals of Generative AI

An Overview on Large Language Models

**Arghavan Moradi Dakhel, Amin Nikanjam, Foutse Khomh,
Michel C. Desmarais, and Hironori Washizaki**

Abstract Generative artificial intelligence (AI), propelled by the advancements in large language models (LLMs), has exhibited remarkable capabilities in various software engineering (SE) tasks and beyond. This development has influenced the research studies in this domain. This chapter offers an overview of LLMs, delving into relevant background concepts while exploring advanced techniques at the forefront of LLM research. We review various LLM architectures, in addition to discussing the concepts of training, fine-tuning, and in-context learning. We also discussed different adaptation approaches to LLMs and augmented LLMs. Furthermore, we delve into the evaluation of LLM research, introducing benchmark datasets and relevant tools in this context. The chapter concludes by exploring limitations in leveraging LLMs for SE tasks.

Keywords Generative AI · Large language models · Transformers · In-context learning

1 Introduction

Generative artificial intelligence (AI) represents a category of AI systems with the ability to create diverse content forms, including text, audio, image, and code [73]. Generative AI models are designed to grasp the patterns and structures present in their training dataset. After the training step, these models can generate new content that exhibits similar characteristics to their training data.

A. Moradi Dakhel (✉) · A. Nikanjam · F. Khomh · M. C. Desmarais
Polytechnique Montréal, Montréal, QC, Canada
e-mail: arghavan.moradi-dakhel@polymtl.ca; amin.nikanjam@polymtl.ca; foutse.khomh@polymtl.ca; michel.desmarais@polymtl.ca

H. Washizaki
Waseda University, Tokyo, Japan
e-mail: washizaki@waseda.jp

Large language models (LLMs), a subset of Generative AI, have demonstrated remarkable proficiency in tasks related to language comprehension and generation [64, 118]. Notably, transformer-based models such as GPT by OpenAI [9] and PaLM by Google [13] have showcased exceptional language generation capabilities. These models excel in various language-oriented tasks such as text generation [35], question answering [66], translation [9], summarization [94], and sentiment analysis [47]. Moreover, LLMs, such as OpenAI's Codex [12] and Meta's LLaMA-2 [87], are designed to automatically generate code in various programming languages through training on extensive open-source projects. These LLMs have been used to successfully generate code for multiple code-related tasks, including implementing specific functionalities [102], generating test cases [91], and fixing buggy code [105].

The exceptional performance of LLMs has sparked a growing interest in harnessing their potential within software engineering (SE), which is not limited to code-related tasks [114, 117]. Researchers have explored new opportunities to leverage LLMs in different phases of the SE life cycle, including software requirements and design (e.g., specifications generation [107] and requirements classification [76]), software development (e.g., code completion [15] and code search [53]), software testing (e.g., vulnerability detection [32] and fault localization [14]), and software maintenance (e.g., program repair [10] and code review [54]).

In this book chapter, we provide an overview of LLMs. We review transformer-based LLMs' architecture, popular LLMs, and various approaches for adapting LLMs, including pre-training, fine-tuning, in-context learning, and augmentation. Additionally, we delve into resource-efficient methods for adapting LLMs, discuss datasets and evaluation approaches applied in different studies that used LLMs, and briefly explore relevant tools and limitations in employing LLMs for SE tasks.

Chapter Organization Section 2 offers an overview of LLMs and their architectures. Section 3 briefly reviews different methods for adaptation of LLMs. We explore the capability of in-context learning in Sect. 4. Augmented LLMs are discussed in Sect. 5. Section 6 presents a brief review of datasets and evaluation techniques that have been used in studies leveraging LLMs. LLM-related tools for SE tasks are explored in Sect. 7. We conclude this chapter by discussing the limitation of leveraging LLMs for SE tasks in Sect. 8.

2 Large Language Models

LLMs represent a revolutionary advancement in natural language processing (NLP), demonstrating capabilities for general-purpose language understanding and generation [64]. LLMs acquire these remarkable abilities by leveraging massive datasets to learn billions of parameters during training, necessitating substantial computational resources for both training and operational phases [11].

These models are artificial neural networks, with the *transformer* architecture [92], such as Bidirectional Encoder Representations from Transformers (BERT) [24], which are (pre-)trained using self-supervised learning and semi-supervised learning. The transformer architecture, characterized by self-attention mechanisms [92], serves as the fundamental building block for language modeling tasks.

This approach has demonstrated effectiveness across broad applications, ranging from language translation to code generation. Notable examples of these models include OpenAI's GPT [9] series (including GPT-3.5 and GPT-4, utilized in ChatGPT), Google's PaLM [13] (deployed in Bard), and Meta's LLaMA [87].

2.1 Tokenization

Tokenization plays a crucial role in NLP by dividing documents, whether they are text or code, into smaller units known as tokens. A token could stand for a word, sub-word, character, or symbol, depending on the model's type and size [4]. This process helps models in effectively managing diverse languages and input formats [63]. There are several tokenization approaches, like WordPiece [81], Byte Pair Encoding (BPE) [82], SentencePiece [49], and Unigram [48].

2.2 Attention Mechanism

The attention mechanism computes a representation of a sequence of tokens in the input by establishing relationships between different tokens in the sequence [68]. This technique serves as a solution to provide multiple meanings or significance to a token, depending on its context and neighboring tokens [92]. It helps learn long-range dependencies in the input sequence, as it allows the model to focus on specific parts of the sequence when processing input, enhancing the model's ability to capture and understand complex relationships within the context [92].

2.3 Encoder and Decoder

The Transformer architecture, which forms the core of LLMs, consists of an encoder and a decoder [92]. This architecture is also known as sequence-to-sequence, allowing it to transform an input sequence of tokens into an output sequence, as seen in translation tasks [70, 115].

Each of these components is comprised of multiple layers of embedding, attention, and feed-forward neural networks [37]. The encoder's primary role is to convert each token in the input sequence into a fixed-length vector, capturing semantic information about each token. Conversely, the decoder is responsible for generating the output sequence of tokens by minimizing the gap between the predicted token and the target token [68, 92]. Two very well-known algorithms used in decoders to generate the sequence of output tokens are greedy search and beam search [42]. Greedy search is a decoding strategy where, at each step, the model selects the token with the highest probability as the next token in the sequence [80]. Greedy search is computationally efficient but may result in sequences that are suboptimal on a global scale, as it does not explore alternative possibilities beyond the current best choice [75]. Beam search is a decoding approach that, instead of selecting only the top-scoring token at each step, maintains a set of the most likely sequences, known as the beam. The beam size determines the number of sequences collected at each step [17, 93].

An Encoder-only architecture, or auto-encoding, focuses on the task of encoding and understanding the input sequence. This architecture is valuable for downstream tasks where contextual representation is crucial, but autoregressive generation in the output is not necessary [109]. For tasks like text classification, name prediction, or sentiment analysis, an encoder-only architecture is useful [33, 108]. BERT (Bidirectional Encoder Representations from Transformers), for example, employs an encoder-only architecture with bidirectional self-attention, allowing it to learn a comprehensive representation of input tokens while considering both the left and right context to learn the embedding vectors [24].

Conversely, a Decoder-only architecture, also known as an auto-regressive model, focuses on creative generation. These models predict the next token in a sequence step by step, generating each token based on the previous tokens [29]. In autoregressive models, the next token is produced using a right-shift method, where the input sequence is shifted to the right by incorporating the generated token into the input sequence [31]. In this approach, each generated token becomes part of the input sequence for predicting the next token, and it allows the model to consider the evolving context in each step, generating tokens based on the input sequence and the tokens generated before. A notable example of a decoder-only model is the Generative Pre-trained Transformer (GPT) [31].

2.4   Activation Functions

Activation functions play an important role in introducing non-linearity into a neural model's decision-making process [68]. These functions are applied to the output of each neuron in a neural network and facilitate the learning of complex patterns and relationships within the data [30]. One widely used activation function in large language models is the Rectified Linear Unit (ReLU), which replaces negative input values with zero while leaving positive values unchanged. Mathematically, this function is expressed as $max(0, x)$ [2]. The choice of an activation function depends on the specific requirements of the model. Different activation functions can yield diverse impacts on the learning process, and their appropriateness may vary based on the architecture and characteristics of the processed data [30].

2.5 Prompt

A prompt is an instruction given to a trained LLM at the inference step that enables the model to generate answers for queries it has never seen before [119]. The output generated by LLM can adapt to the context and instructions provided in the prompt without the need for fine-tuning or alignment. Trained LLMs can be prompted using different setups to generate the best answers [99]. Widely used prompt setups will be explored in Sect. 4.

3 Model Adaption

This section explores various methods for adapting an LLM to a specific downstream task, spanning from pre-training to resource-efficient model adaptation.

3.1 Pre-training

Pre-training in LLMs denotes the initial training phase, encompassing both self-supervised learning, where the model predicts masked words or sequences in unlabeled data, and semi-supervised learning, integrating labeled data to fine-tune the model for specific tasks. The term "pre-training" is employed because it anticipates the need for additional training or post-processing steps to adapt the pre-trained model to the desired task [64]. A widely used pre-training objective for LLMs is Masked Language Modeling (MLM) [16]. In this pre-training technique, the goal is to train the model by predicting tokens that are randomly masked within the input sequence.

3.2 Fine-Tuning

Fine-tuning involves taking pre-trained models and refining them through additional training on smaller, task-specific labeled datasets [64]. This process adapts the models' capabilities and enhances their performance for a particular task or domain. Essentially, fine-tuning transforms general-purpose models into specialized ones. An example of such a task is fine-tuning CodeBERT for defect detection task [69].

3.3 Alignment Tuning

LLMs have the potential to generate outputs that are incorrect, harmful, or biased. Adapting LLMs with human feedback can aid in updating the model parameters to mitigate the occurrence of such outputs [68]. Reinforcement Learning using Human Feedback (RLHF) is a well-known technique employed for alignment tuning in LLMs. In RLHF, a fine-tuned model is further trained with human feedback as a part of the reward system [120]. The RLHF process involves collecting human feedback on the outputs of a fine-tuned model. These feedback responses are then used to learn a reward model that can predict a numerical reward for a generated output. Finally, the model is optimized by incorporating this reward model and leveraging RL techniques [120]. This iterative approach of learning from human feedback contributes to enhancing the model's alignment and adapting the model to avoid generating incorrect, harmful, or biased outputs. Human feedback serves as a valuable source for refining the model's parameters, making it more adept at addressing complex human preferences that may be challenging to capture through traditional reward functions [62].

3.4 Resource-Efficient Model Adaptation

LLMs usually include a large amount of parameters, so conducting the full parameter tuning and deploying them are computationally expensive, in terms of memory and processing resources. Hence, researchers developed various techniques for model adaptation in resource-limited settings, either by parameter-efficient tuning or quantization to reduce the memory footprint of LLMs.

Parameter-efficient techniques for LLMs enable the adaptation of LLMs for downstream tasks at reduced computational costs. Among these techniques, Low-Rank Adaptation (LoRA) [41] receives great attention from the community. LoRA operates by fixing the pre-trained model weights and embedding trainable rank decomposition matrices into the layers of the Transformer architecture. It has found broad adoption in parameter-efficient tuning of open-source LLMs such as LLaMA and BLOOM. Notably, LoRA has been widely applied on LLaMA and its variations. One instance is the development of AlpacaLoRA,[1] which is a LoRA-trained version of Alpaca [86] (a fine-tuned 7B LLaMA model leveraging 52K human demonstrations for instruction following).

Given the substantial memory requirements of LLMs during inference, their deployment in real-world applications becomes costly. Several strategies have been proposed to reduce the memory footprint of LLMs, focusing on a prevalent model compression technique known as model quantization. The aim is to enable the uti-

---

[1] https://github.com/tloen/alpaca-lora.

lization of large-scale LLMs in resource-constrained environments and decreasing inference latency. Two primary approaches to model quantization are:

- Quantization-Aware Training (QAT), which necessitates complete model retraining, like LLM.int8() [22], ZeroQuant [112], and SmoothQuan [106]
- Post-Training Quantization (PTQ), which does not require retraining, like QLoRA [23] and LLM-qat [56]

4 In-Context Learning (ICL)

LLMs demonstrate an ability for In-Context Learning (ICL); meaning that they can learn effectively from a few examples within a specific context. Studies [3, 98, 111] show that LLMs can perform complex tasks through ICL. The fundamental concept of ICL revolves around the model's capacity to learn the patterns through the examples and subsequently make accurate predictions [27]. One advantage of ICL is the possibility of engaging in a dialogue with the model. Second, ICL closely aligns with the decision-making processes observed in humans by learning from analogy [100]. In contrast to traditional training and tuning approaches, ICL operates as a training-free framework, significantly reducing the computational costs associated with adapting the model to new tasks. Moreover, this approach transforms LLMs into black boxes as a service that can be integrated into real-world tasks [85]. Various ICL techniques have been proposed in the literature. In the following section, we will discuss several well-known techniques.

4.1 Few-Shot Learning

Few-shot learning uses a few labeled examples in the prompt to adapt the model for a specific task. This process involves providing contextual demonstration examples as input/output pairs that represent the downstream task. These demonstrations serve to instruct the model on how to reason or use tools and perform actions [3]. This technique enables the use of the same model for various downstream tasks without requiring tuning or changing the model's parameters [9]. The effectiveness of this technique relies on the relevancy of the few examples to the target task, and the format of these examples guides the model in predicting the output format. For instance, authors in [55] employ few-shot learning to demonstrate their method for generating step-by-step solutions that align with the math problems in their training data. The objective of this study is not to impart new skills to the model with few-shot learning; instead, it aims to guide the model in generating solutions in a desired step-by-step format.

4.2 Chain-of-Thought (CoT)

CoT is motivated by the natural step-by-step thinking ability of humans and has been observed to improve the performance of LLMs in solving problems that require multi-step reasoning [98]. The human thought process for tackling a complex problem, such as a complex math problem, involves breaking down the problem into intermediate tasks and solving them to reach the final answer. In CoT, the primary task is decomposed into intermediate tasks, and the LLM then finds answers for these intermediate tasks to resolve the main problem [98]. Another type of CoT is the self-planning approach, which employs LLMs to break down the original task into smaller steps termed plans [46]. The model is then invoked on these provided steps for execution.

4.3 Reasoning+Action (ReAct)

ReAct is an ICL approach that leverages the capabilities of LLMs to generate both reasoning traces and actions on conducting a task in an interleaved manner, which allows the model to engage in dynamic reasoning, creating, maintaining, and adjusting high-level action plan for action (reason to act) [111]. Additionally, ReAct can interact with external environments, such as Wikipedia, to incorporate additional information into its reasoning process (act to reason) [111]. This dynamic interplay between reasoning and action distinguishes ReAct and enhances its performance in tasks requiring decision-making such as question/answering or fact verification [62]. This technique helps overcome the hallucination issue [111].

5 Augmented LLM

LLMs are constrained by their training data. If a user's prompt requires domain-specific knowledge, such as data related to a company's Service Level Agreement (SLA), LLMs may not deliver accurate responses in such cases.

While ICL techniques require users to provide examples in the prompt, such as few-shot learning, augmented LLMs incorporate methods that access external resources and tools to improve the model's performance. This augmentation can be integrated into LLMs either during the training or inference stage [62]. In this section, we explore several categories of augmented LLMs.

5.1 Retrieval Augmented LLM

One of the most common techniques in augmented LLMs is retrieving relevant information from documents. This enables LLMs to more accurately generate output for prompts that require context beyond their training data or to reduce hallucinations in the model's output [8]. This technique also helps bridge the gap between smaller and larger models [43]. Retrieval-augmented LLMs typically consist of two main components: the retriever and the LLM. Various approaches involve incorporating retrieval information into the prompt or using it for fine-tuning either the LLM, the retriever, or both.

The retriever component can either use the prompt as a query [67] or re-prompt the LLM component to generate a query based on the initial prompt [59]. Following this, it applies the query to retrieve documents, which can be general, such as the knowledge base on Wikipedia [111], documents relevant to a specific domain [95], or even a cache of recent prompts [34].

To enhance the retriever's performance, instead of using a sparse bag-of-words vector to find relevant documents [20], all retrieved documents can be encoded into dense vectors [65]. Similarly, the query or prompt can be converted into a dense vector, and then semantic similarity [21] is computed between vectors to identify relevant information.

The retriever can incorporate relevant examples into the prompt to enhance the performance of ICL approaches such as few-shot learning [67]. Another technique involves combining CoT with retrievers. The retriever supports explaining each step in the planning process [38] or guides the reasoning step in CoT [88]. The augmented prompt is then passed to the LLM component to generate the desired output. Notably, these two approaches do not require additional training or tuning.

The retrieval information can also be employed to fine-tune the LLM. An example of such a method is RETRO [8], which is based on the auto-regressive LLM, GPT. RETRO converts external database retrieval into dense vectors, and then it splits input tokens into sequences of chunks, retrieves the nearest neighbors to each chunk in the retrieval database, and encodes them together with input to generate output.

On the flip side, fine-tuning can be applied to the retriever component to enable it to add more relevant examples to the prompt while keeping the LLM frozen. An example of this approach involves employing reinforcement learning techniques, with rewards sent back to the retriever component to improve the relevance of retrieved information for the initial prompt [5]. The other technique involves training both the retriever and LLMs. Retrieval-augmentation generation (RAG) combines a pre-trained retriever with a pre-trained sequence-to-sequence LLM and then fine-tuning them in an end-to-end process on a question-answering task [51].

5.2   Web Augmentation

Instead of solely relying on local storage to retrieve information, various methods involve collecting context relevant to the prompt through Web searches and then incorporating that content into the prompt or using it for fine-tuning the model. This process assists LLMs in generating updated output for prompts, such as inquiries about the temperature. For example, WebGPT [66] can engage with a Web browsing environment to discover answers to questions in the prompt. Another example is BlenderBot [83], which trains a model to generate search queries based on the prompt, then executes the query on a search engine, and incorporates the response relevant to the query into the model through a continuous learning process.

5.3   Tool Augmentation

While RAG relies on a retriever component to provide relevant context for enhancing model performance and refining the inference step, tool augmentation involves using a tool to provide the relevant context. This tool can be applied to the initial output of the LLM to provide feedback or evaluation, thereby augmenting the initial prompt with this feedback and iteratively re-prompting the model to enhance its output [19]. For example, an interpreter could be employed to execute the initial output of the model and augment the initial prompt with an error message, facilitating the model in improving its initial output [79]. Additionally, diverse tools can be employed to execute each step of the prompt after dividing the initial prompt into sub-tasks in CoT setup. An LLM can also serve as a tool, for instance, to generate a plan for a prompt (planning a prompt) [110] or to validate its output using verification questions [25].

6   Dataset and Evaluation

The LLMs used for SE tasks often rely on open-source repositories for training and fine-tuning [12]. Before fine-tuning the model for a specific task, there is a pre-training step on textual data to enhance the language understanding capabilities of the model [91]. Different studies use pre-trained LLMs either for inferring a task or fine-tuning the pre-trained model for specific downstream tasks [26, 74]. Platforms such as GitHub and StackOverflow provide vast code and textual data, serving as resources for tuning LLMs for SE tasks.

Several benchmark datasets are commonly used in evaluating LLMs for diverse SE tasks. Among them, we can point to CodexGLUE [57, 58] dataset, collected for evaluating the general language understanding of LLMs for different code-related tasks. This benchmark includes 14 datasets across 10 different code-related tasks such as clone detection, defect detection, code completion, code translation, and code summarization. For the test case generation task, datasets like ATLAS [97] and Methods2Test [89] are employed to fine-tune and evaluate LLMs for generating test cases in Java. The PROMISE NFR dataset [44], on the other hand, is used in studies leveraging LLMs for classifying project requirements.

Datasets like Humaneval [12] and APPs [39] are also commonly used for evaluating LLMs in tasks requiring code generation, but they often incorporate programming competition tasks. In contrast, CoderEval [113] is a benchmark dataset that collects programming tasks from more real-world programming scenarios.

Regarding the evaluation metrics, given the diversity of SE tasks, a single evaluation metric may not adequately capture the performance of LLMs for different tasks. Studies typically employ a range of metrics based on the specific problem types. Metrics like F1-score or precision find application in tasks such as code classification [40]. For evaluating the generative capability of LLMs, metrics such as BLEU [96], CodeBLEU [78], Exact Match (EM) [90], and Pass@k [12] are commonly used. Metrics like BLEU score and EM are more useful for tasks such as code review or code summarization because the output of the model is textual. But code generation and test generation tasks demand accuracy that extends beyond matching ground truth. An accurate output for these types of tasks should be compiled, effective, and implement the requirements outlined in the task description. Thus, metrics like Pass@k, which execute code on certain test cases, are more practical in these scenarios. In tasks like program repair, the evaluation metric also pertains to the correctness of the code after bug repair [45].

Furthermore, different quality metrics in SE can be employed to evaluate LLM output across different SE tasks. Metrics such as cyclomatic complexity [18], test coverage [79], mutation score [19], code/test smells [84], and vulnerabilities [60, 72] serve as benchmark metrics for assessing the quality of outputs generated by LLMs in diverse SE tasks.

7 Tools or Libraries

Various libraries are available for the training, tuning, and inference of LLMs, including Transformers [101], DeepSpeed [77], BMTrain [7], PyTorch [71], and TensorFlow [1]. Additionally, there are tools designed to facilitate the process of prompting LLMs and building applications with them.

LangChain [50] is a framework tailored for developing applications that leverage LLMs. The primary concept behind this tool involves facilitating the chain of various components around an LLM to build more advanced use cases, such as a Chatbot. LangChain offers diverse prompt templates, short-term and long-term memory access for retrieval setups, and interaction capabilities with different LLMs.

AutoGen [103, 104] is another framework that empowers the development of LLM applications by employing multiple agents capable of communicating with each other to solve different tasks. AutoGen features customizable agents with the core of LLM and also allows human participation and the incorporation of various tools. The framework also supports different prompt templates.

Furthermore, Guidance [36] is a tool that enhances the effective use of various ICL prompts, such as CoT, and simplifies the overall structure for different prompt templates.

The GitHub repository Parameter-Efficient Fine-Tuning (PEFT) [61] provides various efficient tuning approaches for adapting Pre-trained LLMs to downstream applications without fine-tuning all the model's parameters. This repository includes LoRA [41]/AdaLoRA [116] and Prefix Tuning [52]. Additionally, it supports numerous models such as GPT-2 and LLaMA.

8 Discussion and Conclusion

Leveraging LLMs for SE tasks poses several challenges and limitations. One of the challenges is the demand for high-quality data for effective training and tuning of LLMs for different SE tasks. Additionally, the training and tuning processes are resource-intensive and require significant time and computational cost. There is also a lack of effective resource-efficient adaptation methods for LLMs. While the literature has introduced numerous efficient tuning methods as mentioned in Sect. 3.4, the majority of these techniques have been evaluated on small-scale pre-trained language models rather than LLMs. As of now, there remains a notable absence of comprehensive research examining the impact of various efficient tuning methods on large-scale language models across diverse settings or tasks.

Various techniques have been proposed on the prompt side to adapt models for new, unseen tasks, such as ICL. However, one of the limitations of these techniques is the restricted amount of content that can be incorporated into the prompt because of the context window size of LLMs.

On the other side, LLMs are limited by information and knowledge in their training dataset, which limits their adaptability to evolving scenarios. To overcome this limitation, various techniques, like RAG, have been proposed to augment the new information relevant to the prompt into the LLMs either during tuning or inference.

LLMs may also generate hallucinations when producing outputs that are plausible responses but incorrect. Evaluation metrics such as the correct ratio for code generation tasks can aid in detecting hallucinations by identifying code that fails in certain test cases. However, LLMs may occasionally overlook specifications in the task description, which may not be detected with test cases and need human experts to filter them out.

Another limitation pertains to the fact that the outputs of LLMs are sometimes buggy, inaccurate, biased, or harmful. It is necessary to filter these outputs before presenting them to end users. Studies have employed the RLHF technique to enhance the model's output by rewarding good-quality responses. However, a notable limitation is associated with the efforts and time required for learning a reward model based on human feedback.

Moreover, numerous quality evaluation metrics in SE require the execution of the code generated by LLMs, facing challenges when evaluating code that is not self-contained and has dependencies. Exploring the training of a model that can predict code quality could be an interesting direction to address this limitation. Leveraging LLMs as a tool to enhance their own output, such as fixing bugs or generating test cases to evaluate the generated code, also can be beneficial in addressing this limitation.

LLMs also face challenges when addressing complex SE tasks. While these models perform a good performance on benchmark datasets with fewer dependencies that share the same distribution as their training data, they may face challenges in scalability and robustness when deployed in real-world environments, such as software projects. The scalability challenge arises from the size and computational cost of these models, making their deployment and real-time usage challenging. For instance, correctly completing a single programming task may require considering the contexts of various dependencies. As for robustness, the issue lies in the presence of diverse data or prompts in software projects that fall out of the distribution of the LLMs' training data, impacting their performance in real-world environments compared to their performance on benchmark datasets [28].

Another key concern arises from the memorization issue in LLMs, where models generate entire sequences of tokens verbatim from their training data [6]. This problem is triggered, for example, when the prompt precisely matches the content in the model's training data. Consequently, the model generates the sequence of tokens from its training data in the output to complete the prompt rather than generalizing it. Many benchmark datasets in SE are sourced from GitHub or StackOverflow and are already part of the training data for LLMs. Using these benchmarks to evaluate LLMs can impact the quality of evaluation due to the memorization issue. There is a lack of more comprehensive datasets that are not a part of the training data of LLMs to evaluate their performance for different SE tasks. Therefore, another potential future direction could involve constructing benchmark datasets beyond HumanEval to evaluate LLMs for various SE tasks.

References

1. Abadi, M., Barham, P., Chen, J., Chen, Z., Davis, A., Dean, J., Devin, M., Ghemawat, S., Irving, G., Isard, M., et al.: {TensorFlow}: a system for {Large-Scale} machine learning. In: 12th USENIX Symposium on Operating Systems Design and Implementation (OSDI 16), pp. 265–283 (2016)
2. Agarap, A.F.: Deep learning using rectified linear units (ReLU). Preprint (2018). arXiv:1803.08375
3. Ahmed, T., Devanbu, P.: Few-shot training llms for project-specific code-summarization. In: Proceedings of the 37th IEEE/ACM International Conference on Automated Software Engineering, pp. 1–5 (2022)

4. Ali, M., Fromm, M., Thellmann, K., Rutmann, R., Lübbering, M., Leveling, J., Klug, K., Ebert, J., Doll, N., Buschhoff, J.S., et al.: Tokenizer choice for llm training: Negligible or crucial? Preprint (2023). arXiv:2310.08754
5. Bacciu, A., Cocunasu, F., Siciliano, F., Silvestri, F., Tonellotto, N., Trappolini, G.: Rraml: Reinforced retrieval augmented machine learning. Preprint (2023). arXiv:2307.12798
6. Biderman, S., Prashanth, U.S., Sutawika, L., Schoelkopf, H., Anthony, Q., Purohit, S., Raf, E.: Emergent and predictable memorization in large language models. Preprint (2023). arXiv:2304.11158
7. Bmtrain: Efficient training for big models (2021). https://github.com/OpenBMB/BMTrain
8. Borgeaud, S., Mensch, A., Hoffmann, J., Cai, T., Rutherford, E., Millican, K., Van Den Driessche, G.B., Lespiau, J.B., Damoc, B., Clark, A., et al.: Improving language models by retrieving from trillions of tokens. In: International Conference on Machine Learning, pp. 2206–2240. PMLR (2022)
9. Brown, T., Mann, B., Ryder, N., Subbiah, M., Kaplan, J.D., Dhariwal, P., Neelakantan, A., Shyam, P., Sastry, G., Askell, A., et al.: Language models are few-shot learners. Adv. Neural Inf. Process. Syst. **33**, 1877–1901 (2020)
10. Cao, J., Li, M., Wen, M., Cheung, S.c.: A study on prompt design, advantages and limitations of chatgpt for deep learning program repair. Preprint (2023). arXiv:2304.08191
11. Chang, Y., Wang, X., Wang, J., Wu, Y., Zhu, K., Chen, H., Yang, L., Yi, X., Wang, C., Wang, Y., et al.: A survey on evaluation of large language models. Preprint (2023). arXiv:2307.03109
12. Chen, M., Tworek, J., Jun, H., Yuan, Q., Pinto, H.P.d.O., Kaplan, J., Edwards, H., Burda, Y., Joseph, N., Brockman, G., et al.: Evaluating large language models trained on code. Preprint (2021). arXiv:2107.03374
13. Chowdhery, A., Narang, S., Devlin, J., Bosma, M., Mishra, G., Roberts, A., Barham, P., Chung, H.W., Sutton, C., Gehrmann, S., et al.: Palm: Scaling language modeling with pathways. Preprint (2022). arXiv:2204.02311
14. Ciborowska, A., Damevski, K.: Fast changeset-based bug localization with bert. In: Proceedings of the 44th International Conference on Software Engineering, pp. 946–957 (2022)
15. Ciniselli, M., Cooper, N., Pascarella, L., Poshyvanyk, D., Di Penta, M., Bavota, G.: An empirical study on the usage of bert models for code completion. In: 2021 IEEE/ACM 18th International Conference on Mining Software Repositories (MSR), pp. 108–119. IEEE (2021)
16. Clark, K., Luong, M.T., Le, Q.V., Manning, C.D.: Electra: Pre-training text encoders as discriminators rather than generators. Preprint (2020). arXiv:2003.10555
17. Cohen, E., Beck, C.: Empirical analysis of beam search performance degradation in neural sequence models. In: International Conference on Machine Learning. pp. 1290–1299. PMLR (2019)
18. Dakhel, A.M., Majdinasab, V., Nikanjam, A., Khomh, F., Desmarais, M.C., Jiang, Z.M.J.: Github Copilot AI pair programmer: Asset or liability? J. Syst. Software **203**, 111734 (2023)
19. Dakhel, A.M., Nikanjam, A., Majdinasab, V., Khomh, F., Desmarais, M.C.: Effective test generation using pre-trained large language models and mutation testing (2023). https://arxiv.org/abs/2308.16557
20. Dang, V., Bendersky, M., Croft, W.B.: Two-stage learning to rank for information retrieval. In: Advances in Information Retrieval: 35th European Conference on IR Research, ECIR 2013, Moscow, Russia, March 24–27, 2013. Proceedings 35, pp. 423–434. Springer (2013)
21. De Boom, C., Van Canneyt, S., Bohez, S., Demeester, T., Dhoedt, B.: Learning semantic similarity for very short texts. In: 2015 IEEE International Conference on Data Mining Workshop (ICDMW), pp. 1229–1234. IEEE (2015)
22. Dettmers, T., Lewis, M., Belkada, Y., Zettlemoyer, L.: Gpt3. int8 (): 8-bit matrix multiplication for transformers at scale. Adv. Neural Inf. Process. Syst. **35**, 30318–30332 (2022)
23. Dettmers, T., Pagnoni, A., Holtzman, A., Zettlemoyer, L.: Qlora: Efficient finetuning of quantized llms. Preprint (2023). arXiv:2305.14314
24. Devlin, J., Chang, M.W., Lee, K., Toutanova, K.: Bert: Pre-training of deep bidirectional transformers for language understanding. Preprint (2018). arXiv:1810.04805

25. Dhuliawala, S., Komeili, M., Xu, J., Raileanu, R., Li, X., Celikyilmaz, A., Weston, J.: Chain-of-verification reduces hallucination in large language models. Preprint (2023). arXiv:2309.11495
26. Dinella, E., Ryan, G., Mytkowicz, T., Lahiri, S.K.: Toga: A neural method for test oracle generation. In: Proceedings of the 44th International Conference on Software Engineering, pp. 2130–2141 (2022)
27. Dong, Q., Li, L., Dai, D., Zheng, C., Wu, Z., Chang, B., Sun, X., Xu, J., Sui, Z.: A survey for in-context learning. Preprint (2022). arXiv:2301.00234
28. Du, M., He, F., Zou, N., Tao, D., Hu, X.: Shortcut learning of large language models in natural language understanding: A survey. Preprint (2022). arXiv:2208.11857
29. Du, Z., Qian, Y., Liu, X., Ding, M., Qiu, J., Yang, Z., Tang, J.: Glm: General language model pretraining with autoregressive blank infilling. Preprint (2021). arXiv:2103.10360
30. Dubey, S.R., Singh, S.K., Chaudhuri, B.B.: Activation functions in deep learning: A comprehensive survey and benchmark. Neurocomputing **503**, 92–108 (2022)
31. Floridi, L., Chiriatti, M.: Gpt-3: Its nature, scope, limits, and consequences. Minds Mach. **30**, 681–694 (2020)
32. Fu, M., Tantithamthavorn, C.: Linevul: A transformer-based line-level vulnerability prediction. In: Proceedings of the 19th International Conference on Mining Software Repositories, pp. 608–620 (2022)
33. Gao, Z., Feng, A., Song, X., Wu, X.: Target-dependent sentiment classification with bert. IEEE Access **7**, 154290–154299 (2019)
34. Gim, I., Chen, G., Lee, S.s., Sarda, N., Khandelwal, A., Zhong, L.: Prompt cache: Modular attention reuse for low-latency inference. Preprint (2023). arXiv:2311.04934
35. Goyal, T., Li, J.J., Durrett, G.: News summarization and evaluation in the era of gpt-3. Preprint (2022). arXiv:2209.12356
36. Guidance: A programming paradigm to conventional prompting and chaining (2023). https://github.com/guidance-ai/guidance
37. Guo, Y., Zheng, Y., Tan, M., Chen, Q., Li, Z., Chen, J., Zhao, P., Huang, J.: Towards accurate and compact architectures via neural architecture transformer. IEEE Trans. Pattern Anal. Mach. Intell. **44**(10), 6501–6516 (2021)
38. He, H., Zhang, H., Roth, D.: Rethinking with retrieval: Faithful large language model inference. Preprint (2022). arXiv:2301.00303
39. Hendrycks, D., Basart, S., Kadavath, S., Mazeika, M., Arora, A., Guo, E., Burns, C., Puranik, S., He, H., Song, D., et al.: Measuring coding challenge competence with apps. corr abs/2105.09938 (2021). Preprint (2021). arXiv:2105.09938
40. Hou, X., Zhao, Y., Liu, Y., Yang, Z., Wang, K., Li, L., Luo, X., Lo, D., Grundy, J., Wang, H.: Large language models for software engineering: A systematic literature review. Preprint (2023). arXiv:2308.10620
41. Hu, E.J., yelong shen, Wallis, P., Allen-Zhu, Z., Li, Y., Wang, S., Wang, L., Chen, W.: LoRA: Low-rank adaptation of large language models. In: International Conference on Learning Representations (2022). https://openreview.net/forum?id=nZeVKeeFYf9
42. Ippolito, D., Kriz, R., Kustikova, M., Sedoc, J., Callison-Burch, C.: Comparison of diverse decoding methods from conditional language models. Preprint (2019). arXiv:1906.06362
43. Izacard, G., Lewis, P., Lomeli, M., Hosseini, L., Petroni, F., Schick, T., Dwivedi-Yu, J., Joulin, A., Riedel, S., Grave, E.: Few-shot learning with retrieval augmented language models. Preprint (2022). arXiv:2208.03299
44. Jane Cleland-Huang, Sepideh Mazrouee, H.L., Port, D.: The promise repository of empirical software engineering data (2007). https://zenodo.org/records/268542
45. Jiang, N., Liu, K., Lutellier, T., Tan, L.: Impact of code language models on automated program repair. Preprint (2023). arXiv:2302.05020
46. Jiang, X., Dong, Y., Wang, L., Shang, Q., Li, G.: Self-planning code generation with large language model. Preprint (2023). arXiv:2303.06689
47. Kheiri, K., Karimi, H.: Sentimentgpt: Exploiting gpt for advanced sentiment analysis and its departure from current machine learning. Preprint (2023). arXiv:2307.10234

48. Kudo, T.: Subword regularization: Improving neural network translation models with multiple subword candidates. Preprint (2018). arXiv:1804.10959
49. Kudo, T., Richardson, J.: Sentencepiece: A simple and language independent subword tokenizer and detokenizer for neural text processing. Preprint (2018). arXiv:1808.06226
50. Langchain: A primer on developing llm apps fast (2023). https://github.com/langchain-ai/langchain
51. Lewis, P., Perez, E., Piktus, A., Petroni, F., Karpukhin, V., Goyal, N., Küttler, H., Lewis, M., Yih, W.t., Rocktäschel, T., et al.: Retrieval-augmented generation for knowledge-intensive nlp tasks. Adv. Neural Inf. Process. Syst. **33**, 9459–9474 (2020)
52. Li, X.L., Liang, P.: Prefix-tuning: Optimizing continuous prompts for generation. Preprint (2021). arxiv:2101.00190
53. Li, X., Gong, Y., Shen, Y., Qiu, X., Zhang, H., Yao, B., Qi, W., Jiang, D., Chen, W., Duan, N.: Coderetriever: A large scale contrastive pre-training method for code search. In: Proceedings of the 2022 Conference on Empirical Methods in Natural Language Processing, pp. 2898–2910 (2022)
54. Li, Z., Lu, S., Guo, D., Duan, N., Jannu, S., Jenks, G., Majumder, D., Green, J., Svyatkovskiy, A., Fu, S., et al.: Automating code review activities by large-scale pre-training. In: Proceedings of the 30th ACM Joint European Software Engineering Conference and Symposium on the Foundations of Software Engineering, pp. 1035–1047 (2022)
55. Lightman, H., Kosaraju, V., Burda, Y., Edwards, H., Baker, B., Lee, T., Leike, J., Schulman, J., Sutskever, I., Cobbe, K.: Let's verify step by step. Preprint (2023). arXiv:2305.20050
56. Liu, Z., Oguz, B., Zhao, C., Chang, E., Stock, P., Mehdad, Y., Shi, Y., Krishnamoorthi, R., Chandra, V.: Llm-qat: Data-free quantization aware training for large language models. Preprint (2023). arXiv:2305.17888
57. Lu, S., Guo, D., Ren, S., Huang, J., Svyatkovskiy, A., Blanco, A., Clement, C., Drain, et al.: Codexglue: A machine learning benchmark dataset for code understanding and generation (2021). https://github.com/microsoft/CodeXGLUE
58. Lu, S., Guo, D., Ren, S., Huang, J., Svyatkovskiy, A., Blanco, A., Clement, C., Drain, D., Jiang, D., Tang, D., et al.: Codexglue: A machine learning benchmark dataset for code understanding and generation. Preprint (2021). arXiv:2102.04664
59. Ma, X., Gong, Y., He, P., Zhao, H., Duan, N.: Query rewriting for retrieval-augmented large language models. Preprint (2023). arXiv:2305.14283
60. Majdinasab, V., Bishop, M.J., Rasheed, S., Moradidakhel, A., Tahir, A., Khomh, F.: Assessing the security of github copilot generated code—a targeted replication study. Preprint (2023). arXiv:2311.11177
61. Mangrulkar, S., Gugger, S., Debut, L., Belkada, Y., Paul, S., Bossan, B.: Peft: State-of-the-art parameter-efficient fine-tuning methods (2022). https://github.com/huggingface/peft
62. Mialon, G., Dessì, R., Lomeli, M., Nalmpantis, C., Pasunuru, R., Raileanu, R., Rozière, B., Schick, T., Dwivedi-Yu, J., Celikyilmaz, A., et al.: Augmented language models: a survey. Preprint (2023). arXiv:2302.07842
63. Mielke, S.J., Alyafeai, Z., Salesky, E., Raffel, C., Dey, M., Gallé, M., Raja, A., Si, C., Lee, W.Y., Sagot, B., et al.: Between words and characters: a brief history of open-vocabulary modeling and tokenization in nlp. Preprint (2021). arXiv:2112.10508
64. Min, B., Ross, H., Sulem, E., Veyseh, A.P.B., Nguyen, T.H., Sainz, O., Agirre, E., Heintz, I., Roth, D.: Recent advances in natural language processing via large pre-trained language models: A survey. ACM Comput. Surv. **56**(2), 1–40 (2023)
65. Mitra, B., Craswell, N.: Neural models for information retrieval. Preprint (2017). arXiv:1705.01509
66. Nakano, R., Hilton, J., Balaji, S., Wu, J., Ouyang, L., Kim, C., Hesse, C., Jain, S., Kosaraju, V., Saunders, W., et al.: Webgpt: Browser-assisted question-answering with human feedback. Preprint (2021). arXiv:2112.09332
67. Nashid, N., Sintaha, M., Mesbah, A.: Retrieval-based prompt selection for code-related few-shot learning. In: Proceedings of the 45th International Conference on Software Engineering (ICSE'23) (2023)

68. Naveed, H., Khan, A.U., Qiu, S., Saqib, M., Anwar, S., Usman, M., Barnes, N., Mian, A.: A comprehensive overview of large language models. Preprint (2023). arXiv:2307.06435
69. Pan, C., Lu, M., Xu, B.: An empirical study on software defect prediction using codebert model. Appl. Sci. **11**(11), 4793 (2021)
70. Pan, R., Ibrahimzada, A.R., Krishna, R., Sankar, D., Wassi, L.P., Merler, M., Sobolev, B., Pavuluri, R., Sinha, S., Jabbarvand, R.: Understanding the effectiveness of large language models in code translation. Preprint (2023). arXiv:2308.03109
71. Paszke, A., Gross, S., Massa, F., Lerer, A., Bradbury, J., Chanan, G., Killeen, T., Lin, Z., Gimelshein, N., Antiga, L., et al.: Pytorch: An imperative style, high-performance deep learning library. Adv. Neural Inf. Process. Syst. **32**, (2019). arXiv:1912.01703
72. Pearce, H., Ahmad, B., Tan, B., Dolan-Gavitt, B., Karri, R.: Asleep at the keyboard? assessing the security of github copilot's code contributions. In: 2022 IEEE Symposium on Security and Privacy (SP), pp. 754–768. IEEE (2022)
73. Pinaya, W.H., Graham, M.S., Kerfoot, E., Tudosiu, P.D., Dafflon, J., Fernandez, V., Sanchez, P., Wolleb, J., da Costa, P.F., Patel, A., et al.: Generative ai for medical imaging: extending the monai framework. Preprint (2023). arXiv:2307.15208
74. Prenner, J.A., Babii, H., Robbes, R.: Can openai's codex fix bugs? an evaluation on quixbugs. In: Proceedings of the Third International Workshop on Automated Program Repair, pp. 69–75 (2022)
75. Raffel, C., Shazeer, N., Roberts, A., Lee, K., Narang, S., Matena, M., Zhou, Y., Li, W., Liu, P.J.: Exploring the limits of transfer learning with a unified text-to-text transformer. J. Mach. Learn. Res. **21**(1), 5485–5551 (2020)
76. Rahman, K., Ghani, A., Alzahrani, A., Tariq, M.U., Rahman, A.U.: Pre-trained model-based NFR classification: Overcoming limited data challenges. IEEE Access **11**, 81787–81802 (2023)
77. Rasley, J., Rajbhandari, S., Ruwase, O., He, Y.: Deepspeed: System optimizations enable training deep learning models with over 100 billion parameters. In: Proceedings of the 26th ACM SIGKDD International Conference on Knowledge Discovery & Data Mining, pp. 3505–3506 (2020)
78. Ren, S., Guo, D., Lu, S., Zhou, L., Liu, S., Tang, D., Sundaresan, N., Zhou, M., Blanco, A., Ma, S.: Codebleu: a method for automatic evaluation of code synthesis. Preprint (2020). arXiv:2009.10297
79. Schäfer, M., Nadi, S., Eghbali, A., Tip, F.: Adaptive test generation using a large language model. Preprint (2023). arXiv:2302.06527
80. Scholak, T., Schucher, N., Bahdanau, D.: Picard: Parsing incrementally for constrained auto-regressive decoding from language models. Preprint (2021). arXiv:2109.05093
81. Schuster, M., Nakajima, K.: Japanese and korean voice search. In: 2012 IEEE International Conference on Acoustics, Speech and Signal Processing (ICASSP), pp. 5149–5152. IEEE (2012)
82. Sennrich, R., Haddow, B., Birch, A.: Neural machine translation of rare words with subword units. Preprint (2015). arXiv:1508.07909
83. Shuster, K., Xu, J., Komeili, M., Ju, D., Smith, E.M., Roller, S., Ung, M., Chen, M., Arora, K., Lane, J., et al.: Blenderbot 3: a deployed conversational agent that continually learns to responsibly engage. Preprint (2022). arXiv:2208.03188
84. Steenhoek, B., Tufano, M., Sundaresan, N., Svyatkovskiy, A.: Reinforcement learning from automatic feedback for high-quality unit test generation. Preprint (2023). arXiv:2310.02368
85. Sun, T., Shao, Y., Qian, H., Huang, X., Qiu, X.: Black-box tuning for language-model-as-a-service. In: International Conference on Machine Learning, pp. 20841–20855. PMLR (2022)
86. Taori, R., Gulrajani, I., Zhang, T., Dubois, Y., Li, X., Guestrin, C., Liang, P., Hashimoto, T.B.: Stanford alpaca: An instruction-following llama model (2023). https://github.com/tatsu-lab/stanford_alpaca
87. Touvron, H., Martin, L., Stone, K., Albert, P., Almahairi, A., Babaei, Y., Bashlykov, N., Batra, S., Bhargava, P., Bhosale, S., et al.: Llama 2: Open foundation and fine-tuned chat models. Preprint (2023). arXiv:2307.09288

88. Trivedi, H., Balasubramanian, N., Khot, T., Sabharwal, A.: Interleaving retrieval with chain-of-thought reasoning for knowledge-intensive multi-step questions. Preprint (2022). arXiv:2212.10509

89. Tufano, M., Deng, S.K., Sundaresan, N., Svyatkovskiy, A.: Methods2test: A dataset of focal methods mapped to test cases. In: Proceedings of the 19th International Conference on Mining Software Repositories, pp. 299–303 (2022)

90. Tufano, M., Drain, D., Svyatkovskiy, A., Deng, S.K., Sundaresan, N.: Unit test case generation with transformers and focal context. Preprint (2020). arXiv:2009.05617

91. Tufano, M., Drain, D., Svyatkovskiy, A., Sundaresan, N.: Generating accurate assert statements for unit test cases using pretrained transformers. In: Proceedings of the 3rd ACM/IEEE International Conference on Automation of Software Test, pp. 54–64 (2022)

92. Vaswani, A., Shazeer, N., Parmar, N., Uszkoreit, J., Jones, L., Gomez, A.N., Kaiser, Ł., Polosukhin, I.: Attention is all you need. Adv. Neural Inf. Process. Syst. **30**, 1–11 (2017)

93. Vijayakumar, A.K., Cogswell, M., Selvaraju, R.R., Sun, Q., Lee, S., Crandall, D., Batra, D.: Diverse beam search: Decoding diverse solutions from neural sequence models. Preprint (2016). arXiv:1610.02424

94. Wang, B., Xie, Q., Pei, J., Chen, Z., Tiwari, P., Li, Z., Fu, J.: Pre-trained language models in biomedical domain: A systematic survey. ACM Comput. Surv. **56**(3), 1–52 (2023)

95. Wang, Y., Ma, X., Chen, W.: Augmenting black-box llms with medical textbooks for clinical question answering. Preprint (2023). arXiv:2309.02233

96. Wang, Y., Wang, W., Joty, S., Hoi, S.C.: Codet5: Identifier-aware unified pre-trained encoder-decoder models for code understanding and generation. Preprint (2021). arXiv:2109.00859

97. Watson, C., Tufano, M., Moran, K., Bavota, G., Poshyvanyk, D.: On learning meaningful assert statements for unit test cases. In: Proceedings of the ACM/IEEE 42nd International Conference on Software Engineering, pp. 1398–1409 (2020)

98. Wei, J., Wang, X., Schuurmans, D., Bosma, M., Xia, F., Chi, E., Le, Q.V., Zhou, D., et al.: Chain-of-thought prompting elicits reasoning in large language models. Adv. Neural Inf. Process. Syst. **35**, 24824–24837 (2022)

99. White, J., Fu, Q., Hays, S., Sandborn, M., Olea, C., Gilbert, H., Elnashar, A., Spencer-Smith, J., Schmidt, D.C.: A prompt pattern catalog to enhance prompt engineering with chatgpt. Preprint (2023). arXiv:2302.11382

100. Winston, P.H.: Learning and reasoning by analogy. Commun. ACM **23**(12), 689–703 (1980)

101. Wolf, T., Debut, L., Sanh, V., Chaumond, J., Delangue, C., Moi, A., Cistac, P., Rault, T., Louf, R., Funtowicz, M., et al.: Transformers: State-of-the-art natural language processing. In: Proceedings of the 2020 Conference on Empirical Methods in Natural Language Processing: System Demonstrations, pp. 38–45 (2020)

102. Wong, D., Kothig, A., Lam, P.: Exploring the verifiability of code generated by github copilot. Preprint (2022). arXiv:2209.01766

103. Wu, Q., Bansal, G., Zhang, J., Wu, Y., Zhang, S., Zhu, E., Li, B., Jiang, L., Zhang, X., Wang, C.: Autogen: Enabling next-gen llm applications via multi-agent conversation framework. Preprint (2023). arXiv:2308.08155

104. Wu, Q., Bansal, G., Zhang, J., Wu, Y., Zhang, S., Zhu, E., Li, B., Jiang, L., Zhang, X., Wang, C.: Autogen: Enabling next-gen LLM applications via multi-agent conversation framework (2023). https://github.com/microsoft/autogen

105. Xia, C.S., Wei, Y., Zhang, L.: Automated program repair in the era of large pre-trained language models. In: Proceedings of the 45th International Conference on Software Engineering (ICSE 2023). Association for Computing Machinery (2023)

106. Xiao, G., Lin, J., Seznec, M., Wu, H., Demouth, J., Han, S.: Smoothquant: Accurate and efficient post-training quantization for large language models. In: International Conference on Machine Learning, pp. 38087–38099. PMLR (2023)

107. Xie, D., Yoo, B., Jiang, N., Kim, M., Tan, L., Zhang, X., Lee, J.S.: Impact of large language models on generating software specifications. Preprint (2023). arXiv:2306.03324

108. Xu, H., Liu, B., Shu, L., Yu, P.S.: Bert post-training for review reading comprehension and aspect-based sentiment analysis. Preprint (2019). arXiv:1904.02232

109. Yan, H., Deng, B., Li, X., Qiu, X.: Tener: adapting transformer encoder for named entity recognition. Preprint (2019). arXiv:1911.04474
110. Yang, K., Tian, Y., Peng, N., Klein, D.: Re3: Generating longer stories with recursive reprompting and revision. Preprint (2022). arXiv:2210.06774
111. Yao, S., Zhao, J., Yu, D., Du, N., Shafran, I., Narasimhan, K., Cao, Y.: React: Synergizing reasoning and acting in language models. Preprint (2022). arXiv:2210.03629
112. Yao, Z., Yazdani Aminabadi, R., Zhang, M., Wu, X., Li, C., He, Y.: Zeroquant: Efficient and affordable post-training quantization for large-scale transformers. Adv. Neural Inf. Process. Syst. **35**, 27168–27183 (2022)
113. Yu, H., Shen, B., Ran, D., Zhang, J., Zhang, Q., Ma, Y., Liang, G., Li, Y., Xie, T., Wang, Q.: Codereval: A benchmark of pragmatic code generation with generative pre-trained models. Preprint (2023). arXiv:2302.00288
114. Zan, D., Chen, B., Zhang, F., Lu, D., Wu, B., Guan, B., Yongji, W., Lou, J.G.: Large language models meet nl2code: A survey. In: Proceedings of the 61st Annual Meeting of the Association for Computational Linguistics (Volume 1: Long Papers), pp. 7443–7464 (2023)
115. Zhang, J., Luan, H., Sun, M., Zhai, F., Xu, J., Zhang, M., Liu, Y.: Improving the transformer translation model with document-level context. Preprint (2018). arXiv:1810.03581
116. Zhang, Q., Chen, M., Bukharin, A., He, P., Cheng, Y., Chen, W., Zhao, T.: Adaptive budget allocation for parameter-efficient fine-tuning. Preprint (2023). arXiv:2303.10512
117. Zhang, Q., Fang, C., Xie, Y., Zhang, Y., Yang, Y., Sun, W., Yu, S., Chen, Z.: A survey on large language models for software engineering. Preprint (2023). arXiv:2312.15223
118. Zhao, W.X., Zhou, K., Li, J., Tang, T., Wang, X., Hou, Y., Min, Y., Zhang, B., Zhang, J., Dong, Z., et al.: A survey of large language models. Preprint (2023). arXiv:2303.18223
119. Zhou, Y., Muresanu, A.I., Han, Z., Paster, K., Pitis, S., Chan, H., Ba, J.: Large language models are human-level prompt engineers. Preprint (2022). arXiv:2211.01910
120. Ziegler, D.M., Stiennon, N., Wu, J., Brown, T.B., Radford, A., Amodei, D., Christiano, P., Irving, G.: Fine-tuning language models from human preferences. Preprint (2019). arXiv:1909.08593

Part II
Patterns and Tools for the Adoption of Generative AI in Software Engineering

Comparing Proficiency of ChatGPT and Bard in Software Development

Dae-Kyoo Kim

Abstract Generative language-based artificial intelligence models, like ChatGPT and Bard, have gained popularity for their impressive performance across various domains. These models hold the potential for contributing to software development tasks. This chapter presents a comparative study on the proficiency of ChatGPT and Bard in software development, examining their strengths and weaknesses and synergy in their combined use. To facilitate the comparison, we utilize an online tour reservation system (TORS) as a running example. The study found that ChatGPT and Bard have different focuses in requirement analysis and ChatGPT outperforms in design modeling, and they are comparable in implementation and error fixing. However, both models suffer from many inconsistencies particularly between design and implementation, which raises traceability concerns between phases. In both models, human involvement was required to address inconsistency issues and finalize the development.

Keywords Assessment · Bard · ChatGPT · Comparison · Generative language-based artificial intelligence · Software development

1 Introduction

Recently, generative language-based artificial intelligence (Gen-LBAI) models have drawn significant attention due to their impressive performance in various applications across different domains. The potential of Gen-LBAI models to generate humanlike language and perform complex tasks has created considerable interest and exploration in fields such as natural language processing, virtual assistants, and content creation. Researchers and developers are increasingly exploring the

D.-K. Kim (✉)
Department of Computer Science and Engineering, Oakland University, Rochester, MI, USA
e-mail: kim2@oakland.edu

© The Author(s), under exclusive license to Springer Nature Switzerland AG 2024
A. Nguyen-Duc et al. (eds.), *Generative AI for Effective Software Development*,
https://doi.org/10.1007/978-3-031-55642-5_2

capabilities and possibilities offered by Gen-LBAI models to assess their potential for practical use.

Among the well-known models in the field of generative language-based artificial intelligence are ChatGPT-4 [9] and Bard [3]. These models possess the potential to be adopted in the field of software development, offering capabilities that can be harnessed for various tasks such as generating code and fixing bugs. To utilize them effectively, it is necessary to understand their strengths and limitations throughout the software development life cycle, which helps users make proper decisions in taking the outputs of the models.

Several studies (e.g., [1, 6, 7]) evaluated the capabilities of GitHub Copilot [2], an AI-powered code completion tool, focusing on its utilization on software quality, productivity, limitations, and comparisons with human-generated code. Some other studies (e.g., [8, 11]) compared Copilot with other models such as DaVinci [10] and genetic programming (GP) [4] on code generation, tests, and program synthesis.

In this work, we compare the capabilities of ChatGPT and Bard in software development, focusing on requirements analysis, design modeling, and implementation stages. During requirements analysis, we evaluate their abilities to identify ambiguities, differentiate between functional and non-functional requirements, and generate use case specifications. In domain modeling, we assess their capabilities in identifying domain concepts, attributes, and relationships. In design modeling, we evaluate their aptitude in producing detailed design class and sequence diagrams. Finally, in implementation, we analyze their capabilities in implementing the design model and rectifying errors. We use an online tour reservation system (TORS) as a running example.

The findings of the study indicate that ChatGPT and Bard focus on different aspects in requirement analysis and ChatGPT performs somewhat better in design modeling, and they have comparable performance in implementation and error fixing. However, both models suffer from many inconsistencies among generated artifacts, and significant inconsistency was observed between design modeling and implementation, which further leads to traceability concerns between phases. In both models, the *involvement* of the human developer was required to address inconsistency issues and finalize the development. Despite these challenges, it was witnessed that the models have great potential to contribute to software development and their combined use can be effective, especially in requirements analysis and design modeling.

- What are the respective strengths and weaknesses of ChatGPT and Bard in the context of software development?
- How can ChatGPT and Bard be effectively used together for software development?

The remainder of the chapter is organized as follows. Section 2 gives an overview of related work on the utilization of Gen-LBAI models in software development. Section 3 compares the capabilities of ChatGPT and Bard in software development using the TORS system. Section 4 addresses the research questions posed in Sect. 1 based on the findings in Sect. 3. Section 5 concludes the chapter by summarizing key points and discussing the implications of the findings.

2 Related Works

In this section, we give an overview of the existing work that evaluates the performance of Gen-LBAI models in software development.

Dakhel [1] conducted an evaluation of GitHub Copilot as an AI pair programmer, examining its code quality compared to human-generated code. By assessing the solutions generated by Copilot for fundamental programming problems, they reported certain limitations (e.g., incorrectness, complexity) of Copilot and offered some insights on how developers can leverage its capabilities.

Mastropaolo et al. [6] studied the influence of varying natural language descriptions of a function on Copilot's recommendations. They used Java methods with corresponding descriptions and paraphrasing techniques to generate alternative descriptions. The paraphrases produced by the paraphrasing techniques were used for code predictions, and the differences in the recommended code were compared. Their study found that paraphrasing led to different code recommendations in approximately 46% of cases, affecting the accuracy of predictions.

Peng et al. [7] conducted a controlled experiment to examine the impact of Copilot on productivity. Two groups of programmers were tasked with implementing an HTTP server in JavaScript where one group had access to Copilot and the other group did not. They reported that the group utilizing Copilot completed the task 55.8% faster, suggesting the potential of AI-pair programmers to enhance programming productivity.

Wermelinger [11] investigated the performance of Copilot in generating code, tests, and explanations in supporting students to solve CS1 problems and compared it to Davinci, which is a Codex model, in terms of correctness, diversity, and interactive guidance toward correct solutions. They reported that Copilot demonstrated less effectiveness than Davinci on correctness and diversity.

Sobania et al. [8] evaluated Copilot's performance on program synthesis using a set of benchmark problems and compared the results with those of GP reported in the literature. They examined the programs produced by Copilot and GP using the Copilot Extension for Visual Studio Code for correctness. Their study found that Copilot and GP exhibited similar performance on the benchmark problems.

3 Comparing Capabilities of ChatGPT and Bard on Software Development

In this section, we evaluate and compare the capabilities of ChatGPT and Bard on software development using the TORS system. Figure 1 illustrates the approach. Initially, a description of TORS is provided. The description is used as a base for requirements analysis. In this phase, the abilities of ChatGPT and Bards to identify and clarify ambiguities and define functional and non-functional requirements are evaluated. The output of requirements analysis is then used as input for design

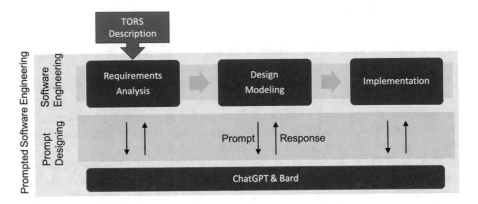

Fig. 1 Research approach

modeling, where ChatGPT and Bard are evaluated for their capabilities to make design decisions such as operation assignment, navigabilities, and data types. The resulting design models are implemented in Java. In this phase, ChatGPT and Bard are evaluated for their abilities to generate code and rectify errors. The output of each phase is evaluated based on object-oriented principles [5] by a software researcher with 32 years of experience in software engineering. For fair comparison, both models were given the same instructions in the experiments.

3.1 Requirements Analysis

In this phase, both models were evaluated for their proficiency in comprehending and analyzing the problem description of the TORS system. The evaluation focuses on identifying ambiguities within the description, rectifying them to enhance the clarity of the problem statement, extracting functional and non-functional requirements from the description, and generating comprehensive and detailed use case specifications. As an input to the models, the description of TORS, as shown in Fig. 2, was given.

Identifying Ambiguities In this task, ChatGPT and Bard were tasked to identify ambiguities in the TORS description. The following prompt was given to both models:

– Prompt: "For the given description, identify ambiguities."

Table 1 shows their outputs. In the outputs, it is observed that ChatGPT focuses more on the technical aspects and functionality (e.g., built-in network, automation level), while Bard considers more user experience and interactions with the system (e.g., user interaction methods in viewing tour information). ChatGPT's output can be more helpful from a system developer perspective to understand the

"Supporting a travel agency, Tour Online Reservation System (TORS) maintains tour information and provides reservation facilities for the people who wish to travel on tours by accessing a built-in network. The system allows users to view information about the tours available and make a reservation on a tour without asking the employees at the agency. Using the system, a user can cancel an existing reservation that the user made. The system also allows a user to send feedback by e-mail to the agency and stores the feedback in the database. Finally, the system allows the employees of the agency to manage customers and tours such as adding, deleting, and updating information on customers and tours. For security purposes, the employees are required to provide login credentials (login ID and password) to access the system."

Fig. 2 Provided description of TORS

implementation aspects of TORS, while Bard's output is more insightful from a user perspective. These observations suggest that their combined use can lead to a more comprehensive description of the system, covering both technical and user-oriented aspects.

Clarifying Ambiguities After identifying ambiguities, both models were instructed to clarify the identified ambiguities. The following prompt was given to the models:

– Prompt: "Clarify the identified ambiguities in the output of the previous prompt."

Table 2 shows the comparison of the produced clarifications. The clarifications by ChatGPT are well aligned with the identified ambiguities, which are from a developer perspective, including built-in network referring to a Web interface, the process being fully automated without requiring employee involvement, built-in email client and CRM in the system, and ways to access the system. Bard also effectively addresses the ambiguities that are from a user perspective, including types of tours and ways to access tour information, make or cancel a reservation, send feedback, manage customer information, and access the system.

Revising Descriptions Based on the produced clarifications, both models were instructed to revise the original description of TORS by incorporating the clarifications. The following prompt was given to the models:

– Prompt: "Revise the original description of TORS by reflecting the clarifications in the output of the previous prompt."

Table 3 shows the revised descriptions. ChatGPT effectively integrated three out of five clarifications, addressing the built-in network, email feedback, and CRM. However, it still falls short in properly incorporating the clarifications regarding human intervention and the security measure. Bard also struggled with integration. Only three out of seven clarifications were properly incorporated. It misses the clarification on types of tours in the revision and only partially integrates the

Table 1 Comparison of identified ambiguities

ChatGPT	Bard
The description mentions that the system "provides reservation facilities for the people who wish to travel on tours by accessing a built-in network." It is not clear what is meant by a "built-in network" and how it relates to the reservation process	The description does not specify what kind of tours are available. Are they domestic or international? Do they include all types of tours, such as sightseeing, adventure, and cultural?
The description states that "the system allows users to view information about the tours available and make a reservation on a tour without asking the employees at the agency." It is not specified if this means that the reservation process is fully automated or if there is still a human intervention involved in the process	The description does not specify how users can view information about the tours. Is there a search function? Can users browse by category?
The description mentions that "the system also allows a user to send feedbacks by email to the agency and stores the feedback in the database." It is not clear if this means that the system has an email client built-in or if it only stores the feedback and the user must use their own email client to send it	The description does not specify how users can make a reservation on a tour. Is there a form to fill out? Do users need to call the travel agency?
The description states that "the system allows the employees of the agency to manage customers and tours such as adding, deleting, and updating information on customers and tours." It is not specified if this means that the system has a built-in CRM or if the employees use an external CRM	The description does not specify how users can cancel an existing reservation. Is there a cancellation form? Do users need to call the travel agency?
The description mentions that "for security purposes, the employees are required to provide login credentials (login ID and password) to access the system." It is not specified if this is the only security measure in place or if there are additional measures such as 2FA or encryption	The description does not specify how users can send feedback to the agency. Is there an email address? Do users need to fill out a form?
	The description does not specify what kind of information employees can manage about customers and tours. Can they update contact information? Can they change the dates of a tour?
	The description does not specify how employees can access the system. Is there a login page? Do they need to use a special app?

clarifications on making a reservation, sending feedback, and accessing the system. Overall, both ChatGPT and Bard had limitations in fully integrating the provided clarifications. However, ChatGPT demonstrated a higher percentage of successfully incorporating clarifications.

Extracting FR and NFR In this task, ChatGPT and Bard were evaluated for their abilities to extract functional requirements (FRs) and non-functional requirements (NFRs). Based on the original description of TORS, they were tasked to identify and distinguish between FRs and NFRs. The following prompt was given to the models:

- Prompt: "For the original description of TORS, identify functional and non-functional requirements."

Table 2 Comparison of produced clarifications

ChatGPT	Bard
Built-in network: The built-in network refers to a Web interface or application that users can access to view information about tours and make reservations Human intervention: The system is fully automated, and users can make reservations without needing to contact the agency employees Email feedback: The system has an email client built-in, and users can send feedback directly through the system, which will be stored in the database CRM: The system has a built-in CRM that the employees of the agency can use to manage customers and tours Security measure: Login credentials (username and password) are the only security measure in place for employees to access the system	What kind of tours are available? TORS offers a variety of tours, both domestic and international. Tours include sightseeing, adventure, and cultural tours How can users view information about the tours? Users can view information about tours by using a search function or browsing by category. The search function allows users to search for tours by destination, date, and other criteria. The browse by category function allows users to view tours by type, such as sightseeing, adventure, and cultural How can users make a reservation on a tour? Users can make a reservation on a tour by filling out a form on the TORS Web site. The form requires users to provide their name, contact information, and the tour they would like to book. Users can also pay for their reservation at the time of booking How can users cancel an existing reservation? Users can cancel an existing reservation by submitting a cancellation request through the TORS Web site. The cancellation request requires users to provide their name, contact information, and the tour they would like to cancel. Users will be refunded for their reservation, minus a cancellation fee How can users send feedback to the agency? Users can send feedback to the agency by emailing their feedback to the agency's address. Feedback can be about the tours, the Web site, or the customer service What kind of information can employees manage about customers and tours? Employees can manage the following information about customers and tours: contact information, dates of tours, and tour prices. Employees can also add, delete, and update information about customers and tours How can employees access the system? Employees can access the system by logging in with their login ID and password. Employees must have a valid login ID and password in order to access the system

In ChatGPT's output, the FRs are deemed comprehensive, but there are some overlaps. For example, *Maintaining tour information* overlaps with *Managing customers and tours*, and *Providing reservation about available tours* overlaps with *Making a reservation on a tour*. These overlaps may have occurred due to the parsing of verbs in the description. Regarding NFRs, ChatGPT seems to have expanded beyond the scope of the original description. The first three qualities (user-friendliness, accessibility, persistency) align with the description, while the rest (availability, reliability, scalability, compatibility, security, efficiency, and tolerance) are more general in nature and not explicitly stated in the description. On the other hand, the FRs produced by Bard do not exhibit any overlaps. However,

Table 3 Comparison of revised descriptions

ChatGPT	Bard
The Tour Online Reservation System (TORS) is a Web-based application that maintains tour information and provides reservation facilities for customers who wish to travel on tours. The system allows customers to view information about the available tours and make a reservation without needing to contact the agency employees. Using the system, customers can also cancel existing reservations they have made. The system also allows customers to send feedbacks by email directly through the system, which will be stored in the database. In addition, the system allows employees of the agency to manage customers and tours such as adding, deleting, and updating information on customers and tours using a built-in CRM. For security purposes, employees are required to provide login credentials (username and password) to access the system	TORS is a Web-based system that allows users to view information about tours, make reservations, cancel reservations, and send feedback to the travel agency. TORS also allows employees of a travel agency to manage customers and tours. Users can view information about tours, such as the dates, times, locations, and prices, by browsing the TORS Web site. To make a reservation, users must first create an account and log in to the TORS Web site. Once they have found the tour they want to book, they can click on the "Book Now" button and follow the instructions. To cancel a reservation, users must first log in to their account and click on the "My Reservations" tab. Once they have selected the reservation they want to cancel, they can click on the "Cancel Reservation" button and follow the instructions. Users can send feedback to the travel agency by logging in to their account and clicking on the "Feedback" tab. Employees of a travel agency can manage customers and tours by viewing customer information, such as contact information and travel history, and tour information, such as dates, times, locations, and prices. They can also add, delete, and update information about customers and tours. Users and employees can access the TORS system through a Web browser by creating an account and logging in using their login credentials.

there are some requirements that are missing. For instance, it fails to capture the requirement of storing feedback in the database and the requirement related to login and authentication. In terms of NFRs, all the identified qualities appear to be of a general nature, such as security, ease of use, reliability, scalability, and availability, which are not specifically stated in the original description. Although ChatGPT had some overlaps in its outputs, overall, they are more complete compared to Bard's outputs, especially for FRs.

Generating Use Case Specifications In this task, ChatGPT and Bard were evaluated for their capabilities to generate use case specifications. For the requirement of making a reservation, they were instructed to produce a detailed use case specification. The following prompt was given to the models:

– Prompt: "For the *"Making a reservation on a tour"* requirement, generate a detailed use case specification."

Table 4 presents the outputs. The use case specification produced by ChatGPT demonstrates a well-structured format with adequate details, following a commonly used form [5]. The preconditions and postconditions align well with the TORS

Table 4 Generated use case specification for *Make Tour Reservation*

ChatGPT	Bard
Tour Reservation Use Case Specification: Title: Make Tour Reservation Primary Actor: Customer Goal: To allow a customer to make a reservation for a tour through Tour Online Reservation System (TORS) Preconditions:	Sure, here is a use case for "make reservations on tours": Actor: User Goal: Make a reservation on a tour Preconditions: The user must have an account with the travel agency Steps:
– Customer has registered in TORS and has a valid login ID and password – Customer has accessed TORS through the built-in network – Tours information is available in TORS	1. The user logs into the travel agency's Web site 2. The user searches for the tour they would like to book 3. The user selects the tour they would like to book
Trigger: Customer logs in to TORS and selects "Make Reservation" option Basic Flow:	4. The user provides their contact information 5. The user selects a payment method 6. The user pays for the reservation 7. The reservation is confirmed
1. Customer logs in to TORS using a valid login ID and password 2. Customer selects "Make Reservation" option 3. TORS displays a list of available tours 4. Customer selects the desired tour 5. TORS displays the tour details and the reservation form 6. Customer fills the reservation form with personal and payment details 7. Customer confirms the reservation 8. TORS verifies the availability of the tour on the selected date and updates the reservation status 9. TORS sends a reservation confirmation email to the customer 10. TORS updates the customer and reservation information in the database	Postconditions: The user has a confirmed reservation on the tour Alternative Flows: If the user does not have an account, they can create an account before making a reservation If the tour is sold out, the user will be notified and will not be able to make a reservation If the user enters incorrect information, they will be prompted to correct the information before making a reservation If the user's payment is declined, they will be prompted to enter a different payment method Exception Handling: If the user encounters an error, they can contact the travel agency's customer service for assistance I hope this use case is clear and concise. Please let me know if you have any questions
Alternative Flows: If the selected tour is not available on the selected date, TORS displays an error message, and the customer needs to select another tour or date If the customer's payment details are invalid, TORS displays an error message, and the customer needs to correct the details Postconditions: The tour reservation is confirmed and updated in TORS The customer receives a reservation confirmation email The customer's and reservation information are updated in the database	

description, and the basic flow effectively depicts the sequence of interactions, including additional details that appear to be inferred from ChatGPT's domain knowledge such as filling out the reservation form in Step 6 (which was not explicitly stated in the original TORS description but added in the revised description), verifying tour availability in Step 7, sending a confirmation in Step 8, and updating information in database in Step 9. Although these additional details are subject to be confirmed by the customer, they contribute to the maturity and richness of the requirements, potentially aiding in the identification of any missing requirements. Alternative flows also provide additional details inferred by ChatGPT, especially for scenarios where the selected tour is not available and payment details are invalid. However, they are somewhat brief and miss steps. Postconditions, which describe any state changes made by the use case, appear reasonable, except the one regarding the customer receiving a reservation confirmation email, which is not necessarily a state change. On the other hand, the specification lacks information on the scope and level of the system under development. The use case specification produced by Bard presents a similar structure to ChatGPT's, adhering to the commonly used form. Compared to ChatGPT's output, Bard's preconditions cover only a single condition similar to the one in ChatGPT's specification. The basic flow generally aligns with the TORS description, incorporating some details inferred from Bard's domain knowledge such as the payment process in Step 5 and 6. However, the sequence lacks interactive system responses, which are crucial from both a user perspective and a development standpoint. On the other hand, the alternative flows appear to be more comprehensive than ChatGPT's, encompassing more scenarios such as users not having an account or entering incorrect information. It is notable that Bard's specification also includes an exception handling section, which resembles the nature of alternative flows. Bard's specification, however, does not include any postconditions. In summary, both ChatGPT and Bard incorporated additional details inferred from their domain knowledge, which contributes to the maturation and enrichment of the requirements, and ChatGPT's specification appears to be more detailed in most aspects, except for alternative flows where Bard's specification offers more comprehensive coverage.

3.2   Domain Modeling

In this phase, we compare the capability of ChatGPT and Bard on constructing UML domain class diagrams that contain domain concepts, attributes, and relationships without any design decisions such as operations, navigabilities, data types, or code-level details such as visibility.

Identifying Domain Concepts   In this task, we evaluate the ability of ChatGPT and Bard to identify domain concepts from the TORS description. The following prompt was given to the models:

– Prompt: "Identify domain concepts from the TORS description."

Table 5 Comparison of identified domain classes

ChatGPT	Bard
Tour: A trip or journey, typically for pleasure, during which a number of different places are visited Reservation: The process of reserving or booking a tour in advance Tour Information: Data and details related to a specific tour, such as its destination, duration, cost, and itinerary Customer: A person who makes a reservation for a tour Feedback: Comments or opinions provided by customers about their experience with the tour or the reservation system Employee: A person who works for the travel agency and manages the tour information and customer data Login credentials: A combination of login ID and password that employees use to access the system Database: A collection of data that is stored and organized in a specific way, used to store and retrieve tour information, customer data, and feedback	Tour: A tour is a journey that is typically organized and led by a tour guide. Tours can be educational, recreational, or cultural Tour information: Tour information includes the destination, date, time, price, and availability of a tour Reservation: A reservation is a booking for a tour. Reservations can be made online or by phone Customer: A customer is a person who makes a reservation for a tour Feedback: Feedback is information that is provided by a customer about a tour. Feedback can be positive or negative Employee: An employee is a person who works for the travel agency. Employees are responsible for managing customers and tours Login credentials: Login credentials are the username and password that are used to access the TORS system

The identified domain concepts along with descriptions are shown in Table 5. Both models successfully identified common domain concepts such as *Tour, Tour Information, Reservation, Customer, Feedback, Employee,* and *Login credentials* with similar descriptions. ChatGPT identified an additional concept *Database*. However, both models failed to identify *System, Reservation facilities, Travel agency,* and *Built-in network*, which are meaningful concepts to the TORS system. These observations hint that both models have competitive proficiency in identifying domain concepts, although there is room for improvement in capturing more relevant concepts.

Identifying Attributes In this task, ChatGPT and Bard were evaluated to identify respective attributes for the identified domain classes. The following prompt was given to the models:

– Prompt: "Identify attributes for the domain classes identified in the previous prompt."

ChatGPT identified a total of 49 attributes for the eight domain classes. Among these attributes, approximately 25 (51%) appear to be drawn from ChatGPT's domain knowledge. Similarly, Bard identified a total of 37 attributes for the seven domain classes, with about 11 (30%) attributes inferred from Bard's domain knowledge. Both models generated by Bard and ChatGPT produced many attributes in common, for instance, (i) *Tour ID, Tour name, Destination, Duration (Date and Time), Cost (Price),* and *Available dates (Availability)* attributes in the *Tour* class; (ii) the *Tour ID, Description,* and *Images* attributes in the *Tour Information* class; and (iii) the *Reservation ID, Tour ID, Customer ID, Reservation date (Date and Time), Number of People,* and *Payment status (Payment method and Status)* attributes in the *Reservation* class. This might imply that both models have acquired similar domain knowledge, likely from comparable sources. The models also produced additional attributes specific to them such as (i) the *Itinerary, Inclusions, Exclusions, Departure location,* and *Available dates* attributes in ChatGPT's outputs and (ii) the *Videos* attribute in Bard's outputs. From these observations, both models are capable of inferring meaningful attributes, many of which are common, but ChatGPT's outputs are a bit more ample than Bard's. It should be noted that any inferred attributes should go through a review and be confirmed by the client before adoption.

Identifying Relationships Based on the identified domain classes, ChatGPT and Bard were instructed to identify their relationships. The following prompt was given to the models:

– Prompt: "Identify relationships for the identified domain classes."

Table 6 presents the identified relationships. Both models identified relationships of (Tour, Reservation), (Tour, Tour Information), (Customer, Reservation), (Customer, Feedback), (Employee, Tour), (Employee, Customer), and (Employee, Login credentials). In addition, ChatGPT also included the relationships of *Database* with *Tour Information, Customer,* and *Feedback,* but did not involve the relationships of the *Database* with *Log credentials* and *Reservation.* There are no additional

Table 6 Comparison of identified relationships

ChatGPT	Bard
Tour and Reservation: A reservation is made for a specific tour	Tours and Tour information: A tour has tour information
Tour and Tour Information: Tour information provides details about a specific tour	Reservations and Tours: A reservation is for a tour
Customer and Reservation: A customer makes a reservation for a tour	Customers and Reservations: A customer makes a reservation
Customer and Feedback: A customer provides feedback about their experience with the tour or the reservation system	Feedback and Customers: A customer provides feedback
Employee and Tour: An employee manages the information and data related to tours	Employees and Customers: An employee manages customers
Employee and Customer: An employee manages the information and data related to customers	Employees and Tours: An employee manages tours
Employee and Login credentials: An employee uses login credentials to access the system	Login credentials and Employees: An employee has login credentials
Tour Information, Customer data and Feedback, and Database: All these are stored in the database	

relationships found in Bard's output. From these observations, it appears that ChatGPT offers slightly more extensive coverage due to the *Database* class.

Inferring Multiplicities In this task, we evaluate the capability of ChatGPT and Bard in "inferring" multiplicities on the ends of the identified relationships. The following prompt was given to the models:

– Prompt: "Determine multiplicities for the relationships identified in the previous prompt."

The majority of the multiplicities inferred by ChatGPT appear reasonable, accompanied by explanations from the perspective of each end of the relationship. For example, the multiplicities of the *Tour to Reservation* relationship are explained as one tour can have many reservations (1:*) from the *Tour* end perspective, and one reservation can only be associated with one tour (*:1) from the *Reservation* end perspective. However, there are notation errors observed in some multiplicities. The notation (*:1) on the *Reservation* end in the *Tour to Reservation* relationship should have been denoted as (1:1) to correspond to the explanation. Similar errors are found on the *Tour* end in the *Tour to Tour Information* relationship and on the *Login credentials* end in the *Employee to Login credentials* relationship. There are also some overly constrained cases. The multiplicity (1) on the *Employee* end in the *Employee to Tour* relationship specifies that one tour can be managed by one employee. However, in general, one tour can be managed by many employees. A similar case is found on the multiplicity (1) on the *Employee* end in the *Employee to Customer* relationship where one customer can be managed by many employees. It is also observed that their corresponding notation (*) on the *Employee* end is inconsistent with the explanation, which should have been denoted as (1) to be consistent. During inferring multiplicities, ChatGPT added an additional relationship between *Feedback* and *Tour*, which was not included in Table 6. This can be viewed as an inconsistency.

On the Bard side, the majority of the inferred multiplicities appear reasonable, and it did not have the errors found in ChatGPT's outputs. However, Bard also contains some overly constrained cases in the relationships of *Reservations and Tours (1:N)*, *Employees and Customers (1:N)*, and *Employees and Tours (1:N)*. For the *Reservations and Tours* relationship, typically, one tour is associated with multiple reservations, which should have been denoted as (N:N). For the relationships of *Employees and Customers* and *Employees and Tours*, ChatGPT had similar issues, and the same justification can apply. From these observations, it can be drawn that both models are capable of inferring multiplicities reasonably, but ChatGPT contains some notation errors and overly constrained cases, while Bard contains only the latter. This highlights the importance of a careful review when adopting inferred multiplicities.

Generating Domain Class Diagrams In this task, we evaluate the capability of ChatGPT and Bard in generating domain class diagrams, which capture a gross view of the problem domain. Based on the identified classes, attributes, and relationships above, the models were instructed to generate a domain class diagram. The following prompt was given to the models:

– Prompt: "Based on the classes, attributes, and relationships identified earlier, generate a domain class diagram."

However, being text-based models, they were unable to produce a visual class diagram. Instead, they provided a textual description of the domain class diagram, as shown in Fig. 3. For better understanding, we manually created class diagrams corresponding to the descriptions as shown in Fig. 4. As domain class diagrams are part of the problem domain, they should not involve any design decisions such as operations, navigability, and data types, which belong to the solution domain.

The diagrams generated by both models do not contain any design decisions, which serves the intended purpose. However, there are some inconsistencies in the generated class diagrams with the previously identified elements. In ChatGPT's diagram, the relationships of the *(Database, Tour)*, em (Database, Reservation), *(Database, Employee)*, and *(Database, Login credentials)* are missing, which were previously identified in Table 6. Similarly, Bard's diagram also lacks the relationship of *(Feedback, Customer)*, which was previously identified in Table 6. Bard's diagram also contains inconsistent attributes. The diagram shows the *Tour Information* attribute in the *Tour* class, but it was not included in Table 5. Bard's model involves association names, which are appropriate and expected for domain models, whereas ChatGPT's model does not. However, Bard's model has the *Feedback* class without any relationships, which is not good. In terms of maturity, ChatGPT's model appears to be more comprehensive, as it depicts more complete relationships among classes. The two models show similar structures that might imply that their domain knowledge was built on similar sources.

3.3   Design Modeling

In this phase, we evaluate the capabilities of ChatGPT and Bard in producing design models in terms of class diagrams and sequence diagrams. Design class diagrams differ from domain class diagrams in that they involve design decisions such as operations, navigabilities, and data types, which are part of human creativity. Hence, a key aspect to observe in this evaluation is how the models handle making design decisions.

Generating Design Class Diagrams The models were evaluated on building design class diagrams based on the domain class diagrams in Fig. 4. The following prompt was given to the models:

– Prompt: "Generate a design class diagram based on the domain class diagram produced earlier."

ChatGPT

The class diagram would consist of several classes, each representing one of the identified concepts (Tour, Reservation, Tour Information, Customer, Feedback, Employee, Login credentials, and Database) and their attributes. The classes would be connected by lines, representing the relationships between the concepts.

For example:

The Tour class would have attributes such as Tour ID, Tour name, Destination, Duration, Cost, Itinerary, Available dates, and Maximum capacity.

The Reservation class would have attributes such as Reservation ID, Tour ID, Customer ID, Reservation date, Number of people, Payment status and would be connected to the Tour class by an association link.

The Tour Information class would have attributes such as Tour ID, Description, Itinerary, Inclusions, Exclusions, Departure location, Available dates, and Images and would be connected to the Tour class by an association link.

The Customer class would have attributes such as Customer ID, Name, Email, Phone number, Address, Payment information, and Reservation history and would be connected to the Reservation class by an association link.

The Feedback class would have attributes such as Feedback ID, Tour ID, Customer ID, Feedback text, Feedback date and would be connected to the Tour class and Customer class by an association link.

The Employee class would have attributes such as Employee ID, Name, Email, Phone number, Address, Role, Login ID, and Password and would be connected to the Tour class, Customer class and Login Credentials class by an association link.

The Login Credentials class would have attributes such as Login ID and Password and would be connected to the Employee class by an association link.

The Database class would have attributes such as Database name, Data structure, Data type, Data security, Backup and recovery system.

Bard

[Tour]
- Tour ID
- Tour name
- Destination
- Date
- Time
- Price
- Availability
- Tour information

[Login credentials]
- Username
- Password

[Tour information]
- Tour ID
- Description
- Images
- Videos

[Tour]
- *has* 1 [Tour information]
- *has* 0.. * [Reservations]

[Reservation]
- Reservation ID
- Tour ID
- Customer ID
- Date
- Time
- Number of people
- Payment method
- Status

[Reservation]
- *is for* 1 [Tour]
- *is made by* 1 [Customer]

[Customer]
- Customer ID
- Name
- Email address
- Phone number
- Address

[Customer]
- *provides feedback for*
0.. * [Tours]

[Feedback]
- Feedback ID
- Customer ID
- Tour ID
- Feedback
- Date

[Employee]
- *manages* * 0.. *
[Customers]
- *manages* * 0.. * [Tours]
- *has* 1 [Login credentials]

[Employee]
- Employee ID
- Name
- Email address
- Phone number
- Address
- Job title

Fig. 3 Comparison of generated domain class diagram descriptions

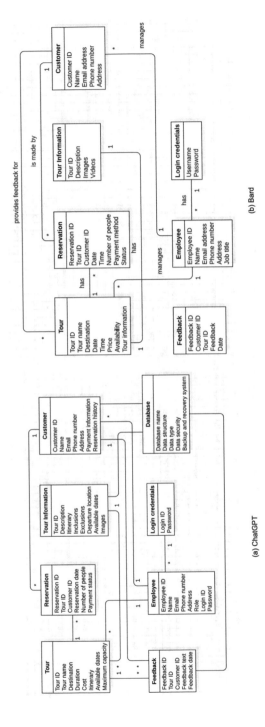

Fig. 4 Manually created domain class diagrams corresponding to the class diagram descriptions in Fig. 3

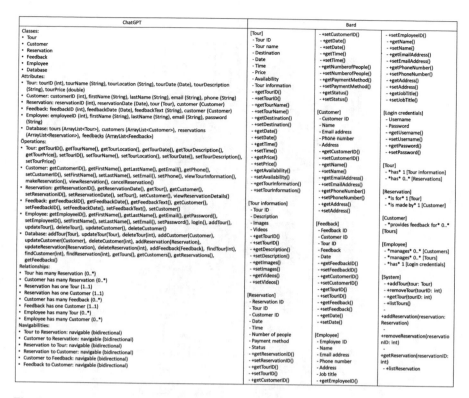

Fig. 5 Comparison of generated design class diagram descriptions

The generated textual descriptions of the design class diagrams are shown in Fig. 5. For better understanding, we manually built graphical diagrams per the generated descriptions as shown in Fig. 6. In ChatGPT's diagram, the attributes that denote relationship roles are represented on association ends (e.g., *tour* in *Reservation*). Getters and setters are excluded by convention. Key points to observe in the diagrams are design decisions made and consistency with the domain class diagrams in Fig. 4.

The diagram generated by ChatGPT involves classes and relationships with operations, data types, multiplicities, and navigabilities. All the classes in the diagram were identified during domain modeling (cf. Table 5), but it does not include the *Tour information* and *Login credentials* classes that were identified during domain modeling, which is an inconsistency. In fact, the missing classes are important data classes that should not be missed. The *Database* class shows no relationships with other classes, which is not good and also inconsistent with the domain model. All the classes in the diagram are defined with operations, which are important design decisions, but most of them are getters and setters for attribute access. The *Reservation*, *Customer*, and *Employee* classes include feature operations such as *viewTourinformation()* and *makeReservation()*, which appear to be derived

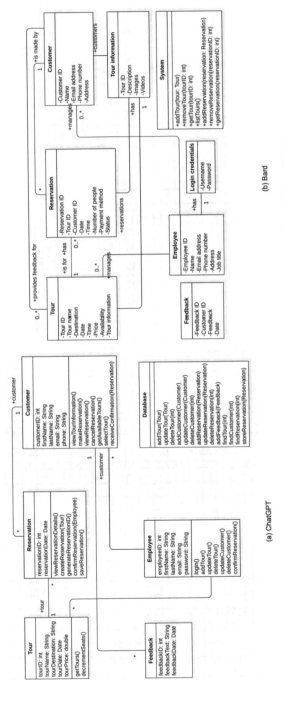

Fig. 6 Manually created design class diagram corresponding to the text-based design class diagram by ChatGPT and Bard

from the TORS description, demonstrating the ability of making design decisions. On the other hand, the operations in the *Database* class appear to be inferred from ChatGPT's domain knowledge, as they are typical data management operations like add, update, and delete. With respect to attributes, all the attributes are appropriately typed and follow a consistent naming convention of using lowercase for the first letter and capitalizing the first letter of each subsequent word, which is impressive. There are also some attributes that denote relationship roles such as the *tour* and *customer* attributes in the *Reservation* class and the *customer* attribute in the *Feedback* class, which should not be included in practice. Regarding relationships, they were all identified during domain modeling (cf. Table 6). However, the description does not include the relationships of (Tour, Tour information), (Tour information, Database), (Customer, Database), and (Feedback, Database) identified in domain modeling. The multiplicities on relationship ends are consistent with those identified during domain modeling (cf. Table 5). However, the multiplicity on the *Employee* end in the *(Employee, Tour)* relationship and the multiplicity on the *Customer* end in the *(Employee, Customer)* relationship are missed. With respect to navigabilities, they are all bidirectional but defined only for the relationships of *(Tour, Reservation)*, *(Customer, Reservation)*, and *(Customer, Feedback)*. The navigabilities for the *(Employee, Tour)* and *(Employee, Customer)* relationships are missed. Overall, the evaluation demonstrates ChatGPT's capability of making appropriate design decisions with some inconsistencies with the domain model.

The diagram generated by Bard includes classes and relationships with visibilities, operations, and multiplicities but lacks data types and navigabilities, which are important design decisions. All the classes that were identified during domain modeling (cf. Table 5) are present, which demonstrates descent consistency. It also introduces a new class *System*, which appears to serves as the facade controller, providing system-level feature operations. However, the class has no relationships with other classes, which is not good. However, except for the *System* class, the operations in all other classes contain only getters and setters with no feature operations, which is not satisfactory from a design decision point of view. The *Public* visibility is used for operations by default. With respect to relationships, they were all identified during domain modeling (cf. Table 6), except for the *(Customer, Tour)* relationship, which is newly added. However, the *(Feedback, Customer)* relationship that was identified in domain modeling is missed. Overall, the evaluation demonstrates the limited capability of Bard on making design decisions on navigabilities and data types with some inconsistencies with the domain model.

In comparison, ChatGPT's diagram is superior to Bard's diagram as it contains more comprehensive design decisions such as data types and navigabilities. Moreover, ChatGPT's diagram better incorporates feature operations across classes, whereas Bard has feature operations only in the *System* class. On the other hand, ChatGPT's diagram lacks visibilities, while Bard's diagram has them. Both diagrams lack return type for operations and contain inconsistencies with from the domain models.

Generating Design Sequence Diagrams In this task, we evaluate the abilities of ChatGPT and Bard on generating design sequence diagrams for behavior modeling, which aims at assigning operations to classes, which is an important design decision. The assigned operations should be consistent with the operations defined in the design class diagrams in Fig. 6. For the evaluation, ChatGPT and Bard were instructed to generate a sequence diagram for the *make tour reservation* use case. The following prompt was given to the models:

– Prompt: "Generate a design sequence diagram for the "Make Tour Reservation" use case specification produced earlier."

The description generated by ChatGPT shows the involved objects and their interactions, but does not clearly show the involved messages and their sequences. On the other hand, Bard's description presents relatively clearly sequences, but messages are not clearly due to the use of an unfamiliar notation (i.e., "->") without explanation. To improve the clarity of message sequences, both models were further instructed to produce explicit message sequences. In the improved message sequences, ChatGPT provides explicit names for operations, but Bard does not. Instead, Bard provides descriptions for operations.

For better understanding, graphical sequence diagrams based on the descriptions and message sequences were created manually as shown in Fig. 7.

The diagram by ChatGPT demonstrates a proper distribution of responsibilities among objects, aligning with the principles of General Responsibilities Assignment Software Patterns (GRASP) [5] (e.g., Information Expert pattern, Creator pattern, Controller pattern). However, there are some drawbacks as well—(i) the sequence should start with the *makeReservation()* operation on the *Customer* object since the scenario is concerned about making a tour reservation; (ii) the sequence of *(getAvailableTours() -> getTours())* is separated from the rest; (iii) the *recieveConfirmation()* message is not involved in any sequence; (iv) the *storeReservation()* message has an inconsistent name with the corresponding *addReservation()* operation in the class diagram in Fig. 6a; and (v) the caller of *receiveConfirmation()* is ambiguous. Nonetheless, overall, ChatGPT's sequence diagram demonstrates appropriate operation assignment and descent consistency with the design class diagram.

The diagram by Bard is more like a system sequence diagram illustrating the interactions between an actor and the system rather than a design sequence diagram. Consequently, the assignment of operations is biased toward the *System* class, which acts as the facade controller. As a result, the design lacks appropriate distribution of operations and object collaboration. Furthermore, none of the messages in the sequence diagram align with the operations defined in the design class diagram (cf. Fig. 6b), leading to significant inconsistencies between the two diagrams.

In summary, ChatGPT's sequence diagram is more practical compared to Bard's in terms of operation assignment and object collaboration. The operations in ChatGPT's diagram are appropriately named and assigned to different classes based on relevant information, which aligns with the principles of GRASP. Also, it demonstrates good consistency with the design class diagram. Contrarily, Bard's sequence diagram is overly focused on the *Customer* and *System* classes, which

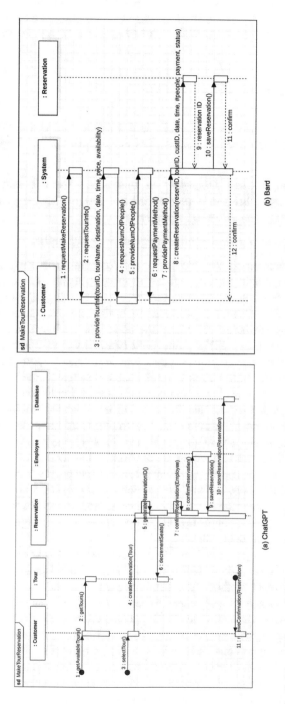

Fig. 7 Manually created design sequence diagram corresponding to the text-based design sequence diagram by ChatGPT and Bard

makes the diagram more like a system sequence diagram in requirements analysis. Furthermore, the operations in Bard's diagram lack proper naming and show significant inconsistency with the design class diagram in terms of operations.

3.4 Implementation

In this phase, we evaluate the ability of ChatGPT and Bard to implement design class diagrams and sequence diagrams. We chose Java for the implementation language.

Implementing Design Class Diagrams In this task, ChatGPT and Bard were assessed for their capabilities in implementing the design class diagrams in Fig. 6. The following prompt was given to the models:

– Prompt: "Implement the design class diagram produced earlier."

Among the generated classes, we chose the *Tour* class for comparison, which contains more comparable characters in terms of code details. The *Customer* class was also chosen for ChatGPT as it contains code details highlighting the coding abilities of ChatGPT. ChatGPT produced a basic implementation of the *Tour* class, incorporating attributes and empty methods. The attributes are defined with code-level details such as visibility and data type. However, some attributes are inconsistent with the class diagram such as *tourDestination* typed with *int*, but its corresponding attribute in the class diagram has a different name *tourDate* typed with *Date*. All the methods were empty in the initial implementation, although they were accompanied by comments outlining the intended implementation for each method. The methods including the constructor were incrementally filled out with specific implementations as further instructions were given. In the *Customer* class, the *cancelReservation* method demonstrates the incorporation of various control structures such as if-else statements, for loops, and nested structures. In the implementation of the *Reservation* class (which is not presented in the figure), the incorporation of data structures such as *List* and *ArrayList* was observed. However, none of the implemented methods match the operations in the design class diagram, which create significant inconsistency.

The implementation generated by Bard encompasses attributes with specified visibility and data types, along with the fully implemented getters, setters, constructor, and *toString()* method. The implementation of the constructor appears appropriate, and the getters and setters follow standard conventions. It is notable that the implementation includes the *toString()* method, which is a common practice to provide a string representation of an object. Also, the implemented methods align well with the operations defined in the design class diagram. However, the implementation lacks the *Tour information* attribute as defined in the class diagram.

In conclusion, Bard's implementation exhibits a more complete code with standard conventions and higher consistency with the design class diagram. On the other hand, ChatGPT's implementation contains incomplete code and more inconsistencies with the design class diagram, which further leads to traceability issues between phases. However, ChatGPT was able to incrementally develop the full implementation with rich code-level details as additional instructions were provided.

Implementing Design Sequence Diagrams In this task, we evaluate the ability of ChatGPT and Bard on implementing design sequence diagrams. For the evaluation, they were instructed to implement the *Make Tour Reservation* sequence diagram in Fig. 7. The following prompt was given to the models:

– Prompt: "Implement the "Make Tour Reservation" design sequence diagram produced earlier."

Table 7 shows the generated implementation. ChatGPT implemented the sequence diagram as part of the driver class *TORS*, which is a new class not included in the class diagram and, thus, does not participate in the sequence diagram. The implementation attempts to follow the sequence in the diagram but does not fully adhere to the intended sequence. Specifically, the diagram specifies that the *createReservation()* method is called within the *selectTour()* method by the *Customer* class, but the implementation shows that the *createReservation()* method is called within the *makeReservation()* method by the *TORS* class, which does not participate in the sequence diagram. This happened as the sequence diagram was implemented solely in a single method, which demonstrates significant inconsistency with the design. Furthermore, the implementation is incomplete in certain parts leaving code sections marked with "...".

Similar to ChatGPT, Bard implemented the sequence diagram as part of the drive class *TourReservationSystem*, which is newly added during implementation and, thus, does not participate in the sequence diagram. Although the sequence diagram is implemented solely within the driver class, the overall sequence of the implementation aligns well with the sequence diagram. This happens because the design sequence diagram was built similar to system sequence diagrams where sequences are captured between only the actor and the system. So, this can be viewed as a wrong design but correct implementation to the design. There also exists an inconsistency where the *status* parameter in the sequence diagram is implemented as updating the tour's availability. Overall, the implementation maintains a descent level of consistency with the sequence diagram in terms of message sequences.

In summary, Bard's implementation exhibits a higher level of consistency with the design compared to ChatGPT. However, Bard's sequence diagram was far more simpler, which makes it easier to be implemented. On the other hand, ChatGPT's sequence diagram was more realistic and practical, but its implementation had significant inconsistency with the design. Both ChatGPT and Bard incorporated data generation in the driver class, which was impressive.

Fixing Errors The generated code by ChatGPT and Bard contained a number of errors of different kinds, including missing import statements, missing modifiers

Table 7 Comparison of generated code for *MakeTourReservation* sequence diagram

ChatGPT	Bard

public void makeReservation(Tour tour) {
 	
// retrieve available tours
 	
ArrayList<Tour> availableTours = tour.getAvailableTours();
 	
// select a tour
 	
Tour selectedTour = ...;
 	
// create a reservation for the tour
 	
Reservation reservation = new Reservation();
 	
String reservationId = reservation.createReservation(selectedTour);
 	
// decrement available seats for the selected tour
 	
tour.decrementAvailableSeats(selectedTour);
 	
// confirm the reservation
 	
Employee employee = new Employee();
 	
employee.confirmReservation(reservationId);
 	
// save the reservation in the database
 	
reservation.saveReservation(reservationId);
 	
}
	public void makeReservation(Customer customer, Tour tour, int numberOfPeople, PaymentMethod paymentMethod) {
	
	// Check if the tour is available
	
	if (!tour.isAvailable()) {
	
	throw new IllegalStateException("Tour is not available");
	
	}
	
	// Check if the number of people is less than or equal to the capacity of the tour
	
	if (numberOfPeople > tour.getCapacity()) {
	
	throw new IllegalStateException("Number of people exceeds tour capacity");
	
	}
	
	// Create a new reservation object
	
	Reservation reservation = new Reservation(
	
	customer.getCustomerID(),
	
	tour.getTourID(),
	
	numberOfPeople,
	
	paymentMethod
	
	);
	
	// Add the new reservation to the list of reservations
	
	reservations.add(reservation);
	
	// Update the tour's availability
	
	tour.setAvailable(false);
	
	// Send a confirmation message to the customer
	
	System.out.println("Reservation created successfully!");
	}

(e.g., static), undefined variables (e.g., symbol errors), undefined data types (e.g., undefined enumerations), undefined methods (e.g., missing getters and setters), parameter mismatches (e.g., redundant arguments, type mismatches, ordering mismatches), and misuse of methods and constructors in library classes (e.g., *Date*, *Time*). However, they were able to fix the majority of the errors effectively (more than 90%), which was impressive. In Bard, sometimes, the fixed code did not contain any change, and further instructions had to be given until a proper fix was incorporated. Such an issue did not occur with ChatGPT. Although both models successfully addressed most errors individually, the fixes were made piecemeal for each specific error, which led to many inconsistencies among fixes, which introduced new errors, and further fixes had to be introduced for the errors. This cycle continued until the human developer intervened and resolved the errors manually. In summary, both ChatGPT and Bard demonstrated competitive capabilities in fixing individual errors, but human involvement was required to finalize the implementation and make it executable.

4   Discussion

Based on the findings in Sect. 3, we answer the research questions posed in Sect. 1 as follows.

What Are the Respective Strengths and Weaknesses of ChatGPT and Bard in the Context of Software Development? In requirements analysis, ChatGPT focused more on technical aspects and functionality, while Bard was concerned more on user experience and system interactions. ChatGPT performed slightly better in clarifying ambiguities in requirements, incorporating clarifications into requirements, extracting FRs and NFRs, and generating use case specifications. In domain modeling, Bard's model was easier to understand due to the inclusion of association names. However, ChatGPT's model offers a more comprehensive structure with more relationships among classes. In design modeling, ChatGPT produced more mature and practical designs compared to Bard. ChatGPT's design class diagram incorporates more design decisions of different kinds than Bard's. In terms of design sequence diagrams, ChatGPT's diagram demonstrates more collaborative behaviors among objects, while Bard's diagram primarily focuses on interactions between two objects, resembling a system sequence diagram used in requirements analysis. In implementation, Bard's implementation was more consistent to the design with standard coding practice. In contrast, ChatGPT's implementation was less complete in the initial implementation, but with further instructions, it incrementally evolved to the mature level with rich code-level details. In error fixing, ChatGPT slightly outperformed Bard in terms of accuracy. However, both models suffered from significant inconsistency between the design and implementation, which further raises traceability issues between phases.

How Can ChatGPT and Bard Be Effectively Used Together for Software Development? It is found that ChatGPT and Bard focus on different aspects (technical aspects in ChatGPT and user aspects in Bard) in requirements analysis, which suggests that their combined use can help cover more comprehensive aspects and achieve balanced analysis of requirements. ChatGPT is more mature in design modeling in terms of making design decisions, while Bard can supplement additional design elements (e.g., classes, attributes, operations, relationships). Both ChatGPT and Bard demonstrate comparable capabilities in generating code and fixing errors, with limited benefits in their combined use.

Threats to Validity The prompts used in this work are designed to be sequential where the output of an earlier prompt is used as input for a later prompt, simulating the forward engineering in the development process. Different approaches may yield different outputs. The findings are based on only one case study, and thus, the assessment is not general enough. The assessment was carried out by a single researcher with 32 years of experience in software engineering. Different assessment results may be drawn by other researchers.

5 Conclusion

The findings in this study suggest that ChatGPT and Bard had different focuses in requirement analysis, ChatGPT performed slightly more effectively in design modeling, and they are comparable in implementation and error fixing. However, both models suffer from many inconsistencies among generated artifacts, and significant inconsistency was observed between design and implementation, which further leads to traceability concerns between phases. In both models, the involvement of the human developer was required to address inconsistency issues and finalize the development. Despite these challenges, it was witnessed that the models have great potential to contribute to software development and their combined use can be effective particularly in requirements analysis and design modeling. Further studies with more case studies are needed to generalize the assessment and provide statistical support. More focused studies targeting specific activities in a phase can be valuable, such as applying design patterns in the design phase and refactoring code in the implementation phase. Also, the testing phase, which is not covered in this work, needs investigation. For more comprehensive comparison, other models such as GitHub Copilot [2] can be included.

References

1. Dakhel, A.M., Majdinasab, V., Nikanjam, A., Khomh, F., Desmarais, M.C., Jiang, Z.M.: GitHub copilot AI pair programmer: asset or liability? J. Syst. Software, 111734 (2023)
2. GitHub: Github copilot (2021). https://copilot.github.com/

3. Google: Bard (2023). https://bard.google.com
4. Koza, J.R.: Genetic programming as a means for programming computers by natural selection. Stat. Comput. **4**, 87–112 (1994)
5. Larman, C.: Applying UML and Patterns: An Introduction to Object-Oriented Analysis and Design and Iterative Development, 3rd edn. Prentice Hall, New Jersey (2004)
6. Mastropaolo, A., Pascarella, L., Guglielmi, E., Ciniselli, M., Scalabrino, S., Oliveto, R., Bavota, G.: On the robustness of code generation techniques: An empirical study on Github copilot. Preprint (2023). arXiv:2302.00438
7. Peng, S., Kalliamvakou, E., Cihon, P., Demirer, M.: The impact of AI on developer productivity: Evidence from Github copilot. Preprint (2023). arXiv:2302.06590
8. Sobania, D., Briesch, M., Rothlauf, F.: Choose your programming copilot: a comparison of the program synthesis performance of Github copilot and genetic programming. In: Proceedings of the Genetic and Evolutionary Computation Conference, pp. 1019–1027 (2022)
9. Team, O.: Openai: Advances in large language models (2021). https://chat.openai.com/
10. Team, O.: Openai: models (2022). https://platform.openai.com/docs/models/overview
11. Wermelinger, M.: Using GitHub copilot to solve simple programming problems. In: Proceedings of the 54th ACM Technical Symposium on Computing Science Education, vol. 1, pp. 172–178 (2023)

DAnTE: A Taxonomy for the Automation Degree of Software Engineering Tasks

Jorge Melegati ⓘ and Eduardo Guerra ⓘ

Abstract Software engineering researchers and practitioners have pursued manners to reduce the amount of time and effort required to develop code and increase productivity since the emergence of the discipline. Generative language models are another step in this journey, but it will probably not be the last one. In this chapter, we propose DAnTE, a Degree of Automation Taxonomy for software Engineering, describing several levels of automation based on the idiosyncrasies of the field. Based on the taxonomy, we evaluated several tools used in the past and in the present for software engineering practices. Then, we give particular attention to AI-based tools, including generative language models, discussing how they are located within the proposed taxonomy and reasoning about possible limitations they currently have. Based on this analysis, we discuss novel tools that could emerge in the middle and long term.

Keywords Software engineering automation · AI for software engineering · Generative AI

1 Introduction

Human history is defined by the use of tools. From the use of rudimentary stones for preparing food in the Paleolithic to rockets taking us to space today, tools have been used to augment our capabilities or even to give us newer and more complex ones. As with any other human activity, software engineering (SE) has also experienced, since its inception, the continuous creation of tools to increase productivity, reduce errors, and facilitate the work of those involved in the activity. High-level programming languages, integrated development environments (IDEs), and frameworks, just to name a few, allowed the development of increasingly complex software systems with reduced effort and time spent [28]. For at least a

J. Melegati (✉) · E. Guerra
Free University of Bozen-Bolzano, Bolzano, Italy
e-mail: jorge.melegati@unibz.it; eduardo.guerra@unibz.it

© The Author(s), under exclusive license to Springer Nature Switzerland AG 2024
A. Nguyen-Duc et al. (eds.), *Generative AI for Effective Software Development*,
https://doi.org/10.1007/978-3-031-55642-5_3

53

decade, researchers have been exploring the use of artificial intelligence (AI) to support SE tasks [31]. The emergence of a novel generation of AI tools, driven by generative large language models (LLMs), promises to be a disruption on how software is developed, intensifying this tendency. Some research has investigated how developers have employed different tools, such as IDEs [17], and even code generation tools [37]. However, a framework to understand the evolution of these tools, including generative AI, still lacks.

In this chapter, based on a literature review of taxonomies in SE and other fields, we propose DAnTE, a taxonomy of SE automation tools that considers the whole evolution of these tools, positioning generative AI-based tools in a historical continuum. DAnTE consists of six levels of degree of automation: No automation (Level 0), Informer (Level 1), Suggester (Level 2), Local generator (Level 3), Global generator (Level 4), and Full generator (Level 5). To evaluate the taxonomy, we use it to classify two sets of tools focused on different SE activities: coding and testing. This utility demonstration indicates that the taxonomy could be used for classifying different tools for the automation of diverse SE tasks with clear advantages over the existent classification schemes described in the literature. Practitioners could employ it for evaluating and choosing tools to be used in different contexts. The taxonomy could be also useful for classifying research endeavors and guiding the development of novel tools.

2   Background and Related Work

2.1   Taxonomies

A taxonomy is a classification system defined by a collection of classes [22, 36]. A class is a set of properties shared by a set of instances [20, 22], where "an instance can be a material object, action, event, or any other phenomenon" [20]. Taxonomies are useful since they serve two functions: cognitive efficiency and inference support [20, 22]. Cognitive efficiency regards the possibility of remembering features of classes (a smaller number) instead of instances (a larger number) [20]. For example, a class "cat" already describes a set of characteristics, such as having whiskers and meowing, so we do not need to store the information that each cat we know has whiskers and meows, and we only store that a specific cat is an instance of the class "cat" and, consequently, has whiskers and meows. Inference regards the possibility of deducing unobserved properties of an instance based on the class it pertains or "about other (concurrent) phenomena, about possible future states of us and our environment" [20]. In the previous example, once we know that a particular animal is a cat, we can infer, based on the characteristics of the class, that it has whiskers and meows, for example. In the SE field, taxonomies are useful because "they provide concepts and technical language needed for precise communication and education." Specifically, a taxonomy for the automation degree of tasks could help practitioners

Table 1 Levels of automation used in the AI-SEAL taxonomy [8]

	Level description
1	Human considers alternatives, makes and implements decision
2	Computer offers a set of alternatives, which human may ignore in making decision
3	Computer offers a restricted set of alternatives, and human decides which to implement
4	Computer offers a restricted set of alternatives and suggests one, but human still makes and implements final decision
5	Computer offers a restricted set of alternatives and suggests one, which it will implement if human approve
6	Computer makes decision but gives human option to veto before implementation
7	Computer makes and implements decision but must inform human after the fact
8	Computer makes and implements decision and informs human only if asked to
9	Computer makes and implements decision and informs human only if it feels this is warranted
10	Computer makes and implements decision if it feels it should and informs human only if it feels this is warranted

choose tools to be used in their projects, researchers to develop novel solutions, and educators to prepare the future actors for these tasks.

In the SE literature, there are taxonomies focused on related topics. Feldt et al. [8] proposed AI-SEAL, a taxonomy for the use of AI in SE, consisting of three facets: point of application, type of AI applied, and level of automation. Point of application regards "when" and "on what" the tool is being applied, i.e., process, product, or runtime. Type of AI applied represents the type of AI technology used, for instance, connectionist or symbolist. Finally, the level of automation, described in Table 1, regards to which extent the tool assists the human in performing the task. The scale is adapted from the ten levels of automation in human-computer interaction proposed by Sheridan and Verplank [29]. The adoption of a taxonomy proposed for another field has the positive aspect of having been evaluated; however, even if it is related to the topic, it does not consider the specificalities of the new field, in our case, SE. Another issue is the focus on AI, neglecting the long history of tools developed for SE automation.

Savary-Leblanc et al. [25] performed a systematic mapping study on the employment of software assistants in SE. They classified assistants into three types: informer systems, passive recommender systems, and active recommender systems. Informer systems simply display the results of data analysis without any side effect. Passive recommender systems analyze data and potentially produce one or several alternatives for a decision-making problem. Finally, an active recommender system could also implement the decision. As examples of active recommender systems, the paper refers to tools that suggest code completion and code refactoring but also code documentation. Given the recent advances of generative LLMs, this class might accommodate several tools that have really different capabilities, such as code completion tools based on stemming and full-fledged code generation solutions based on LLMs.

Bosch et al. [4] proposed that there are three distinct approaches to software development: requirement-driven, outcome/data-driven, and AI-driven development. In the requirement-driven approach, software is built based on requirements collected from stakeholders and specified as input for the team. In data-driven development, teams work toward pre-defined metrics and experiment with different solutions to improve them. In the AI-driven development, teams employ AI techniques "such as machine learning and deep learning to create components" based on data. Although these approaches define an evolution of SE, it is coarse-grained by considering one level of AI-use without considering cases in which AI is used to support, for example, requirement-driven development.

Tanimoto [32, 33] proposed a hierarchy for liveness, i.e., the ability to modify a running program, in visual programming. It contains six levels: (1) informative; (2) informative and significant; (3) informative, significant, and responsive; (4) informative, significant, responsive, and live; (5) tactically predictive; and (6) strategically predictive. In the first level, the visual representation of the program is only used by the developer for comprehending and documenting the program [32]. In the second level, the representation is the actual implementation of the program and will be used to perform the computation. In the third level, any change to representation triggers the execution or re-execution of the associated parts of the system after a period of time. In Level 4, the system would not wait and would be updated as soon as changes were made. In Level 5, the system is able to predict the next developer action, possibly suggesting multiple alternatives, planning "ahead slightly to discover possible nearby program version" useful for the developer [33]. Finally, in Level 6, the system would be able to make predictions regarding a larger unit of software, synthesizing information from the software behavior and "a large knowledge base" [33].

From the above, the taxonomies used in SE were either (1) imported from other fields, such as human-computer interaction [8], without proper consideration of the idiosyncrasies of SE, or (2) they were limited in the scope as the one of Savary-Leblanc et al. [25], which considers only a small number of types. For example, assistants with different levels of automation could be classified as active recommender systems. Therefore, there is a clear need of an improved taxonomy, focused on SE tasks, taking into consideration the last developments in the field of LLMs and generative AI in general.

Taxonomies for the automation of tasks have also been proposed in other fields. A notorious example is the taxonomy for driving automation systems [12] proposed by SAE International and recognized as a standard by ISO. The document describes six levels of driving automation: the first level (0) describes no automation; Level 1 regards when there is driver assistance; Level 2 stands for partial driving automation;

Level 3, conditional driving automation; Level 4, high driving automation; and finally, Level 5, which regards full driving automation. The classification is based on how much the driver participates in the process. Even though it is simple, consisting of only one dimension, the taxonomy has been employed by the industry and governments [43].

2.2 Automation of SE Tasks

In her seminal paper on an engineering discipline for software, Shaw [28] reviews how SE evolved until that moment, including a discussion on the tools used. In the beginning, around 1960, programs were small, and tools consisted mainly of assemblers and core dumps. Around 1970, programs became more complex, including more algorithms and data structures, but still usually consisted of individual effort. In this period, tools like higher-level programming languages and compilers emerged. Around 1980, systems became even more complex, with some running continuously, and were the result of team efforts, leading to the emergence of the IDEs. For example, Teitelman and Masinter [34], in a paper from 1981, describe an integrated environment for the Lisp language. The tool allowed programmers to switch between tasks, such as debugging and editing. In the following years, IDEs became more sophisticated. In the 2000s, programmers could, for example, in Eclipse, perform several tasks, such as navigating the code structure and perform automatic refactoring [17]. More recently, the increased usage of dynamic languages, such as JavaScript [35], led to the emergence of linters, simple static analysis tools that "flag non-complex programming errors, best practices, and stylistic coding standards" [9].

With the advancements in AI, researchers have been proposing tools to automatically generate code, for example, IntelliCode [31]. These tools have started to move to the industry, especially as add-ons to IDEs, such as GitHub Copilot,[1] which could be used in, for example, Visual Studio and IntelliJ. The recent emergence of LLMs with tools like OpenAI's ChatGPT could represent another leap in this evolution. Researchers have already investigated its potential use for SE tasks, such as architecture [1] and testing [42]. More in this regard can be found in other chapters of this book.

3   Research Method

Taxonomies can be created based on several research methods, either as secondary studies or primary studies, employing diverse data collection methods, such as interviews, observation, questionnaires, or archival analysis [22, 36]. Secondary

---

[1] https://github.com/features/copilot.

studies are considered one of the best options to generate a taxonomy, given its speed, connection with existing theories, and greater rigor [22]. A natural choice would be to conduct a systematic review or mapping study in SE literature to identify tools that automate processes. However, the SE literature breadth and the interval of time that should be considered, given the goal of considering all attempts for automating the different tasks, would lead to a massive number of papers to be analyzed. Ralph [22] suggest that taxonomies can be created "by synthesizing, combining, refining or adapting existing theories from SE or reference disciplines." Given the success of the taxonomy for autonomous driving, suggested by its adoption by industry and governments [43], we decided to take it as a reference to build a similar taxonomy to SE automation.

To perform this adaptation, we performed a literature review focusing specially on secondary studies that classified, to some extent, automation tools for SE, as described in Sect. 2. We also reviewed primary studies, especially recent ones that focused on novel solutions, such as ChatGPT, which, given the short time interval since the launch, would probably not be reported in scientific published secondary studies. Then, using the taxonomy of driving automation, we compared the different tools, grouping them according to levels of automation. Based on this process, we propose a taxonomy for the automation degree of SE tasks described below.

To evaluate the taxonomy, we identified some tools regarding two SE activities, namely, coding and testing, and classified them according to the taxonomy's classes. We aim to demonstrate that it fulfills the criteria suggested by Ralph [22], i.e., (1) its class structure should reflect "similarities and dissimilarities between instances," (2) its classes facilitate the inference of properties of an instance based on how it has been classified, and (3) it is effective regarding the proposed purpose. Considering different approaches for taxonomy evaluation [36], this evaluation study can be classified as a utility demonstration, in which the taxonomy's utility is demonstrated by actually classifying subject matter examples [30, 39]. The tools used in the evaluation were taken from academic reports in the existing literature, but tools considered as state-of-practice, used by industry, were also considered.

4   DAnTE: A Taxonomy for SE Automation

DAnTe, a Degree of Automation Taxonomy for software Engineering, consists of six levels, from a level in which no automation is employed (Level 0) to a level with complete automation (Level 5). As the level increases, on the one hand, tools are able to perform more tasks with a greater level of autonomy, and on the other hand, the responsibilities of developers decrease. Figure 1 summarizes all the levels. The name refers to Dante Alighieri (c. 1265–1321), an Italian poet who wrote the *Divine Comedy*, considered by many the greatest literary work in the Italian language. In the *Comedy*, Dante describes hell, purgatory, and heaven as containing different levels.

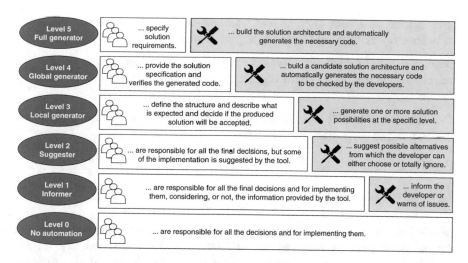

Fig. 1 DAnTE and its six levels of automation degree

4.1 Level 0: No Automation

This level considers the scenario with a total lack of automation or support tools. A typical example is a developer or development team employing simple text editors to create code. This scenario represents how software was developed in the early days of computing, especially before the advent of IDEs [34]. Except for educational settings and new approaches, we do not expect to find software being professionally developed in such a way nowadays. However, we believe it is important to have this level in the taxonomy as a baseline for the other levels. We also highlight that the software development activity started at this level and new software development platforms might start here.

Developer Involvement The developer is completely responsible for performing the tasks and making all the decisions required to achieve the goals.

Tool Involvement No tool is employed to automate the process.

4.2 Level 1: Informer

This level represents the situations in which automatic tools are able to provide developers useful information; however, they are not able to suggest improvements. Some examples are tools included in simple IDEs that manage to statically check the code syntax and warn the user of problems but are not able to propose fixes. However, this level is not limited to static checks, and this information might also be extracted at runtime. An example would be information about test code coverage. More recent tools at this level are tools that automatically identify software vulnerabilities and warn developers of such issues.

Developer Involvement The developer is responsible for performing the task and making all the decisions needed considering, or not, the information provided by the tool.

Tool Involvement The tool informs the developer or warns of issues, but is not able to produce suggestions for fixing them.

4.3   Level 2: Suggester

At this level, tools are able not only to identify issues but also to propose solutions for the developers. In other words, the tool is able to automatically suggest modifications to the code originally created by the developer. Besides that, the decision to incorporate or not the suggestions is made by the developer. There are several examples in modern IDEs, such as auto-completion tools or refactoring suggesters. Another example is DependaBot,[2] a tool for GitHub that automatically identifies dependencies for the project in a repository that could be updated and suggests the most recent versions by automatically updating dependencies files.

Developer Involvement The developer is responsible for performing the tasks, but the tool is able to, automatically or not, suggest modifications.

Tool Involvement The tool suggests one or more possible alternatives from which the developer can either choose one or, even, ignore all of them.

4.4   Level 3: Local Generator

At this level, tools are able to automatically perform tasks in a constrained situation with limited scope. This task can be based on the current state of the artifacts or based on a brief description provided by the developer. At a module, component, or solution level, the developer, or development team, is still responsible for the conception. An example is the GitHub Copilot that, at the moment of writing, is able to compose methods, functions, or even classes, based on comments or function signatures; however, the overall structure of the code is defined by the developer. Another example will be tools that automatically detect problems, like in the previous level, but autonomously decide to change the code to correct or improve it.

---

[2] https://github.com/dependabot.

Developer Involvement Developers define the structure at a certain level and describe either in natural language or a domain-specific language what is expected. They decide if the proposed solution will be accepted or, in case many possibilities are given by the tool, which one will be used. In some situations, the developer might also fix issues or adapt the solution to other parts of the system. For example, in the case of code generation, the developer could perform variable renaming to adapt the names to other parts of the system.

Tool Involvement Given a description for a task with limited scope, the tool is able to generate one or more possibilities of solutions.

4.5   Level 4: Global Generator

Tools at this level might be able to produce complete solutions given a description in a natural or domain-specific language. However, a developer still needs to verify and, if needed, modify the solution. The tools could recognize that specific parts of the system are beyond their capabilities and recommend that developers should implement these parts. Currently, some informal reports are evaluating the use of LLMs, such as ChatGPT, to achieve this level, with still modest results, without any reported usage in real projects. Other tools at this level are limited to specific scenarios, such as no-code tools.

Developer Involvement The developer only provides the solution specification and verifies the generated solution.

Tool Involvement The tool implements a solution, including any necessary architecture and code, to be checked by developers.

4.6   Level 5: Full Generator

In this final level, tools would be able to develop a complete solution relying mainly on interactions with developers using natural language instead of programming language, representing a shift on the level of abstraction required for coding. This change is similar to the emergence of high-level programming languages that allowed most of the developers to not handle assembly languages, restricting it to specific cases. In the future, programming languages might become just another intermediate step that could be inspected but would not be the standard approach to develop software. Figure 2 illustrates this scenario. Depending on its scope, it is expected that a tool could generate all the artifacts needed for the system, which, besides source code, can also include others, such as models and documentation. Currently, some no-code tools might be able to perform similar tasks in really restricted contexts.

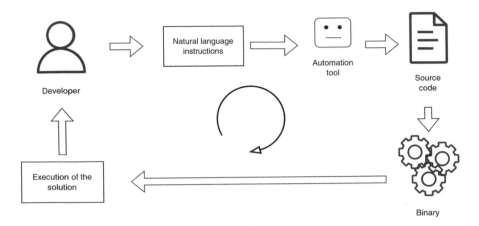

Fig. 2 Possible scenario of coding tool at Level 5 of automation

Developer Involvement The developer only needs to specify the solution requirements to the tool in a natural language.

Tool Involvement The tool builds the solution architecture and automatically generates the necessary code.

5   Evaluation

To evaluate DAnTE, we performed an utility demonstration [36], i.e., we applied it to classify tools and approaches on two SE activities: coding and testing. In the following sections, we present each level for both activities.

5.1   Level 0

Coding At this stage, no automation is foreseen. For coding, this scenario consists of developers using simple text editors, without any specific features for handling code, such as syntax checker, to write code. In the early days of software development, around the 1960s, until the beginning of the 1980s, programs were small and generally done as an individual effort [28]. The need for larger systems and development teams led to the emergence of development environments and integrated tools [28]. Since then, it is hard to imagine software being produced without any supporting tool, except for small educational tasks.

Testing This scenario consists of developers elaborating the code of automated tests manually, using only the requirements and information about the testing API.

Only a testing framework, such as JUnit [6], is used to provide some structure to the tests. The setup for the tests and the verification are configured through code. The developer has no aid on the test structure and its coverage.

5.2 Level 1

Coding In this level, tools inform developers about potential issues but are not able to make any suggestions for fixing them. For coding, this level include tools or simple code editors that, for instance, are able to identify syntax errors or the use of non-existent variables or functions. A contemporary example is the use of linters, "lightweight static analysis tools that employ relatively simple analysis to flag non-complex programming errors, best practices, and stylistic coding standards" [9]. These tools are especially useful for dynamically typed languages to warn about errors that, in these languages, would be only observed in runtime. ESLint[3] for JavaScript and Pylint for Python[4] are some examples.

Testing In this scenario, the development environment can provide some additional information about the tests that can guide the developer to create the tests and the test code. An example of a feature present in some tools that can help for a better test code is automated test smell detection [19, 21]. This information can guide the developer to create a cleaner code and a more efficient test suite. Another useful information that can be provided is code coverage [26], which is usually shown visually in the IDE through the lines of code being covered by the tests or not. Based on that, the developer might add new tests or modify the existing ones to achieve the desired test coverage.

5.3 Level 2

Coding At this level, tools not only identify issues but make suggestions that could be accepted or not by the developer. Regarding coding, tools that leverage similar scenarios in a limited context to make suggestions of modifications on the code for the developer are included at this stage. These processes are implemented using heuristics relying on similarity. A clear example is auto-completion tools in IDEs. Once the developer starts typing, the tool looks for similar terms from the language or elements in the project that could complete what the developer wanted to do. Another example could be automatic refactoring that, for example, has been for long supported by the Eclipse IDE for Java [40]. In this case, developers select pieces of

---

[3] https://eslint.org/.

[4] https://www.pylint.org/.

code and which type of refactoring they wish to perform; the tool, then, suggests the refactoring based on pre-defined rules, and the developer can accept or not the suggested modifications.

Testing Tools that can provide suggestions to create or improve the tests should be included in this level. Similar to coding, there are suggested refactorings specific to test code that can be applied automatically by the tools [14, 41]. Another kind of tool that fits into this level is the creation of test templates. Most IDEs provide the feature of creating test classes based on the structure of the class under test, suggesting test methods to be created. The test template generation might also consider other factors, such as test names [44].

5.4   Level 3

Coding Tools that are able to generate solutions for different SE activities should be included at this level. For coding, tools that can generate code for a given limited scenario, generally restricted to a few lines of code and few degrees of freedom, should be categorized in this level. An example is GitHub Copilot, which creates the code of a function based on a comment or the signature provided by the developer. The developer can also select one of many solutions suggested by the tool. GitHub Copilot's suggestions have low complexity code that could be further simplified or that relies on undefined helper methods [18]. It has been also observed that it struggles to combine methods to form a solution [16].

Testing At this level, test code is automatically generated for limited and specific contexts, such as unit tests of isolated classes and methods [15]. These tools usually consider the internal structures of the test target, generating test suites trying to maximize coverage [5, 10]. Some preliminary research also explored the usage of LLMs, based on ChatGPT, for unit test generation [42] with promising results. Even if some results indicate that the coverage of generated test suites is similar to manually created tests [13], other studies show that several faults were not detected by these automatically generated tests [27]. For instance, these tools have difficulties generating tests with good coverage when the inputs need a specific format or type to reach a given code branch.

5.5   Level 4

Coding Starting from this level on, at the time of writing, no tools fulfill the needs in a complete way. For coding, a tool at this level should be able to, given a description, develop the overall solution, including the design and implementation. In an object-oriented scenario, it would propose the classes, their interactions, and also the implementation of the methods. However, the tool would not guarantee the correctness, and developers should still check the proposed design and implementation. Several researchers and practitioners have experimented with ChatGPT to investigate whether the tool is able to support the development of a software system architecture, e.g., [1]; however, the results at the time of writing did not support the capacity of the tool to fulfill this goal. Another example is AgentGPT,[5] a tool that allows the configuration and deployment of AI agents based on a natural language chat with the developer.

Testing Tools at this level should be able to create tests not only for a class or a method but considering the whole application. In that scope, we can find tools that generate functional tests for specific kinds of applications, like Web apps [7] and REST APIs [2]. For more specific cases, it is possible to find test generation for non-functional aspects, like a proposal to generate tests to detect leaks in Android applications [45]. Even if we have some test generation tools that could be classified at this level for targeting the application as a whole, they are still specific to platforms and focus the tests on a single aspect.

5.6 Level 5

Since no tool currently reaches this degree of automation for code or test generation, it is hard to predict how the process of humans interacting with the tools would be when this level is reached. Based on the currently existing tools that are still in the previous levels, it is expected that they will follow an iterative process in which, based on the generated artifact, the user will provide feedback and more information to evolve it further in the desired direction employing natural language.

Coding At this final stage of the evolution of automatic generation, tools should be able to completely and reliably develop a software solution based on a natural language description of the required features. As in the driving automatic scenario in which, at the last level, it is only needed to define the destination, code generation tools in Level 5 simply require the goals to generate the final solution. The advancements of LLMs might lead to this stage in medium or long term. Another set of tools hinting how these tools could be are low-code/no-code platforms [23, 24], such as Mendix[6] and OutSystems.[7] By leveraging model-driven engineering, automatic code generation, cloud infrastructures, and graphical abstractions, these tools allow the development of fully functional applications by end users with no particular programming background [24]. However, these platforms require that users model the domain, define the user interface, and specify business logic [24]. Level 5 tools

---

[5] https://agentgpt.reworkd.ai/.

[6] https://www.mendix.com/.

[7] https://www.outsystems.com/.

would leverage natural language processing to perform these steps automatically based on, e.g., a chat with users.

Testing For the full generation of automated tests, the tool is expected to evaluate the application structure and generate automated tests at different levels. The tests should be generated in an executable specification using a general-purpose programming language or a tool-specific one. Additionally, its scope should not be limited to functional tests, also considering other non-functional aspects, such as security and performance. Current test generation tools focus on generating a specific type of test, usually with a limited scope regarding the platform on which it acts, like for REST API tests [3, 38]. For tools at the fifth level, it is expected that, for a given feature, they could generate unit tests exploring more low-level technical details, such as the interaction with user interface components and database, but also at a higher-level functional scenarios that verify not only the integration between the units but also their collaboration in delivering the expected functionality. For quality attributes, an initial set of metrics would be collected and presented to the user, which could refine the tests with incremental interactions with the tool. For example, after a presentation of performance measurements, more details about load and interaction would generate more specific scenarios. Currently, no tool reaches this degree of automation for test generation.

6   Discussion

The taxonomy proposed in this chapter, DAnTE, aimed to increase cognitive efficiency and facilitate inferences, as is the general case for taxonomies [22], for the specific case of automation of SE tasks. The validation performed through a utility demonstration, i.e., by classifying coding and testing tools, demonstrated that different tools, even for distinct tasks, share similarities and that the taxonomy could be employed to group them in categories, facilitating comparison.

Comparing with the existing taxonomy for the application of AI for SE tasks, i.e., AI-SEAL [8], and the classification of assistants for SE [25], DAnTE has some advantages. It has less steps when compared to AI-SEAL, and they are similar to those of a taxonomy of another field, i.e., driving automation. This aspect facilitates the comprehension by practitioners also by giving an analogy. In particular, the taxonomy development was based on the parsimony principle, which favors the simplest explanation possible [11], as the reduced number of levels show. Besides that, the proposed steps were redesigned with concepts and terminology related to SE, and not simply adapted from another field, as human-computer interaction. The number of steps allows, however, to differentiate tools that in the classification proposed for software assistants would be grouped together. Most, if not all, tools classified in the levels above 2 would be classified as active recommender systems even though, as our examples show, they have very different capabilities and degree of automation.

When classifying some practices in Levels 4 and 5, we could observe that some tools are probably going to be able to perform diverse tasks, such as coding and testing. Therefore, a possible further development of the taxonomy could consider the capacity of a tool of fulfilling multiple tasks rather than, for example, the point of application of the AI-SEAL taxonomy.

Ralph [22] identifies five possible errors when creating taxonomies: inclusion, exclusion, combination, differentiation, and excess. An inclusion error happens when an instance is included in a class even though it is not similar to other instances of the class, while an exclusion error occurs when an instance is not grouped with other instances similar to it. In the utility demonstration we performed, we presented the differences among the tools that made us grouped them together or apart. Combination errors happen when not similar instances are grouped together. In this regard, DAnTE is an improvement regarding the existent classification of software assistants, in the sense that it differentiates tools with different degrees of automation. Differentiation errors represent the cases when similar instances are separated in different classes. Based on our discussion above, we argue that the proposed taxonomy avoids this error that is possible when using AI-SEAL and its ten levels of automation by reducing the number of steps and providing an analogy. Finally, an excess regards cases when a class has no instances. Although Level 5 might fit this definition, it is useful to guide the development of new tools that, based on the rapid development of generative AI and LLMs, we expect to have them available in the near future.

7 Conclusions

This chapter presented DAnTE, a taxonomy for the automation degree of SE tasks, by leveraging a taxonomy for driving automation and reviewing similar works for SE. We performed an initial evaluation based on utility demonstration, i.e., by classifying coding and testing tools, reaching promising results. The taxonomy could help the comparison of diverse tools. It could also help practitioners understand what they could expect from different tools and facilitate the decision process of tool selection. The taxonomy also hints the next steps of automation of SE tasks, guiding practitioners and researchers alike in the development of novel tools.

Given the limited space, we were not able to present the use of the taxonomy for other SE tasks. However, our preliminary results indicate that it is useful to classify diverse tools. This classification can support the decision-making processes of development teams regarding which tools they should adopt, allowing the comparison among different tools and also between a tool and the development context. For example, depending on the availability of developers or the specificity of the domain, tools at different levels might be more adequate. The taxonomy also guide the development of new tools, providing the requirements that a new tool should fulfill to different itself at a distinct level from the competitors. Although not its focus, the taxonomy could bring implications to process taxonomies, such as the

Capability Maturity Model Integration (CMMI). Future work could investigate how tools at different levels influence development processes. A comprehensive analysis might indicate that the emergence of Level 4 or 5 tools could lead to the merge of different tasks as our evaluation showed, i.e., coding tools that already test the code produced. The taxonomy could be also further developed, probably including other dimensions, such as the type of AI applied. For example, the capability of a tool of performing more than a task, as described above, might indicate a valuable dimension for the classification of these tools. As the generative AI technology advances and new tools for SE tasks are proposed, future work could investigate the addition of new dimensions for the taxonomy.

References

1. Ahmad, A., Waseem, M., Liang, P., Fahmideh, M., Aktar, M.S., Mikkonen, T.: Towards human-bot collaborative software architecting with ChatGPT. In: Proceedings of the 27th International Conference on Evaluation and Assessment in Software Engineering, pp. 279–285. ACM, New York (2023). https://doi.org/10.1145/3593434.3593468
2. Arcuri, A.: RESTful API automated test case generation. In: 2017 IEEE International Conference on Software Quality, Reliability and Security, pp. 9–20. IEEE, New York (2017)
3. Arcuri, A.: RESTful API automated test case generation with EvoMaster. ACM Trans. Softw. Eng. Methodol. (TOSEM) 28(1), 1–37 (2019)
4. Bosch, J., Olsson, H.H., Crnkovic, I.: It takes three to tango: requirement, outcome/data, and AI driven development. In: Software-intensive Business Workshop on Start-ups, Platforms and Ecosystems (SiBW 2018), pp. 177–192. CEUR-WS.org, Espoo (2018)
5. Braione, P., Denaro, G., Mattavelli, A., Pezzè, M.: Sushi: a test generator for programs with complex structured inputs. In: Proceedings of the 40th International Conference on Software Engineering: Companion Proceedings, pp. 21–24 (2018)
6. Cheon, Y., Leavens, G.T.: A simple and practical approach to unit testing: the JML and JUnit way. In: ECOOP 2002—Object-Oriented Programming: 16th European Conference Málaga, Spain, June 10–14 Proceedings, pp. 231–255. Springer, Berlin (2002)
7. Dallmeier, V., Pohl, B., Burger, M., Mirold, M., Zeller, A.: WebMate: web application test generation in the real world. In: 2014 IEEE Seventh International Conference on Software Testing, Verification and Validation Workshops, pp. 413–418. IEEE, New York (2014)
8. Feldt, R., de Oliveira Neto, F.G., Torkar, R.: Ways of applying artificial intelligence in software engineering. In: Proceedings of the 6th International Workshop on Realizing Artificial Intelligence Synergies in Software Engineering, pp. 35–41. ACM, New York (2018). https://doi.org/10.1145/3194104.3194109
9. Ferreira Campos, U., Smethurst, G., Moraes, J.P., Bonifacio, R., Pinto, G.: Mining rule violations in JavaScript code snippets. In: 2019 IEEE/ACM 16th International Conference on Mining Software Repositories (MSR), pp. 195–199. IEEE, New York (2019). https://doi.org/10.1109/MSR.2019.00039
10. Fraser, G., Arcuri, A.: EvoSuite: automatic test suite generation for object-oriented software. In: Proceedings of the 19th ACM SIGSOFT Symposium and the 13th European Conference on Foundations of Software Engineering, pp. 416–419 (2011)
11. Gori, M., Betti, A., Melacci, S.: Learning principles. In: Machine Learning, pp. 53–111. Elsevier, Amsterdam (2024). https://doi.org/10.1016/B978-0-32-389859-1.00009-X
12. Taxonomy and definitions for terms related to driving automation systems for on-road motor vehicles. Standard, International Organization for Standardization, Geneva (2021)

13. Kracht, J.S., Petrovic, J.Z., Walcott-Justice, K.R.: Empirically evaluating the quality of automatically generated and manually written test suites. In: 2014 14th International Conference on Quality Software, pp. 256–265. IEEE, New York (2014)

14. Marinke, R., Guerra, E.M., Fagundes Silveira, F., Azevedo, R.M., Nascimento, W., de Almeida, R.S., Rodrigues Demboscki, B., da Silva, T.S.: Towards an extensible architecture for refactoring test code. In: Computational Science and Its Applications–ICCSA 2019: 19th International Conference, Saint Petersburg, Russia, July 1–4, 2019, Proceedings, Part IV 19, pp. 456–471. Springer, Berlin (2019)

15. McMinn, P.: Search-based software test data generation: a survey. Softw. Test. Verif. Reliab. **14**(2), 105–156 (2004)

16. Moradi Dakhel, A., Majdinasab, V., Nikanjam, A., Khomh, F., Desmarais, M.C., Jiang, Z.M.J.: GitHub Copilot AI pair programmer: Asset or Liability? J. Syst. Softw. **203**, 111734 (2023). https://doi.org/10.1016/j.jss.2023.111734

17. Murphy, G., Kersten, M., Findlater, L.: How are Java software developers using the Eclipse IDE? IEEE Softw. **23**(4), 76–83 (2006). https://doi.org/10.1109/MS.2006.105

18. Nguyen, N., Nadi, S.: An empirical evaluation of GitHub copilot's code suggestions. In: Proceedings of the 19th International Conference on Mining Software Repositories, pp. 1–5. ACM, New York (2022). https://doi.org/10.1145/3524842.3528470

19. Palomba, F., Zaidman, A., De Lucia, A.: Automatic test smell detection using information retrieval techniques. In: 2018 IEEE International Conference on Software Maintenance and Evolution (ICSME), pp. 311–322. IEEE, New York (2018)

20. Parsons, J., Wand, Y.: Using cognitive principles to guide classification in information systems modeling. MIS Q. **32**(4), 839 (2008). https://doi.org/10.2307/25148874

21. Peruma, A., Almalki, K., Newman, C.D., Mkaouer, M.W., Ouni, A., Palomba, F.: tsDetect: an open source test smells detection tool, pp. 1650–1654. ESEC/FSE 2020, Association for Computing Machinery, New York (2020). https://doi.org/10.1145/3368089.3417921

22. Ralph, P.: Toward methodological guidelines for process theories and taxonomies in software engineering. IEEE Trans. Softw. Eng. **45**(7), 712–735 (2019). https://doi.org/10.1109/TSE.2018.2796554

23. Rokis, K., Kirikova, M.: Challenges of low-code/no-code software development: a literature review. In: Lecture Notes in Business Information Processing, vol. 462 LNBIP, pp. 3–17. Springer International Publishing, New York (2022). https://doi.org/10.1007/978-3-031-16947-2_1

24. Sahay, A., Indamutsa, A., Di Ruscio, D., Pierantonio, A.: Supporting the understanding and comparison of low-code development platforms. In: 2020 46th Euromicro Conference on Software Engineering and Advanced Applications (SEAA), pp. 171–178. IEEE, New York (2020). https://doi.org/10.1109/SEAA51224.2020.00036

25. Savary-Leblanc, M., Burgueño, L., Cabot, J., Le Pallec, X., Gérard, S.: Software assistants in software engineering: a systematic mapping study. Softw. Pract. Experience **53**(3), 856–892 (2023). https://doi.org/10.1002/spe.3170

26. Shahid, M., Ibrahim, S.: An evaluation of test coverage tools in software testing. In: 2011 International Conference on Telecommunication Technology and Applications Proceedings of CSIT, vol. 5. sn (2011)

27. Shamshiri, S., Just, R., Rojas, J.M., Fraser, G., McMinn, P., Arcuri, A.: Do automatically generated unit tests find real faults? an empirical study of effectiveness and challenges (t). In: 2015 30th IEEE/ACM International Conference on Automated Software Engineering (ASE), pp. 201–211. IEEE, New York (2015)

28. Shaw, M.: Prospects for an engineering discipline of software. IEEE Softw. **7**(6), 15–24 (1990). https://doi.org/10.1109/52.60586. http://ieeexplore.ieee.org/document/60586/

29. Sheridan, T.B., Parasuraman, R.: Human-automation interaction. Rev. Hum. Factors Ergon. **1**(1), 89–129 (2005). https://doi.org/10.1518/155723405783703082

30. Šmite, D., Wohlin, C., Galviņa, Z., Prikladnicki, R.: An empirically based terminology and taxonomy for global software engineering. Empir. Softw. Eng. **19**, 105–153 (2014)

31. Svyatkovskiy, A., Deng, S.K., Fu, S., Sundaresan, N.: IntelliCode compose: code generation using transformer. In: Proceedings of the 28th ACM Joint Meeting on European Software Engineering Conference and Symposium on the Foundations of Software Engineering, pp. 1433–1443. ACM, New York (2020). https://doi.org/10.1145/3368089.3417058
32. Tanimoto, S.L.: VIVA: a visual language for image processing. J. Vis. Lang. Comput. **1**(2), 127–139 (1990). https://doi.org/10.1016/S1045-926X(05)80012-6
33. Tanimoto, S.L.: A perspective on the evolution of live programming. In: 2013 1st International Workshop on Live Programming, LIVE 2013—Proceedings, pp. 31–34 (2013). https://doi.org/10.1109/LIVE.2013.6617346
34. Teitelman, W., Masinter, L.: The Interlisp programming environment. Computer **14**(4), 25–33 (1981). https://doi.org/10.1109/C-M.1981.220410
35. Tomasdottir, K.F., Aniche, M., van Deursen, A.: Why and how JavaScript developers use linters. In: 2017 32nd IEEE/ACM International Conference on Automated Software Engineering (ASE), pp. 578–589. IEEE, New York (2017). https://doi.org/10.1109/ASE.2017.8115668
36. Usman, M., Britto, R., Börstler, J., Mendes, E.: Taxonomies in software engineering: a Systematic mapping study and a revised taxonomy development method. Inf. Softw. Technol. **85**, 43–59 (2017). https://doi.org/10.1016/j.infsof.2017.01.006
37. Vaithilingam, P., Zhang, T., Glassman, E.L.: Expectation vs. experience: evaluating the usability of code generation tools powered by large language models. In: CHI Conference on Human Factors in Computing Systems Extended Abstracts, pp. 1–7. ACM, New York (2022). https://doi.org/10.1145/3491101.3519665
38. Viglianisi, E., Dallago, M., Ceccato, M.: Resttestgen: Automated black-box testing of RESTful APIs. In: 2020 IEEE 13th International Conference on Software Testing, Validation and Verification (ICST), pp. 142–152. IEEE, New York (2020)
39. Wheaton, G.R., Fleishman, E.A.: Development of a Taxonomy of Human Performance: A Review of Classificatory Systems Relating to Tasks and Performance. Clearinghouse, Mumbai (1968)
40. Xing, Z., Stroulia, E.: Refactoring practice: how it is and how it should be supported—an eclipse case study. In: IEEE International Conference on Software Maintenance (ICSM), pp. 458–467 (2006). https://doi.org/10.1109/ICSM.2006.52
41. Xuan, J., Cornu, B., Martinez, M., Baudry, B., Seinturier, L., Monperrus, M.: B-refactoring: automatic test code refactoring to improve dynamic analysis. Inf. Softw. Technol. **76**, 65–80 (2016)
42. Yuan, Z., Lou, Y., Liu, M., Ding, S., Wang, K., Chen, Y., Peng, X.: No more manual tests? evaluating and improving ChatGPT for unit test generation. arXiv preprint arXiv:2305.04207 (2023)
43. Zanchin, B.C., Adamshuk, R., Santos, M.M., Collazos, K.S.: On the instrumentation and classification of autonomous cars. In: 2017 IEEE International Conference on Systems, Man, and Cybernetics (SMC), pp. 2631–2636. IEEE, New York (2017). https://doi.org/10.1109/SMC.2017.8123022
44. Zhang, B., Hill, E., Clause, J.: Automatically generating test templates from test names (n). In: 2015 30th IEEE/ACM International Conference on Automated Software Engineering (ASE), pp. 506–511. IEEE, New York (2015)
45. Zhang, H., Wu, H., Rountev, A.: Automated test generation for detection of leaks in android applications. In: Proceedings of the 11th International Workshop on Automation of Software Test, pp. 64–70 (2016)

ChatGPT Prompt Patterns for Improving Code Quality, Refactoring, Requirements Elicitation, and Software Design

Jules White, Sam Hays, Quchen Fu, Jesse Spencer-Smith, and Douglas C. Schmidt

Abstract This chapter presents design techniques for software engineering, in the form of prompt patterns, to solve common problems that arise when using large language models (LLMs) to automate common software engineering activities, such as ensuring code is decoupled from third-party libraries and creating API specifications from lists of requirements. This chapter provides two contributions to research on using LLMs for software engineering. First, it provides a catalog of patterns for software engineering that classifies patterns according to the types of problems they solve. Second, it explores several prompt patterns that have been applied to improve requirements elicitation, rapid prototyping, code quality, deployment, and testing.

Keywords Large language models · Prompt patterns · Prompt engineering · Software engineering · ChatGPT

1 Introduction

Overview of LLMs and Prompts for Automating Software Engineering Tasks
Large language models (LLMs) [4] are rapidly being adopted by software developers and applied to generate code and other artifacts associated with software engineering. Popular examples of LLM-based tools applied for these purposes include ChatGPT [3] and GitHub Copilot [1]. Initial research indicates that these chat-assisted artificial intelligence (AI) tools can aid a range of common software development and engineering tasks [6].

Key to the adoption of these tools has been the creation of LLMs and IDE-integrated services around them. Any user can access these complex LLM capabilities by simply typing a message to ChatGPT and/or opening popular integrated

J. White (✉) · S. Hays · Q. Fu · J. Spencer-Smith · D. C. Schmidt
Department of Computer Science, Vanderbilt University, Nashville, TN, USA
e-mail: jules.white@vanderbilt.edu; quchen.fu@vanderbilt.edu; george.s.hays@vanderbilt.edu; jesse.spencer-smith@vanderbilt.edu; douglas.c.schmidt@vanderbilt.edu

development environments (IDEs) [1, 2, 18], such as IntelliJ [13] and Visual Studio Code. Leveraging these capabilities previously required much more time and effort. In addition, prior state-of-the-art LLMs were not widely accessible to users.

Interacting with an LLM in general involves feeding it "prompts" [14], which are natural language instructions used to provide context to the LLM and guide its generation of textual responses. In a chat-assisted LLM environment, a prompt is a message that a user sends to an LLM, such as ChatGPT, Claude, or Bard. The remainder of this chapter focuses on the ChatGPT chat-assisted LLM.

In the context of software engineering, a prompt is a natural language instruction given to an LLM to facilitate its generation of requirements, code, and software-related artifacts (such as documentation and build scripts), as well as to simulate certain aspects of a software system. Prompts are thus a form of programming used to instruct an LLM to perform software engineering tasks. For example, in an IDE environment (such as Copilot [1]), a prompt can be a comment, method definition, or source file.

One way to use prompts in the software development life cycle is to ask an LLM directly to provide some information or generate some code. Another use of prompts is to dictate rules for the LLM to follow going forward, such as conforming to certain coding standards. Both types of prompts program the LLM to accomplish a task. The second type of prompt, however, customizes future interactions with the LLM by defining additional rules to follow or information to use when performing subsequent tasks. We cover both types of patterns in this chapter.

Overview of Prompt Patterns for Software Engineering Tasks This chapter builds on our prior work that introduced the concept of *prompt patterns* [24], which are reusable prompt designs to solve problems in LLM interaction. Similar to software patterns [10, 20], prompt patterns codify sound design experience, thereby providing a reusable solution to common problems in LLM interaction, such as ensuring that software adheres to certain design principles, programming paradigms, and/or secure coding guidelines.

Software developers and engineers can use prompt patterns to establish rules and constraints that improve software quality attributes (such as modularity or reusability) when working with LLMs. For example, prompt patterns can ensure that generated code (or user-provided code being refactored) separates business logic from code with side effects (e.g., file system access, database access, network communication, etc.). These types of constraints make business logic easier to test and reason about since it is decoupled from harder-to-test and harder-to-understand side-effecting code. Prompt patterns can also require that third-party libraries have intermediate abstractions inserted between the libraries and the business logic depending on them to ensure the code is not tightly coupled to external dependencies that would otherwise limit its portability and reusability.

Toward a Prompt Pattern Catalog for Software Engineering This chapter extends our prior work [24] by focusing on creating a catalog of prompt patterns that can be applied collaboratively throughout the software life cycle. We introduce a variety of prompt patterns in this chapter, ranging from patterns that simulate and reason about systems early in the design phase to patterns that help alleviate issues with LLM token limits when generating code. In addition, we explore relationships between patterns by examining patterns compounds and sequences that are most effective when employed in combination with each other.

The remainder of this chapter is organized as follows: Section 2 gives an overview of prompt pattern structure and functionality; Sect. 3 introduces the catalog of prompt patterns covered in the chapter; Sect. 4 describes prompt patterns used during requirements elicitation and system design; Sect. 5 describes prompt patterns that help LLMs generate higher quality code and refactor human-produced code; Sect. 6 compares our research on prompt patterns with related work; and Sect. 7 presents concluding remarks and lessons learned.

2 Prompt Pattern Structure and Functionality

Prompt patterns are documented using a similar structure to software patterns, with analogous versions of the name, classification, intent, motivation, structure, example implementation, and consequences. Each of these sections for the prompt pattern form is described briefly below:[1]

- **A name and classification**. The name provides a unique identifier for the pattern that can be referenced in discussions and the classification groups the pattern with other patterns based on the types of problems they solve. The classification used in this chapter is shown in Table 1.
- **The intent and context** captures the problem that the pattern solves and the goals of the pattern.
- **The motivation** explains the rationale and importance of the problem that the pattern is solving.
- **The structure and key ideas**. The structure describes the fundamental contextual information that needs to be provided by the LLM to achieve the expected behavior. These ideas are listed as a series of statements but can be reworded and adapted by the user, as long as the final wordings convey the key information.
- **Example implementation** shows specific implementations of the pattern and discusses them.
- **Consequences** discusses the pros and cons of using the pattern and discussion of how to adapt the pattern for different situations.

Prompt patterns can take various forms. In the context of patterns that enable LLMs to perform software engineering tasks, a prompt typically starts with a conversation scoping statement, such as "from now on," "act as a X," "for the next

---

[1] Our prior work [24] defines the fundamental structure of a prompt pattern and compares it with software patterns. We briefly define prompt patterns for completeness below, but we refer the reader to our prior work for additional details.

Table 1 Classifying prompt patterns for automating software engineering tasks

Requirements Elicitation	Requirements Simulator
	Specification Disambiguation
	Change Request Simulation
System Design and Simulation	API Generator
	API Simulator
	Few-shot Example Generator
	Domain-Specific Language (DSL) Creation
	Architectural Possibilities
Code Quality	Code Clustering
	Intermediate Abstraction
	Principled Code
	Hidden Assumptions
Refactoring	Pseudo-code Refactoring
	Data-guided Refactoring

four prompts," etc. These statements direct the LLM to change its operation going forward based on the prompt being provided. For example, the following prompt pattern is an adaptation of the *Output Automater* pattern [24] that uses "from now on" to automate production of a list of dependencies for generated code:

> from now on, automatically generate a python requirements.txt file that includes any modules that the code you generate includes.

After the initial conversational scoping statement, the prompt includes a number of statements that provide the ground rules the LLM should follow in output generation and prompt flow for software engineering tasks. These output rules may include one or more conditional statements indicating when specific rules should be applied. For example, the following prompt:

> From now on, whenever you generate code that spans more than one file, generate a python script that can be run to automatically create the specified files or make changes to existing files to insert the generated code.

Normally, a user must manually open and edit multiple files to add generated code that spans multiple files to a project. With the above prompt, ChatGPT will generate a script to automate opening and editing each file for the user and eliminate potential manual errors. The prompt is scoped to "from now on" and then includes a conditional "whenever you generate code that spans more than one file," followed by the rule to generate a python script. This prompt form is an example of the *Output Automator* pattern from [24], applied to software engineering.

3 A Catalog of Prompt Patterns for Automating Software Engineering Tasks

This section summarizes our catalog of 14 prompt patterns that have been applied to solve common problems in the domain of conversational LLM interaction and output generation for automating common software tasks. We partitioned these 14 prompt patterns into four categories to help pattern users navigate and apply these patterns more effectively. Table 1 outlines the initial classifications for the catalog of prompt patterns for automating software engineering tasks identified by our work with ChatGPT (GPT 3.5-turbo GPT-4).

Two areas of LLM usage in the domain of software engineering that have received scant attention thus far include (1) requirements elicitation and (2) system design and specification. These areas represent some of the most important aspects of software engineering, however, and commonly yield changes late in the development cycle that cause schedule overruns, unanticipated costs, and risk. The *Requirements Elicitation* patterns listed in Table 1 aid in creating requirements and exploring their completeness with respect to desired system capabilities and accuracy. Other patterns in this category use an LLM as a trusted intermediary to reason about the impact of changes.

The *System Design and Simulation Patterns* patterns category listed in Table 1 explores patterns that address issues creating concrete design specifications, domain-specific languages, and exploring alternative architectures. The section demonstrates ways to simulate aspects of a system to help identify deficiencies early in the life cycle, i.e., when they are less costly and disruptive to remediate.

Considerable concern [2, 5, 18] has risen regarding the quality of code produced by LLMs, as well as written via collaborations between humans and LLMs. The *Code Quality* patterns category introduces several patterns that improve both LLM and human-generated code. LLMs can often reason effectively about abstraction, as well as generate relatively modular code. The patterns listed in this category in Table 1 help ensure certain abstraction and modularity attributes are present in code, e.g., they facilitate replacement of third-party libraries by introducing an interface between them and business logic.

Finally, the *Refactoring* patterns listed in Table 1 provide various means to refactor code using LLMs effectively. LLMs like ChatGPT have a surprisingly powerful understanding of abstract coding constructs, such as pseudo-code. Innovative pattern-oriented approaches to refactoring are therefore discussed to allow specification of refactoring at a high level, such as using pseudo-code to describe code structure.

All examples in this chapter were tested with the ChatGPT LLM. Our process for identifying and documenting these patterns combined exploring community-posted prompts on the Internet and creating independent prompts to support our own software engineering work with ChatGPT. Our broader goal is to codify a catalog of software engineering prompt patterns that can be easily adapted or reused for various LLMs, much like how classic software patterns can be implemented independently in various programming languages.

4   System Requirements and Architecture Patterns

This section describes prompt patterns used during requirements elicitation and system design.

4.1   The Requirements Simulator Pattern

Intent and Context

The *Requirements Simulator* pattern allows stakeholders to explore the requirements of a software-reliant system interactively to determine if certain functionality is captured properly. The simulation output should provide additional details regarding the initial requirements and new requirements added to accomplish the tasks the stakeholders tried to perform in the simulation. The goal of this pattern is to aid in elicitation and analysis of the completeness of software requirements.

Motivation

Changes late in a software system's development are generally more expensive to remediate than early in the development phase. Unfortunately, many requirement changes are made late in the development cycle when they are more costly to fix. A common source of issues with requirements is that the requirements do not adequately describe the needs of the system. The motivation of the *Requirements Simulator* pattern is to use an LLM to simulate interactions with the system based on descriptions of the tasks that a user might want to perform and identify missing requirements.

Structure and Key Ideas

The fundamental contextual statements are as follows:

Requirements Simulator Pattern

1. I want you to act as the system
2. Use the requirements to guide your behavior
3. I will ask you to do X, and you will tell me if X is possible given the requirements.
4. If X is possible, explain why using the requirements.
5. If I can't do X based on the requirements, write the missing requirements needed in format Y.

Example Implementation

A sample implementation of the *Requirements Simulator* pattern is shown below. This implementation focuses on task-based exploration of the system's capabilities. It also specifically refines the format of the requirements to be user stories, so the LLM will produce requirements in the desired format.

The prompt implementation assumes that the requirements have been given to the LLM prior to use of the prompt. The requirements could be typed in manually or generated by ChatGPT through a series of prompts asking for requirements related to a particular system. Any approach will work as long as the requirements are in the current context of the prompt.

> Now, I want you to act as this system. Use the requirements to guide your behavior. I am going to say, I want to do X, and you will tell me if X is possible given the requirements. If X is possible, provide a step-by-step set of instructions on how I would accomplish it and provide additional details that would help implement the requirement. If I can't do X based on the requirements, write the missing requirements to make it possible as user stories.

An extension to this implementation is to include a screen-oriented exploration of the system. Whereas the prior example focuses more on interrogating the system to see if a task is possible, the example below walks the user through individual screens. This approach of screen-by-screen walkthrough is similar to classic text-based adventure games, such as Zork.

> Now, I want you to act as this system in a text-based simulator of the system. Use the requirements to guide your behavior. You will describe the user interface for the system, based on the requirements, and what I can do on each screen. I am going to say, I want to do X, and you will tell me if X is possible given the requirements and the current screen. If X is possible, provide a step-by-step set of instructions how I would accomplish it and provide additional details that would help implement the requirement. If I can't do X based on the requirements, write the missing requirements to make it possible as user stories. Whenever the state of the user interface changes, update the user on what they are looking at.
> Tell me what I am looking at in the system and ask me what I want to do.

This pattern showcases two unique exploration methods. First, the task-based exploration handles tasks and investigates their feasibility. Second, the screen-based exploration focuses on helping the user imagine an interface-driven walk-through of system functionalities akin to a textual adventure game. Each has its merits depending on the use case; task-based explorations are better for back-end services, whereas screen-based explorations are suited for front-end or user-interface heavy applications.

Consequences

The *Requirements Simulator* pattern enables simulation of a software-reliant system in greater levels of fidelity as the requirements are expanded. Since requirements can be rapidly expanded with this pattern through interactive exploration, the simulation of the system gains fidelity throughout the simulation. This iterative process allows rapid generation of large requirement sets.

However, a limitation of using this pattern in isolation is that the descriptions of the system are purely textual, which may provide insufficient information to capture all requirements accurately. One way to overcome this limitation and help write better requirements and later generate design mockups is to combine this pattern with the *Visualization Generator* pattern [24] This combination of patterns enables simulation of the system, as well as possible visualizations of each screen generated by another AI tool, such as Dall-E, Midjourney, or Stable Diffusion. A modified prompt that combines the *Requirements Simulator* and *Visualization Generation* patterns would be:

> . . . In addition to the textual screen description, provide a Dall-E prompt that I can use to generate wireframes of what the screen might look like.

A sample output of combining these two patterns when used in an exploration of a Web application with Twitter-like functionality for socially sharing ChatGPT prompts is shown below:

> **ChatGPT:** Sure, I can provide a DALL-E prompt to generate a wireframe for the screen description. Here is the DALL-E prompt for the screen where users can delete their prompts: A wireframe of the "My Prompts" screen where users can see a list of their own prompts. Each prompt is displayed with its title and description. Next to each prompt is a "Delete" button that users can click to remove the prompt from the social network. At the bottom of the screen, there is a "Back" button that users can click to return to the previous screen.

The resulting wireframe generated with Midjourney rather than Dall-E is shown in Fig. 1. This figure shows the generated image is a rough interpretation of possible realizations of the prompt. However, such visualizations may be easier to reason about than textual descriptions, which can spur productive discussions between participants. In addition, the randomness in image generation may yield unexpected layouts or user interface approaches that may inspire new ideas.

4.2   The Specification Disambiguation Pattern

Intent and Context

The *Specification Disambiguation* pattern causes the LLM to review specifications provided to a developer or development team by non-technical or semi-technical personnel. The goal is to ensure any areas of potential miscommunication or ambiguity are caught early and clarified.

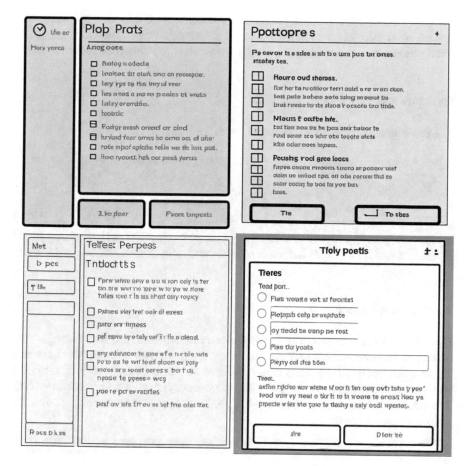

Fig. 1 Wireframe samples generated from combining the requirements simulator and visualization generator patterns

Motivation

Creating a specification (which could take the form of requirements or non-formal description of the system) is complicated since errors, areas of ambiguity, and/or omissions are often not discovered until after a system is initially implemented and deployed. In many cases, developers make assumptions that enable them to implement ambiguous ideas, even if those assumptions do not align with the original specification designers intention. Even experienced system designers and software engineers are prone to ambiguous language and incomplete specification, particularly for ultralarge-scale systems [8].

It is common for software developers to work with one or more product or project managers who generate requirements and provide those to the developers. Often, these requirements stem from discussions with customers, and there may be a loss of meaningful context in the capture and delivery of those requirements. The *Specification Disambiguation* pattern helps automate some of the work needed to clarify requirement specifications, ideally before they are delivered to developers.

Structure and Key Ideas

The fundamental contextual statements are as follows:

Specification Disambiguation Pattern

1. Within this scope
2. Consider these requirements or specifications
3. Point out any areas of ambiguity or potentially unintended outcomes

Example Implementation

Here we consider a scenario in which a non-technical product manager has consulted with customers and tried to capture the essence of their requirements. These requirements have been communicated in natural language unsuitable for software requirements due to inconsistent context (i.e., the *what*, not the *how*). The product manager may request additional areas of clarification by posing the following prompt to the LLM:

> The following will represent system requirements. Point out any areas that could be construed as ambiguous or lead to unintended outcomes. Provide ways in which the language can be more precise.

By providing the prompt above along with the captured requirements, the LLM can provide results of interest to the product manager. For example, if some requirement specifications were:

1. Create a user interface that allows file uploads via Web browser.
2. Keep the files secure.
3. Make sure the files are movie file types.
4. Files can be no larger than 100 MB

The LLM would provide a path for the product manager to bolster the requirement specifications prior to providing them to the development team. For example, the LLM might suggest

> The system requirement to "Keep the files secure" could be made more precise by specifying which security measures should be implemented to ensure the files are kept secure. For example: "Implement access control and encryption measures to ensure that uploaded files can only be accessed by authorized users and are protected against unauthorized access or tampering."

Follow-up questions such as "provide example requirements for a system that accepts file uploads by logged-in users, and keeps the files secure the entire time" may then be posed to guide product manager decision-making and ensure the requirements delivered to developers are more precise and actionable.

Consequences

The *Specification Disambiguation* pattern helps overcome errors, areas of ambiguity, and/or omissions in requirement specifications by providing an automated "devil's advocate" that can attempt to find points of weakness in a requirement specification. In addition, whereas social concerns (such as the concern of questioning a more senior developer) may cause developers to not ask questions, LLMs do not suffer from these same biases and reservations.

A particularly compelling use of the *Specification Disambiguation* pattern is integrating two separate systems, such as two different development teams building separate parts of a system using a common integration specification. This pattern can be used independently by the team members to collect potential ambiguities and then bring them to a joint meeting before kicking off development to discuss. The LLM can serve as an unbiased source of topics of discussion for a kickoff.

This pattern is also helpful when a specification is being developed for an external audience (such as consumers of an unreleased API) who are not involved in the specification writing process. In this case, developers may not be able to talk to the target consumers due to secrecy or lack of an audience for the product and thus lack the mean to easily get external feedback on the specification. This patterns allows the LLM to serve as a representative for external users.

The *Specification Disambiguation* pattern is also effective when combined with the *Persona* [24], *API Generator*, and *API Simulator* or *Requirements Simulator* patterns. Ambiguities can be further discovered by interactively simulating the system or converting it into an API specification. Each transforming the specification into another format through one of these prompt patterns can help identify ambiguities that are uncovered through this pattern since the transformation may produce an unexpected reification of the requirements. In addition, the *Persona* pattern [24] can be used to consider potential ambiguities from different perspectives.

A drawback of the *Specification Disambiguation* pattern arises when the user assumes that the LLM's output is comprehensive and complete. Developers might assume that the LLM has identified all possible ambiguities, which may not be the case. As a result, unnoticed ambiguities might still exist after using the pattern. Moreover, LLMs are trained on large datasets, but they might not understand specific domain or contextual nuances as well as a human would. Consequently, there may be occasions where the LLM misinterprets specifications and inaccurately flags non-ambiguities as ambiguous or vice versa.

4.3 The API Generator Pattern

Intent and Context

The *API Generator* pattern generates an application programming interface (API) specification, such as a REST API specification, from natural language requirement statements or descriptions of the system. The goal of this pattern is to allow developers to rapidly explore multiple possible API designs, formalize API design earlier, and produce a starting point for manual refinement of the design.

Motivation

Designing a complete API specification to support a set of requirements—or even a high-level description of a software-reliant system—often involves manual effort. If this level of effort is significant, then (1) fewer potential designs may be explored, (2) systematic API specifications may be deferred until after key portions of the system are implemented, and/or (3) *ad hoc* alignment and integration of disparate systems, services, or modules may use the code as the only source of truth. A key motivation for applying the *API Generator* pattern is to dramatically reduce and/or eliminate the cost of the API creation, so these specifications are created earlier, and careful thought goes into their design.

Structure and Key Ideas

The fundamental contextual statements are as follows:

API Generator Pattern

1. Using system description X
2. Generate an API specification for the system
3. The API specification should be in format Y

Example Implementation

A sample implementation of the *API Generator* pattern showing a prompt to generate an OpenAPI specification, which is a specification for a REST API, is shown below:

Generate an OpenAPI specification for a web application that would implement the listed requirements.

The implementation uses a concrete format for the specification, OpenAPI, and assumes that the requirements for the system were previously discussed. Typically, the *API Generator* pattern is used after a discussion of the requirements or even a simple textual description of a system, such as "a web application for a customer relationship management system." The more detailed the list of requirements, the more accurate the generated API will be, although developers can perform thought experiments and simulations with prompts as simple as "generate an OpenAPI specification for a web application related to cooking."

Consequences

The *API Generator* pattern enables developers and/or teams to rapidly create multiple potential API designs and compare/contrast them before selecting their final design. In contrast, writing these APIs manually is tedious, so developers often only have time to write and explore a limited number of API design options. In general, providing developers with tools to experiment with different API designs from a system description or requirements list is a powerful tool.

Another benefit of the *API Generator* pattern is that developers may choose to write the API specification after the code is implemented because they do not want to spend time specifying the same information twice (i.e., once in the API specification and again in the actual code). By automating API production, developers are incentivized to create API specifications earlier in the design process. Although existing (i.e., non-LLM) tools can generate an API specification from code, they still require the initial production of code. Moreover, tools that can generate skeletons of code from the API specification can be combined with this pattern to accelerate the API implementation compare with writing it manually.

This pattern can be combined effectively with the *API Simulator* pattern described in Sect. 4.4 to both generate and evaluate the proposed specification. Simulating the API can allow developers to get a sense of the "ergonomics" of the API and evaluate how hard it is to accomplish various tasks in code. The API can also be refactored through the LLM using the *Data-guided Refactoring* pattern described in Sect. 5.6.

Applying the *API Generator* pattern provides the benefits to the design and development process discussed above. As with all tools and processes, however, it also has potential drawbacks and considerations. For example, LLMs may produce inconsistent API designs when given similar or updated requirements. These inconsistencies make it hard to maintain consistency across a project or large code base and could potentially lead to confusion during the comparison and selection of final API design or in ensuring different teams use a consistent API design strategy. The LLM will likely require significant context to ensure consistency across API generations.

4.4   The API Simulator Pattern

Intent and Context

The *API Simulator* pattern causes the LLM to simulate the API from a specification, thereby enabling developers to interact immediately with an API and test it through a simulation run by the LLM. LLMs possess powerful—and often largely unrecognized—capabilities to generate synthetic data and tailor that data to natural language descriptions of scenarios. In addition, LLMs can help developers explore a simulated API by synthesizing sample requests, as well as providing usage guidance and explaining errors.

Motivation

Although tools are available to simulate an API [12], they require setup to use and may have limited ability to generate effective synthetic data. Current infrastructure for simulating APIs also often just supports strict interaction, typically through HTTP or code, rather than a more fluid interface based on a combination of pseudo-operations and concrete operation specification. Early interaction with an API design can aid developers in uncovering issues, omissions, and awkward designs.

Structure and Key Ideas

The fundamental contextual statements are as follows:

API Simulator Pattern

1. Act as the described system using specification X
2. I will type in requests to the API in format Y
3. You will respond with the appropriate response in format Z based on specification X

Example Implementation

An example implementation of the *API Simulator* pattern that asks an LLM to simulate a REST API based on an OpenAPI specification is shown below. This implementation specifies that requests to the system will be typed in as HTTP requests and that the system should output the HTTP response. It is also possible to have the LLM generate a description of state changes in the system as the simulation, data saved, etc. Similarly, the specification of the user input could be simply a description of what a user is doing with the API or a Web client.

> Act as this web application based on the OpenAPI specification. I will type in HTTP requests in plain text and you will respond with the appropriate HTTP response based on the OpenAPI specification.

The specification can take a number of forms, such as a programmatic interface or a common API specification domain-specific language, such as OpenAPI [17]. In the example above, the OpenAPI specification for an HTTP API is used. Requests can then be input to the LLM, which then replies with the corresponding HTTP responses.

Consequences

The *API Simulator* pattern enables users to customize their interactions or scenarios of interaction with an LLM using natural language, which may be easier than trying to accomplish the same thing in code. For example, users can tell the LLM, "for the following interactions, assume that the user has a valid OAuth authorization token for the user Jill" or "assume that 100 users exist in the system and respond to requests with sample data for them." More complex customization can also be performed, such as "assume the users are from a set of 15–25 families and come from multiple countries in North America."

Interactions with a simulated API can be done through either a rigorous programmatic form, such as "strictly interpret my input as an HTTP request and reject any malformed requests" or "I am going to only provide pseudo data for the input and you should fix any formatting issues for me." The flexibility of interacting with the LLM simulation and customizing it via natural language facilitates rapid exploration of an API.

Another benefit of the *API Simulator* pattern arises when combining it with other patterns so users can (1) have the LLM create examples of usage that are later used as few-shot examples [23] in future prompts or (2) leverage the LLM to reason about how hard or easy it is to accomplish various tasks in code. In particular, combining this pattern with the *Change Request Simulation* pattern described in Sect. 4.8 allows users to reason about the effort needed to accommodate changing assumptions later in the software life cycle.

One important consideration is that the simulation will not be completely accurate, so fine-grained analysis cannot be performed. It is important to ensure that the analysis done with the simulation is at a high level and mainly used for thinking through how interactions with the interface will work, sequencing, etc. Users should not infer other properties of the interface, such as performance, based on the simulation.

The *API Simulator* pattern, like any tool or process, has potential drawbacks and considerations, despite its advantages. For example, users might start relying heavily on simulated results, disregarding the fact that simulations may not accurately reflect the behavior of a deployed API. This overreliance could lead to unrealistic expectations about system behavior or performance. Moreover, this pattern is driven by the LLM, which is not designed to provide in-depth, detailed analysis of API behavior, such as exact performance metrics and fine-grained error conditions. Therefore, users may erroneously assume that the simulated performance is representative of the actual API when implemented.

4.5   Pattern: Few-shot Code Example Generation

Intent and Context

The *Few-shot Code Example Generation* pattern instructs the LLM to generate a set of usage examples that can later be provided back to the LLM as examples in a prompt to leverage few-shot learning [23], which provides a limited set of example training data in a prompt to an LLM. In the software domain, the few-shot examples are proper usage of code that an LLM can learn from. In some cases, these examples can convey the function and use of code in a more space/token-efficient manner than the actual code itself.

This pattern leverages the LLM itself to generate few-shot examples that can later be provided in a prompt, in lieu of writing the actual code. In response, an LLM can reason about the original code more effectively. These examples can be helpful to remind the LLM of the design/usage of the system that it designed in prior conversations.

Motivation

LLMs typically have a limit on the number of tokens (e.g., words or symbols) that can be input in a single prompt. Since a large software system or module may exceed an LLM's token limit, it may be necessary to describe design or programming aspects (such as a module, class, set of functions, etc.) within the LLM's token limit to use it properly. This overrunning of the token limit necessitates a way to remind the LLM of prior decisions it made in the past.

One approach to solve the token limit problem is to provide few-shot training examples in a prompt that are based on the usage of the code, API, state transitions, or other specification usage examples. These examples can demonstrate proper usage and train the LLM on the fly to use the related design or code properly. However, manually generating few-shot examples may not be feasible, which motivates the *Few-shot Code Example Generation* pattern.

Structure and Key Ideas

The fundamental contextual statements are as follows:

> **Few-shot Code Example Generation Pattern**
> 1. I am going to provide you system X
> 2. Create a set of N examples that demonstrate usage of system X
> 3. Make the examples as complete as possible in their coverage
> 4. (Optionally) The examples should be based on the public interfaces of system X
> 5. (Optionally) The examples should focus on X

Example Implementation

The example implementation below generates few-shot examples of using a RESTful API and focuses the examples on the creation of new users:

> I am going to provide you code. Create a set of 10 examples that demonstrate usage of this OpenAPI specification related to registration of new users.

These examples could then be used in later prompts to the LLM to remind it of the design of the API with regard to the creation of users. Providing the examples may be more concise and convey more meaning than natural language statements that try to convey the same information.

In another example, the *Few-shot Code Example Generation* pattern implementation asks the LLM to create few-shot examples for usage of portion of code:

> I am going to provide you code. Create a set of 10 examples that demonstrate usage of this code. Make the examples as complete as possible in their coverage. The examples should be based on the public interfaces of the code.

One valuable use of the LLM examples is to teach the LLM about the same code in future interactions. It is common to need to teach an LLM about code, and one way to teach it is with natural language documentation. However, documentation is often not information dense and can use significant context in a prompt to the LLM. In contrast, code examples can be information-rich and token-efficient relative to natural language, particularly when the examples convey important meaning, such as ordering of operations, required data, and other details, which are concise when described in code but overly verbose in natural language. The *Few-shot Code Example Generation* pattern aids in creating examples that can be provided to the LLM to either remember or learn how to use a library, interface, or other code artifact.

Consequences

The *Few-shot Code Example Generation* pattern can be used early in the design cycle to help capture expected usage of a system and then later provide a usage-based explanation back to the LLM to highlight its past design decisions. When combined with patterns, such as the *API Simulator* pattern, developers can rapidly interact with the system and record the interactions and then supplement them with additional generated examples.

This pattern is best applied when example usage of the system also conveys important information about constraints, assumptions, or expectations that would require more tokens to express in another format, such as a written natural language description. In some cases, a document, such as an OpenAPI specification, may be more token-efficient for conveying information. However, example usage has been shown to be an effective way of helping an LLM perform problem-solving [27], so this pattern may be a useful tool even when it is not the most token-efficient mechanism for conveying the information.

The *Few-shot Code Example Generation* pattern yields many advantages, particularly helping LLMs understand and operate on code. However, developers may face challenges in creating code examples that cover all possible use cases, scenarios, or edge cases. As a result, the LLM may hallucinate when faced with situations not covered by the examples, which can negatively affect downstream behaviors since inaccurate code examples or examples containing bad practices could mislead the LLM later. Likewise, the LLM could amplify these mistakes by using those examples as the basis for future code generations, potentially creating bigger problems.

4.6   The Domain-Specific Language (DSL) Creation Pattern

Intent and Context

The *Domain-Specific Language (DSL) Creation* pattern enables an LLM to create its own domain-specific language (DSL) that both it and users can leverage to describe and manipulate system concepts, such as requirements, deployment aspects, security rules, or architecture in terms of modules. The LLM can then design and describe the DSL to users. In addition, the examples and descriptions the LLM generates can be stored and used in future prompts to reintroduce the DSL to the LLM. Moreover, the examples the LLM generates will serve as few-shot examples for future prompts.

Motivation

DSLs can often be used to describe aspects of a software-reliant system using more succinct and token-efficient formats than natural language, programming languages, or other formats [19]. LLMs have a maximum number of "tokens," which corresponds to the maximum size of a prompt, and creating more token-efficient inputs is important for large software projects where all the needed context may be hard to fit into a prompt. Creating a DSL, however, can be time-consuming. In particular, the syntax and semantics of the DSL (e.g., its metamodel) must be described to an LLM a priori to enable subsequent interactions with users.

Structure and Key Ideas

The fundamental contextual statements are as follows:

DSL Creation Pattern

1. I want you to create a domain-specific language for X
2. The syntax of the language must adhere to the following constraints
3. Explain the language to me and provide some examples

Example Implementation

A sample implementation of the *Domain-Specific Language (DSL) Creation* pattern creating a DSL for requirements is shown below. This implementation adds a constraint that the DSL syntax should be YAML-like, which aids the LLM in determining what the textual format should take. An interesting aspect of this is that "like" may yield a syntax that is not valid YAML but looks similar to YAML.

> I want you to create a domain-specific language to document requirements. The syntax of the language should be based on YAML. Explain the language to me and provide some examples.

Another implementation approach is to ask the LLM to create a set of related DSLs with references between them. This approach is helpful when you need to describe related aspects of the same system and want to trace concepts across DSL instances, such as tracing a requirement to its realization in an architectural DSL describing modules. The LLM can be instructed to link the same concept together in the DSLs through consistent identifiers so that concepts can be tracked across DSL instances.

Consequences

The *Domain-Specific Language (DSL) Creation* pattern may facilitate system design without violating token limits. The specific syntax rules that are given to the LLM must be considered carefully, however, since they directly influence the space efficiency of the generated DSL. Although users of a DSL may only need to express relevant concepts for a designated task, this high concept density may not translate into the token efficiency of a textual representation of such concepts. For example, an XML-based syntax for a DSL will likely be much more space consumptive than a YAML-based syntax.

Token efficiency in a DSL design can be improved via conventions and implicit syntax rules. For example, positional conventions in a list can add meaning rather than marking different semantic elements in the list via explicit labels. The downside, however, is that the DSL may be harder to interpret for users unfamiliar with its syntax, although this problem can be rectified by using the *Few-shot Code Example Generation* pattern in Sect. 4.5 to create examples that teach users how to apply the DSL. Combining these two pattern also helps the LLM self-document usage of the pattern for later prompting based on the DSL.

The *Domain-Specific Language (DSL) Creation* pattern provides substantial benefits, particularly when dealing with complex systems that might require multiple DSLs for different aspects. However, there are potential drawbacks that may arise. For example, introducing multiple DSLs may increase the overall complexity of a system, particularly for human developers that did not create the DSLs. Understanding and maintaining multiple DSLs, and their references, can be hard for humans over a project life cycle. Each DSL has its own structure and syntax rules, which developers need to understand to supervise the LLM effectively.

4.7   The Architectural Possibilities Pattern

Intent and Context

The *Architectural Possibilities* pattern generates several different architectures for developers to consider, with little effort on the part of developers. An "architecture" can be very open-ended, and it is up to the developer to explain to the LLM what is meant by this term. A developer may desire seeing alternative architectures for how code is laid out into files, communication is performed between modules, or tiers in a multi-tiered system.

The intent of this pattern, therefore, is to allow the developer to explore any of these architectural aspects of the system with the LLM. Moreover, developers can interactively refine architectural suggestions by adding further constraints or asking the LLM to describe the architecture in terms of a different aspect of the system, such as file layout, modules, services, communication patterns, infrastructure, etc.

Motivation

Devising software architectures often requires considerable cognitive effort on the development team, particularly when architectures are mapped all the way to system requirements. Developers may therefore only consider a relatively small number of possible architectures when designing a software-reliant system due to the effort required to generate such architecture. In addition, developers may not have familiarity with architectures that could be a good fit for their systems and hence would not explore these architectural possibilities. Since architecture plays such an important role in software-reliant system design, it is important to facilitate exploration of many different alternatives, including alternatives that developers many not be familiar with.

Structure and Key Ideas

The fundamental contextual statements are as follows:

Architectural Possibilities Pattern

1. I am developing a software system with X for Y
2. The system must adhere to these constraints
3. Describe N possible architectures for this system
4. Describe the architecture in terms of Q

Example Implementation

The example implementation below explores architectures related to using a Web application built on a specific set of frameworks:

> I am developing a python web application using FastApi that allows users to publish interesting ChatGPT prompts, similar to twitter. Describe three possible architectures for this system. Describe the architecture with respect to modules and the functionality that each module contains.

The implementation specifies that the architecture should be described in terms of the modules and functionality within each module. The "with respect to" portion of the pattern is important to guide the LLM's output to appropriately interpret the term architecture. The same prompt could be changed to ask for architecture in terms of the REST API, interaction of a set of services, communication between modules, data storage, deployment on virtual machines, or other system aspects. The "with respect to" focuses the output on which of the many aspects the architecture is being explored in terms of.

Consequences

Performance-sensitive applications can use the *Architectural Possibilities* pattern to propose possible architectures to meet performance goals and then generate experiments, in the form of code, to test each architecture. For example, a cloud application might be implementable as (1) a monolithic Web application and run in a container or (2) a series of microservices in a microservice architecture. The LLM can first generate a sample implementation of each architecture and then generate a script to deploy each variation to the cloud and test it under various workloads. In addition, the workload tests could allow for comparative cost analysis from the resulting expenses incurred in the cloud. The *Architectural Possibilities* pattern is particularly powerful when combined with this type of LLM-based rapid implementation and experimentation.

Another way to expand this rapid architectural experimentation capability is to combine it with the *API Generator* pattern described in Sect. 4.3 and *API Simulator* pattern described in Sect. 4.4. The architecture can serve as the basis of the API generation, which can then be simulated. This approach allows developers to see what the realization and use of this architecture from a code perspective might look like. Likewise, the *Change Request Simulator* pattern described in Sect. 4.8 can be employed to reason about how hard/easy it would be to change different assumptions later given a proposed architecture.

Since an LLM may not fully understand the specific detailed requirements and constraints of the system, some of the proposed architectures may not suitable, leading to wasted time and effort. This drawback of the *Architectural Possibilities* pattern can be combated by giving additional context during the generation of the alternatives, but the onus is on the user to provide the relevant context. In addition, an LLM can only propose architectures based on the information it has been trained on and/or provided as context to user prompts. Its output may therefore not include newer or less well-known architectural patterns that could be a good fit for a given project.

4.8   The Change Request Simulation Pattern

Intent and Context

The *Change Request Simulation* pattern helps users reason about the complexity of a proposed system change, which could be related to requirements, architecture, performance, etc. For example, this pattern helps users reason about what impact a given change might have on some aspect of the system, such as which modules might need changing. This pattern is particularly helpful when a group of stakeholders need to discuss a possible requirements change, where the LLM serves as a (potentially) unbiased estimator of the scope and impact of the change.

Motivation

In many situations, it may not be immediately clear to stakeholders what the impact of a change would be. Without an understanding of a change's impact, however, it is hard to reason about the associated effects on schedule, cost, or other risks. Getting rapid feedback on potential impacts can help stakeholders initiate the appropriate conversations and experiments to better determine the true risk of the change. Distrust between users may also complicate the discussion of the change and necessitate an "unbiased" external opinion.

Structure and Key Ideas

The fundamental contextual statements are as follows:

Change Request Simulation Pattern

1. My software system architecture is X
2. The system must adhere to these constraints
3. I want you to simulate a change to the system that I will describe
4. Describe the impact of that change in terms of Q
5. This is the change to my system

Example Implementation

In this example implementation, the prompt refers back to a previously generated OpenAPI specification [17] as the basis of the simulation:

> My software system uses the OpenAPI specification that you generated earlier. I want you to simulate a change where a new mandatory field must be added to the prompts. List which functions and which files will require modifications.

The prompt above focuses the simulation on how the change will impact various functions and files in the system. This approach allows stakeholders to estimate the cost of a change by examining the complexity of the referenced files, functions, and the total count of each. Alternatively, in cases where the entire affected section of code can fit into the prompt, the LLM can be asked to identify lines of code that may require changing.

Consequences

The hardest part of applying the *Change Request Simulation* pattern is establishing enough context for the LLM to reason about a proposed change. This pattern works best, therefore, when it is employed with other **System Design** category patterns, such as the *API Generator* in Sect. 4.3, where conversation history can be used to seed the analysis. The more concrete the change description is in relation to the context, the more likely the LLM can provide a reasonable estimate of change impact.

The *Change Request Simulation* pattern can also be used to reason either (1) abstractly about a software-reliant system in terms of modules or (2) concretely in terms of files, functions, and/or lines of code. Existing LLMs have token limits that only consider a limited amount of information about a system. Large sweeping changes to a system can generally only be reasoned about at a higher level of abstraction since the detailed information needed to implement such changes would exceed an LLM's token limit. Within a smaller set of files or features, however, an LLM may be able to reason precisely about what needs to change.

One way to handle the tension between token limits and detailed output is to apply the *Change Request Simulation* pattern iteratively to zoom in and out. Initially, an abstract analysis is performed to identify features, modules, etc. that need to change. The prompt is then modified to refine the context to a specific module or feature and obtain greater detail from the LLM. This process can be repeated on individual parts of the module or feature until sufficient detail is obtained. Likewise, this process can be repeated for each high-level module to estimate the overall impact of a proposed change.

Applying the *Change Request Simulation* pattern is reliant on providing the LLM with enough context to reason about the proposed changes. The more detailed this context is, the better the LLM can evaluate the possible impact of the change. Providing enough context can be hard as users must present clear, detailed, and specific scenarios. Moreover, the fidelity of the LLM's output depends on the accuracy of the context given.

5   Code Quality and Refactoring Patterns

This section describes prompt patterns that help LLMs generate higher-quality code and refactor human-produced code.

5.1   The Code Clustering Pattern

Intent and Context

The *Code Clustering* pattern separates and clusters code into packages, classes, methods, etc. based on a particular property of the code, such as separating pure code (i.e., code with no side effects) and impure code (i.e., code with side effects) [22], business logic from database access, HTTP request handling from business logic, etc. The *Code Clustering* pattern defines the expected cluster properties to the LLM and then asks the LLM to restructure the code automatically to realize the desired clustering. This pattern helps ensure that LLM-generated code exhibits desired the clustering and can also be used to refactor human-produced code to add the clustering that wasn't originally present.

Motivation

How software is decomposed and clustered into packages, classes, methods, etc. has a significant impact on how easily the code can be changed, extended, and easily maintained. By default, an LLM will not have guidelines on the decomposition/clustering needs for an application. This lack of context can lead an LLM to produce code that appears monolithic, brittle, messy, and generally low quality. A key motivation for applying the *Code Clustering* pattern, therefore, is to provide the missing clustering context an LLM needs to generate higher quality code.

Structure and Key Ideas

The fundamental contextual statements are as follows:

> **Code Clustering Pattern**
> 1. Within scope X
> 2. I want you to write or refactor code in a way that separates code with property Y from code that has property Z.
> 3. These are examples of code with property Y.
> 4. These are examples of code with property Z.

Example Implementation

A sample implementation of the *Code Clustering* pattern is shown below:

> Whenever I ask you to write code, I want you to write code in a way that separates functionality with side-effects, such as file system, database, or network access, from functionality without side-effects.

Some common properties that are effective in generating higher-quality code with this pattern include:

- *Side effects*, where code is decomposed into functions to isolate code with side effects from code that is pure business logic so that it is easier to test and reason about in isolation,
- *Tiers*, where code is decomposed based on a layered architecture, such as the business logic tier and the data management tier,
- *Features*, where code is grouped into cohesive features that are isolated in separate files or groups of files.

One way to specify the properties used for this decomposition is by defining one property as the absence of the other property. In the implementation example above, the "side effects" property is clearly defined. The "without side effects" property is defined as the converse of the side effects property. A common form of implementation is to define properties that are opposites of each other.

Many other properties can be used to separate and cluster code as long as they are describable to an LLM. Well-understood properties, such as side effects, are likely to have been concepts that were present in the LLM's training set, so they will require less prompt design work for the LLM to reason about. Custom properties can be reasoned about through a combination of natural language description and few-shot examples. The *Code Clustering* pattern can be combined with the *Few-shot Code Example Generator* pattern in Sect. 4.5 to create code samples that demonstrate the desired property-based clustering and then use them in the *Code Clustering* pattern for in-context learning of the property.

Consequences

The *Code Clustering* pattern can dramatically improve the quality of LLM-produced code. Unless the LLM is told otherwise, its code will solve the problem at hand and often does not solve structuring problems, such as separating pure and impure functions, that it has not been asked to solve. The *Code Clustering* pattern surfaces a key issue in LLM software engineering, i.e., an LLM's output is only as good as the prompt it is given. Implicit knowledge (e.g., the project requires code that exhibits certain clustering properties) will not be known to the LLM unless this information is provided to it in a prompt.

The *Code Clustering* pattern depends crucially on understanding implicit requirements, such as coding conventions, architectural constraints, separation of concerns, etc. An LLM may be unaware of these implicit requirements unless users explicitly mention them in the prompt. Making the LLM understand how the implicit requirements may require substantial space in the prompt. LLMs have limitations in learning and understanding the semantics behind code structuring and clustering that are not yet fully understood, so they may not always be capable of autonomously defining meaningful clusters even when given significant context.

5.2   The Intermediate Abstraction Pattern

Intent and Context

The *Intermediate Abstraction* pattern instructs an LLM to not tightly couple some aspects of generated code by introducing an intermediate abstraction. This intermediate abstraction helps ensure that certain aspects of the code can be changed more easily at a later point in time. Abstraction and modularity are fundamental components of high-quality maintainable and reusable code. Code should be written in a way that isolates cohesive concepts into individual classes or methods so that edits can be isolated in scope. In addition, when working with an LLM, refactoring existing code is easier if refactorings can be isolated to a single function or method that needs to be modified, replaced, or added.

Motivation

Be default, LLMs often generate code that is highly procedural and directly translates the requirements spelled out in the prompt into code. In particular, the implementation may not have sufficient abstraction or modularity, making it hard to maintain. Moreover, as an LLM is continually prompted to add features to the code, it may produce increasingly long methods with little separation of concepts into packages, classes, or other abstractions that facilitate long-term maintainability.

Structure and Key Ideas

The fundamental contextual statements are as follows:

Intermediate Abstraction Pattern

1. If you write or refactor code with property X
2. that uses other code with property Y
3. (Optionally) Define property X
4. (Optionally) Define property Y
5. Insert an intermediate abstraction Z between X and Y
6. (Optionally) Abstraction Z should have these properties

Example Implementation

A sample implementation of the *Code Clustering* pattern is shown below:

> Whenever I ask you to write code, I want you to separate the business logic as much as possible from any underlying third-party libraries. Whenever business logic uses a third-party library, please write an intermediate abstraction that the business logic uses instead so the third-party library could be replaced with an alternate library if needed.

A common risk in software is third-party libraries since their dependencies are not directly under the control of a developer, thereby creating project risk. For example, a third-party library developer introduces changes to its dependencies that make it hard to incorporate into an existing project and limit access to future security updates in the new version. This example implementation uses the LLM to insert an intermediate abstraction to mitigate this type of risk.

Consequences

The *Code Clustering* pattern can aid in producing high-quality code. By explicitly instructing an LLM to structure its output in a certain way (e.g., separating pure and impure functions), the resulting code can adhere to best practices and be easier to understand and maintain. Another benefit of this pattern is that it can help ensure consistency, particularly in large projects where multiple LLMs or even human developers might be involved. Consistent code is more predictable and easier to understand.

However, the *Code Clustering* pattern may not be able to design a good abstraction simply from analysis of a single third-party library that provides a given capability. For example, different dependencies may have different fundamental architectures and interfaces. One way to address this heterogeneity is to leverage the *Few-shot Example Generator* pattern in Sect. 4.5 to create examples of other comparable third-party libraries and their usage and then ask the LLM to refactor the interface so it can be implemented with any alternatives.

5.3 The Principled Code Pattern

Intent and Context

The *Principled Code* pattern uses well-known names for coding principles to describe the desired code structure without having to explicitly describe each individual design rule. For example, an organization may want to ensure that their code follows SOLID [15] design principles.[2] The goal is to ensure that generated, refactored, and reviewed code adheres to the expected design principles.

Motivation

Writing software with good design characteristics is important to maintain a code base effective. However, developers may not be able to easily articulate and specify all the rules and patterns for what constitutes good design. Many articles and books have been written to explain how good design practices can be applied to different languages, frameworks, platforms, etc. The motivation for the Principled Code pattern is to enable developers to define these rules in natural language, as long as they know the commonly accepted name of the design method.

Structure and Key Ideas

The fundamental contextual statements are as follows:

Principled Code Pattern

1. Within this scope
2. Generate, refactor, or create code to adhere to named Principle X

Example Implementation

A sample implementation of the *Principled Code* pattern is shown below:

From now on, whenever you write, refactor, or review code, make sure it adheres to SOLID design principles.

---

[2] The SOLID code refers to software that applies the following design principles: (1) Single responsibility, (2) Open-closed, (3) Liskov substitution, (4) Interface segregation, and (5) Dependency inversion.

This example uses the SOLID design principles as the desired design guidelines. This named design methodology informs the LLM of the underlying principles that code it generates should follow.

Consequences

The *Principled Code* pattern works best with LLMs trained on a substantial volume of written material that explains the application of the named principle to a range of code bases. The more well-known the design principle(s), the more examples the LLM will likely have been trained on. The availability of training examples is particularly important for less mainstream languages or languages with more uncommon designs, such as Prolog or Clojure.

This situation is similar to the *Persona Pattern* presented in our prior work [24], where users describe the desired output using a well-known name. A consequence of the *Principled Code* pattern is that it only works with well-known named descriptions of code qualities that existed before the LLM was trained. Newer coding or design styles that came after the training date will not be accessible through this pattern. However, other approaches could be used to leverage in-context learning and few-shot examples to incorporate these inaccessible named coding or design styles.

5.4 The Hidden Assumptions Pattern

Intent and Context

The *Hidden Assumptions* pattern has an LLM identify and describe any assumptions made in a section of code. The pattern helps users identify these assumptions or remind them of assumptions they may have forgotten about. By showing key assumptions from the code to users, the LLM can help ensure users account for these assumptions in their decisions related to their code.

Motivation

Any code, regardless if it is produced by a human or LLM, may have hidden assumptions that user must understand. If users are unaware of these assumptions, however, they may use, modify, or otherwise leverage the code incorrectly. Hidden assumptions are particularly risky for LLM-generated code, where users may have less familiarity with what is being produced for them.

Structure and Key Ideas

The fundamental contextual statements are as follows:

Hidden Assumptions Pattern

1. Within this scope
2. List the assumptions that this code makes
3. (Optionally) Estimate how hard it would be to change these assumptions or their likelyhood of changing

Example Implementation

Several sample implementations of the *Hidden Assumptions* pattern are shown below, starting with this one:

List the assumptions that this code makes and how hard it would be to change each of them given the current code structure.

This first example focuses on listing assumptions that may be hard to change in the future. This refinement of the pattern helps make developers aware of liabilities in the code with respect to future change. If one of the assumptions is hard to change—but developers expect this aspect will need to change—they can request the LLM to refactor it to remove this flawed assumption.

A second example of the *Hidden Assumptions* pattern shows how it can be used to aid in refactoring code from being tightly coupled to an underlying database:

List the assumptions in this code that make it hard to change from a MongoDB database to MySQL.

With this example, the LLM will list assumptions that are tightly coupling to a specific database. User could then take this list and use it as the basis for refactoring, e.g., by asking the LLM to refactor the code to eliminate the listed assumptions.

Consequences

The *Hidden Assumptions* pattern enables the discovery of presuppositions or hidden assumptions present in the code. These insights can be invaluable in understanding the background context and underlying functioning of the code in question. Uncovering hidden assumptions of the code helps ensure that it is used, modified, or referenced correctly, mitigating the risk of misuse due to misunderstood or overlooked assumptions.

However, the *Hidden Assumptions* pattern may not identify all hidden assumptions in the code. For example, there may be code outside of what is in the context provided to the LLM that is needed to identify the assumption. The risk of this pattern is that developers will take it as a source of truth for all assumptions in the code, rather than flagging of some possible assumptions for consideration by developers.

5.5   The Pseudo-code Refactoring Pattern

Intent and Context

The *Pseudo-code Refactoring* pattern give users fine-grained control over the algorithm, flow, or other aspects of the code, while not requiring explicit specification of details. It also allows users to define pseudo-code for one or more details of generated or refactored code. The LLM is expected to adapt the output to fit the pseudo-code template while ensuring the code is correct and runnable.

Motivation

In many cases, users may have strong opinions or specific goals in the refactoring or generation of code that are tedious to describe—and duplicative of an LLM's work—if it were necessary to type the exact code structures they wanted. In particular, the benefit of using an LLM is reduced if developers must do as much coding work as the LLM to specify what they want. The motivation of the *Pseudo-code Refactoring* pattern is to provide a middle ground that allows greater control over code aspects without explicit coding and considering all the details.

Structure and Key Ideas

The fundamental contextual statements are as follows:

> **Pseudo-code Refactoring Pattern**
>
> 1. Refactor the code
> 2. So that it matches this pseudo-code
> 3. Match the structure of the pseudo-code as closely as possible

Example Implementation

A sample implementation of the *Pseudo-code Refactoring* pattern is shown below:

> Refactor the following code to match the following psuedo-code. Match the structure of the pseudo-code as closely as possible.

```
files = scan_features()
for file in files:
    print file name
for file in files:
    load feature
    mount router
create_openapi()
main():
    launch app
```

In this example, the prompt is asking the LLM to refactor a much larger body of code to match the structure of the pseudo-code. The pseudo-code defines the outline of the code, but not the details of how individual tasks are accomplished. In addition, the pseudo-code does not provide exact traceability to which lines are part of the described functionality. The LLM determines what the intent of the refactoring is and how to map it into the current code provided to it.

Consequences

The *Pseudo-code Refactoring* pattern enables more precise control over code generation or refactoring. It empowers users to influence the algorithm's flow, structure, or other aspects without going into exhaustive details. The pattern also boosts efficiency by enabling users to outline pseudo-code structures that the LLM can populate. This pseudo-code reduces duplicate work and saves time since developers need not program the full code structure that they desire.

The *Pseudo-code Refactoring* pattern can trigger more substantial refactoring than what is outlined in the pseudo-code. For example, rewriting the code to match the pseudo-code may require the LLM to remove a method and split its code between two other methods. However, removing the method could then change the public interface of the code.

5.6   The Data-Guided Refactoring Pattern

Intent and Context

The *Data-guided Refactoring* pattern allow users to refactor existing code to use data with a new format. Rather than specifying the exact logic changes needed to use the new format, users can provide the new format schema to the LLM and ask the

LLM to make the necessary changes. This pattern helps automate code refactoring for the common task of incorporating changes to data formats.

Motivation

Refactoring code to use a new input or output data structure can be tedious. When communicating with an LLM, explaining the explicit refactoring steps to may also require more time than actually conducting the needed steps. The *Data-guided Refactoring* pattern provides a concise way of explaining to the LLM what refactoring is needed. Since changing data formats can have such a large-scale impact on a system, this pattern can automate these refactorings, potentially reducing costs and accelerating overall system development.

Structure and Key Ideas

The fundamental contextual statements are as follows:

> **Data-guided Refactoring Pattern**
>
> 1. Refactor the code
> 2. So that its input, output, or stored data format is X
> 3. Provide one or more examples of X

Example Implementation

An example implementation of the *Data-guided Refactoring* pattern is shown below:

> Let's refactor execute_graph() so that graph has the following format {'graph':{ ...current graph format... }, 'sorted_nodes': { 'a': ['b','c'...],... }}

This example asks the LLM to refactor a method to use a different format for the graph. In the example, the specific use of the graph format is not defined, but could potentially be input, output, or internal to the method. All the different uses of the graph would be supportable by the pattern. In addition, the implementation uses ellipses to indicate portions of the data structure, which allows the LLM to fill in user intent with concrete details.

Consequences

The *Data-guided Refactoring* pattern reduces the manual effort to specify refactoring for many types of code changes necessitated by a change in data format. In many cases, the refactoring can be completely automated through this process, or at least boostrapped, thereby accelerating and potentially reducing the cost of changing data formats.

While LLMs can operate with many different schemas and refactor code accordingly, they may struggle with complex or niche data formats different from what the LLM saw in its training data. Developers may therefore need to provide additional guidance or instruction in these cases. Moreover, an LLM might not understand the full implications of the data format change and may not refactor all necessary parts of the code, leading to an inconsistent codebase that uses multiple data formats at different points in the code.

6 Related Work

Software patterns [10, 20] have been studied extensively and shown their value in software engineering. Software design patterns have also been specialized for other types of non-traditional uses, such as designing smart contracts [26, 28]. Prompt design patterns for software engineering are complementary to these, although not focused on the design of the system itself but on the interactions with an LLM to produce and maintain software-reliant systems over time.

Prompt engineering is an active area of study, and the importance of prompts is well understood [7]. Many problems cannot be solved by LLMs unless prompts are structured correctly [9]. Some work has specifically looked at prompting approaches to help LLMs learn to leverage outside tooling [27]. Our work complements these approaches, focusing on specific patterns of interaction that can be used to tap into LLM capabilities to solve specific problems in software engineering.

Much discussion on LLM usage in software engineering to date has centered on the use of LLMs for code generation and the security and code quality risks associated with that usage. For example, Asare et al. [2] compared LLM code generation to humans from a security perspective. Other research has examined the quality of generated answers and code from LLMs [5, 9, 11, 16] and interaction patterns for fixing bugs [21, 25]. Our research draws inspiration from these explorations and documents specific patterns that can be used to improve code quality and help reduce errors. Moreover, as more prompt patterns are developed, different patterns can be quantitatively compared to each other for effectiveness in solving code quality issues.

7   Concluding Remarks

Ever since ChatGPT was released to the public in November 2022, much attention [1, 2, 18] has focused on the mistakes that LLMs make when performing software engineering tasks particularly with respect to generating code with defects and/or security vulnerabilities. As shown in this chapter, however, prompt patterns can be used to help alleviate many of these mistakes and reduce errors. Moreover, prompt patterns can tap into LLM capabilities that are hard to automate using existing technologies, including simulating a system based on requirements, generating an API specification, and pointing out assumptions in code.

The following are lessons learned thus far from our work on applying ChatGPT to automate common software engineering tasks:

- **Prompt engineering is crucial for unlocking the full capabilities of LLMs for software engineering tasks**. The prompt patterns described in this chapter codify effective prompt design techniques that can help address common software engineering challenges. Thoughtful prompt design is key to tapping into ChatGPT's strengths.
- **Prompt patterns enable rapid exploration and experimentation throughout the software life cycle**. Patterns like the *API Generator*, *API Simulator*, and *Architectural Possibilities* allow developers to experiment rapidly with multiple designs and approaches early in the life cycle. This agility can accelerate development and lead to better solutions.
- **Integrating prompt patterns together into pattern catalogs can further enhance their effectiveness**. This chapter discusses chaining prompt patterns together, such as combining the *Requirements Simulator* and *Visualization Generator* patterns. These sequences and combinations of patterns can build upon each other to accomplish more complex goals.
- **The depth of capabilities of LLMs, such as ChatGPT, is not widely or fully understood or appreciated**. LLMs hold immense potential for helping to automate common tasks throughout the software engineering life cycle. Many LLM capabilities have the potential to accelerate software engineering, not just by generating code but by making rapid experimentation at many different levels of abstraction possible. A key to leveraging these capabilities is to codify an effective catalog of prompts and guidance on how to combine them at different stages of the software life cycle to improve software engineering.
- **Significant human involvement and expertise is currently necessary to leverage LLMs effectively for automating common software engineering tasks**. The tendency of ChatGPT to "hallucinate" confidently and enthusiastically when generating incorrect output requires close scrutiny from human users at this point. While prompt patterns can help mitigate some of these issues, much further work is needed on other aspects of prompt engineering (such as quality assurance and versioning) to ensure output of LLMs is accurate and helpful in practice.

We encourage readers to test the prompt patterns described in this chapter by using ChatGPT to replicate our findings in their own domains and environments.

References

1. GitHub Copilot . Your AI pair programmer. github.com/features/copilot
2. Asare, O., Nagappan, M., Asokan, N.: Is GitHub's copilot as bad as humans at introducing vulnerabilities in code? arXiv preprint arXiv:2204.04741 (2022)
3. Bang, Y., Cahyawijaya, S., Lee, N., Dai, W., Su, D., Wilie, B., Lovenia, H., Ji, Z., Yu, T., Chung, W., et al.: A multitask, multilingual, multimodal evaluation of ChatGPT on reasoning, hallucination, and interactivity. arXiv preprint arXiv:2302.04023 (2023)
4. Bommasani, R., Hudson, D.A., Adeli, E., Altman, R., Arora, S., von Arx, S., Bernstein, M.S., Bohg, J., Bosselut, A., Brunskill, E., et al.: On the opportunities and risks of foundation models. arXiv preprint arXiv:2108.07258 (2021)
5. Borji, A.: A categorical archive of ChatGPT failures. arXiv preprint arXiv:2302.03494 (2023)
6. Carleton, A., Klein, M.H., Robert, J.E., Harper, E., Cunningham, R.K., de Niz, D., Foreman, J.T., Goodenough, J.B., Herbsleb, J.D., Ozkaya, I., Schmidt, D.C.: Architecting the future of software engineering. Computer **55**(9), 89–93 (2022)
7. van Dis, E.A., Bollen, J., Zuidema, W., van Rooij, R., Bockting, C.L.: ChatGPT: five priorities for research. Nature **614**(7947), 224–226 (2023)
8. Feiler, P., Sullivan, K., Wallnau, K., Gabriel, R., Goodenough, J., Linger, R., Longstaff, T., Kazman, R., Klein, M., Northrop, L., Schmidt, D.: Ultra-Large-Scale Systems: The Software Challenge of the Future. Software Engineering Institute, Carnegie Mellon University, Pittsburgh (2006)
9. Frieder, S., Pinchetti, L., Griffiths, R.R., Salvatori, T., Lukasiewicz, T., Petersen, P.C., Chevalier, A., Berner, J.: Mathematical capabilities of ChatGPT. arXiv preprint arXiv:2301.13867 (2023)
10. Gamma, E., Johnson, R., Helm, R., Johnson, R.E., Vlissides, J.: Design patterns: elements of reusable object-oriented software. In: Pearson Deutschland GmbH (1995)
11. Jalil, S., Rafi, S., LaToza, T.D., Moran, K., Lam, W.: ChatGPT and software testing education: Promises & perils. arXiv preprint arXiv:2302.03287 (2023)
12. Kendar, R.: Httpansweringmachine. github.com/kendarorg/HttpAnsweringMachine (2022), accessed on March 11, 2023
13. Krochmalski, J.: IntelliJ IDEA Essentials. Packt Publishing Ltd, Mumbai (2014)
14. Liu, P., Yuan, W., Fu, J., Jiang, Z., Hayashi, H., Neubig, G.: Pre-train, prompt, and predict: a systematic survey of prompting methods in natural language processing. ACM Comput. Surv. **55**(9), 1–35 (2023)
15. Marshall, D., Bruno, J.: Solid Code. Microsoft Press, New York (2009)
16. Nair, M., Sadhukhan, R., Mukhopadhyay, D.: Generating secure hardware using ChatGPT resistant to CWES. In: Cryptology ePrint Archive (2023)
17. OpenAPI Initiative: OpenAPI Specification (2021). https://www.openapis.org/, accessed on March 11, 2023
18. Pearce, H., Ahmad, B., Tan, B., Dolan-Gavitt, B., Karri, R.: Asleep at the keyboard? assessing the security of GitHub copilot's code contributions. In: 2022 IEEE Symposium on Security and Privacy (SP), pp. 754–768. IEEE, New York (2022)
19. Schmidt, D.C.: Guest editor's introduction: model-driven engineering. IEEE Comput. **39**(2), 25–31 (2006)
20. Schmidt, D.C., Stal, M., Rohnert, H., Buschmann, F.: Pattern-Oriented Software Architecture, Patterns for Concurrent and Networked Objects. Wiley, New York (2013)

21. Sobania, D., Briesch, M., Hanna, C., Petke, J.: An analysis of the automatic bug fixing performance of ChatGPT. arXiv preprint arXiv:2301.08653 (2023)
22. Wadler, P.: The essence of functional programming. In: Proceedings of the 19th ACM SIGPLAN-SIGACT Symposium on Principles of Programming Languages, pp. 1–14 (1992)
23. Wang, Y., Yao, Q., Kwok, J.T., Ni, L.M.: Generalizing from a few examples: a survey on few-shot learning. ACM Comput. Surv. (CSUR) **53**(3), 1–34 (2020)
24. White, J., Fu, Q., Hays, S., Sandborn, M., Olea, C., Gilbert, H., Elnashar, A., Spencer-Smith, J., Schmidt, D.C.: A prompt pattern catalog to enhance prompt engineering with ChatGPT. arXiv preprint arXiv:2302.11382 (2023)
25. Xia, C.S., Zhang, L.: Conversational automated program repair. arXiv preprint arXiv:2301.13246 (2023)
26. Xu, X., Pautasso, C., Zhu, L., Lu, Q., Weber, I.: A pattern collection for blockchain-based applications. In: Proceedings of the 23rd European Conference on Pattern Languages of Programs, pp. 1–20 (2018)
27. Yao, S., Zhao, J., Yu, D., Du, N., Shafran, I., Narasimhan, K., Cao, Y.: React: synergizing reasoning and acting in language models. arXiv preprint arXiv:2210.03629 (2022)
28. Zhang, P., White, J., Schmidt, D.C., Lenz, G.: Applying software patterns to address interoperability in blockchain-based healthcare apps. CoRR **abs/1706.03700** (2017). http://arxiv.org/abs/1706.03700

Requirements Engineering Using Generative AI: Prompts and Prompting Patterns

Krishna Ronanki (ID), **Beatriz Cabrero-Daniel** (ID), **Jennifer Horkoff** (ID), and **Christian Berger** (ID)

Abstract [**Context**] Companies are increasingly recognizing the importance of automating Requirements Engineering (RE) tasks due to their resource-intensive nature. The advent of GenAI has made these tasks more amenable to automation, thanks to its ability to understand and interpret context effectively. [**Problem**] However, in the context of GenAI, prompt engineering is a critical factor for success. Despite this, we currently lack tools and methods to systematically assess and determine the most effective prompt patterns to employ for a particular RE task. [**Method**] Two tasks related to requirements, specifically requirement classification and tracing, were automated using the GPT-3.5 turbo API. The performance evaluation involved assessing various prompts created using 5 prompt patterns and implemented programmatically to perform the selected RE tasks, focusing on metrics such as precision, recall, accuracy, and F-Score. [**Results**] This paper evaluates the effectiveness of the 5 prompt patterns' ability to make GPT-3.5 turbo perform the selected RE tasks and offers recommendations on which prompt pattern to use for a specific RE task. Additionally, it also provides an evaluation framework as a reference for researchers and practitioners who want to evaluate different prompt patterns for different RE tasks.

Keywords Requirements engineering · Generative AI · Prompt patterns · Prompt engineering · Large language models

1 Introduction

Researchers in Requirements Engineering (RE) have been exploring the use of machine learning (ML) and deep learning (DL) methods for various RE tasks, including requirements classification, prioritization, tracing, ambiguity detection, and modelling [1]. However, the majority of existing ML/DL approaches are based

K. Ronanki (✉) · B. Cabrero-Daniel · J. Horkoff · C. Berger
University of Gothenburg, Gothenburg, Sweden
e-mail: krishna.ronanki@gu.se

© The Author(s), under exclusive license to Springer Nature Switzerland AG 2024
A. Nguyen-Duc et al. (eds.), *Generative AI for Effective Software Development*,
https://doi.org/10.1007/978-3-031-55642-5_5

on supervised learning, which requires huge amounts of task-specific labelled training data. But the lack of open-source RE-specific labelled data makes it difficult for RE researchers and practitioners to develop, train, and test advanced ML/DL models [1] for their effective usage in RE tasks.

Utilizing pre-trained generative artificial intelligence (GenAI) models like large language models (LLM) for performing RE tasks removes the need for large amounts of labelled data. Pre-trained LLMs are also observed to increase developer productivity [13] and reduce code complexity [12] among other things. The adoption of these LLMs in practical settings is also growing thanks to the development of IDE-integrated services around them [18]. Recent LLMs are demonstrating increasingly impressive capabilities when performing a wide range of tasks [3]. These capabilities can be further improved in NLP tasks just by carefully crafting the input given to the model [8].

To interact with an LLM, one typically provides instructions written in natural language (NL) [18], referred to as prompts. The emerging practice of utilizing carefully selected and composed NL instructions to achieve the desired output from a GenAI model such as a pre-trained LLM is called prompt engineering [10]. However, the problem with NL instructions is that they can be ambiguous in some contexts, i.e., some of the words in the instruction can have multiple interpretations, which vary according to the context. One of the major risks of having an instruction that can be interpreted in different ways is that the LLM might interpret the instruction in a way that is different from the users'. This might lead to an output generation that is considered unexpected and/or undesirable by the user. Despite the existence of empirically validated prompt engineering techniques like zero-shot, few-shot [3], and chain-of-thought prompting [16], prompt engineering is still more of an art than science. Even the order in which the samples are provided in a few-shot setting can make the difference between near state-of-the-art and random guess performance [11].

One potential way to mitigate the challenges with the ambiguous nature of current prompt engineering practices is to develop a structured approach for crafting the NL prompts. However, to define and establish a prompt structure that can be generalized, it is crucial to identify any underlying patterns within the prompts that consistently generate desirable output for a given task. Different prompts need to be tested in order to see what different outputs they may lead to, thereby discovering any discrepancies between what is assumed or expected and what is understood by the models [4]. This led to the development of prompt patterns. Prompt patterns can be defined as codified reusable patterns that can be applied to the input prompts to improve the desirability of the generated output while reducing the gap between the user's expected output and the model's generated output [17].

Recognizing prompt patterns that consistently produce desirable output so that practitioners can leverage the numerous benefits of using these LLMs in RE tasks has significant value. Our work investigates and presents which prompt patterns can be used to produce outputs that are desirable and conform to users' expectations when using LLMs for two RE tasks. We chose the GPT 3.5-turbo model (which we will refer to as "the model" from now on for the rest of the chapter) as our choice of LLM, which we accessed through the API to perform the RE tasks. The two RE tasks we chose to focus on in this study are (a) binary requirements classification and (b) identifying requirements that are dependent on each other (requirements traceability task). We measure the performance of the patterns' implementation in these tasks using measures like precision, recall, accuracy, and F-score. We evaluate the performance of the model at different temperature settings to understand its effect on prompt patterns' performance. We recommend prompt patterns that achieve the best performance scores for the selected RE tasks in our experimental configuration. We also propose a framework to evaluate a prompt pattern's effectiveness for any RE task based on the methodology we employed for this study. To that end, we aim to answer the following research questions:

RQ1- What prompt patterns can be recommended for RE researchers and practitioners for binary requirements classification and requirement traceability tasks?

RQ2- How to evaluate a prompt pattern's effectiveness in performing any RE task?

2 Background

Our approach toward designing the binary requirements classification and requirements traceability tasks for our experimental setup involves influences from requirements Information Retrieval (IR). In the context of requirements IR, classification involves categorizing requirements into different groups [20]. Requirements classification and IR share common principles related to information organization, search and retrieval, and semantic understanding among other things. IR methods are also used to search for specific traceability information during software development, helping stakeholders locate related artefacts and trace the relationships between them.

2.1 Prompt Engineering

Prompt engineering [10] or prompt programming [15] or prompting is an emerging practice in which carefully selected and composed sentences are used to achieve the desired output (the process of engineering a natural language prompt). Prompt engineering allows the model's users to express their intent in plain language, rather than a specially designed programming language [7]. Prompt engineering is still more of an art than science, but few techniques have been empirically validated in experimental settings to improve the GenAI model's performance.

Zero-Shot Prompting In its most basic form, zero-shot prompting involves using natural language sentences to convey the "problem to be solved" or the "expected output," without providing any examples [7]. It is a technique modelled after Zero-Shot Learning (ZSL), which directly applies previously trained models to predicting both seen and unseen classes without using any labelled training instances [9].

Few-Shot Prompting Few-shot prompting builds on zero-shot prompting by conveying the "problem to be solved" or the "expected output" using a few demonstrations of the task (examples) at inference time as conditioning [14].

Chain-of-Thought Prompting Chain-of-thought prompting is a technique that is observed to enhance the reasoning capabilities of an LLM. Using this technique, the user constructs the prompts in a way that makes the model generate a coherent series of intermediate reasoning steps that lead to the final answer for the task at hand [16].

2.2   Generative AI Model Temperature

Temperature of a GenAI model is a parameter that controls the randomness of the model's output. When adjusting the temperature setting of a GenAI model, which ranges from 0.0 to 1.0, one is essentially controlling the randomness of the model's responses. Higher temperatures (e.g., 0.8 or 1.0) result in more diverse and "creative" responses, while lower temperatures (e.g., 0.2 or 0.5) produce more focused and deterministic responses. In our study, we evaluate the performance of the model in performing the selected RE tasks while implementing all five patterns over three temperature settings. The three temperature settings are 0.0 (lowest), 0.4 (default), and 1.0 (highest).

2.3   Related Work

There are several works in the existing literature that focus on the application of LLMs for various IR-specific software engineering (SE), while few focus on RE tasks like binary and multiclass classification of requirements. Zhang et al. [20] empirically evaluate ChatGPT's performance on requirements IR tasks. Under the zero-shot setting, their results reveal that ChatGPT's performance in IR tasks has high recall but low precision. They posit their evaluation provides preliminary evidence for designing and developing more effective requirements IR methods based on LLMs. Alhoshan et al. [1] report an extensive study using the contextual word embedding-based zero-shot learning (ZSL) approach for requirements classification. The study tested this approach by conducting more than 360 experiments using four language models with a total of 1020 requirements and found generic language models trained on general-purpose data perform better than domain-specific language models under the zero-shot learning approach. Their results show that ZSL achieves F-Scores from 66% to 80% for binary and multiclass classification tasks.

To the best of the authors' knowledge, there are no works that focus on measuring the performance of LLMs in requirements traceability tasks. A systematic mapping study (SMS) performed by Li et al. [19] presents 32 machine learning (ML) technologies and 7 enhancement strategies for establishing trace links through their work. Their results indicate that ML technologies show promise in predicting emerging trace links by leveraging existing traceability information within the requirements. They identified three studies that they classified under the "semantically similar words extraction" enhancement strategy.

White et al. [17] present prompt design techniques for software engineering in the form of patterns to automate common software engineering activities using LLMs. Prompt patterns serve as a means of knowledge transfer, similar to software patterns, by offering reusable solutions to common problems related to generating output and engaging with LLMs. They establish a framework for documenting prompt patterns that can be adapted to various domains, providing a systematic approach for structuring prompts to tackle a range of issues. The academic literature presents and discusses a catalogue of patterns that have proven successful in enhancing the quality of LLM-generated conversations.

Despite these studies, to our knowledge, there are no works that focus on measuring the performance of an LLM in performing a certain RE task while using a specific prompt pattern to craft your input prompts. This is crucial since there is an opportunity to identify prompt patterns that work better in comparison to others for particular RE tasks.

3 Methodology

3.1 Experiment Design

We selected five prompt patterns for our experiments with the RE tasks, (1) Cognitive Verifier, (2) Context Manager, (3) Persona, (4) Question Refinement, and (5) Template, out of 16 patterns presented by White et al. [17]. They have been selected on the basis of the descriptions for each prompt pattern provided by the authors, which include the intent and motivation behind the pattern's proposal, the structure and key ideas that the pattern represents, an example implementation of the pattern in practice, and the observed consequences of the pattern's implementation in practice. We used these five patterns to craft prompts for the selected RE tasks and presented these prompts in Table 1. We performed each experiment five times using each of the prompts presented in Table 1, gathering the model's replies and computing the aggregated performance measures (precision, recall, accuracy, and F-score) for each run.

Table 1 Prompts table

Pattern	Classification	Tracing
Cognitive verifier	Classify the given list of requirements into functional (labelled as F) and non-functional requirements (labelled as NF). Ask me questions if needed to break the given task into smaller subtasks. All the outputs to the smaller subtasks must be combined before you generate the final output	List the IDs of requirements that are related to the [deprecated] feature in the requirements specification document below. Ask me questions if needed to break down the given task into smaller subtasks. All the outputs to the smaller subtasks must be combined before you generate the final output
Context manager	Classify the given list of requirements into functional (labelled as F) and non-functional requirements (labelled as NF). When you provide an answer, please explain the reasoning and assumptions behind your response. If possible, address any potential ambiguities or limitations in your answer, in order to provide a more complete and accurate response	List the IDs of requirements that are related to the [deprecated] feature from the requirements specification document below. When you provide an answer, please explain the reasoning and assumptions behind your response. If possible, address any potential ambiguities or limitations in your answer in order to provide a more complete and accurate response
Persona	Act as a requirements engineering domain expert, and classify the given list of requirements into functional (labelled as F) and non-functional requirements (labelled as NF)	Act as a requirements engineering domain expert, and list the IDs of requirements that are dependent on the [deprecated] feature in the following requirements specification document
Question refinement	Classify the given list of requirements into functional (labelled as F) and non-functional requirements (labelled as NF). If needed, suggest a better version of the question to use that incorporates information specific to this task, and ask me if I would like to use your question instead	List the IDs of requirements that are related to the [deprecated] feature from the requirements specification document below. If needed, suggest a better version of the question to use that incorporates information specific to this task, and ask me if I would like to use your question instead
Template	Read the following list of requirements, and return the IDs of non-functional requirements only. Write the result as a list like (ID=X) (ID=Y) (ID=Z), where X, Y, and Z are IDs of non-functional requirements	List the IDs of requirements that are related to the [deprecated] feature in the requirements specification document below. Follow the provided template when generating the output: ID list: X.X.X.X; X.X.X; X.X.X.X; etc.

3.2 Datasets

We used the PROMISE dataset [5] for the classification task and the PURE dataset for the requirements traceability task as they have been widely used in literature. The PROMISE dataset, which is available in .arff file format, was converted into .csv format. The CSV file (ground truth for our experiment) had a total of 621 requirements, out of which 253 requirements were functional requirements labelled as F and 368 were non-functional requirements labelled as NF.

The PURE dataset [6] is composed of public requirements documents retrieved from the Web. The documents cover multiple domains, have different degrees of abstraction, and range from product standards to documents of public companies, to university projects. A general XML schema file (XSD) was also defined to represent these different documents in a uniform format. From this dataset, we chose a subset of the dataset where each requirement in the System Requirements Specification (SRS) documents has a numerical ID in the format of X.X.X.X. These IDs (trace links as we will call them from now on) were used to establish a reference point, helping identify which requirements in the SRS documents are connected or dependent on one another. For example, if requirement A contains any reference to requirement B, then requirement A also had a trace link referencing requirement B in the X.X.X.X format. We used this information to construct the ground truth for the traceability task.

3.3 Tasks

We begin the study by conducting a series of controlled experiments with the model for two tasks, (i) Binary Classification of Functional Requirements (FR) and Non-Functional Requirements (NFR) and (ii) Requirements Traceability, described in more detail below.

Binary Classification of Functional and Non-Functional Requirements The task aims to distinguish Functional Requirements (FR) from Non-Functional Requirements(NFR), assuming that a requirement belongs to either the FR or NFR class. The PROMISE NFR dataset [5] was used for this purpose. The process we followed is:

1. We wrote a Python program that randomly picks 50 requirements from a CSV file. This CSV file contains 621 unlabelled requirements, the same 621 requirements that make up the PROMISE dataset.
2. We also input a prompt that we created using one of five patterns right into the program.
3. We use the model through the API to perform the classification task. We do this five times, and each time, the program chooses a different set of 50 requirements randomly.
4. The program then automatically compares the classification results with the ground truth results from the PROMISE dataset.
5. We repeated this whole process five times, once for each of the prompt patterns we were testing.

Requirements Traceability For this task, we had two sets of software requirement specifications (SRS) taken from the PURE dataset [6]: one for a home temperature control system called "THEMAS" and the other for defining a game interface and its functionalities, known as "QHEADACHE." The process we followed is:

1. For consistency, we manually formatted these SRS files and removed any unnecessary information, like hyperlinks.
2. We then created modified versions of these documents, referred to as "THEMAS clean" and "QHEADACHE clean," where we removed trace links.
3. We provided these cleaned documents, without trace links, to the model programmatically.
4. The model was given a requirement (randomly selected from the input documents) and asked to identify all related or dependent requirements.
5. We repeated this process five times for each prompt pattern, with a different randomly selected set of requirements each time.
6. This entire procedure was repeated five times, once for each prompt pattern we were testing.

3.4 Performance Metrics

The RE field has often adopted IR's measures, i.e., precision, recall, and the F-measure, to assess the effectiveness of any tool [2]. Since both tasks selected and defined for our study are related to requirements IR, we also used precision, recall, F-Score, and accuracy to measure the performance of the model in performing both the RE tasks using the five prompt patterns. These measures were computed programmatically by comparing the model's outputs with the ground truth.

Consider a scenario where an analyst wants to identify all NFRs in a specification. In this scenario, a high recall indicates that the majority of the NFRs selected were accurately categorized as NFRs. Conversely, a low recall suggests that the majority of requirements were misclassified, with FRs being mistakenly identified as NFRs. A high precision signifies that most of the requirements classified as NFRs by the LLM are indeed NFRs. On the contrary, a lower precision suggests that a number of requirements identified as NFRs by the LLM are, in fact, FRs.

Consider a scenario where a requirement is marked as "deprecated." In this scenario, it is important to trace all affected dependencies, i.e., find all requirements associated with the deprecated requirement. In this context, a high recall would signify that the majority of the associated or dependent requirements have been appropriately identified. Conversely, a low recall would indicate that only a limited number of the connections have been recognized. Precision provides a measure of the accuracy of retrieved links in relation to the dataset. A high precision indicates that a significant portion of the retrieved results indeed align with the dataset's true links. On the other hand, a low precision implies that a considerable number of the retrieved results are not truly linked and should not have been flagged.

The F-score is the harmonic mean of precision and recall that takes both false positives and false negatives into account. It combines both of them into a single metric to provide a balanced evaluation of a model's performance.

3.5   Threats to Validity

While this study provides an analysis of prompt patterns in the context of binary requirements classification and tracing dependent requirements using LLMs, it is essential to acknowledge and address potential threats to the validity of the findings.

Internal Validity There is a possibility for the existence of a degree of uncertainty in the ground truth since the data in our chosen datasets are labelled by humans(contributing authors of the dataset). Inter-rater variability and potential labelling bias could impact the reliability of performance metrics. The preprocessing steps applied to the data, such as cleaning, could influence the model's ability to capture complex patterns as well. The prompts crafted and presented in Table 1 using the prompt patterns are also subject to the authors' capabilities and competence with the task at hand.

External Validity Given the unique nature of some RE tasks, the findings from this study may not always generalize beyond binary requirements classification and tracing dependent requirements.

Construct Validity The findings of this study may be constrained by the characteristics and representativeness of the datasets in use. Since we used a GPT model, there is a possibility that the datasets we used could have been part of the training data for the GPT model. Next, the choice of prompt patterns is a critical aspect of this study. The selected patterns may not fully encompass the spectrum of possible patterns, potentially leading to an incomplete representation of LLM performance for the selected RE tasks.

4   Results and Analysis

This section presents the aggregated results from the described experiments. Section 4.1 presents the performance measures of the model in performing the two RE tasks using the five selected prompt patterns. Section 4.2 presents recommendations for RE researchers and practitioners on which prompt patterns to use for the selected RE tasks based on our analysis of the results obtained, answering **RQ1**. We abstract our methodology and present it as a framework to evaluate the performance of any prompt pattern for a chosen RE task in Sect. 4.3, answering **RQ2**.

4.1   Prompt Patterns' Performance for the Selected RE Tasks

Tables 2 and 3 present the performance measures of the model using all five prompt patterns in the binary requirements classification task and requirements traceability task, respectively. The red column represents the value of the metric

Table 2 Performance measures of the model using all five prompt patterns in binary requirements classification

Prompt Pattern	Precision	Recall	F-Score	Accuracy
Cognitive Verifier	61.7% 76.7%	87.1% 83.3%	81.6% 79.9%	78.0% 74.8%
Context Manager	80.6% 79.4%	73.0% 72.4%	76.6% 75.6%	73.6% 71.6%
Persona	71.9% 79.9%	81.0% 86.9%	76.2% 80.4%	71.2% 76.0%
Question Refinement	84.6% 80.8%	71.7% 76.6%	77.6% 78.7%	76.0% 74.4%
Template	75.0% 68.0%	91.0% 89.9%	82.2% 76.1%	77.2% 68.8%

Table 3 Performance measures of the model using all five prompt patterns in requirements traceability

Prompt Pattern	Precision	Recall	F-Score	Accuracy
Cognitive Verifier	35.2% 37.2%	61.5% 63.2%	44.8% 46.8%	88.9% 89.5%
Context Manager	28.5% 29.9%	59.8% 61.3%	36.7% 38.5%	85.0% 85.8%
Persona	41.3% 38.5%	76.9% 76.1%	53.7% 51.0%	90.4% 89.4%
Question Refinement	43.2% 43.4%	62.4% 64.0%	51.0% 53.2%	91.3% 91.8%
Template	38.9% 36.7%	61.5% 62.6%	47.2% 47.3%	89.9% 90.9%

Table 4 Standard deviation of performance measures for the five prompt patterns in binary requirements classification task

Binary requirements classification	P-STDEV	R-STDEV	F-STDEV	A-STDEV
Cognitive verifier	1.9%	2.0%	1.7%	1.7%
Context manager	3.7%	13.5%	7.7%	2.0%
Persona	5.4%	0.1%	2.8%	3.3%
Question refinement	2.0%	2.5%	0.5%	0.8%
Template	5.3%	0.8%	3.5%	4.8%

Table 5 Standard deviation of performance measures for the five prompt patterns in requirements traceability task

Tracing dependant requirements	P-STDEV	R-STDEV	F-STDEV	A-STDEV
Cognitive verifier	3.7%	1.0%	3.0%	1.1%
Context manager	2.5%	4.5%	2.1%	1.4%
Persona	3.8%	2.7%	3.9%	1.4%
Question refinement	1.2%	1.7%	1.1%	0.3%
Template	3.9%	3.3%	3.3%	1.5%

for the temperature setting of 1.0, the green column represents the value of the metric for the temperature setting of 0.4, and the blue column represents the value of the metric for the temperature setting of 0.0. Tables 4 and 5 present the standard deviations of precision, recall, F-Score, and accuracy measures across the three temperature settings, denoted by P-STDEV, R-STDEV, F-STDEV, and A-STDEV, respectively.

The precision, recall, and F1 scores, which serve as crucial indicators of the model's performance, consistently exhibit higher values in the binary requirements classification task as compared to the tracing of dependent-requirements task. Observations from the results presented above underscore the model's ability to discern and classify binary requirements effectively, demonstrating a higher precision in isolating relevant instances and a better recall in identifying all pertinent cases. A major observation deviation from this is the higher accuracy scores the model achieved for all patterns for the requirements traceability task in comparison to the binary requirements classification task. This rather significant deviation might be the result of the model being more adept at accurately predicting false negatives than identifying true positives, true negatives, and false positives. This leads to a scenario where not wrongly predicting non-existing trace links between two requirements within the SRS documents results in higher accuracy scores. This is why we focus our analysis and base our observations more on precision, recall, and F-score measures than accuracy.

Cognitive Verifier Pattern From Table 2, we can see that the recall is higher than precision when implementing this pattern for binary requirements classification. This holds true for all three temperature settings. This means that the model is observed to be more adept at categorizing NFRs accurately as NFRs (predicting true positives) than making sure the categorized NFRs are indeed NFRs (predicting true positives as well as false negatives) using the Cognitive Verifier pattern.

The variability in standard deviation scores, as seen in Table 4, suggests that the effectiveness of these patterns is sensitive to the temperature setting. A higher standard deviation score indicates lower dependability in the model's classification results at varying temperature settings. The standard deviation scores of precision, recall, F-score, and accuracy are no more than two percentage points for this pattern. This means that the effect of temperature on the model's performance is low when using this pattern, indicating a higher dependability in binary requirements classification.

When it comes to the requirements traceability task, this pattern yielded higher precision, recall, F-score, and accuracy at higher temperature settings, as seen in Table 3. The standard deviation of recall and accuracy is observed to be lower compared to the standard deviation of precision and F-score as observed in Table 5. This indicates this pattern is not as good at performing requirements traceability as it is at binary requirements classification.

Context Manager Pattern From Table 2, we observe that precision increases by 6% between low- and high-temperature settings, while recall sees a significant drop from 73% to 49%. The F-score and accuracy also drop with an increase in temperature but not as significantly as recall. The standard deviation scores of precision, recall, F-score, and accuracy also vary significantly as in from Tables 4 and 5. These inconsistent results and high variability across standard deviation measures indicate that this pattern is not a very dependable pattern to use when performing binary requirements classification.

When looking at the requirements traceability task, this pattern yielded the lowest precision, recall, and F-score values among all the patterns. Only the accuracy scores are somewhat closer to the accuracy values of other patterns. Therefore, this pattern might not be a suitable choice for performing requirements traceability either.

Persona Pattern The performance of the model when using the Persona pattern is better than the Context Manager pattern, but not as good as the Cognitive Verifier pattern. It has a higher precision value compared to the Cognitive Verifier, but the standard deviation of precision values is almost three times that of the Cognitive Verifier pattern. This suggests that when the temperature is not known or adjustable, the Persona pattern might not be the most dependable if precision is more important. A major observation is the almost negligible effect the temperature setting has on the recall, standing at 0.1%. This means the Persona pattern has the ability to make the model predict true positives with the same level of accuracy with little to no impact from varying the model's temperature.

The Persona pattern yielded the highest recall scores compared to the other patterns when it comes to requirements traceability task. The standard deviation of precision, recall, and F-score is between 3% and 4%, which is the second highest among the chosen patterns. The Persona pattern does not seem to be a great choice when performing requirements tracing, unless the focus is solely on achieving a high recall. Even then, we recommend a lower model temperature setting to achieve the best results.

Question Refinement Pattern The Question Refinement Pattern yielded the highest average precision scores in comparison to other patterns. The recall, F-score, and accuracy are slightly lower than the Cognitive Verifier pattern but also slightly higher than the other patterns. The standard deviation of precision and recall are around 2% and 2.5%, but for F-score and accuracy, they are under 1.0%. This means this pattern can be considered a dependable pattern to use when performing binary requirements classification with a statistically insignificant effect of varying the model's temperature.

Even in the requirements traceability task, this pattern yielded the highest average precision, F-score, and accuracy values in comparison to other patterns. It also achieved the lowest standard deviation scores for all the performance metrics, making it the top choice for implementation for requirements traceability task.

Template Pattern Finally, coming to the Template pattern, it has the highest observed recall measures across all three temperature settings among all patterns tested. The standard deviation of recall is also very low, indicating the model can predict true positives with the same level of accuracy with little to no impact from varying the model's temperature. However, the precision and accuracy are below 70% at default and higher-temperature settings. It has a significant amount of standard deviation for precision, F-score, and accuracy across temperatures. This makes us question the pattern's ability to make the model yield consistent results when performing binary requirements classification.

The template pattern does not show any noteworthy improvement in results when it comes to the requirements traceability task. The standard deviation scores of precision, recall, and F-score are all above 3%, with none of the performance metrics achieving higher scores in comparison to other patterns.

4.2 Recommendations

Based on our analysis of the results presented in Table 2, we can say that the **Cognitive Verifier** pattern and the **Question Refinement** pattern are better suited for the binary requirements classification task at any temperature setting compared to the **Context Manager**, the **Template**, and the **Persona** patterns.

Similarly, we can say that the **Question Refinement** pattern is the most consistent and reliable pattern among the five for tracing dependent requirements followed by the **Cognitive Verifier** and the **Persona** pattern. The **Context Manager** pattern and the **Template** pattern are the least reliable pattern for this task (Table 6).

Overall, the **Question Refinement** pattern shows consistent results across both the classification and requirements traceability tasks. The **Cognitive verifier** pattern and the **Persona pattern** obtained higher performance scores in binary requirements classification, although their performance in tracing dependent requirements was

Table 6 Rank based prompt pattern recommendation for overall and individual tasks

Rank	Binary classification	Tracing	Overall
1st	Question Refinement	Question Refinement	Question Refinement
2nd	Cognitive Verifier	Cognitive Verifier	Cognitive Verifier
3rd	Persona	Persona	Persona
4th	Template	Template	Template
5th	Context Manager	Context Manager	Context Manager

reduced. The **Context Manager** pattern was found to have a greater degree of variability in its STDEV measures for both tasks. Our results indicate this pattern may not be the best-suited pattern for performing the selected requirements engineering tasks.

4.3 Evaluation Framework

In order to evaluate the effectiveness of prompt patterns for any RE task, we propose adopting a framework similar to the methodology used in this chapter.

- **Step-1:** Curate a dataset for the task in question, comprising two distinct versions. The first version should contain the ground-truth annotations, while the second version should be cleaned to remove any identifiers that helped in establishing the ground truth. This version will serve as input data provided to the GenAI model through a program script.
- **Step-2:** Create a program script[1] that mimics the RE task's underlying logic. The script should be designed to leverage the capabilities of the GenAI model via an API call function. Clearly specify the desired output format within the prompt embedded in the code script. Ensure that the script is capable of taking the second version of the dataset as input and generating results using the GenAI model.
- **Step-3:** Execute the code script created in the previous step to generate results. The script should make API calls to the GenAI model, using the specified prompt pattern.
- **Step-4:** Conduct a comparative analysis of the obtained results against the ground-truth annotations (from the first version of the dataset). This analysis will provide insights into how well the GenAI model performed in relation to the ground truth.
- **Step-5:** Use the comparative assessment results to evaluate the effectiveness of the prompt pattern(s) in the context of the specific RE task.

---

[1] https://github.com/beatrizcabdan/GenAI4REtasks

By analyzing the requirements and objectives of the task, one can determine whether the nature of the task leans more toward binary classification or requirements traceability. Based on this, our recommendations for which prompt patterns to apply may hold. However, the results of this study may not consistently apply to other situations. When confronted with a novel RE task that cannot be framed as a requirements IR task, it is advisable to experiment with the patterns and evaluate the effectiveness of patterns in the context of the specific task and dataset as suggested in our evaluation framework.

5 Discussion

The results of our research study shed light on the effectiveness of different prompt patterns in the context of RE tasks, specifically focusing on binary requirements classification and requirements traceability. In the following, we will delve into the implications of these findings and their practical applications in real-world practice.

Our study revealed that the **Cognitive Verifier** and **Question Refinement** patterns achieved the best results in binary requirements classification. These patterns provide a reliable and consistent approach to achieving accurate and reliable classifications. In real-world RE practice, RE practitioners can consider adopting either the **Cognitive Verifier** or **Question Refinement** pattern for tasks that involve binary classification. For instance, when evaluating software requirements for compliance with specified standards, these patterns could be used to streamline the classification process, reducing manual effort and potential errors. The **Persona** pattern seems to exhibit better results at lower-temperature settings compared to higher-temperature settings, indicating it is better suited to classification tasks where less creative and more definitive responses are required.

In the case of requirements traceability, our findings indicate that the **Question Refinement** pattern outperforms others. This suggests that when the RE task involves establishing relationships and dependencies between various requirements, using the **Question Refinement** pattern is the most effective option. For RE teams tasked with tracing dependencies among requirements, the **Question Refinement** pattern has significantly better performance compared to other patterns. This is particularly valuable in complex projects where understanding how changes in one requirement may impact others is critical.

Since the performance measures were calculated automatically using the dependencies provided in the datasets, we did not manually investigate the requirements that were misidentified as dependent (or independent). Further work, particularly work focusing specifically on traceability, should look closer to investigate the reasons behind the misclassification. The sensitivity of the prompt used to generate some artefacts using LLMs or any other GenAI model opens up possibilities where minimal changes to the prompt can result in significant differences in the quality of the output as well as the performance of the model. This experimental study was limited to examining the effect of pattern-level variations on the prompts used

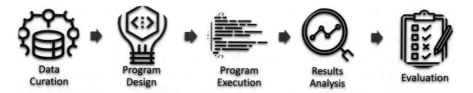

Fig. 1 Prompt pattern effectiveness evaluation framework

and did not look into the specific wording of the prompts, in order to keep the experimental results tractable. It is equally important to remember that using LLMs for RE tasks should be limited to assisting relevant RE stakeholders with appropriate human oversight mechanisms in place instead of automating these tasks. Therefore, the usefulness of LLMs, and subsequently, prompt patterns that are used to craft the prompts to interact with the LLMs, comes with limitations and needs more dedicated research results to discuss it in depth.

While our study provides insights into the effectiveness of specific patterns, it is essential to acknowledge the unique nature of various RE tasks. Not all tasks can be framed as requirements IR tasks. Therefore, organizations should consider an analysis of their specific RE requirements and objectives. When confronted with novel RE tasks, teams can follow a structured approach similar to our proposed framework presented in Fig. 1 to identify the most suitable prompt pattern. By breaking down the workflow and considering the task's nature, they can adapt and experiment with different patterns to optimize results. This iterative process allows for continuous improvement in the choice of patterns for specific tasks.

6 Conclusion

In conclusion, the insights garnered from this study offer guidance for practitioners seeking to leverage prompt patterns for using GenAI in RE tasks. Our research offers recommendations on the selection and adoption of prompt patterns for real-world RE tasks. We suggest that the Question Refinement pattern might serve as a suitable compromise for both tasks. Moreover, the chapter presents an evaluation framework based on the methodology used in our study on how one might evaluate and decide which prompt pattern could be the most effective for a new RE task, one that considers the trade-offs between precision, recall, and accuracy. Practitioners/other researchers can use this framework as a guideline for assessing the suitability of prompt patterns for their unique RE tasks. By understanding the strengths and limitations of different patterns and employing a structured evaluation framework, organizations can enhance the efficiency and accuracy of their RE processes, ultimately leading to improved software development outcomes and project success.

The insights presented can lay the foundation for several avenues of future research, aiming to deepen our understanding of prompt patterns and further enhance the performance of GenAI in RE. Future investigations could delve into a more exhaustive exploration of prompt patterns, potentially identifying novel approaches. An ensemble approach, combining the merits of different patterns, may mitigate the limitations associated with individual patterns and contribute to a more robust and adaptable classification framework. Future research could focus on optimizing the balance; exploring strategies that prioritize comprehensive recall without compromising precision or accuracy, which could lead to more context-aware and adaptable models; and synthesizing new prompt patterns and evaluation framework. Another avenue of further research is to establish the boundary of LLMs' application in RE activities with appropriate human oversight mechanisms in place to ensure the ethical and responsible application of these technologies.

Acknowledgments This work was supported by the Vinnova project ASPECT [2021-04347].

References

1. Alhoshan, W., Ferrari, A., Zhao, L.: Zero-shot learning for requirements classification: an exploratory study. Inf. Software Technol. **159**, 107202 (2023)
2. Berry, D.M., Cleland-Huang, J., Ferrari, A., Maalej, W., Mylopoulos, J., Zowghi, D.: Panel: context-dependent evaluation of tools for NL RE tasks: recall vs. precision, and beyond. In: 2017 IEEE 25th International Requirements Engineering Conference (RE), pp. 570–573 (2017). https://doi.org/10.1109/RE.2017.64
3. Brown, T., Mann, B., Ryder, N., Subbiah, M., Kaplan, J.D., Dhariwal, P., Neelakantan, A., Shyam, P., Sastry, G., Askell, A., et al.: Language models are few-shot learners. Adv. Neural Inf. Process. Syst. **33**, 1877–1901 (2020)
4. Cheng, Y., Chen, J., Huang, Q., Xing, Z., Xu, X., Lu, Q.: Prompt Sapper: A LLM-Empowered Production Tool for Building AI Chains. Preprint (2023). arXiv:2306.12028
5. Cleland-Huang, J., Mazrouee, S., Liguo, H., Port, D.: NFR (2007). https://doi.org/10.5281/zenodo.268542
6. Ferrari, A., Spagnolo, G.O., Gnesi, S.: PURE: a dataset of public requirements documents. In: 2017 IEEE 25th International Requirements Engineering Conference (RE), pp. 502–505 (2017). https://doi.org/10.1109/RE.2017.29
7. Fiannaca, A.J., Kulkarni, C., Cai, C.J., Terry, M.: Programming without a programming language: challenges and opportunities for designing developer tools for prompt programming. In: Extended Abstracts of the 2023 CHI Conference on Human Factors in Computing Systems, CHI EA '23. Association for Computing Machinery, New York, NY, USA (2023). https://doi.org/10.1145/3544549.3585737
8. Haque, M.U., Dharmadasa, I., Sworna, Z.T., Rajapakse, R.N., Ahmad, H.: "I think this is the most disruptive technology": Exploring Sentiments of ChatGPT Early Adopters Using Twitter Data. Preprint (2022). arXiv:2212.05856
9. Lampert, C.H., Nickisch, H., Harmeling, S.: Learning to detect unseen object classes by between-class attribute transfer. In: 2009 IEEE Conference on Computer Vision and Pattern Recognition, pp. 951–958. IEEE (2009)
10. Liu, V., Chilton, L.B.: Design guidelines for prompt engineering text-to-image generative models. In: Proceedings of the 2022 CHI Conference on Human Factors in Computing Systems, CHI '22. Association for Computing Machinery, New York, NY, USA (2022). https://doi.org/10.1145/3491102.3501825

11. Lu, Y., Bartolo, M., Moore, A., Riedel, S., Stenetorp, P.: Fantastically Ordered Prompts and Where to Find Them: Overcoming Few-shot Prompt Order Sensitivity. Preprint (2021). arXiv:2104.08786
12. Nguyen, N., Nadi, S.: An empirical evaluation of GitHub copilot's code suggestions. In: Proceedings of the 19th International Conference on Mining Software Repositories, MSR '22, pp. 1–5. Association for Computing Machinery, New York, NY, USA (2022). https://doi.org/10.1145/3524842.3528470
13. Peng, S., Kalliamvakou, E., Cihon, P., Demirer, M.: The Impact of AI on Developer Productivity: Evidence from GitHub Copilot. Preprint (2023). arXiv:2302.06590
14. Radford, A., Wu, J., Child, R., Luan, D., Amodei, D., Sutskever, I., others: Language models are unsupervised multitask learners. OpenAI Blog 1(8), 9 (2019)
15. Reynolds, L., McDonell, K.: Prompt programming for large language models: beyond the few-shot paradigm. In: Extended Abstracts of the 2021 CHI Conference on Human Factors in Computing Systems, CHI EA '21. Association for Computing Machinery, New York, NY, USA (2021). https://doi.org/10.1145/3411763.3451760
16. Wei, J., Wang, X., Schuurmans, D., Bosma, M., ichter, b., Xia, F., Chi, E., Le, Q.V., Zhou, D.: Chain-of-thought prompting elicits reasoning in large language models. In: Koyejo, S., Mohamed, S., Agarwal, A., Belgrave, D., Cho, K., Oh, A. (eds.) Advances in Neural Information Processing Systems. vol. 35, pp. 24824–24837. Curran Associates, Inc., New York (2022). https://proceedings.neurips.cc/paper_files/paper/2022/file/9d5609613524ecf4f15af0f7b31abca4-Paper-Conference.pdf
17. White, J., Fu, Q., Hays, S., Sandborn, M., Olea, C., Gilbert, H., Elnashar, A., Spencer-Smith, J., Schmidt, D.C.: A Prompt Pattern Catalog to Enhance Prompt Engineering with ChatGPT (2023). https://doi.org/10.48550/arXiv.2302.11382
18. White, J., Hays, S., Fu, Q., Spencer-Smith, J., Schmidt, D.C.: ChatGPT Prompt Patterns for Improving Code Quality, Refactoring, Requirements Elicitation, and Software Design (2023). https://doi.org/10.48550/arXiv.2303.07839
19. Xu, C., Li, Y., Wang, B., Dong, S.: A systematic mapping study on machine learning methodologies for requirements management. IET Software 17(4), 405–423 (2023). https://doi.org/10.1049/sfw2.12082
20. Zhang, J., Chen, Y., Niu, N., Wang, Y., Liu, C.: Empirical Evaluation of ChatGPT on Requirements Information Retrieval Under Zero-Shot Setting (2023). https://doi.org/10.48550/arXiv.2304.12562

Advancing Requirements Engineering Through Generative AI: Assessing the Role of LLMs

Chetan Arora, John Grundy, and Mohamed Abdelrazek

Abstract Requirements Engineering (RE) is a critical phase in software development including the elicitation, analysis, specification, and validation of software requirements. Despite the importance of RE, it remains a challenging process due to the complexities of communication, uncertainty in the early stages, and inadequate automation support. In recent years, large language models (LLMs) have shown significant promise in diverse domains, including natural language processing, code generation, and program understanding. This chapter explores the potential of LLMs in driving RE processes, aiming to improve the efficiency and accuracy of requirements-related tasks. We propose key directions and SWOT analysis for research and development in using LLMs for RE, focusing on the potential for requirements elicitation, analysis, specification, and validation. We further present the results from a preliminary evaluation, in this context.

Keywords Requirements engineering · Generative AI · Large language models (LLMs) · Natural language processing · Software engineering

1 Introduction

Requirements Engineering (RE) is arguably the most critical task in the software development process, where the needs and constraints of a system are identified, analyzed, and documented to create a well-defined set of requirements [19]. Organizations and project teams often overlook or do not understand the significance of RE and its impact on project success [24]. Some underlying reasons for the lack of effort and resources spent in RE include (i) time, budget, and resource

C. Arora (✉) · J. Grundy
Monash University, Melbourne, VIC, Australia
e-mail: chetan.arora@monash.edu; john.grundy@monash.edu

M. Abdelrazek
Deakin University, Geelong, VIC, Australia
e-mail: mohamed.abdelrazek@deakin.edu.au

constraints; (ii) inadequate training and skills; (iii) uncertainty and ambiguity in early stages, which teams consider as challenging, causing them to cut corners in the RE process; (iv) inadequate tools and automation support [5]; and (v) emphasis on an implementation-first approach instead [14]. These lead to significant challenges in the later stages of development as issues related to inconsistent, incomplete, and incorrect requirements become increasingly difficult to resolve, resulting in increased development costs, delays, and lower-quality software systems [19].

In this chapter, we contend that the recent advances in large language models (LLMs) [13] might be revolutionary in addressing many of these RE-related challenges noted above, though with some caveats. LLMs are advanced AI models designed to process and generate human language by learning patterns and structures from vast amounts of text data. These models have made significant strides in natural language processing (NLP) tasks and are particularly adept at handling complex language-based challenges. LLMs, including OpenAI's Generative Pre-trained Transformer (GPT) series and Google's Bidirectional Encoder Representations from Transformers (BERT) [8] and LaMDA [23], learn to comprehend and generate human language by predicting the most probable next word in a given sequence, capturing the probability distribution of word sequences in natural language (NL). OpenAI's ChatGPT[1] and Google's Bard[2], built on the advancements of the LLMs, are examples of chatbot platforms designed to facilitate interactive and dynamic text-based conversations. When a user provides input to ChatGPT or Bard, the model processes the text and generates a contextually appropriate response based on the patterns learned during the training process.

A large majority of requirements are specified using NL. LLMs thus have the potential to be a "game-changer" in the field of RE. This could be by automating and streamlining several crucial tasks and helping to address many of the RE challenges mentioned earlier. With the focus on automated code generation using LLMs, delivering concise and consistently unambiguous specifications to these models (as prompts) becomes paramount. This underscores the ever-growing significance of RE in this new era of generative AI-driven software engineering. This chapter explores the potential of LLMs to transform the RE processes. We present a SWOT (strengths, weaknesses, opportunities, and threats) analysis for applying LLMs in all key RE stages, including requirements elicitation, analysis, and specification. We also discuss examples from a preliminary evaluation as motivation for using LLMs in all RE stages.

Preliminary Evaluation Context We performed a preliminary evaluation on a real-world app (pseudonym ActApp), encouraging patients with type-2 diabetes (T2D) to remain active. To ensure that the app is effective, engaging, and personalized, the ActApp team implemented a machine learning (ML) model in the background to learn from user behavior and preferences and suggest appropriate

---

[1] https://chat.openai.com/.

[2] https://bard.google.com/.

reminders and activities. The team has a mix of experienced engineers and an ML scientist (with little understanding of RE). Our preliminary evaluation and the examples in the chapter are done using ChatGPT (GPT-3.5).

Structure Section 2 provides an overview of our vision of the role of LLMs in RE process. Sections 3, 4, 5, and 6 cover the four major RE stages, i.e., elicitation, specification, analysis, and validation, respectively. Section 7 presents our preliminary evaluation results. Section 8 covers the lessons learned, and Sect. 9 concludes the chapter.

2 LLMs-Driven RE Process

Figure 1 provides an overview of our vision of an LLMs-driven RE process (an adaptation of RE process by Van Lamsweerde [24]). The RE process can be broadly divided into four stages: requirements elicitation (domain understanding and elicitation), specification (specification and documentation), analysis (evaluation and negotiation), and validation (quality assurance). We note that the exact instantiation and contextualization of LLMs in RE will depend on the problem domain and the project. For instance, implementing the LARRE framework for ActApp might be different from a safety-critical system. We, in this book chapter, provide a broad perspective on the role of LLMs in RE, which should be applicable to a wide range of projects, as the RE stages discussed are common and can be generalized across domains and systems, with finer refinements required in some cases.

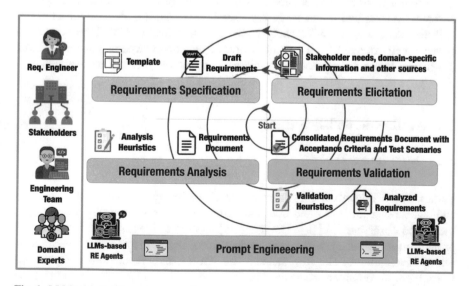

Fig. 1 LLMs-driven RE process overview

LLMs can be employed differently for automating RE tasks, e.g., as they have been successfully applied for ambiguity management [9]. In this chapter, we specifically focus on prompting by requirements analysts or other stakeholders directly on generative AI agents, e.g., ChatGPT or fine-tuned LLMs RE agents built on top of these agents. One would generate multiple agents based on LLMs for interaction (via prompting) with the stakeholders (e.g., domain experts, engineering teams, clients, requirements engineers, and end users) and potentially with each other for eliciting, specifying, negotiating, analyzing, validating requirements, and generating other artefacts for quality assurance. Prompting is a technique to perform generative tasks using LLMs [11]. Prompts are short text inputs to the LLM that provide information about the task the LLM is being asked to perform. Prompt engineering is designing and testing prompts to improve the performance of LLMs and get the desired output quality. Prompt engineers use their knowledge of the language, the task at hand, and the capabilities of LLMs to create prompts that are effective at getting the LLM to generate the desired output [26]. Prompt engineering involves selecting appropriate prompt patterns and prompting techniques [26]. Prompt patterns refer to different templates targeted at specific goals, e.g., Output Customization pattern focuses on tailoring the format or the structure of the output by LLMs. Other generic templates include formatting your prompts consistently in "Context, Task and Expected Output" format. For instance, one can use a *persona* for output customization, wherein the agent plays a certain role when generating the output, e.g., the patient in ActApp. Prompting technique refers to a specific strategy employed to get the best output from the LLM agents. Some of the well-known prompting techniques include zero-shot prompting [18], few-shot prompting [16], chain-of-thought prompting [25], and tree-of-thought prompting [27]. In this context, prompt engineering combinations must be empirically evaluated in RE for different systems and domains. In each section, we explore the role of LLMs in each RE stage with a SWOT analysis. The insights for the SWOT analysis were systematically derived from a combination of our direct experiences with LLMs, feedback gathered from practitioner interactions, and our preliminary evaluation.

3   Requirements Elicitation

3.1   Elicitation Tasks

Requirements Elicitation encompasses pre-elicitation groundwork (as-is analysis and stakeholder analysis) and core elicitation activities with stakeholders (interviews and observations) [19]. The main objective is to identify and document the project information, system needs, expectations, and constraints of the solution under development. The key tasks in elicitation include domain analysis, as-is analysis, stakeholders analysis, feasibility analysis, and conducting elicitation sessions with the identified stakeholders using techniques such as interviews and observations. While the elicitation process is methodical, it is inherently dynamic, often necessitating iterative sessions as requirements evolve and new insights emerge from stakeholders. Requirements elicitation is also intensely collaborative, demanding constant feedback and validation from diverse stakeholders to ensure clarity and alignment. Some prevalent challenges associated with requirements elicitation involve the lack of domain understanding [21], unknowns (i.e., known and unknown unknowns) [22], communication issues due to language barriers or technical jargon [6], and lack of a clear understanding of what needs to be built in early stages [10]. In addition, the current elicitation techniques fall short in human-centric software development, i.e., ensuring adequate representation from all potential user groups based on their human-centric factors, such as age, gender, culture, language, emotions, preferences, accessibility, and capabilities [12]. External influences, such as evolving legal stipulations and legal compliance, also play a pivotal role in shaping the elicitation process. Furthermore, with the rapidly advancing technological landscape, the existing elicitation processes often fail to capture the system requirements precisely, e.g., in the case of AI systems, bias, ethical considerations, and integration of undeterministic AI components in larger software systems [2].

3.2 Role of LLMs

LLMs can address numerous key challenges in the elicitation phase, including domain analysis. LLMs can rapidly absorb vast amounts of domain-specific literature, providing a foundational structuring and acting as a proxy for domain knowledge source [15]. They can assist in drawing connections, identifying gaps, and offering insights based on the existing literature and based on automated tasks such as as-is analysis, domain analysis, and regulatory compliance. In addition to stakeholder communication, leveraging LLMs would require other inputs such as existing domain or project-specific documentation (e.g., fine-tuning LLMs) and regulations (e.g., GDPR). While LLMs have access to the domain knowledge, it is difficult to replace domain specialists' intuition, experience, and expertise. For example, in ActApp , the nuanced understanding of how specific exercises influence a patient's glucose or hormonal levels rests with medical professionals such as endocrinologists, who are irreplaceable in RE.

LLMs help identify unknowns by analyzing existing documentation and highlighting areas of ambiguity or uncertainty. LLMs can help with the completion or suggest alternative ideas that the requirements analysts might have otherwise missed, drawing on their large corpus of training data and connections. LLMs can assist with translating complex technical jargon into plain language and aiding stakeholders from different linguistic backgrounds, e.g., translating medical terminology in ActApp for requirements analysts or translating domain information from one language to another.

LLMs play a vital role in human-centric RE. They can analyze diverse user feedback, like app reviews, ensuring all user needs are addressed. LLMs can also simulate user journeys considering human-centric factors, but this necessitates resources such as app reviews, persona-based use cases, and accessibility guidelines. For emerging technologies, LLMs need regular updates, a challenging task since automated solutions might be affected by these updates. The use of LLMs in requirements elicitation also warrants ethical scrutiny. LLMs may introduce or perpetuate biases as they are trained on vast internet data. Ensuring the ethical use of LLMs means avoiding biases and guaranteeing that the stakeholders' inputs are managed according to the data privacy and security guidelines. LLMs output should be viewed as complementary to human efforts. Requirements analysts bring domain expertise, cultural awareness, nuanced understanding, and empathetic interactions to the table, ensuring that software requirements cater to the diverse and evolving needs of end users. This synergy of humans and generative AI is crucial in human-centric software development.

Example Prompt for requirements generation. *I am developing an app called ActApp. ActApp is a real-time application for T2D patients to ensure an active lifestyle. The app gives timely reminders for working out, health & disease management. Act and respond as an ActApp user with the persona provided below in JSON format. The main aim is to elicit the requirements from your perspective. The generated requirements should each be associated with a unique id, and rationale.*
{ "persona":{ "name": "Jane Doe", "age": "65", "gender": "Female", "location": "Canada", "occupation": "Retired", "medical info": ..., "lifestyle": ..., "goals": ... "work": "sedentary", "challenges": ... } }

Example For the ActApp, LLMs are used to gather information from various stakeholders, including patients and carers. The agent can conduct virtual interviews with the stakeholders (for a given persona, as exemplified below), asking targeted questions to identify their needs, preferences, and concerns. For instance, the agent may inquire users about desired features and data privacy concerns. Additionally, LLMs can analyze and synthesize information from online forums, social media, reviews from similar apps, and research articles on disease management to extract insights into common challenges patients face and best practices for care. This information can generate preliminary requirements (e.g., R1 and R2 below), which can be refined in later stages.

ActApp Example Information and Early Requirements.
Key stakeholders (identified based on initial app ideas): Patients, carers, app developers, ML scientists, and healthcare professionals, e.g., endocrinologists.
R1. The patients should receive a notification to stand up and move around if they have been sitting for long.
R2. The patients should not receive notifications when busy.

SWOT Analysis: LLMs for Requirements Elicitation

[Strengths]

- *Interactive Assistance*: Can actively assist in elicitation, asking probing questions and generating diverse potential requirements based on initial inputs – leading to uncovering unknowns.
- *Efficient Data Processing*: Facilitate round-the-clock elicitation, rapidly processing large volumes of elicitation data in varied formats.
- *Domain Knowledge*: Can rapidly absorb and understand domain-specific literature and automate tasks based on the absorbed literature.
- *Assisting Multilingual and Multicultural Stakeholders*: Can accurately translate complex technical jargon into plain language and aid stakeholders' communication even with diverse backgrounds.

[Weaknesses]

- *Lack of Empathy and Nuance*: Do not possess human empathy and might miss out on emotional cues or implicit meanings.
- *Lack of Domain Expertise*: While LLMs understand domain knowledge, they cannot replace the intuition and experience of domain experts.
- *Misinterpretation Risks*: The potential for misinterpreting context or over-relying on existing training data without considering unique project nuances.

[Opportunities]

- *Real-time Documentation and Processing*: Can document requirements and analyze feedback in real time, ensuring thoroughness and accuracy.
- *Human-centric Elicitation*: By analyzing diverse user feedback, LLMs can ensure all user needs are considered, promoting a holistic approach to elicitation.

[Threats]

- *Over-reliance and Trust Issues*: Excessive dependence might lead to missing human-centric insights, and some stakeholders might hesitate to engage with AI.
- *Data Security and Privacy Concerns*: Eliciting requirements via LLMs could raise data confidentiality issues, especially with sensitive information (e.g., in public LLMs-based agents like ChatGPT and Bard).
- *Potential Biases*: May inadvertently introduce or perpetuate biases in the elicitation process if trained on biased data or past flawed projects.
- *Regular Updates and Compatibility*: Given the stochastic nature of LLMs, the regular updates might lead to technical issues and inconsistency in project requirements. On the other hand, outdated LLMs are suboptimal for RE.

---

4 Requirements Specification

4.1 Specification Tasks

Requirements Specification translates the raw, elicited requirements information into structured and detailed documentation, serving as the system design and implementation blueprint. LLMs can contribute to this process by helping generate well-structured requirements documents that adhere to established templates and guidelines, e.g., the "shall" style requirements, user story formats, EARS template [17], or specific document templates, e.g., VOLERE [20]. Given a project's context, the informal NL requirements need to be converted into structured specifications—both what the system should do (functional requirements) and the quality attributes or constraints the system should possess (non-functional requirements).

Requirements analysts must maintain consistency in terminology and style throughout the document to enhance readability and clarity. In this stage, requirements can be prioritized considering stakeholder needs, project constraints, and strategic objectives. This phase is exacting, as ambiguities or errors can lead to significant project delays and escalated costs in later stages. Moreover, it is essential to balance the level of detail (too granular or too abstract) and ensure that non-functional requirements like security and usability are adequately addressed and not sidelined. Additional tasks such as generating requirements glossary, examples, and rationale and developing user personas to ensure that the human-centric aspects are duly covered are often performed during or immediately after requirements specification.

4.2   Role of LLMs

LLMs can streamline the specification process. The unstructured requirements from the elicitation stage can be automatically formatted into structured templates like EARS or user stories (see the example prompt below for EARS and the example for user stories). They can further assist in categorizing requirements into functional and non-functional and classifying NFRs like performance, ethical requirements, and usability. LLMs can automate other tasks during specification, e.g., generating glossary, rationale, and examples, developing personas [29]. Another advantage of LLMs is their ability to cross-check requirements against existing standards, regulatory guidelines, or best practices. For a health-focused app like ActApp, LLMs can ensure alignment with health data privacy standards and medical device directives.

LLMs can also suggest requirements prioritization by analyzing technical dependencies, project goals, and historical data. However, generating requirements prioritization requires several SE roles and deep-seeded expertise. Hence, the results produced by LLMs might be inaccurate. On similar lines, while LLMs can enhance the speed and consistency of specification, there is a risk of "over-automation," i.e., overlooking some crucial aspects or over-trusting the requirements produced by LLMs. For instance, determining the criticality of specific NFRs—like how secure a system needs to be or how scalable—often requires human expertise. LLMs can aid the process, but decisions should be validated by domain experts familiar with the project context. Similarly, for compliance issues, it is essential to have domain experts validate the results.

Example Prompt. Using the EARS template defined by the BNF grammar below, generate the <requirement> from the unformatted requirement - "The patients should not receive notifications when busy."
<requirement> ::= <ubiquitous> | <event-driven> | <state-driven> | <optional> | <unwanted>
<ubiquitous> ::= "The system shall <action>."
<event-driven> ::= "When <event>, the system shall <action>."
<state-driven> ::= "While <state>, the system shall <action>."
<optional> ::= "The system shall <action>."
<unwanted>::= "The system shall <preventive-action> to <unwanted-outcome>."

<action> ::= <verb-phrase>
<event> ::= <noun-phrase>
<state> ::= <noun-phrase>
<preventive-action> ::= <verb-phrase>
<unwanted-outcome> ::= <noun-phrase>
<verb-phrase> ::= "a verb phrase"
<noun-phrase> ::= "a noun phrase"
Example Output: "When patient is driving, ActApp shall not send notifications."

Example In ActApp, the LLMs can generate refined requirements as user stories (desired by ActApp team members). The requirements document may include sections such as an introduction, a description of ActApp stakeholders, a list of functional and non-functional requirements, a list of ActApp features with priorities, and any constraints or assumptions related to the development process. For non-functional requirements, such as data privacy for patients' health information, LLMs can cross-reference with regulations, e.g., HIPAA or GDPR to ensure compliance [1].

ActApp Example (as user story for functional requirements).
R1.1. As a user, I want to receive a notification to move if I have been sitting for 60 minutes, so that I will be active.
R1.2. As a carer, I want ActApp to notify me if the patient continues to remain inactive after receiving a notification to move, so that I can intervene.
NFR1.1: The app shall encrypt all data during transmission and storage to ensure patient privacy and comply with GDPR guidelines.

We note that for SWOT analysis in subsequent phases, we attempt to reduce overlap (to the best extent possible). For instance, almost all threats from elicitation are also applicable for specification.

```
┌──────────────────────────────────────────────────────────────────────┐
│           SWOT Analysis: LLMs for Requirements Specification           │
│                                                                        │
│ [Strengths]                                                            │
│ • Automation: Can streamline converting raw requirements into struc-   │
│   tured formats, such as EARS or user stories. Can generate additional │
│   artefacts, e.g., glossaries and personas, from converted require-    │
│   ments and domain information.                                        │
│ • Compliance Check: Can cross-reference requirements against standards │
│   and regulatory guidelines, ensuring initial compliance.             │
│ • Requirement Classification: Can categorize requirements into func-   │
│   tional and non-functional, further classifying them.                │
│ • Initial Prioritization: Can suggest requirement prioritization based │
│   on dependencies, project goals, and historical data.                │
│ [Weaknesses]                                                           │
│ • Depth of Domain Expertise: While LLMs have vast knowledge, they      │
│   might not fully capture the nuances of specialized domains.          │
│ • Over-Automation Risk: Sole reliance on LLMs might lead to overlook-  │
│   ing crucial requirements or business constraints.                   │
│ • Ambiguity Handling: May sometimes struggle with ambiguous or con-    │
│   flicting requirements, necessitating human intervention.            │
│ [Opportunities]                                                        │
│ • Continuous Feedback: Can aid in real-time documentation and specifi- │
│   cation updates as requirements evolve.                              │
│ • Human-Centric Focus: Can help maintain a human-centric outlook in    │
│   the specification stage by generating alternate requirements for     │
│   different user groups.                                              │
│ [Threats]                                                              │
│ • Ambiguities in Structured Requirements: Can generate requirements in │
│   specific formats. However, the generated requirements can have       │
│   unintentional ambiguities (if the model is not fine-tuned adequately)│
│   or other quality issues (e.g., inconsistencies due to the limited    │
│   'memory' of LLMs).                                                   │
│ • Over-specification: Known to be verbose [31], which can easily lead  │
│   to over-defined requirements, and consequently lead to a rigid       │
│   system design.                                                      │
│ • Missing Non-functional Requirements: Non-functional (unlike func-    │
│   tional) requirements rely on a deeper understanding of the system's  │
│   context, which LLMs might miss or inadequately address.             │
└──────────────────────────────────────────────────────────────────────┘
```

5 Requirements Analysis

5.1 Analysis Tasks

Requirements analysis focuses on understanding, evaluating, and refining the gathered requirements to ensure they are of high quality, i.e., coherent, comprehensive, and attainable, before moving to the design and implementation stages. An integral component of this phase is the automated evaluation of requirements quality. This includes addressing defects like ambiguity resolution, ensuring consistency, and guaranteeing completeness. Deficiencies in this phase can affect subsequent artefacts, leading to project delays, budget overruns, and systems misaligned with stakeholder expectations. The main challenges of NL requirements are ambiguity, incompleteness, inconsistency, and incorrectness, which lead to misinterpretations, untestable requirements, untraced requirements to their origin, no consensus among stakeholders on what needs to be built, and conflicting requirements. Constantly evolving requirements further exacerbate all these issues. At times, documented requirements or underlying assumptions might inadvertently overlook potential risks or dependencies. In such instances, it becomes crucial to identify these risks and introduce new requirements as countermeasures. Analysis of requirements, for instance, getting an agreement on conflicting requirements, requires negotiation. Negotiation is the key to resolving all conflicts, and the stakeholders converge on a unified set of requirements. From a human-centric RE perspective, the analysis stage must prioritize users' emotional, cultural, and accessibility needs. This entails scrutinizing user feedback for inclusivity, vetting ethics, and bias concerns—especially in AI-based software systems [3]—and analyzing requirements against prevailing accessibility guidelines.

5.2   Role of LLMs

LLMs come into play as powerful tools to automate the quality evaluation process:

1. **Automated Evaluation for Quality Assurance:** LLMs can automatically assess the quality of requirements, flagging any ambiguities, vague terms, inconsistencies, or incompleteness, and highlight gaps or overlaps.
2. **Risk Identification and Countermeasure Proposal:** LLMs, when equipped with domain knowledge, can identify potential risks associated with requirements or their underlying assumptions. Drawing from historical data or known risk patterns, LLMs can suggest new requirements that act as countermeasures to mitigate those risks, ensuring system design and operation robustness.
3. **Conflict Resolution and Negotiation:** By identifying areas of contention, LLMs can facilitate the negotiation process. Multiple LLM agents can be employed to negotiate the requirements, suggest compromises, and simulate various scenarios, helping stakeholders converge on a unified set of requirements.
4. **Human-centric Requirements Enhancement:** LLMs can evaluate requirements to ensure they cater to diverse user needs, accessibility standards, and user experience guidelines. LLMs can also suggest requirements that enhance the software's usability or accessibility based on user personas or feedback. Moreover, they can evaluate requirements for biases or potential ethical concerns, ensuring that the software solution is inclusive and ethically sound.

5. **Change Impact Analysis:** LLMs offer real-time feedback in requirements refinement, enhancing the efficiency of the iterative analysis and maintaining stakeholder alignment. The change impact analysis process implemented as continuous feedback cycle via LLMs ensures consistency. LLMs can further proactively predict requirements changes improving the quality of requirements.

Example Prompt.
Context: For the ActApp system, we need to negotiate and prioritize requirements (FR1-FR7 and NFR1-NFR5) that ensure the system caters to the patient's health needs while maintaining usability and data privacy.
Task: Create two agents: Agent1 (A1) represents the primary user (a T2D patient). Agent2 (A2) represents the system's software architect. A1 and A2 will negotiate and discuss FR1 - FR7 to determine a priority list. During this negotiation, A1 will focus on the user experience, health benefits, and practical needs, while A2 will consider technical feasibility, integration with existing systems, and the architectural perspective. The agents can sometimes have differing opinions, leading to a more nuanced and realistic discussion. No decisions should violate NFR1 - NFR5.
Expected Output Format: FRs in decreasing order of priority, and include the rationale for priority order based on the negotiation outcomes between A1 and A2.

Example In the context of ActApp, LLMs can (i) identify and resolve ambiguities or inconsistencies in the requirements, such as conflicting preferences of patients or unclear feature descriptions; (ii) highlight any dependencies and requisites, e.g., a secure data storage system to support medical data storage; and (iii) generate missed ethical and regulatory concerns related to data storage.

ActApp Analysis Examples.
Identify the missing information from R1.2 and NFR1.1 in Section 4, wherein in R1.2 - the information on how long after the initial notification the system should wait before notifying the carer is missing, and in NFR1.1, no information about data retention and deletion were specified, with regards to GDPR.

SWOT Analysis: LLMs for Requirements Analysis

[Strengths]

- *Automation Support*: Can automatically and efficiently assess and enhance the quality of requirements, addressing ambiguities, inconsistencies, incompleteness, potential risks and countermeasures, and conflicts.
- *Consistency*: Unlike human analysts who might have varying interpretations or might overlook certain aspects due to fatigue or bias, LLMs provide consistent analysis, ensuring uniformity in the analysis process.
- *Historical Data Analysis*: Can draw insights from historical project data, identifying patterns, common pitfalls, or frequently occurring issues and provide proactive analysis based on past experiences.
- *Support Evolution and Continuous Learning*: Provide real-time feedback during iterative requirements analysis, predicting possible changes and ensuring consistency. As LLMs are exposed to more data, they can continuously learn and improve, ensuring their analysis is refined.

[Weaknesses]

- *Lack of Nuanced Domain Understanding*: Can process vast amounts of information but might miss or get confused on subtle nuances or domain context that a human analyst would catch, leading to potential oversights.
- *Difficulty with Ambiguities*: Struggle with inherently ambiguous or conflicting requirements, potentially leading to misinterpretations for all analysis tasks.
- *Limited Context/Memory*: Have a limited "window" of context they can consider at any given time. This means that when analyzing large requirements documents as a whole, they might lose context on earlier parts of the document, leading to potential inconsistencies or oversights. They don't inherently "remember" or "understand" the broader context beyond this window, which can be challenging when ensuring coherence and consistency across the document.

[Opportunities]

- *Continuous Refinement*: As requirements evolve, LLMs can provide real-time feedback on the quality and consistency of these requirements.
- *Integration with Development Tools*: Can be integrated with software development environments, offering real-time requirement quality checks during the software development lifecycle.
- *Collaborative Platforms*: Can facilitate better stakeholder collaboration by providing a unified platform for requirements analysis, negotiation, and refinement.

[Threats]

- *Over-automation*: Risk of sidelining human expertise in favor of automated checks, potentially leading to overlooked requirements defects.
- *Regulatory Issues*: Certain industries, domains or certification bodies might have regulatory or compliance concerns related to using LLMs for critical RE tasks.

6   Requirements Validation

6.1   Validation Tasks

Requirements validation ensures that the documented requirements accurately represent the stakeholders' needs and are ready for the subsequent design and implementation stages. Validating requirements often involves intricate tasks like reviewing them with stakeholders, inspecting them for defects, ensuring their traceability to their origins (or other artefacts), and defining clear acceptance criteria and test scenarios.

The primary challenge in the validation phase revolves around ensuring the requirements are devoid of gaps due to stakeholders "real" expectations and tacit assumptions. Requirements might be interpreted differently by stakeholders, leading to potential misalignments. The dynamic nature of projects means that requirements evolve, further complicating the validation process. Occasionally, requirements or their underlying assumptions might inadvertently miss certain constraints or dependencies. This leads to further issues for validation tasks. In such cases, it is imperative to identify these gaps and refine the requirements accordingly.

6.2   Role of LLMs

LLMs can assist in the validation phase in several nuanced ways. As highlighted in the Analysis phase, LLMs can aid in the manual review and inspections by flagging potential ambiguities, inconsistencies, or violations based on predefined validation heuristics. LLMs can be utilized to simulate stakeholder perspectives, enabling analysts to anticipate potential misinterpretations or misalignments. For instance, by analyzing historical stakeholder feedback, LLMs can predict potential areas where clarifications might be sought from the perspective of a given stakeholder. With their ability to process vast amounts of data quickly, LLMs can assist in requirements traceability to other artefacts, e.g., design documents and regulatory codes. LLMs can further assist in formulating clear and precise acceptance criteria based on the documented requirements. They can also propose test scenarios, ensuring a comprehensive validation suite. Furthermore, LLMs can scan the requirements to identify and flag any overlooked human-centric aspects, constraints, or dependencies, ensuring a more comprehensive validation. While LLMs can facilitate most validation tasks, as noted above, a major weakness of LLMs in this context is that the validation tasks often require an overall picture of the project, domain, and stakeholders' viewpoints—it is extremely difficult for LLMs to work at that level of abstraction, which typically requires manual effort from numerous stakeholders.

SWOT Analysis: LLMs for Requirements Validation

[Strengths]
- *Alternate Perspectives*: Can simulate multiple stakeholder perspectives and ensure that all requirements are vetted from different viewpoints.
- *Proactive Feedback*: Can provide real-time feedback during validation sessions, enhancing stakeholder engagement.

[Weaknesses]
- *Depth of Context Understanding*: While adept at processing text, LLMs are not able to process the tacit knowledge in RE, the domain and the business context.

[Opportunities]
- *Interactive Validation Workshops*: Can be integrated into workshops to provide instant feedback, enhancing the validation process.
- *Gap Analysis Enhancements*: Can assist in refining requirements by highlighting overlooked aspects or potential improvements.
- *(Semi-)Automated Acceptance and Testing Artefacts Generation*: Can lead to a substantial effort saving in V&V activities and concomitantly higher quality software products by generating acceptance criteria and test scenarios.

[Threats]
- *Excessive False Positives*: Likely to generate too many potential issues, leading to an unnecessary overhead of addressing false positives and slowing down the validation process – rendering the added value for automation moot.
- *Stakeholder Misrepresentation*: Might not accurately capture the unique concerns or priorities of specific stakeholders (when simulating stakeholder perspectives), leading to a skewed validation process.

Example Prompt.

Context: For the ActApp system, we need to perform the validation on all the requirements specified in the system (FR1 - FR50) and (NFR1 - NFR28). The goal is to identify the gaps in all the requirements from three different stakholders' perspectives, the software developer, the ML scientist and the product owner.

Task: Imagine all three stakeholders are answering this question. For each requirement, all stakeholders will write down the gaps in the requirement based on their role, and then share it with the group. Then all stakeholders will review the inputs in the group and move to the next step. If any expert doesn't have any gap identified or a concern they can skip the discussion on that requirement.

Expected Output Format: For all gaps agreed upon by all stakeholders, export the issue with the requirement id.

Example In ActApp, LLMs can generate acceptance criteria. Also, LLMs can uncover gaps—in our preliminary LLMs evaluation, the ActApp team figured it needed to comply with Australia's Therapeutic Goods Act (TGA) regulation.

Example Acceptance Criteria.

R1.1-AC1 Accurately detect when the user has been sitting for 60 continuous mins.
R1.1-AC2 Notifications can be toggled on or off by user.
R2-AC1 Accurately identifies when the user is driving.

7   Preliminary Evaluation

We conducted a preliminary evaluation of LLMs in RE on a real-world system (ActApp). We note that the purpose of this evaluation was not to conduct a comprehensive assessment of LLMs in RE. Instead, we focused primarily on the feasibility of integrating LLMs into requirements elicitation. The rationale is that the applicability of LLMs to the remaining RE stages is relatively intuitive, thanks in part to the extensive history and well-established methodologies of applying NLP techniques to these stages [28, 30]. Thus, we deemed exploring LLMs in requirements elicitation to be the essential first step.

Data Collection Procedure   The main goal of our data collection procedure was to establish the user requirements in ActApp and analyze the performance of ChatGPT for requirements elicitation. Our team had access to three ActApp experts—the project manager, an ML scientist, and a software engineer. These experts met with a researcher, Katelyn (pseudonym), to articulate the project's focus. The meetings were part of a broader context of understanding the RE processes. ChatGPT was not mentioned to experts to avoid bias. Katelyn engaged in four two-hour meetings with the experts, where they presented an overview of the project, system users, user requirements, and software features.

We used ChatGPT to simulate the initial stages of requirements elicitation, wherein requirements engineers acquire project knowledge from stakeholders, review existing documentation, and formulate user requirements and core functionalities. The process involved four participants: Jorah and Jon, both seasoned software/requirements engineers, and Arya and Aegon, both early-stage RE and NLP research students. They were given a project overview from Katelyn and asked to start a ChatGPT session, introducing themselves as developers of the ActApp project. Guided by the project brief, they interacted with ChatGPT to elicit user-story-style requirements over a 45-minute session. Subsequently, Katelyn examined the requirements generated by the participants using ChatGPT against the actual project requirements.

Results   Overall, 20 key user requirements were identified in ActApp by Katelyn with the experts. Katelyn mapped the requirements Jorah, Jon, Arya, and Aegon elicited against these 20 requirements. Each requirement in the elicited set was categorized as a full match, partial match, or no match. It should be noted that a "full match" did not imply an exact syntactic duplication of the original requirement but rather captured its essence effectively. Likewise, a "partial match" indicated that only a part of the original requirement's essence was captured. We note that in our calculation of precision and recall, each full match is weighted as 1 true positive (TP) and each partial match is weighted as 0.5 TP. Katelyn further classified all "no match" requirements as superfluous or potentially relevant (for further expert vetting if required). Table 1 shows the overall results from the four participants. The results clearly show the significance of experience while using ChatGPT in this preliminary evaluation. While none of the participants could elicit most

Table 1 Evaluation results

Participant	Elicited	Full match	Partial match	Potentially relevant	Superfluous/ redundant	Precision	Recall
Jorah	14	11	1	0	2	82%	58%
Jon	17	7	4	2	4	53%	45%
Arya	14	3	2	1	8	29%	20%
Aegon	27	2	4	1	20	15%	20%

requirements, it is important to note that with a project brief and one interaction session, the experienced participants could get almost half the relevant requirements, emphasizing the feasibility of LLMs for RE.

8 Lessons Learned

Our preliminary evaluation provided insights and highlighted challenges noted below.

Role of Prompts and Contextual Information LLMs depend heavily on comprehensive prompts and the availability of contextual information to generate meaningful output. Slightly different prompts can produce very different outputs. A thorough empirical evaluation of prompt engineering is necessary for employing LLM agents.

Experience Matters Experienced requirements engineers were more successful in formulating prompts, interpreting responses, and getting quality output, despite the project background being uniform across participants. This highlights the importance of experience and training in RE teams.

LLMs Capabilities Our preliminary evaluation underlined the capability of LLMs to discover "unknown" requirements, addressing a significant challenge in RE. We found four "potentially relevant" requirements for future stages in ActApp, which were not part of the original set, from three participants. We surmise that LLMs may assist interpreting and generating text for varied stakeholders, which can be key in reducing communication barriers inherent in diverse project teams. However, managing many "false positive" candidate requirements will require care to ensure engineers are not overloaded with many irrelevant or semi-inaccurate requirements.

LLM Problems LLMs have some inherent issues, such as systematic inaccuracies or stereotypes in the output (influenced by the training data [7]), and the limited context length, e.g., ChatGPT has a limit of 32K tokens, which although enough but still might make it difficult to process large documents or maintain task context in a session. All participants reported issues with maintaining the context of ActApp system in the evaluation session and noticed inaccuracies.

Domain Understanding RE requires an excellent understanding of the underlying domain for eliciting and specifying correct and complete requirements. An LLM's training on specific domain knowledge may be limited and requires addressing to incorporate domain knowledge via experts, other sources, or fine-tuned LLMs. Access to large amounts of training data to fine-tune a custom LLM may be a challenge.

Automation Bias Humans often display unfounded trust in AI [4], e.g., the LLMs-generated requirements in our case. For example, upon completing the session, Arya and Aegon displayed a remarkable degree of confidence in their elicited requirements.

Security, Privacy, and Ethical Issues Requirements are by their very nature mission-critical for software engineering and incorporate much sensitive information. Disclosure via public LLMs may result in IP loss, security breaches in deployed systems, organizational and personal privacy loss, and other concerns. Who "owns" requirements generated by LLMs from training data from unknown sources?

9   Conclusion

In this chapter, we explored the transformative potential of LLMs at various stages of RE. Our exploration positioned that LLMs have the potential to enhance several RE tasks by automating, streamlining, and augmenting human capabilities. Their capability to simulate stakeholder perspectives, generate alternative requirements, address requirements quality, cross-reference with standards, and generate structured documentation is revolutionary. However, we also cautioned against unchecked optimism (using detailed SWOT analysis) that LLMs are not the "silver bullet" for solving all RE problems and in fact have threats of their own. Specific challenges and threats associated with their application in RE include understanding deep-seeded domain nuances, understanding the overall context, over-automation, over-specification, and losing the human-centric view of requirements. The chapter further outlines lessons learned from applying LLMs in a real-world project on RE for ActApp app for T2D patients.

References

1. Abualhaija, S., Arora, C., Sleimi, A., et al.: Automated question answering for improved under-standing of compliance requirements: A multi-document study. In: International Requirements Engineering Conference (RE'22) (2022)
2. Ahmad, K., Abdelrazek, M., Arora, C., et al.: Requirements engineering framework for human-centered artificial intelligence software systems. Appl. Soft Comput. **143**, 110455 (2023a)

3. Ahmad, K., Abdelrazek, M., Arora, C., et al.: Requirements engineering for artificial intelligence systems: A systematic mapping study. Inf. Software Technol. **158**, 107176 (2023b)
4. Akter, S., McCarthy, G., Sajib, S., et al.: Algorithmic bias in data-driven innovation in the age of AI. Int. J. Inf. Manag. **60**, 102387 (2021)
5. Arora, C., Sabetzadeh, M., Briand, L., et al.: Automated checking of conformance to requirements templates using natural language processing. IEEE Trans. Software Eng. (TSE'15) **41**(10), 944–968 (2015)
6. Arora, C., Sabetzadeh, M., Briand, L., et al.: Automated extraction and clustering of requirements glossary terms. IEEE Trans. Software Eng. **43**(10), 918–945 (2017)
7. Borji, A.: A categorical archive of chatgpt failures. Preprint (2023). arXiv:230203494
8. Devlin, J., Chang, M.W., Lee, K., et al.: BERT: Pre-training of deep bidirectional transformers for language understanding (2018). arXiv:181004805
9. Ezzini, S., Abualhaija, S., Arora, C., et al.: Automated handling of anaphoric ambiguity in requirements: A multi-solution study. In: 2022 IEEE/ACM 44rd International Conference on Software Engineering (2022)
10. Gorschek, T., Wohlin, C.: Requirements abstraction model. Requir. Eng. **11**, 79–101 (2006)
11. Hariri, W.: Unlocking the potential of chatgpt: A comprehensive exploration of its applications, advantages, limitations, and future directions in natural language processing (2023). https://doi.org/10.48550/arXiv.2304.02017
12. Hidellaarachchi, D., Grundy, J., Hoda, R., et al.: The effects of human aspects on the requirements engineering process: A systematic literature review. IEEE Trans. Software Eng. **48**(6), 2105–2127 (2022)
13. Jurafsky, D., Martin, J.H.: Speech and Language Processing, 3rd edn. (2020). https://web.stanford.edu/~jurafsky/slp3/ (last visited 2021-06-04)
14. Laplante, P.A., Kassab, M.H.: Requirements Engineering for Software and Systems. CRC Press, Boca Raton (2022)
15. Luitel, D., Hassani, S., Sabetzadeh, M.: Using language models for enhancing the completeness of natural-language requirements. In: Requirements Engineering: Foundation for Software Quality: 29th International Working Conference (2023)
16. Ma, H., Zhang, C., Bian, Y., et al.: Fairness-guided few-shot prompting for large language models. Preprint (2023). arXiv:230313217
17. Mavin, A., Wilkinson, P., Harwood, A., et al.: Easy approach to requirements syntax (ears). In: 2009 17th IEEE International Requirements Engineering Conference, pp. 317–322. IEEE (2009)
18. Pan, W., Chen, Q., Xu, X., et al.: A preliminary evaluation of ChatGPT for zero-shot dialogue understanding. Preprint (2023). arXiv:230404256
19. Pohl, K.: Requirements Engineering, 1st edn. Springer, New York (2010)
20. Robertson, J., Robertson, S.: Volere. Requirements Specification Templates (2000)
21. Sawyer, P., Sommerville, I., Viller, S.: Capturing the benefits of requirements engineering. IEEE Software **16**(2), 78–85 (1999)
22. Sutcliffe, A., Sawyer, P.: Requirements elicitation: Towards the unknown unknowns. In: International Requirements Engineering Conference (RE'13) (2013)
23. Thoppilan, R., De Freitas, D., Hall, J., et al.: Lamda: Language models for dialog applications. Preprint (2022). arXiv:220108239
24. van Lamsweerde, A.: Requirements Engineering: From System Goals to UML Models to Software Specifications, 1st edn. Wiley, New York (2009)
25. Wei, J., Wang, X., Schuurmans, D., et al.: Chain of thought prompting elicits reasoning in large language models (2022). CoRR abs/2201.11903. https://arxiv.org/abs/2201.11903
26. White, J., Fu, Q., Hays, S., et al.: A prompt pattern catalog to enhance prompt engineering with chatgpt. Preprint (2023). arXiv:230211382
27. Yao, S., Yu, D., Zhao, J., et al.: Tree of thoughts: Deliberate problem solving with large language models. Preprint (2023). arXiv:230510601

28. Zamani, K., Zowghi, D., Arora, C.: Machine learning in requirements engineering: A mapping study. In: 2021 IEEE 29th International Requirements Engineering Conference Workshops (REW), pp 116–125. IEEE (2021)
29. Zhang, X., Liu, L., Wang, Y., et al.: Personagen: A tool for generating personas from user feedback. In: 2023 IEEE 31st International Requirements Engineering Conference (RE), pp 353–354. IEEE (2023)
30. Zhao, L., Alhoshan, W., Ferrari, A., et al.: Natural language processing for requirements engineering: A systematic mapping study. ACM Comput. Surv. (CSUR) **54**(3), 1–41 (2021)
31. Zheng, L., Chiang, W.L., Sheng, Y., et al.: Judging llm-as-a-judge with mt-bench and chatbot arena. Preprint (2023). arXiv:230605685

Part III
Generative AI in Software Development:
Case Studies

Generative AI for Software Development: A Family of Studies on Code Generation

Arghavan Moradi Dakhel, Amin Nikanjam, Foutse Khomh, Michel C. Desmarais, and Hironori Washizaki

Abstract The rapid advancements in generative artificial intelligence (AI) offer multiple opportunities for its application in various domains, including software engineering (SE). This chapter explores the benefits and challenges of utilizing generative AI for different activities in the software development cycle that involve code generation. We review different approaches leveraging generative AI, either independently or in combination with traditional SE techniques, to complete a diverse set of tasks including feature implementation, generating test cases, and repairing programs. Additionally, we discuss the potential pitfalls of using generative AI to perform such SE tasks, as well as the quality of the code generated by these models. Finally, we explore research opportunities in harnessing generative AI, with a particular emphasis on tasks that require code generation.

Keywords Large language model · Code generation · Code quality · Test generation

1 Introduction

Various phases of software development necessitate code generation, spanning from code completion to software testing. Code generation involves the transformation of intended logic into executable programs [3]. Automating the process of code generation has been a long-standing dream in software engineering (SE), ultimately aiming to speed up programming activities and enhance developer productivity.

A. Moradi Dakhel (✉) · A. Nikanjam · F. Khomh · M. C. Desmarais
Polytechnique Montréal, Montréal, QC, Canada
e-mail: arghavan.moradi-dakhel@polymtl.ca; amin.nikanjam@polymtl.ca;
foutse.khomh@polymtl.ca; michel.desmarais@polymtl.ca

H. Washizaki
Waseda University, Tokyo, Japan
e-mail: washizaki@waseda.jp

The advancement of generative artificial intelligence (AI) has brought profound transformation across various stages of the software development cycle [19, 63]. Large language models (LLMs) featuring transformer architecture and billions of parameters stand as a remarkable advancement in the realm of generative AI, enabling these models to generate diverse lines of code [9, 50]. This convergence bears the potential to reshape the essential steps in software development that require code generation by using LLMs as an AI programming assistant [5, 22].

Task specification or user intention can be fed to LLMs using natural language description [9] or a set of input/output examples [6], commonly referred to as prompt. LLMs show desired performance in various SE tasks ranging from crafting code to implementing a specific functionality [59], generating test cases [54], or repairing bugs [60]. In addition, using LLM as an AI programming assistant has shown benefits in improving the productivity and efficiency of developers [65]. In turn, this allows developers to focus on high-level design considerations and problem-solving tasks [31, 59].

While the usage of LLM as an AI programming assistant is promising, challenges persist in evaluating the quality of its generated code. Ensuring that the generated code with LLM is not only syntactically correct but also semantically meaningful and aligned with the intended functionality poses significant challenges. Furthermore, code generated by LLMs, much like human-written code, can introduce bugs [10] and security vulnerabilities [41] and increase maintainability and testability efforts [10, 47].

This book chapter examines the quality of code generated by LLMs as an AI programming assistant within two critical steps of the software development life cycle: feature implementation and software testing. Furthermore, we glimpse into the potential of leveraging LLMs for program repair. Finally, we provide a range of suggestions and strategies to improve the quality of code generated by LLMs for these two types of SE tasks. In particular, our focus is directed toward addressing the following research questions (RQs):

RQ1: How can LLMs be employed to generate reliable code for implementing a functionality?

We explore generating code with LLMs on certain programming tasks and revisit the assessment of different quality metrics applied to the output of LLMs, including bug repairing cost, code complexity, and diversity [10]. Furthermore, we show how employing an SE program repair tool can improve the reliability of code generated by LLMs.

RQ2: How can LLMs be employed for generating effective test cases?

We leverage LLMs to automatically generate test cases and review the effectiveness of their test cases in revealing bugs. We also examine a prompt-based learning strategy for enhancing the effectiveness of test cases produced by LLMs, harnessing the power of mutation testing (MT) [11].

Chapter Organization Section 2 presents an overview of various studies leveraging LLMs for code generation in SE tasks. Section 3 briefly describes the outline of the research methodology followed in our studies to address the research questions.

The key insights from the book chapter are discussed in Sect. 4. Section 5 concludes the chapter.

2 Related Work

In this section, we discuss the related works on leveraging LLMs on different SE tasks.

2.1 Different LLMs for Code Generation

In SE, many efforts have aimed to automate code generation over the years. Early efforts formulated the task of code generation as a search-based problem, wherein the objective is to discover a program within a predefined search space of a programming language that satisfies all constraints derived from the functionality that the code should provide [17]. Subsequent efforts shifted toward input/output task specifications and collected a set of expressions from the pool of possible expressions in a programming language that transfers the input examples into output examples [18].

The advancement of generative AI has brought a profound transformation in developing intelligent assistant tools for automatic code generation that incorporate LLMs. Various LLMs exhibit remarkable performance in code generation tasks in SE. Table 1 shows a list of well-known LLMs for code generation tasks, along with their prevalent use cases. An early undertaking on pre-training transformers with code content is CodeBERT [16]. CodeBERT is an auto-encoding LLM based on BERT architecture [12]. Its pre-training phase encompasses 6M (Million) code snippets and 2M pairs of natural language and code snippets, across 6 programming languages. Its pre-training data are all extracted from the CodeSearchNet [21] dataset gathered from GitHub public repositories. It has found application in diverse code classification tasks such as code review classification [55], prediction of flaky tests [2], defect detection [39], and also in code retrieval tasks [8]. While CodeBERT continues to stand out as a practical, open-source, and lightweight model, well suited for a variety of tasks that require code representation [13, 64], its maximum length of tokens limits its usage for diverse code generation tasks.

One of the very powerful LLMs is OpenAI's Codex [9], which has been extensively applied across various SE tasks involving code generation [29, 37]. Codex is a GPT-based autoregressive LLM [6] with up to 12B (Billion) parameters that are fine-tuned on 54M public repositories from GitHub. OpenAI provides two versions of Codex: *code-davinci-002* and *code-cushman-001*. The former stands as the more capable model, with a maximum context length of 4k, whereas the latter is

Table 1 Common LLMs for SE tasks involving code generation

Model	Architecture	Transformer type	Parameter size	Max length	Common use case
CodeBERT	BERT	Encoder-only (auto-encoding)	125M	512	Classification tasks: code vulnerability classification Information Retrieval tasks: code search
Codex	GPT	Decoder-only (auto-regressive)	12M-12B	4K	Generation Task (left-to-right): code completion and code generation
CodeT5	T5	Encoder-Decoder (sequence-to-sequence)	60M, 220M and 770M	1K	Code Translation, Code Summarization, question/answering
Llama-2-chat	Llama	Decoder-only (auto-regressive)	7B–70B	4K	Dialog use case on variety of generative tasks including code generation, code summarization, code translation

limited to 2k. Notably, Codex powers GitHub Copilot,[1] an in-IDE developer coding assistant that was released on June 29, 2021.

A new release of GitHub Copilot is "Copilot Chat,"[2] which is tuned with human feedback for dialog use cases. Copilot Chat can be employed for a wide range of coding-related tasks. Depending on the specific context of the task, it offers responses such as generating code snippets to implement specific functionalities, providing natural language explanations for code segments, suggesting unit tests, or repairing a buggy code.

Although Codex and its collaborative tool, Copilot, indicate promising performance across a range of code generation tasks, their lack of open-source availability renders them unsuitable for tasks that involve a tuning step.

CodeT5 operates as a sequence-to-sequence LLM [57]. CodeT5 employed code-specific knowledge and proposed a novel-type identifier-aware approach as part of its training objective. It is built upon the T5 architecture and is well suited for tasks revolving around the generation of a new sequence in response to an input sequence. An illustrative example of such tasks is code translation [58], code summarization [1], or generative question answering [61]. The updated version of CodeT5, called CodeT5+, has been trained on a larger volume of data,

---

[1] https://copilot.github.com/

[2] https://docs.github.com/en/copilot/github-copilot-chat

encompassing 115M code files sourced from GitHub[3] and it is configurable to decode-only or encode-only architecture as well. Although CodeT5 is an open-source model that makes it suitable for studies that require fine-tuning, it cannot compete with Codex in Code generation tasks.

Llama-2 is a powerful and open-source LLM that has been introduced by Meta. It is an auto-regressive model, spanning a parameter range from 7B to 70B. [50]. The fine-tuned version of llama-2, known as llama-2-chat, is iteratively tuned using Reinforcement Learning with Human Feedback (RLHF). This process optimizes the model specifically for dialog use cases, spanning different types of tasks, including programming [50]. The dialog model gives the possibility of defining three roles: *System, User*, and *Assistant*. The system role helps specify the task type or the programming language that meets the user's intention.

2.2   Generate Code with LLMs to Implement a Functionality

One of the primary use cases of automatic code generation in the SE development life cycle is to generate a code snippet that implements a particular functionality. Various initiatives have concentrated on leveraging LLM to generate code that aligns with a natural language description of a programming task, called prompt [22, 45, 59]. The experiences of developers in using tools such as Copilot or ChatGPT show that these tools assist them in quickly completing programming tasks [5, 31]. Other studies show that these tools save developers' efforts in online searching and offer a good starting point for implementing task descriptions [4, 56].

Although LLMs provide numerous insights into completing programming tasks, different studies show that LLM suggestions can occasionally be plagued by bugs, non-compilable code, or misalignment with task descriptions [56]. In addition to the model's performance, which can affect the correctness of the output of LLMs, another factor that can impact the correctness of outputs is the complexity or ambiguity of the prompt [25, 62]. The evaluation of different studies shows that sometimes the code generated by LLMs fails to meet some of the conditions described in the prompt [10].

Various approaches have been employed to address this limitation, including few-shot learning [6] and self-planning [24]. In the former, diverse task-representative examples, as input/output pairs, are incorporated into the prompt. The latter approach involves breaking down original tasks into smaller steps using LLMs and calling them plans. While both approaches have shown improvements in the rate of accurate solutions generated by LLMs, they also have their own limitations. The few-shot learning approach's drawback lies in the diversity of tasks, which may require a diverse range of illustrative examples in the prompt. Meanwhile, the self-planning approach's limitation pertains to evaluating the correctness of the

---

[3] https://huggingface.co/datasets/codeparrot/github-code

generated step-by-step plan and ensuring that the newly decomposed prompt aligns with the primary intent.

Apart from providing incorrect suggestions, studies show that LLMs also generate code that is complex [37], inefficient [45], and prone to reproducing vulnerabilities and various Common Weakness Enumerations (CWEs) [41]. Consequently, in addition to a set of test cases used to evaluate the correctness of suggestions, various tools and methods are also necessary to filter out low-quality suggestions.

2.3   Generate Test Cases with LLMs

Following LLM's good performance in code synthesis, another realm of code-related tasks that have gained from the emergence of LLM is software testing. Testing constitutes an important yet costly phase in the SE development life cycle. An ongoing endeavor in this field involves fine-tuning pre-trained code-generating LLMs, using a dataset containing pairs of methods and tests [53]. This process aims to generate test cases [52] or assertions [13, 54]. The performance of these fine-tuned models has been evaluated in their ability to produce tests that "exactly match" with specific ground truths. However, it's important to highlight that training and fine-tuning are resource-intensive in terms of time and space, and they also require additional data.

A less expensive but effective approach involves employing few-shot prompting for test generation. For instance, a study by Nashid et al. [36] introduced dynamic few-shot learning to produce assertions. This technique involves dynamically selecting pairs of illustrative examples similar to the Program Under Test (PUT) from a pool of examples. This method outperforms zero-shot prompting, in generating test assertions that are exactly matched to a set of ground truths. However, the study did not check if generated tests are syntactically correct, functional, and effective in revealing bugs.

CODAMOSA [29] leverages LLM to expand the search space of a search-based automatic test generation tool whenever its generated test case stalls improving the test coverage. Despite the enhanced test coverage gained by this suggested approach, the proposed test cases lack test oracles or assertions. MuTAP [11] is another study that leveraged LLM to generate test cases. The study assesses the effectiveness of test case generation by LLM in bug detection while also presenting an MT-based approach to enhance the effectiveness of test cases, including assertions, in revealing bugs.

2.4   Program Repair with LLMs

Another domain within the SE development life cycle that has been influenced by LLM is program repair. Automatic program repairs aid developers in enhancing code reliability. Various LLMs such as CodeT5 [23, 60], Codex [43], or Chat-

GPT [49] have been employed for program repair. Their results show that directly applying LLMs for automatic program repairs outperformed different state-of-the-art tools across various levels of granularity: producing complete patches, inline repairs with provided prefixes and suffixes for buggy functions, and repairing individual lines [60].

The adoption of retrieval few-shot learning, which exhibits improvements in test case generation, also yields interesting outcomes in the program repair [26, 36]. Fine-tuning pre-trained LLM with bug-repair datasets is another effort in this area [23]. While fine-tuning shows some improvement in program repair compared to direct LLM prompting and state-of-the-art program repair tools, it is expensive and demands a considerable volume of data.

LLMs are also employed for repairing bugs in both programs and test cases that have been generated by LLMs themselves [32, 46]. This is accomplished by re-prompting the LLMs with, for example, the inclusion of error details in the prompt.

3   Research Method

In this section, our attention shifts toward a more comprehensive discussion about the process of generating code using LLMs and the assessment of the quality of their suggestions. We delve into two of our studies in this domain [10, 11] along with their findings across three different coding-related tasks: functional implementation, test case generation, and program (test) syntax repair. Figure 1 shows an overview of our research method.

3.1   First Study: Quality of Code Generated by LLM Compared to Humans

As discussed in Sect. 2, if LLMs such as Copilot are aimed to function as an AI coding assistant, the excellence of the code they produce as an AI pair programmer will inevitably influence the quality of SE projects. In this section, our objective is to generate code with LLM to implement various Python programming tasks and assess the quality of the generated code in comparison to human-written code. Furthermore, we use an SE tool to repair the buggy code snippets generated by LLMs, enhance the reliability of its suggestions, and offer practical advice to practitioners and developers to maximize the benefits of LLMs when implementing a functionality. To carry out this study, we adopt the following methodology.

LLM We select Copilot as a candidate due to its widespread adoption among developers as an AI pair programming tool [4, 22, 65] and the possibility of using it as an in-IDE LLM-based coding assistant tool.

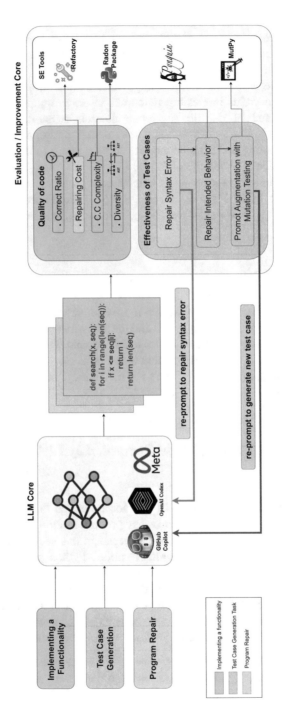

Fig. 1 The proposed methodology for generating and evaluating code with LLMs

Dataset We select a dataset, named Refactory, from a Python programming course including five different programming assignments [20]. This dataset offers several advantages that render it well suited for our study. Firstly, it includes student submissions for each assignment, categorized as correct and buggy, providing a valuable basis for comparison with human-written code, which constitutes the primary objective of this study. Students can be considered novice developers. Furthermore, for every assignment, a series of unit tests, generated by humans, are available that are beneficial in assessing the accuracy of code generated by Copilot. Moreover, the task descriptions within this dataset are human-written, mitigating the likelihood of memorization-related issues [7].

Experimental Setup Within the dataset, each assignment has a corresponding description provided to the students. We use the same description of each programming task on Copilot in five distinct attempts. In each attempt, we collect its top ten suggestions. We adhere to Copilot's default configuration, which returns a maximum of ten suggestions for a given task specification in each attempt. In aggregate, we collect 50 solutions for each task. Given that the number of student submissions for each task provided in the dataset exceeds 50, we downsample the student submissions to 50 to have an equal number of samples for both students and Copilot in the experiment.

Evaluation Criteria We employ the following criteria to compare Copilot's suggestions with students' submissions:

- **Correctness Ratio (CR):** This metric signifies the fraction of correct solutions among the entire set of suggestions provided by Copilot and students' submissions for a programming task.
- **Repairing Cost:** We leverage a bug repairing tool [20] to gauge the extent to which we can repair the buggy code generated by Copilot. This assessment also explores the potential of existing SE tools to enhance the reliability of code generated by Copilot. Additionally, we conducted an assessment of the cost associated with repairing bugs in buggy Copilot-generated code as compared to students' submissions. We present the following metric for this purpose:
  Repair Rate: The fraction of buggy code that passed all test cases after the repair process.
  Average Repair Time: The average execution time taken to repair a buggy program in seconds.
  Relative Patch Size: The Tree-Edit-Distance (TED) between the Abstract Syntax Trees (AST) of a buggy code and the AST of its repaired version, normalized by the AST size of the buggy code.
- **Cyclomatic Complexity:** McCabe's Cyclomatic Complexity or CC serves as a code quality metric that assesses the complexity of a code snippet [14]. Assessing the complexity of code snippets enables us to estimate the necessary effort for incorporating new features into the code. To calculate CC, we utilize a Python package called RADON [44].

- **Diversity:** While increasing the number of generated solutions by LLMs for a programming task results in an increased number of correct solutions passing all test criteria [9, 30], it is not known that this leads to a broader array of solution variations or merely replicating previous ones. To delve deeper into this inquiry, we undertake a comparison of the AST of all correct suggestions (i.e., different attempts with Copilot and students' submissions). We eliminate the AST leaves representing variables and function names, as well as other linguistic components like comments and docstrings.

3.2   Second Study: Quality of Test Cases Generated by LLMs Compared to an Automatic Test Generation Tool

MT evaluates the quality and effectiveness of test cases. MT operates by introducing artificial modifications resembling actual bugs into the PUT, resulting in a buggy code referred to as a "Mutant" [40]. If a mutant survives on all the test cases in a unit test for a given PUT, it signifies that the unit test has failed to detect the mutant. Surviving mutants highlight the shortcomings of test cases, indicating the necessity of either incorporating new test cases or enhancing existing ones.

In the second part of our study, our attention shifts to generating test cases with LLMs and assessing their quality in revealing bugs [11]. We employ MT to evaluate the capability of test cases generated by LLMs in detecting bugs, after applying some post-processing steps to enhance generated test cases. Our method comprises the following sequence of steps:

1. **Initial Prompt:** For generating the initial prompt, we use two different techniques:
   Zero-shot learning: A natural language instruction such as "generate test cases for the following function" followed by the PUT.
   Few-shot learning: Our few-shot prompt consists of a set of three pairs of methods along with their corresponding test unit, serving as illustrative examples [1]. These examples remain constant, and for each new PUT, we append the PUT to the end of the few-shot prompt.
2. **Large Language Model Component (LLMC):** We utilize two LLMs: Codex [9] and llama-2-chat [50]. We call the initial prompt on LLMC, gather its output, and transmit it to the subsequent step.
3. **Repair syntax error:** The test cases generated by LLMC may have syntax errors. We leverage the potential of LLM in program repair [46, 60] by re-prompting the LLMC to fix the syntax errors. This process starts by parsing the generated test cases. If any syntax error arises, we re-prompt the LLMC with an instruction akin to "fix the syntax error in the following code," followed by the erroneous test cases. If the LLMC remains unsuccessful in fixing the syntax error after ten

attempts, we resort to the Python parser to identify the erroneous line. We retain the lines prior to the erroneous line, ensuring they remain free of syntax errors.

4. **Repair Intended behavior:** It is possible that certain test cases within the unit test exhibit unintended behavior. First, we exclude test cases with incorrect test input, such as when the PUT expects a list of integers but the test input is a string, or if the PUT expects two inputs but the test case invokes the PUT with only one input. Next, we aim for the test cases with incorrect asserted output. It refers to those test cases in which their asserted output may not be matched with the expected output of the PUT. To address this unintended behavior, we draw inspiration from Pynguin [33], an automated test generation tool for the Python language. The approach operates by gathering the test input from the test case, executing the PUT with the provided test input, and subsequently comparing the expected output of the PUT (returned values) with the asserted output (test output). If they are not equal, we repair the test case by replacing its asserted output with the expected output.

5. **Mutation Testing (MT):** We use MutPy [35], a tool designed for implementing MT. To assess the effectiveness of test cases, we calculate Mutation Score (MS), which is the ratio of killed mutants out of all mutants of a PUT [40]. If the MS of a unit test is below 100%, we proceed to transmit the test cases and the surviving mutants to the "Prompt Augmentation," step 6. Otherwise, we send the test cases to "Oracle Minimization," step 7.

6. **Prompt Augmentation:** This step focuses on improving the effectiveness of the unit test using surviving mutants. To achieve this, we augment the initial prompt by incorporating the unit test and one of the surviving mutants. Then, we re-prompt LLMC using these augmented prompts. After collecting the new test cases, we iterate through steps 3, 4, 5, and, if necessary, step 6 with another surviving mutant until either the MS reaches 100% or all the surviving mutants of the PUT have been incorporated into the initial prompt.

7. **Oracle minimization:** The test cases generated by the LLMC often contain redundant assertions. Additionally, the augmentation process might introduce further redundant test cases. To avoid confusing developers, similar to previous tools that generate mutation-driven test oracles [40], we employ a Greedy technique to reduce the number of assertions. This final step helps eliminate redundant test cases and their assertions that do not contribute to improving the MS.

Evaluation: To assess the test cases generated by our proposed method, we utilize two different datasets. The first one is the HumanEval dataset [9], which serves as a benchmark for evaluating LLMs. It has 164 human-written programming problems at easy-to-medium levels. Each problem has different attributes such as descriptions and reference solutions. We treat each task within the HumanEval dataset as a PUT and evaluate the effectiveness of test cases generated by LLMs in detecting injected bugs (mutants) of the tasks within this dataset.

Furthermore, we employ the tasks contained in the Refactory dataset, i.e., the same dataset utilized in the first part of our study, as PUT and generate test cases for those tasks with our proposed method. Subsequently, we apply these test cases, both before and after the augmentation step, to the buggy code of students within the dataset. In addition, we apply the test cases on the buggy code that we collected from Copilot in the first study. This dataset enables us to evaluate the effectiveness of test cases generated by LLMs in revealing real bugs within students' code submissions, as well as the buggy code generated by an LLM like Copilot. We employ Pynguin [33], a state-of-the-art automatic test case generation tool, as the comparable tool in this study.

4   Result and Discussions

In this section, we present the results of our research in addressing the questions posed at the beginning of this chapter. Subsequently, we delve into the significant takeaways from our findings and present key insights that can benefit practitioners and researchers.

4.1   Results

In this section, we will share our findings from two studies aimed at addressing the two following research questions:

RQ1: How can LLMs be employed to generate reliable code for implementing a specific functionality?
The results of our first study in Table 2 show that Copilot's CR in solving the programming assignments lags behind students at 36.4% compared to 59%.

However, 💡 leveraging an SE program repair tool significantly increases the correctness of Copilot's suggestions from 36.4 to 98.5%, achieving a success rate of 95% in terms of repair rate. Moreover, the cost of repairing buggy code, quantified in terms of repair time and Repair Patch Size (RPS), is lower for the buggy code generated by Copilot in comparison to the buggy submissions of students.

Our observation also indicates that 💡 Copilot generates solutions that are easier to understand and also employs more Pythonic programming keywords in contrast to the student code [10]. This contrast is evident in the Cyclomatic Complexity (CC) metric average across various tasks in Table 2. While both students' and Copilot's CC values remain below 10, which can be attributed to the simplicity of the tasks, the code generated by Copilot represents lower CC on average compared to the students.

Table 2 Copilot's suggestions compared to students' submissions. CR@k denotes the proportion of accurate solutions among Copilot's suggestions, collected from the top-k suggestions across all five attempts

Candidate	Correctness ratio			Repairing cost			Cyclomatic complexity
	$CR@1$	$CR@5$	$CR@10$	$RepRate$	$AvgTime$	$AvgRPS$	CC
Copilot	5.2%	21.6%	36.4%	**95%**	**4.94**	**0.33**	**2.81**
Students	–	–	**59%**	89%	6.48	0.35	3.87

While Copilot asserts the elimination of duplicate solutions from its top ten suggestions, ⑨ our results in Fig. 2 show the continued presence of duplicates within such suggestions. This discrepancy stems from Copilot's reliance on token sequence comparison to identify and eliminate duplicates. As an illustration, consider the last attempt, "atp5" for q3 in Fig. 2, among 28 correct solutions generated by Copilot, only two remain unique. In contrast, for students out of 22 accurate solutions, 21 exhibited uniqueness. This result is also evident in another study that users report Copilot gets into loops of suggesting the same thing [5].

The findings of the first study are based on the earliest release of Copilot (v1.7). Although subsequent releases have introduced modifications that could influence result replication, the methodology remains applicable to any of Copilot's releases and other LLMs for the purpose of evaluating the quality of its generated code.

RQ2: How can LLM be employed for generating effective test cases?

The findings from our second study, as presented in Table 3, explain that ⑨ both of the selected LLMs in our investigation—Codex and llama-2-chat—are capable of generating test cases that exhibit higher effectiveness compared to those produced by Pynguin. This enhanced effectiveness is observed after implementing refining steps (Before-Augment), namely, the repair of syntax errors and the repair of intended behavior. Additionally, ⑨ augmenting prompt with surviving mutants (After-Augment) further contributes to the enhancement of test case effectiveness.

For instance, when utilizing llama-2-chat with a few-shot initial prompt approach, the MS improves from 85.16 to 93.57% for tasks within the HumanEval dataset. Furthermore, the outcomes obtained from human-written buggy code in students' submissions and Copilot-generated buggy code validate the enhanced effectiveness of the test cases in identifying bugs.

4.2 Practical Suggestions

In this section, we formulate practical suggestions. Our findings also propose practical suggestions for developers and practitioners to maximize the benefit of using LLMs for real-world programming tasks.

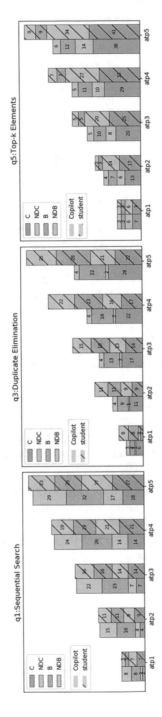

Fig. 2 The cumulative distribution of solutions by Copilot and students across three selected programming tasks. Correct (C), Non-duplicate Correct (NDC), Buggy (B), and Non-duplicate Buggy (NDB). Attempts (atp) for students equal to a random sample set of their submission [10]

Table 3 Evaluation result of test cases generated by Codex and llama-2-chat 7B. The total number of mutants in HumanEval dataset is 1260 [11]

Prompt	Model	Method	Mutants(HumanEval)		Buugycode(refactory)	
			$MS(\%)$	#killedmut	Human	Copilot
–	–	Pynguin	65.94%	649	78.78%	75.92%
Zero-shot	Codex	Before-augment	76.82%	749	79.87%	76.85%
		After-argument	89.13%	869	84.03%	82.40%
Zero-shot	llama-2-chat	Before-augment	84.04%	1059	86.43%	79.62%
		After-augment	91.98%	1159	93.22%	87.03%
Few-shot	Codex	Before-augment	82.73%	829	82.51%	79.62%
		After-augment	92.02%	922	89.41%	100%
Few-shot	llama-2-chat	Before-augment	85.16%	1073	88.42%	87.96%
		After-augment	93.57%	1179	94.91%	100%

Using Programming-Specific Instructions in the Prompt This suggestion is based on the results that we find for one of the programming tasks in our dataset with the objective specified as *"... sort the people in an order such that the older people are at the front of the list... "*. In this case, we observed that Copilot failed to generate code with the correct sorting order, instead retaining the default ascending order in the majority of its generated code. As a result, many of Copilot's solutions for this task did not pass the test cases.

In a new scenario ⑨ , we modified the programming task description by changing *"... older people are at the front..."* to *"... descending order..."* and repeated the process with Copilot to generate solutions. This simple adjustment significantly improved the CR from 14 to 79%.

This improvement underscores the existence of certain details and keywords in problem descriptions that may be obvious to humans but are not always considered by Copilot and maybe other LLMs. Consequently, enhancing the prompt with more specific programming instructions can enhance the CR of code generated by LLMs.

Separating Functions into Distinct Prompts In another programming task named "Unique Birthday", the prompt requested the implementation of three distinct functions: *"unique_day"*, *"unique_month"*, and *"contains_unique _day"*. While all the students managed to interpret and adhere to these requirements, Copilot failed to comprehend these requirements as described in the prompt, which specified the creation of three separate functions. Copilot's CR for this task stood at zero because all of its generated solutions combined the entire task into a single function.

In another scenario ⑨, we break down the task description into three separate prompts for each function: *"unique_day"*, *"unique_month"*, and *"contains_unique _day"*. These prompts were structured as follows:

- **unique_day:** Given a day and a list of possible birth dates, the function should return True if there is only one potential birthday with that day and False otherwise.

- **unique_month:** Given a month and a list of possible birth dates, the function should return True if there is only one potential birthday within that month and False otherwise.
- **contains_unique_day:** Given a month and a list of possible birth dates, the function should return True if there is only one potential birthday with that specific month and day and False otherwise.

We began with the prompt of the *"unique_day"* function, placed at the beginning of the source file, and accepted Copilot's first suggested solution. We followed the same process for the *"unique_month"* and *"contains_unique_day"* functions. In this scenario, the CR for *"unique_day"*, *"unique_month"*, and *"contains_unique_day"* amounted to 88%, 0%, and 40%, respectively.

While this approach improved the CR for two of the prompts, the CR for *"unique_month"* remained at zero. In the rest of this section, we delve into this case and explore a practical approach to enhance the CR in this specific experiment.

Incorporating Input and Expected Output Pairs in the Prompt As Copilot failed to generate any correct solutions for *"unique_month"* prompt in the previous scenario, we conducted a manual review of Copilot's suggested solutions. Our observation revealed that in all the buggy solutions, Copilot incorrectly identified the order of input items in the function as it was expected in the unit tests. An example of such a unit test is provided below. As it is shown in this unit test, for each tuple within the list of birthdays, such as *("January", "1")*, Copilot mistakenly assigned the second item as the birthday month, whereas it should have been the first item in the tuple:

- unique_month (Month = "January", Birthdays = [("January","1"), ("January", "2")]).

In a new scenario 💡, we incorporated the above unit test as a sample input within the prompt of *"unique_month"* positioned at the end of the prompt. This alteration significantly improved the CR of this function elevating it from 0 to 91%. This outcome underscores the value of including sample input or unit tests in the problem description, as it aids Copilot in generating more accurate solutions.

Incorporating Error Messages and Error Line in the Prompt for Code Repair In our second study, during the *"Repair Syntax Error"* phase, we employed a prompt for LLMC that simply instructed as *"fix the syntax error in the following code"*. The average success rate for code repair using the "llama-2-chat" model stood at 31.64% using this prompt.

Previous studies have already shown that including error messages in the prompt can enhance the ability of LLMs to detect bugs in their generated code [46]. Consequently, in a new scenario 💡, we augmented the initial prompt by including the specific syntax error message and error line. We then repeated the process using the "llama-2-chat" model, resulting in a notable improvement in the repair rate to 64.11%.

The Benefit of Dialog LLM Our results in the second study indicate that ⑨ the dialog setup of llama-2-chat provides the flexibility to assign distinct roles to each component of the augmented prompt. For instance, by assigning the initial unit test generated by the model to the assistant role during the prompt augmentation process, the likelihood of repeating the initial tests in the generated output is reduced, while the chance of generating new test cases for detecting surviving mutants is increased.

4.3 Discussion

While LLMs as AI programming assistant tools generate code snippets that are competitive with human-written code across various quality metrics, they still produce code that is buggy, non-optimal, ineffective, syntactically incorrect, or misaligned with intended functionality [10]. Developers express that when employing Copilot to fulfill programming tasks, they find themselves *less in coding and more in reviewing*[5]. Another study highlights that among the various possible interactions with LLMs, up to 34% of developers' engagements with LLMs involve debugging, testing, and validating suggestions [34].

The investigation of the findings of our two studies suggests that ⑨ applying diverse post-processing steps, such as employing a tool to repair buggy code generated by LLMs or re-prompting the LLM to repair syntax errors in its own suggestions, can enhance the reliability in the code generated by LLMs. Furthermore, for test cases ⑨ , augmenting the prompt with information like surviving mutants can improve the effectiveness of the test cases in revealing bugs.

One limitation of our two studies is the absence of a dataset from an industrial context that includes programming task statements along with their corresponding code. As a result, we chose to follow the approach of previous research in software engineering by using traditional programming tasks, such as those in the HumanEval dataset [9], to evaluate the effectiveness of LLM-based tools [38, 48, 56].

The focus of this chapter is not on the type or difficulty level of programming tasks that LLMs can handle but rather on the quality of the code they generate when used as AI pair programmers. We also explore methods to enhance this code quality and enhance developers' reliability on tools incorporating LLMs for code generation. Therefore, we selected datasets for which LLMs are capable of producing answers to their programming tasks. While these tasks might not represent all the programming tasks a professional developer encounters, they enable us to evaluate the capabilities and limitations of LLMs. Furthermore, we provide recommendations to developers on how to effectively utilize this tool in actual software projects. However, readers need to acknowledge these limitations when attempting to generalize our results to more complex tasks.

Another limitation might stem from the quality metrics used in our first study. Although we employed a range of quantitative metrics, drawing inspiration from previous research in software engineering, to compare Copilot's code with that produced by humans [15, 27, 38], the selected metrics primarily focus on functional suitability and maintainability. However, in accordance with ISO/IEC 25010 and relevant studies [51], there are other quality characteristics to consider, including usability of software systems [28], performance efficiency, and security concerns, which we have deferred to future works.

Overall, our results show that 💡 even though post-processing steps or prompt augmentation lead to enhanced reliability and effectiveness, it remains crucial for an expert to validate the final suggestions. A human study reveals that while participants using LLM-based code assistance exhibit more confidence in generating accurate code compared to those without such tools, their code is significantly less correct upon actual evaluation [42].

💡 Relying solely on LLM-based code assistance might pose a risk in SE projects, particularly when novice developers put complete trust in its suggestions, potentially overlooking buggy or suboptimal solutions due to their limited expertise [10]. As emphasized by D. Wong et al. [59], while LLM-based code assistance like Copilot is indeed a powerful tool for code-related tasks, it should not be *flying the plane by itself.*

5   Conclusion

In this chapter, we have reviewed the utilization of generative AI to automate various activities within the SE development life cycle that require code generation. The primary objective is to assess and improve the quality of the generated code. The scope of this book chapter is confined to two specific SE tasks despite the extensive application of LLMs within the SE development life cycle: firstly, generating code using LLMs to implement functionality and, secondly, generating test cases. Furthermore, we glimpse into the potential of leveraging LLMs for program repair.

Our studies present the advantage of applying post-processing steps by employing different SE tools to improve the quality of LLMs generated code. This is achieved through the exploration of automated repair techniques for repairing buggy code generated by LLMs to enhance correctness, consequently, the reliability of the suggestions, as well as the advantage of MT to enhance the effectiveness of the test cases generated by them. A comparison of the repair cost between buggy code generated by LLMs and that by humans reveals that repairing LLM-generated code is often easier, given that LLM-generated bugs are frequently attributable to minor oversights or the missing of specific corner cases in the provided prompt. Additionally, the findings indicate that enhancing the prompt with surviving mutants can assist LLMs in generating more effective unit tests by creating novel test cases capable of detecting the surviving mutants. This underscores the advantage of employing LLMs as the core of an automatic test generation tool, as conventional automatic generation tools lack access to the insights embedded in surviving mutants.

Although our studies propose solutions to enhance the quality of LLM suggestions, there are interesting research lines that can be tackled in the future to reduce the time that developers spend on debugging and verifying the output of LLMs. Firstly, leveraging LLMs to effectively repair buggy code through a more comprehensive methodology, evolving bug localization, and subsequent repair has the competence of further investigation. Secondly, the exploration of assertions in test cases beyond primitive assertions presents an engaging area for future research. Finally, the techniques outlined in this chapter to generate test cases with LLMs rely on a correct solution, akin to other state-of-the-art automatic test generation tools that require a specification of correctness. Exploring more independent approaches to generate test cases using LLMs for code snippets, even in the presence of bugs, holds promise. The existing LLMs excel in code synthesizing capabilities. Therefore, rather than investing in the training or tuning of new models, forthcoming research could redirect their attention toward exploring alternative prompt-based techniques by leveraging diverse SE tools.

References

1. Ahmed, T., Devanbu, P.: Few-shot training llms for project-specific code-summarization. In: Proceedings of the 37th IEEE/ACM International Conference on Automated Software Engineering, pp. 1–5 (2022)
2. Akli, A., Haben, G., Habchi, S., Papadakis, M., Le Traon, Y.: Flakycat: Predicting flaky tests categories using few-shot learning. In: 2023 IEEE/ACM International Conference on Automation of Software Test (AST). pp. 140–151. IEEE, Piscataway (2023)
3. Alur, R., Bodik, R., Juniwal, G., Martin, M.M., Raghothaman, M., Seshia, S.A., Singh, R., Solar-Lezama, A., Torlak, E., Udupa, A.: Syntax-Guided Synthesis. IEEE, Piscataway (2013)
4. Barke, S., James, M.B., Polikarpova, N.: Grounded copilot: how programmers interact with code-generating models. Proc. ACM Programm. Lang. 7(OOPSLA1), 85–111 (2023)
5. Bird, C., Ford, D., Zimmermann, T., Forsgren, N., Kalliamvakou, E., Lowdermilk, T., Gazit, I.: Taking flight with copilot: early insights and opportunities of ai-powered pair-programming tools. Queue 20(6), 35–57 (2022)
6. Brown, T., Mann, B., Ryder, N., Subbiah, M., Kaplan, J.D., Dhariwal, P., Neelakantan, A., Shyam, P., Sastry, G., Askell, A., et al.: Language models are few-shot learners. Adv. Neural Inf. Process. Syst. 33, 1877–1901 (2020)
7. Carlini, N., Ippolito, D., Jagielski, M., Lee, K., Tramer, F., Zhang, C.: Quantifying memorization across neural language models (2022). arXiv preprint arXiv:2202.07646
8. Chai, Y., Zhang, H., Shen, B., Gu, X.: Cross-domain deep code search with meta learning. In: Proceedings of the 44th International Conference on Software Engineering, pp. 487–498 (2022)
9. Chen, M., Tworek, J., Jun, H., Yuan, Q., Pinto, H.P.D.O., Kaplan, J., Edwards, H., Burda, Y., Joseph, N., Brockman, G., et al.: Evaluating large language models trained on code (2021). arXiv preprint arXiv:2107.03374
10. Dakhel, A.M., Majdinasab, V., Nikanjam, A., Khomh, F., Desmarais, M.C., Jiang, Z.M.J.: Github Copilot AI pair programmer: asset or liability? J. Syst. Softw. 203, 111734 (2023)

11. Dakhel, A.M., Nikanjam, A., Majdinasab, V., Khomh, F., Desmarais, M.C.: Effective test generation using pre-trained large language models and mutation testing (2023). https://arxiv.org/abs/2308.16557
12. Devlin, J., Chang, M.W., Lee, K., Toutanova, K.: Bert: Pre-training of deep bidirectional transformers for language understanding (2018). arXiv preprint arXiv:1810.04805
13. Dinella, E., Ryan, G., Mytkowicz, T., Lahiri, S.K.: Toga: A neural method for test oracle generation. In: Proceedings of the 44th International Conference on Software Engineering, pp. 2130–2141 (2022)
14. Ebert, C., Cain, J., Antoniol, G., Counsell, S., Laplante, P.: Cyclomatic complexity. IEEE Softw. **33**(6), 27–29 (2016)
15. Fakhoury, S., Roy, D., Hassan, A., Arnaoudova, V.: Improving source code readability: Theory and practice. In: 2019 IEEE/ACM 27th International Conference on Program Comprehension (ICPC), pp. 2–12. IEEE, Piscataway (2019)
16. Feng, Z., Guo, D., Tang, D., Duan, N., Feng, X., Gong, M., Shou, L., Qin, B., Liu, T., Jiang, D., et al.: Codebert: A pre-trained model for programming and natural languages (2020). arXiv preprint arXiv:2002.08155
17. Green, C.: Application of theorem proving to problem solving. In: Readings in Artificial Intelligence, pp. 202–222. Elsevier, Amsterdam (1981)
18. Gulwani, S.: Automating string processing in spreadsheets using input-output examples. ACM Sigplan Notices **46**(1), 317–330 (2011)
19. Hou, X., Zhao, Y., Liu, Y., Yang, Z., Wang, K., Li, L., Luo, X., Lo, D., Grundy, J., Wang, H.: Large language models for software engineering: A systematic literature review (2023). arXiv preprint arXiv:2308.10620
20. Hu, Y., Ahmed, U.Z., Mechtaev, S., Leong, B., Roychoudhury, A.: Re-factoring based program repair applied to programming assignments. In: 2019 34th IEEE/ACM International Conference on Automated Software Engineering (ASE), pp. 388–398. IEEE, Piscataway (2019)
21. Husain, H., Wu, H.H., Gazit, T., Allamanis, M., Brockschmidt, M.: Codesearchnet challenge: Evaluating the state of semantic code search (2019). arXiv preprint arXiv:1909.09436
22. Imai, S.: Is github copilot a substitute for human pair-programming? An empirical study. In: Proceedings of the ACM/IEEE 44th International Conference on Software Engineering: Companion Proceedings, pp. 319–321 (2022)
23. Jiang, N., Liu, K., Lutellier, T., Tan, L.: Impact of code language models on automated program repair (2023). arXiv preprint arXiv:2302.05020
24. Jiang, X., Dong, Y., Wang, L., Shang, Q., Li, G.: Self-planning code generation with large language model (2023). arXiv preprint arXiv:2303.06689
25. Jones, E., Steinhardt, J.: Capturing failures of large language models via human cognitive biases. Adv. Neural Inf. Process. Syst. **35**, 11785–11799 (2022)
26. Joshi, H., Sanchez, J.C., Gulwani, S., Le, V., Verbruggen, G., Radiček, I.: Repair is nearly generation: Multilingual program repair with llms. In: Proceedings of the AAAI Conference on Artificial Intelligence, vol. 37, pp. 5131–5140 (2023)
27. Kim, S., Whitehead Jr, E.J.: How long did it take to fix bugs? In: Proceedings of the 2006 International Workshop on Mining Software Repositories, pp. 173–174 (2006)
28. Komiyama, T., Fukuzumi, S., Azuma, M., Washizaki, H., Tsuda, N.: Usability of software–intensive systems from developers' point of view: Current status and future perspectives of international standardization of usability evaluation. In: Human-Computer Interaction. Design and User Experience: Thematic Area, HCI 2020, Held as Part of the 22nd International Conference, HCII 2020, Copenhagen, Denmark, July 19–24, 2020, Proceedings, Part I 22, pp. 450–463. Springer, Berlin (2020)
29. Lemieux, C., Inala, J.P., Lahiri, S.K., Sen, S.: Codamosa: Escaping coverage plateaus in test generation with pre-trained large language models. In: International Conference on Software Engineering (ICSE) (2023)

30. Li, Y., Choi, D., Chung, J., Kushman, N., Schrittwieser, J., Leblond, R., Eccles, T., Keeling, J., Gimeno, F., Dal Lago, A., et al.: Competition-level code generation with alphacode. Science **378**(6624), 1092–1097 (2022)
31. Liang, J.T., Yang, C., Myers, B.A.: Understanding the usability of AI programming assistants (2023). arXiv preprint arXiv:2303.17125
32. Liventsev, V., Grishina, A., Härmä, A., Moonen, L.: Fully autonomous programming with large language models (2023). arXiv preprint arXiv:2304.10423
33. Lukasczyk, S., Fraser, G.: Pynguin: Automated unit test generation for python. In: Proceedings of the ACM/IEEE 44th International Conference on Software Engineering: Companion Proceedings, pp. 168–172 (2022)
34. Mozannar, H., Bansal, G., Fourney, A., Horvitz, E.: Reading between the lines: Modeling user behavior and costs in ai-assisted programming (2022). arXiv preprint arXiv:2210.14306
35. Mutpy: A mutation testing tool for Python 3.x source code. https://github.com/mutpy/mutpy (2019)
36. Nashid, N., Sintaha, M., Mesbah, A.: Retrieval-based prompt selection for code-related few-shot learning. In: Proceedings of the 45th International Conference on Software Engineering (ICSE'23) (2023)
37. Nguyen, N., Nadi, S.: An empirical evaluation of github copilot's code suggestions. In: Proceedings of the 19th International Conference on Mining Software Repositories, pp. 1–5 (2022)
38. Nguyen, N., Nadi, S.: An empirical evaluation of GitHub Copilot's code suggestions. In: Accepted for Publication Proceedings of the 19th ACM International Conference on Mining Software Repositories (MSR), pp. 1–5 (2022)
39. Pan, C., Lu, M., Xu, B.: An empirical study on software defect prediction using codebert model. Appl. Sci. **11**(11), 4793 (2021)
40. Papadakis, M., Kintis, M., Zhang, J., Jia, Y., Le Traon, Y., Harman, M.: Mutation testing advances: An analysis and survey. In: Advances in Computers, vol. 112, pp. 275–378. Elsevier, Amsterdam (2019)
41. Pearce, H., Ahmad, B., Tan, B., Dolan-Gavitt, B., Karri, R.: Asleep at the keyboard? assessing the security of github copilot's code contributions. In: 2022 IEEE Symposium on Security and Privacy (SP), pp. 754–768. IEEE, Piscataway (2022)
42. Perry, N., Srivastava, M., Kumar, D., Boneh, D.: Do users write more insecure code with ai assistants? (2022). arXiv preprint arXiv:2211.03622
43. Prenner, J.A., Babii, H., Robbes, R.: Can openai's codex fix bugs? An evaluation on quixbugs. In: Proceedings of the Third International Workshop on Automated Program Repair, pp. 69–75 (2022)
44. Radon: A python tool to compute various metrics from the source code. https://radon.readthedocs.io/en/latest (2019)
45. Sakib, F.A., Khan, S.H., Karim, A.: Extending the frontier of chatgpt: Code generation and debugging (2023). arXiv preprint arXiv:2307.08260
46. Schäfer, M., Nadi, S., Eghbali, A., Tip, F.: Adaptive test generation using a large language model (2023). arXiv preprint arXiv:2302.06527
47. Siddiq, M.L., Santos, J., Tanvir, R.H., Ulfat, N., Rifat, F.A., Lopes, V.C.: Exploring the effectiveness of large language models in generating unit tests (2023). arXiv preprint arXiv:2305.00418
48. Sobania, D., Briesch, M., Rothlauf, F.: Choose your programming copilot: A comparison of the program synthesis performance of github copilot and genetic programming (2021). arXiv preprint arXiv:2111.07875
49. Sobania, D., Briesch, M., Hanna, C., Petke, J.: An analysis of the automatic bug fixing performance of chatgpt arxiv (2023). arXiv preprint arXiv:2301.08653
50. Touvron, H., Martin, L., Stone, K., Albert, P., Almahairi, A., Babaei, Y., Bashlykov, N., Batra, S., Bhargava, P., Bhosale, S., et al.: Llama 2: Open foundation and fine-tuned chat models (2023). arXiv preprint arXiv:2307.09288

51. Tsuda, N., Washizaki, H., Honda, K., Nakai, H., Fukazawa, Y., Azuma, M., Komiyama, T., Nakano, T., Suzuki, H., Morita, S., et al.: Wsqf: Comprehensive software quality evaluation framework and benchmark based on square. In: 2019 IEEE/ACM 41st International Conference on Software Engineering: Software Engineering in Practice (ICSE-SEIP), pp. 312–321. IEEE, Piscataway (2019)

52. Tufano, M., Drain, D., Svyatkovskiy, A., Deng, S.K., Sundaresan, N.: Unit test case generation with transformers and focal context (2020). arXiv preprint arXiv:2009.05617

53. Tufano, M., Deng, S.K., Sundaresan, N., Svyatkovskiy, A.: Methods2test: A dataset of focal methods mapped to test cases. In: Proceedings of the 19th International Conference on Mining Software Repositories, pp. 299–303 (2022)

54. Tufano, M., Drain, D., Svyatkovskiy, A., Sundaresan, N.: Generating accurate assert statements for unit test cases using pretrained transformers. In: Proceedings of the 3rd ACM/IEEE International Conference on Automation of Software Test, pp. 54–64 (2022)

55. Turzo, A.K., Faysal, F., Poddar, O., Sarker, J., Iqbal, A., Bosu, A.: Towards automated classification of code review feedback to support analytics (2023). arXiv preprint arXiv:2307.03852

56. Vaithilingam, P., Zhang, T., Glassman, E.L.: Expectation vs. experience: Evaluating the usability of code generation tools powered by large language models. In: Chi Conference on Human Factors in Computing Systems Extended Abstracts, pp. 1–7 (2022)

57. Wang, Y., Wang, W., Joty, S., Hoi, S.C.: Codet5: Identifier-aware unified pre-trained encoder-decoder models for code understanding and generation (2021). arXiv preprint arXiv:2109.00859

58. Wang, C., Yang, Y., Gao, C., Peng, Y., Zhang, H., Lyu, M.R.: No more fine-tuning? an experimental evaluation of prompt tuning in code intelligence. In: Proceedings of the 30th ACM Joint European Software Engineering Conference and Symposium on the Foundations of Software Engineering, pp. 382–394 (2022)

59. Wong, D., Kothig, A., Lam, P.: Exploring the verifiability of code generated by github copilot (2022). arXiv preprint arXiv:2209.01766

60. Xia, C.S., Wei, Y., Zhang, L.: Automated program repair in the era of large pre-trained language models. In: Proceedings of the 45th International Conference on Software Engineering (ICSE 2023). Association for Computing Machinery, New York (2023)

61. Yu, T., Gu, X., Shen, B.: Code question answering via task-adaptive sequence-to-sequence pre-training. In: 2022 29th Asia-Pacific Software Engineering Conference (APSEC), pp. 229–238. IEEE, Piscataway (2022)

62. Zamfirescu-Pereira, J., Wong, R.Y., Hartmann, B., Yang, Q.: Why johnny can't prompt: how non-AI experts try (and fail) to design llm prompts. In: Proceedings of the 2023 CHI Conference on Human Factors in Computing Systems, pp. 1–21 (2023)

63. Zheng, Z., Ning, K., Chen, J., Wang, Y., Chen, W., Guo, L., Wang, W.: Towards an understanding of large language models in software engineering tasks (2023). arXiv preprint arXiv:2308.11396

64. Zhou, X., Han, D., Lo, D.: Assessing generalizability of codebert. In: 2021 IEEE International Conference on Software Maintenance and Evolution (ICSME), pp. 425–436. IEEE, Piscataway (2021)

65. Ziegler, A., Kalliamvakou, E., Li, X.A., Rice, A., Rifkin, D., Simister, S., Sittampalam, G., Aftandilian, E.: Productivity assessment of neural code completion. In: Proceedings of the 6th ACM SIGPLAN International Symposium on Machine Programming, pp. 21–29 (2022)

BERTVRepair: On the Adoption of CodeBERT for Automated Vulnerability Code Repair

Nguyen Ngoc Hai Dang, Tho Quan Thanh, and Anh Nguyen-Duc

Abstract Vulnerable code continues to have a significant impact to software quality, leading to serious consequences such as economic loss, privacy breaches, and threats to national security. Traditional methods of detecting and addressing software security issues are often time-consuming and resource-intensive. This research aims to examine the effectiveness of generative-based methods, particularly those leveraging generative (DL) models like CodeBERT, in repairing code and addressing software vulnerabilities. Our research question (RQ) is: Can the adoption of CodeBERT extend the capabilities of vulnerability code repair, and, if so, to what extent? We proposed a new approach called BERTVRepair that adopts CodeBERT and state-of-the-art transfer learning and tokenization methods to generate vulnerable code patches. We performed an experiment to compare the performance of BERTVRepair with existing models. We showed a marginal improvement in accuracy and perplexity. We conclude that using generative-based methods like CodeBERT, with its code embedding extraction and transfer learning approaches, can potentially enhance the process of software vulnerability repair. This research contributes to adopting large programming language models into software engineering tasks, such as automated code repair.

Keywords Code LLM · BERT · Large language model · Code repair · Vulnerability

N. N. H. Dang (✉) · T. Q. Thanh
Ho Chi Minh University of Technology, Ho Chi Minh City, Vietnam

Vietnam National University, Ho Chi Minh City, Vietnam
e-mail: qttho@hcmut.edu.vn

A. Nguyen-Duc
University of South Eastern, Notodden, Norway
e-mail: anh.nguyen.duc@usn.no

© The Author(s), under exclusive license to Springer Nature Switzerland AG 2024
A. Nguyen-Duc et al. (eds.), *Generative AI for Effective Software Development*,
https://doi.org/10.1007/978-3-031-55642-5_8

1 Introduction

In today's technologically driven society, software systems play a pivotal role in almost every aspect of our daily lives, from communication, work, learning, and entertainment to critical infrastructure [1, 2]. Software vulnerability is a security flaw, glitch, or weakness in software code that could be exploited by an attacker [3]. These vulnerabilities, if exploited, can lead to severe consequences, including economic loss, privacy breaches, and threats to national security [4]. While detecting software security issues can be done during and after software release, addressing security issues early in the development process saves time and resources [3].

By actively searching for security issues, developers can uncover and address potential flaws before the software is deployed, reducing the risk of exploitation by malicious actors [5]. Once security issues are detected, code repair comes into play. Code repair, or program repair, also known as automated program repair or software patching, refers to the process of automatically identifying and fixing software bugs or defects without manual intervention [6]. This may involve activities such as patching code, implementing security controls, updating dependencies, or improving the overall design of the software. Automated code repair can be classified into template-based and generative-based. Generative-based repair uses machine learning (ML), particularly DL, to generate fixes for bugs [7, 8]. Unlike template-based methods, generative approaches do not rely on predefined patterns but learn from data to create fixes.

The adoption of deep learning (DL) is a novel and promising approach for an efficient and effective way of identifying and rectifying these vulnerabilities [6, 9–14]. Among these, CodeBERT represents a novel approach in code repair, utilizing the power of code embeddings derived from DL models to understand and fix vulnerabilities in software systems.

We want to examine the performance of generative-based methods, particularly those that leverage DL models like CodeBERT, in repairing code and addressing security vulnerabilities. CodeBERT's unique aspect is its use of code embeddings, which represent source code in a format that DL models can process. This question investigates whether the use of a specific code embedding approach can enhance the effectiveness of vulnerability code repair.

Research Question Can adopting CodeBERT extend the vulnerability code repair capabilities and, if yes, to what extent?

The remainder of the paper is structured as follows: Sect. 2 is a literature review. Section 3 is our proposed approach. Section 4 presents our experiment design. Section 5 is the result, and Sect. 6 concludes the paper.

2 Background

This section provides basic knowledge about Transformer architecture and BERT model (Sect. 2.1), a description of CodeBERT and UnixCoder (Sect. 2.2), and recent research on automated code repair (Sect. 2.3).

2.1 Transformer Architecture and BERT Model

This section presents fundamental DL architectures that provide the foundation for our approach, which are the Transformer architecture and BERT model.

Transformer

Although the RNN model combined with attention is widely applied to Seq2Seq problems and has achieved quite good results, this architecture still has some major drawbacks:

- An RNN node only receives semantic information from previous nodes (words on the left) and lacks information from nodes located after (words on the right). Although the bidirectional RNN variant [15] can somewhat solve this problem, it increases the computation time while the information is still transmitted indirectly.
- The model calculates sequentially: the result of the current calculation depends on the result of the previous calculation. Therefore, data from different transmissions cannot be performed in parallel, leading to not fully utilizing the GPU.
- It can "forget" or "lose" data when information is transmitted through many network nodes during the calculation due to too large or too small derivatives (vanishing/exploding gradient [16]). This hinders the embedding of context information of words in the sentence for the word representation vector. Although some variants of RNN such as GRU [17] and LSTM [18] have the ability to selectively decide to keep/discard information at each network node as presented in the previous chapter, when going through many intermediate nodes, the information is still lost a lot.

To overcome these drawbacks, in 2017, the research team of Google Brain introduced the Transformer model [19]. This model is gradually being widely used in the field of natural language processing—NLP [19]—and even Image Processing (Computer Vision, CV) [20]. Like RNN networks, Transformer is designed to handle sequential data, such as tasks like machine translation or automatic summarization in the field of NLP. However, unlike RNN, Transformer does not require sequential data to be processed in order. For example, if the input data is a natural language sentence, Transformer does not need to process the beginning of the sentence before the end of the sentence. Because of this feature, Transformer allows many parallel calculations and therefore reduces training time. Especially the operation mechanism of Transformer allows information at each network node to be aggregated in both directions at the same time in a quite natural way, thereby significantly improving performance when applied to machine learning problems. The Transformer model also follows the seq2seq architecture, but with Encoder and Decoder built from scaled dot-product attention and feed-forward blocks as shown in Fig. 1. Besides the modules commonly found in neural network architectures, Transformer introduces three new techniques:

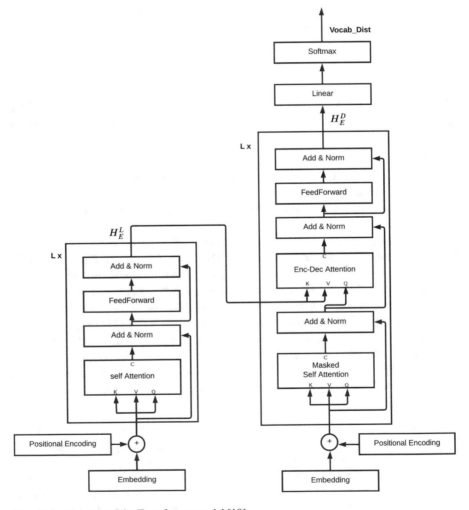

Fig. 1 Architecture of the Transformer model [19]

- *Scaled dot-product attention technique*: This technique allows Transformer to perform two-way attention mechanism and has the ability to parallelize. This technique is used in Self-Attention, Masked Self Attention, and Encoder-Decoder Attention (or Cross-Attention) modules.
- *Multi-head technique*: This is simply applying Self-Attention multiple times (each time is called a head) and aggregating the results, similar to the mechanism of applying multiple filters and aggregating the results of CNN. Thanks to its distinctive attention mechanism, the Multi-head calculation process on Transformer can also be parallelized.
- *Positional Encoding mechanism*: This mechanism allows encoding position information into input vectors.

BERT

Since the advent of the Transformer model, many large language models have been pre-trained on Transformer. Typical examples are BERT [21] using the encoder architecture of Transformer, GPT-2 [22] using the decoder architecture of Transformer, Transformer XL [23] using the recurrent decoder architecture based on the decoder of Transformer. Applying these large language models to downstream applications has yielded impressive results in many NLP problems. Since 2018, Devlin and colleagues proposed the Pre-training of Deep Bidirectional Transformers for Language Understanding (BERT) model [21]. BERT is trained on a large amount of data and can be seen as a pre-trained model that is often fine-tuned with some simple neural layers to create state-of-the-art models that solve various problems in the field of natural language processing such as question answering [24] or language inference [25]. BERT uses the same architecture as the encoder block of Transformer and is trained on two objectives: masked language modeling (MLM) and next sentence prediction (NSP). For the MLM objective, BERT will randomly mask 15% of the tokens in the input sequence (with 80% of them actually being replaced by the token [MASK], 10% of the tokens being randomly replaced by another token, and 10% remaining unchanged), and then BERT is trained to predict the masked tokens based on the context of the surrounding tokens. Therefore, the output of BERT can be used as an embedding layer that has been embedded with contextual information from both directions, thanks to the self-attention mechanism in each Transformer encoder layer. Figure 2 illustrates how BERT predicts and trains for this objective. After the input data passes through the Encoding layers of Transformer, we will get the final embedding vectors. These embedding vectors continue to go through an FC layer to create the probability distribution vectors of the vocabulary at the corresponding position in the sentence. This is also BERT's prediction for the probability of occurrence of each word at the output position of the model. BERT will compare the predicted probability of the word appearing at the [MASK] position and compare it with the corresponding word in the ground truth to determine the loss value for this training and update the corresponding weight.

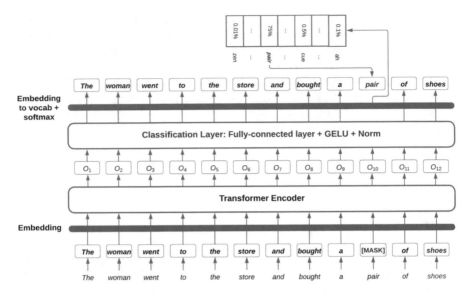

Fig. 2 Overview of the prediction and training process of the BERT model

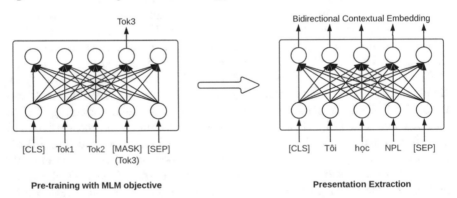

Fig. 3 Thanks to the MLM objective and the encoder architecture of Transformer, BERT can be used as an embedding block to extract contextual information from both sides

Therefore, BERT is a large AutoEncoding language model, often used to create representations for text to continue serving other problems.

For the NSP objective, the model takes as input pairs of sequences separated by the token [*SEP*] and is trained to predict whether they are two consecutive sequences or not as shown in Fig. 3. To train, the model will select some pairs of consecutive sentences and some pairs of random sentences with the ground-truth value determined by the token [*CLS*]. By changing the meaning of the token [*CLS*] with the corresponding inputs, we can train BERT for other *supervised learning* problems. The two objectives MLM and NSP can be trained simultaneously when training BERT with a corpus.

With the two training objectives, BERT offers the following advantages.

- The MLM training strategy helps BERT efficiently represent the contextual semantics of the training corpus, which are encoded as embedding vectors. Once applied in another corpus, such that one of programming languages, this strategy can help embed the corresponding semantics of the training corpus.
- The NSP training strategy allows BERT to train another supervised task, which takes advantage of the semantic encoding offered by MLM. By controlling the meaning of the $[CLS]$ token, one can leverage BERT-based model for other supervised task.

2.2 CodeBERT

The success of BERT in NLP has led to CodeBERT model for code generation [26]. This model borrows the same design and training process of Roberta [27] in the context of multilingualism. CodeBERT is trained on two types of data: the code segments and their documentation. CodeBERT is trained with a dataset that is a mixture of programming languages with no indication in the model to differentiate between these languages.

Training of code and documentation use the same tokenization process as in a standard text processing pipeline. The generated sequences of tokens would then be inserted with some special tokens formulating the following sequence, which is used as input for the model, and the model would need to output (1) dense vector representations of both code tokens and word tokens along with (2) the representation of $[CLS]$ stated in [26]. In order to generate such representation, the model is trained on two learning objectives: masked language modeling and replaced token detection.

$$[CLS], w_1, w_2, \ldots, w_n, [SEP], c_1, c_2, c_n, [EOS]$$

CodeBERT applies masked language modeling on corpus of programming languages to "learn" the representation of these programming languages. For the replaced token prediction objective, CodeBERT adapts the next token prediction objective from BERT to train a vector representation for $[CLS]$ token.

UnixCoder [28] is another large programming languages model that leverages the AST representation of code segments, which is described in Fig. 4, along with the comments to learn the embeddings in two pre-training tasks.

- The first one is a contrastive learning task in which the model tries to optimize a cosine loss that measures the sum of the similarity of all vectorized input in a training batch. The input of this task, which is shown in Fig. 5, is fed into the model that composes of a concatenation of the flattened AST representation of a code segment and the comment describing the code segment.

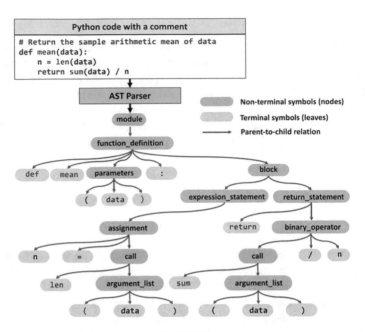

Fig. 4 A Python code with its comment and AST [28]

Fig. 5 Input for contrastive learning task of UnixCoder [28]

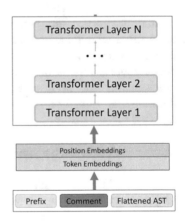

- The second pre-training task is the conditional text generation that makes the model learn to generate the respective comment with the flattened AST of the code segment.

2.3 Code Repair

Methods used for creating code patches can be classified into template-based and generative-based.

Template-Based Code Repairs

Template-based patching involves using predefined templates or patterns to guide the creation of code patches. These templates provide a structure or framework for making specific modifications to the code. Developers can fill in the template with the necessary changes based on the identified security issues. This approach simplifies the patching process by providing a consistent and predictable format, making it easier to apply fixes across different codebases. Template-based patching is especially useful for addressing common security vulnerabilities that have well-defined solutions.

A notable system that falls into this category is VuRLE [29] generated patches using the template-based method that includes two phases: learning phase and repair phase. In the learning phase, the method mines the training data to create repair templates that are retrieved for patches generated in the later phase. This method uses a tree as source code representation, and it is created using GumTree. Figure 6 shows an overview of the two-phase workflow along with the necessary steps to transform the data in each phase.

In the learning phase, VuRLE will mine the data and generate the patch templates, which will then be fine-grained in a later phase for creating respective patches. Pairs of buggy code and its patch are fed into GumTree to create edit sequences fixing the buggy code. These edit sequences will be used to create graphs by forming edges between sequence pairs with the longest overlapping sub-

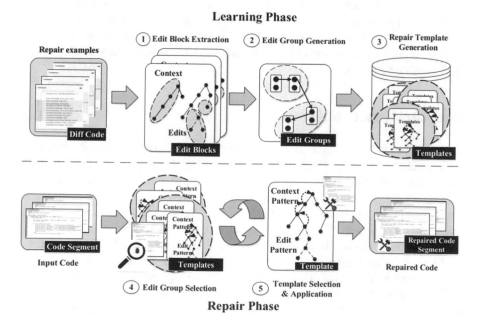

Fig. 6 Workflow of VuRLE [29]

sequence. The graphs of edit sequences are then split into connected components, and DBSCAN is used to cluster these components into edit groups. For each pair of edit sequences in the edit groups, a template is created by identifying the longest overlapping edit sub-sequence and the context of this sub-sequence. The editing context is also the output of GumTree that specifies the locations of edit operations in the code segments.

In the repair phase, we will find the appropriate templates for each unseen bad code segment based on their similarity with the known bad code in the learning phase data set. After that, the chosen template will then be further fine-grained to match the bad code. Templates are selected by comparing the input code with edit groups' templates mined in the learning process. The input code then used the transformative operations specified in the templates' edit pattern to create code patches and only keep patches that do not contain redundant code

Source Code Embeddings

Source code embedding is a NLP concept about the transformation of source code into numerical representations, making it understandable and processable by ML algorithms. This enables the creation of dense vector representation of language learning by training the model on a huge corpus, resulting in a general-purpose representation that can preserve the semantic relationships between words to the extent that these relationships can be expressed through the arithmetic operations [30]. However, in order to learn such representations, the requirements are (1) an enormous amount of data and (2) unlimited computing resources; due to these reasons, these pre-trained models are normally provided by tech giants like Google with their BERT architecture, and its usages in different tasks have been pushing performance boundaries.

Generative-Based Code Repairs

Generative-based patching takes an automated and algorithmic approach to creating code patches. Instead of relying on predefined templates, this approach leverages ML techniques, code analysis, and algorithms to generate patches automatically. Generative-based patching involves analyzing the codebase, identifying problematic areas, and generating code changes that address the detected security issues. This approach can be more flexible and adaptive, as it can handle a wider range of vulnerabilities and adapt to different programming languages and code structures.

Most of the generative-based methods use the encoder-decoder framework as the design blueprint for their models. Recently, with the reported improvement in terms of speed and performance provided by the transformer module in all areas of DL. It is not a surprise that the generative models for vulnerability repairing problems are also based on transformers, and we will dive into the details of such models in this section. Methods mentioned in this section follow the encoder-decoder scheme of the sequence-to-sequence framework and use transfer learning from code repairing task to vulnerabilities repairing task. Due to the commons in their design, we will go through them using a three-phase structure: pre-processing, pre-training and then fine-tuning for transfer learning, and patch generation.

SeqTrans

SeqTrans [31] used transfer learning to fine-tune the model that first trained on the bug repairing task to the vulnerabilities repairing task; for that reason, each task will need a separate data set. In reported experiments, the model trained on bug repairing task using the Tufano [32] dataset, and then in the fine-tuning phase, the Ponto [33] dataset is used, with both of these dataset being source code of Java language.

Before going into the details of this method, let us look at the general design of the architecture in Fig. 7.

Tokenization and Normalization Although SeqTrans does not use tree representation of the source codes, the GumTree algorithm is still used to map the AST nodes of the source and patch so that the diff context can be extracted using a commercial tool Understand. Each sample from both datasets of bug repair and vulnerability repair is represented as a list of code segment pairs

$$CP = (st_{src}, st_{dst})_1, \ldots, (st_{src}, st_{dst})_n$$

These code pairs are further fine-grained to construct the def-use chains, which are the assignment of some value to a variable containing all variable definitions from the vulnerable statement [31] turning the code pairs into. Figure 8 shows a sample of code pair input for the model, in which all global variable definitions

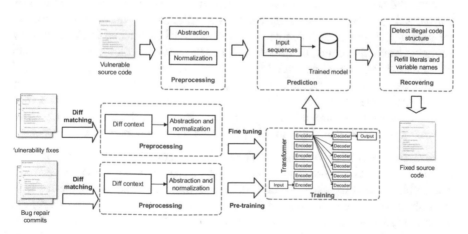

Fig. 7 Architecture of SeqTrans [31]

Fig. 8 Input of SeqTrans

```
Test.Java: source
class Foo {
    int i;
    int k;
    String test;
    public void clear(String test){
        test = " ";
    }
    private String foo(int i, int k,) {
        if(i == k) return i-k;
    }
}
                                    ⇓
Test.Java: buggy body
int i;
int k;
String test;
private String foo(int i, int k,) {
    if(i == k) return i-k;
}
```

Fig. 9 Normalized code
segment [34]

```
Test.java: source
private String foo(int i, int k) {
    if(i == 0) return "Foo!";
    if(k == 1) return 0;}
                    ⇓
Test.java: normalized source
private String foo(int var1, int var2) {
    if(var1 == num1) return "str";
    if(var2 == num2) return num1;}
```

and statements have dependencies with the vulnerability statements preserved while other statements in the same method discarded

$$CP = ((def_1, \ldots, def_n, st_{src}), (def_1, \ldots, def_n, st_{dst}))_1, \ldots,$$

$$((def_1, \ldots, def_n, st_{src}), (def_1, \ldots, def_n, st_{dst}))_n$$

After the code pairs dataset has been created, each code segment would first be normalized to reduce the vocabulary size of the dictionary, which also determines the output vectors size as it denotes the probability of each token in the dictionary being the predictions; this, in turn, would ease the models training processed: each literal and strings would be turned into $num_1, \ldots, num_n$, and $str_1, \ldots, str_2$, and variable name would be replaced with $var_1, \ldots, var_n$ as shown in Fig. 9; however, these "placeholders" will later be replaced back with their real value using mappings generated during this normalization process. At this state, the input is ready to be tokenized with Byte Pair Encoding [34] along with the dictionary of the dataset.

Pre-training and Fine-Tuning SeqTrans is designed using transformer modules as building blocks, whose details have been discussed in the previous sections. The architecture is the same for both the pre-training and fine-tuning phases with the only differences in the dataset, batch size, and number of training steps: the pre-training model is trained with a batch size of 4096 for 300k steps, and fine-tuning model is trained with a batch size of 4096 for extra 30k steps [31]. The

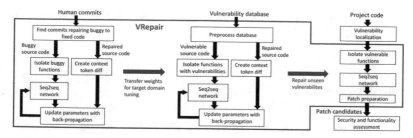

Fig. 10 The VRepair pipeline

implementation of SeqTrans is done with OpenNMT[1], and the framework offers a low code solution to configure the model architecture using configuration files, some of the main configurations used to build the model listed by the authors in [31].

- Word vector size: 512
- Attention layers: 6
- Size of hidden transformer feed-forward: 2048
- Dropout: 0.1
- Batch size: 4096
- Train steps: 300000
- Learning rate decay: 0.5
- Optimizer: Adam

VRepair

VRepair is one of the most state-of-the-art algorithms for automated vulnerability repair that leverages a Transformer-based Neural Machine Translation (NMT) [35]. VRepair's architecture is the same as SeqTrans, and the main difference is in the way VRepair performs pre-processing and source code representation. For SeqTrans, the code pairs are generated using GumTree, a syntax tree differencing tool for detecting changes between two versions of source code, and further fine-grained to extract the reference chains before being tokenized, while in VRepair, source code is handled just like natural language, and the tokenizing process is applied directly to the vulnerable code segments and their respective patches with additional special tokens in both the buggy code segments and patches.

Figure 10 shows both the pre-training and fine-tuning process of VRepair, in which we can see the similarity with SeqTrans [31] apart from the preprocessing step. With VRepair, the additional tokens serve the function of localizing the buggy segments in the input code and reduce the difficulty of the generative task by setting up the model only to learn to generate the modified segments instead. Moreover, representing multiple changes to a function, which in turn allows vulnerabilities

---

[1] https://opennmt.net/

fixes across multiple lines within a single code block, provides robustness to the existing models [29, 36, 37].

3 Our Proposal: BERTVRepair

We argue that using embeddings created by CodeBERT would be beneficial for vulnerability repair due to the effective use of large-scale embeddings for models of downstream tasks with low resources in many NLP problems. With the availability of large-scale code language models trained on large datasets on code generation tasks such as code repairing and/or masked token prediction, we can leverage them as embeddings for models of vulnerability repairing that have limited datasets, with the premise that the upstream and downstream tasks are similar in terms of objectives and data. On the similarity between data, we know vulnerability is a type of bug that can be the target of security exploitation, which poses a much more difficult challenge to identifying and generating patches manually.

We proposed a new approach, titled BERTVRepair (BERT model for Vulnerability Repair), that adopts CodeBERT for vulnerability code repair. The approach includes code preprocessing, tokenization, and code embedding extraction, as shown in Fig. 11.

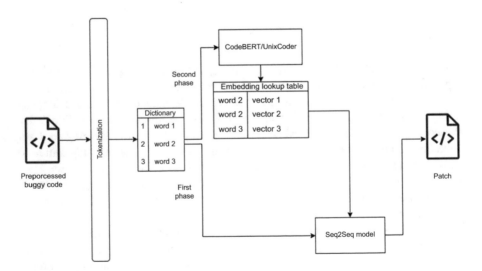

Fig. 11 Design of our pipeline

3.1 Code Preprocessing and Tokenization

We treat source code along with its patch as plain texts shown in Fig. 12 and tokenize them using a byte-pair encoding algorithm. Before the tokenization process, we have an extra preprocessing step that adds two special tokens to the original dataset, which are the input sequence and target sequence. This processing step is done before we extract the embeddings from data using programming language models.

- In the input sequence shown in Fig. 13, $< StarLoc >$ and $< EndLoc >$ will be added to the location identified as vulnerable, and there is also an additional indicator "CWE-xxx," which specifies the type of vulnerability.
- For the target sequence shown in Fig. 14, we use two new unique tokens $< ModStart >$ and $< ModEnd >$ and change the target sequence to only contain the modifications needed. There are three types of modifications to be made to the input to create a patch, which is shown in Fig. 15, leading to three types of format of the target sequence, each indicating a type of modification made to the input sequence.

Hypothetical buggy source code:

```
int getVal(int *array, int len, int index) {
    if (index < len)
    {
        return array[index];
    } else {
        return index;
    }
}
```

Hypothetical repaired function:

```
int getVal(int *array, int len, int index) {
    if (index < len && index >= 0)
    {
        return array[index];
    } else {
        return -1;
    }
}
```

(a)

(b)

Fig. 12 An example of buggy code and its patch. (**a**) An example of buggy code. (**b**) An example of patch

```
CWE-119 int getVal ( int * array, int len, int index)
{ <StartLoc> if (index < len) <EndLoc> { return
array [ index ] ; } else { return index ; } }
```

Fig. 13 An example of input sequence

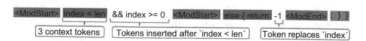

Fig. 14 An example of output sequence

Fig. 15 Syntax for three
types of modification

Type	Syntax
Add	<ModStart> *context new*
Delete	<ModStart> *context* <ModEnd> *context*
Replace	<ModStart> *context new* <ModEnd> *context*

3.2 Code Embedding Extraction

The embeddings extracted from language models such as CodeBERT are stored as a lookup table of the vocabulary of the corpus; therefore, we are required first to extract the vocabulary of words that exist in the corpus, which should include the newly added tokens. Each word in the vocabulary is represented by a vector shown in Fig. 11, which has a size of 768 and represents the semantic representation learned by the pretraining tasks of programming language models.

In this process, we use two different large language models to extract embeddings from; one is CodeBERT [26], and the other is Unixcoder [28]; both of these are trained on a large dataset of programming languages including the ones in our vulnerability dataset. The main difference between these two pre-trained is the type of input on which they trained; the information that CodeBERT used to train includes both natural language and programming language, while Unixcoder is trained on programming language only. This difference stems from the fact that they aim at optimizing their performance on different tasks; the first one emphasizes code summarization, while the latter is better at autoregressive tasks such as code completion.

The extracted embeddings representing the entire vocabulary in the corpus are stored as a lookup table, which will later be used as input during the training process of the downstream translation model of vulnerability repairing. One thing to note here is that the programming language models used in our experiments have their tokenizers and dictionaries. Therefore, the input tokenized by OpenNMT's tokenizer might further be tokenized in these language models, which leads the output tensors to have shape nx768, in which n is the number of tokens created from the input token. For example, the token *word*1 might further be tokenized into *subword*1 and *subword*2, making the output tensor of the language models have the size of 2x768. To create an embedding of size 1x768 representing one single token in our dictionary, we use two methods to aggregate the language models' output tensors. First, we take the mean of the output tensor along the second dimension. The code snippet of this method is shown below, in which the `tokenizer` is the tokenizer used by the programming language model to map the `vocab` in the vulnerability dataset into indexes respective to the dictionary of the programming language models. These indexes are then fed into the language models to get the output tensor whose mean is taken along the second dimension.

Listing 1.1 Extracting the embeddings using mean

```
code_tokens = tokenizer.tokenize(vocab)
tokens_ids = tokenizer.convert_tokens_to_ids(code_tokens)
context_embeddings = model(torch.tensor(tokens_ids)[None,:])[0]
context_embeddings = torch.mean(context_embeddings,dim=1).ravel()
vul_embs[idx,:] = context_embeddings
```

Second, whenever we feed a token in our dictionary into the language models, we concatenate it with a special token named [cls], which intuitively represents the semantic information of the entire tokens. By using this method, we only need to use the first row of the language model output to act as the embedding. The code snippet of this method resembles the first method with the only difference in the additional [cls] token used as embedding.

Listing 1.2 Embeddings with the concatenated token

```
code_tokens = tokenizer.tokenize(vocab)
tokens = [tokenizer.cls_token]+code_tokens
tokens_ids = tokenizer.convert_tokens_to_ids(tokens)
context_embeddings = model(torch.tensor(tokens_ids)[None,:])
    [0][0,0]
vul_embs[idx,:] = context_embeddings
```

4 Experiments

The experiment design is as follows. First, we replicate the experiments reported by the authors of VRepair on a downscaled network due to our limited computing resources [38]. The network used in these experiments is the transformer-based neural translation network built using the OpenNMT-py framework. Second, we use the embeddings created from programming language models as input to the VRepair architecture and compared the result of this pipeline with the previous one.

4.1 Dataset

We used the existing dataset provided by VRepair, which are Big-Vul [39] and CVE-fixes [40], for training the neural translation network [35]. The big-Vul dataset was created by crawling CVE databases and extracting vulnerability-related information such as CWE ID and CVE ID. Big-Vul contains 3754 different vulnerabilities across 348 projects categorized into 91 different CWE IDs, with a time frame spanning from 2002 to 2019. CVEfixes dataset is collected in a way similar to the Big-Vul dataset. This dataset contains 5365 vulnerabilities across 1754 projects categorized into 180 different CWE IDs, with a time frame spanning from 1999 to 2021. In our research, we only conducted the experiments on Big-vul to narrow down the scope of experiments in this thesis and then left the experiments on a more diverse dataset in future works.

4.2 Model Training

To train and validate our experiments, we split the datasets into training data, validation data, and test data with 70% for training, 10% for validation, and 20% for testing. In the Big-vul dataset, we will have 2228 samples as training data, 318 samples as validation data, and 636 samples as testing data.

4.3 Evaluation Metrics

OpenNMT-py framework [41] reports two measures, the perplexity (PPL) and the accuracy during training and validation. PPL is a measure of how uncertain the network is that the predicted outcome is correct. Low PPL means low uncertainty, while high PPL means high uncertainty. Luong et al. report that the translation quality is connected to the PPL [42], where they claim that if a model has a low PPL, its translation will be of higher quality. The PPL is defined in Eq. 1, in which the network's uncertainty of the generated document D is measured by the joint probability of all words in that document, normalized by the number of words N_d in the document:

$$\text{Perplexity(D)} = \exp\left(-\frac{\sum_{d=1}^{|D|} \log P(w_d)}{\sum_{d=1}^{|D|} N_d}\right) \tag{1}$$

Another metric, accuracy, is calculated by:

$$\text{Accuracy}(Y, \hat{Y}) = 100 * \frac{\text{Number of correct token in } \hat{Y}}{\text{Number of token in } Y} \tag{2}$$

where $\hat{Y}$ is the predicted output sequence and Y is the target sequence. The way accuracy is calculated makes it a metric that does not give much insight into the results and the model's performance. The reason is that even if all the tokens present in the target sequence, Y, are present in the predicted sequence $\hat{Y}$, the positions of each token can be different from the target sequence, and the accuracy will still be 100%.

BLEU score [43] is a metric that is used specifically for evaluating the quality of text in the machine translation problem, which is based on calculating the predictions' precision on an n-length subsequence of the prediction sequence. The precision metric in the context of machine translation is the number of words in the predicted tokens that also appear in the target sequence. The calculation of the BLEU score is done using the following Eq. 3, in which N is the length of the subsequence in the predicted sequence:

$$\text{BLEU} = e^{\frac{1}{N}\sum_{n=1}^{N} P_n} \tag{3}$$

4.4 Environment

All of our experiments are conducted on a machine with 32G of RAM and one NVIDIA Quadro RTX 6000 24GB GDDR6. To train, predict, and create the vocabularies for both embedding extraction along our translation model, we use the OpenNMT-py framework [41]. It is a neural machine translation framework built on top of Pytorch [44]. The programming language models used in our experiments are all accessible through the Hugging Face hub and implemented with the Transformers framework [45].

5 Result

Table 1 shows the results of our replicating experiments with VRepair on a downscale version of the Transformer architecture. Table 2 shows a complete set of our hyperparameters used in these experiments.

We ran multiple experiments trying our different configurations of some of the hyperparameters, which were also experiments in [38], to understand better the architecture performance when training without using the embeddings from CodeBERT [26] and UnixCoder [28]. We report the model performance using token-level accuracy, perplexity, and training time in Table 3 with the best configuration highlighted, which has a token-level accuracy of 50.229%. However, the high perplexity value in these results indicates that the models are not certain in their predictions.

Table 3 shows the pipeline that leverages the embeddings extracted from CodeBERT and UnixCoder as input for the downstream task. However, in these experiments, we choose only one set of hyperparameters from the configurations in

Table 1 Experiments replicating the VRepair pipeline

Learning rate	Hidden size	Sequence length	Accuracy (%)	Perplexity	Training time (s)
0.0005	256	2000	49.948	662.939	14,139
0.0005	256	5000	48.418	266.025	16,035
0.0005	512	2000	49.9271	156.912	20,589
0.0005	512	5000	47.3147	420.41	25,231
0.0005	1024	2000	36.2927	56.8428	39,582
0.0005	1024	5000	35.127	391.112	69,404
0.0001	256	2000	49.6669	2359.81	26,604
0.0001	256	5000	48.1266	9126.37	26,552
0.0001	**512**	**2000**	**50.229**	**527.823**	**24,343**
0.0001	512	5000	49.49	727.988	27,938
0.0001	1024	2000	49.3443	172.811	37,475
0.0001	1024	5000	49.6774	212.39	37,279

Bold values shows the best accuracy

Table 2 Complete set of
hyperparameters used in our
models built by OpenNMT-py

Hyperparameter	Value
src _vocab _size	2000
tgt _vocab _size	2000
src _seq _length	Varied
tgt _seq _length	100
batch _size	4
valid _batch _size	1
train _steps	Varied
valid _steps	Varied
save _checkpoint _steps	valid _steps
early _stopping	2
early _stopping _criteria	accuracy
keep _checkpoint	3
optim	adam
learning _rate	Varied
learning _rate _decay	0.9
label _smoothing	0.1
param _init	0
param _init _glorot	true
encoder _type	transformer
decoder _type	transformer
enc _layers	3
dec _layers	3
heads	4
rnn _size	Varied
word _vec _size	rnn _size
transformer _ff	1024
dropout	0.1
attention _dropout	0.1
copy _attn	true
position _encoding	true

the first phase, in which the learning rate is set to 0.0005, the hidden size is 768, and the sequence length is 2000. The reason behind this is that we just want to clarify the effect of using embeddings on the downstream model, and using the same hyperparameters helps us correctly attribute any improvement in terms of performance to the use of embeddings. Along with that, as mentioned in the earlier section, we also chose to reduce the training iteration from 100000 in the previous experiments to 20000 with the same justification mentioned.

As mentioned in Sect. 3.2, we fed each word in the vocabulary into the programming language model to get the representation of the word; however, each of these models has its own input specification, leading to the differences in output. The experiments denoted with postfix (1) using the embeddings extracted from the first method, which is aggregation along the second dimension of the language models

Table 3 Experiments with embeddings as input

Embedding	Accuracy (%)	PPL	Training time (s)	EM (out of 316)	BLEU score
Unixcoder (1)	41.7881	128.627	15,964	12	23.73
CodeBERT (1)	45.6078	654.327	21,596	17	27.123
CodeBERT (2)	**46.3884**	**890.801**	**22,175**	**23**	**30.128**
None	44.9833	122.637	3932	18	24.83

Bold values shows the best results

output tensor, and the one with postfix (2) is using the [*cls*] token as embedding. Similar to the first phase of our experiment, results in our second phase are also reported on token-level accuracy, perplexity, and training time. In addition, we also report the models' performance on their capability to generate the perfect patches that entirely match the samples' labels. The results show that the use of embeddings extracted from CodeBERT by the latter method does help improve the performance slightly.

The code snippet below is an example of the perfect patches generated from the models using samples from the validation dataset, which has the format described in Sect. 3.1. In this specific example, the predict sequence indicates that the generated patch will insert `memset` between `stride )` ; and `( input` , at every place in the original code that has such pattern

Listing 1.3 Sample output
```
<S2SV_ModStart> stride ) ; memset <S2SV_ModEnd> ( input ,
```

Results from both of these experiments (Tables 1 and 3) show that the use of pre-trained embeddings does only marginal improvement compared to training the models from scratch in terms of models' performance and training time. We argue that the similarity between code repairing and vulnerability repairing tasks is not close enough for the embeddings to be used as a medium for transferring information to improve the training process of the vulnerability repairing model. The experiments in our second phase that use embeddings only show a slight increase in BLEU score and exact match when compared to the vanilla pipeline, although the BLEU score reaching 30 in Table 3 is considered to be understandable according to [46]. The high perplexity in the results of both phases of the experiments shows that the models are not certain in their predictions, which means the probability of the correctly predicted token is not much larger than others.

6   Conclusions

Generative-based methods in code repair research leverage the recent development of ML due to the large and easily accessible amount of dataset, i.e., code, software defects, and documentation [47, 48], to archive significant improvement in prediction accuracy and model quality. While vulnerability in source code is also a type of bug, it is more difficult to detect and patch due to the endeavor to exploit the application for security errors taking more time. This led to the fact that the available labeled dataset of vulnerability source code is sparse compared to the generic bugs, which makes the application of deep networks in the problem of vulnerability repairing become limited. The literature review has shown that most of the noticeable research on code repairing or vulnerability repairing recently focused on learning the patterns in the dataset from the perspective of natural language in which the input is either represented as lists of tokens or an abstract syntax tree.

We attempted to improve the performance of a state-of-the-art model VRepair, in which a transformer-based model is trained to generate vulnerability code patches. We proposed BERTVRepair, a model that leverages the embeddings extracted from CodeBERT and UnixCoder to serve as a medium for transferring knowledge learning from a larger dataset to a vulnerability-repairing task. However, it seems that the code embeddings do not offer a significant improvement on the task, and while conducting this research, we also find out that researchers have also conducted the same experiments [49] on the tasks of vulnerability detections and archived the same analysis as our experiments.

Our work can be used as justification that the task of vulnerability repairing and code understanding tasks do not have close proximity. However, due to the complex nature of the vulnerability, we can try to lower the tasks' proximity by focusing on one type of vulnerability most likely to resemble a code understanding task. Another approach can also be considered, which is doing feature engineering on the vulnerability dataset using traditional machine learning methods, and the justification is that the complex nature of vulnerability can be further explored through the use of code representation like dataflow suggested in [50].

References

1. Nguyen Duc, A., Chirumamilla, A.: Identifying security risks of digital transformation - an engineering perspective. In: Pappas, I.O., et al. (eds.) Digital Transformation for a Sustainable Society in the 21st Century, Cham, pp. 677–688 (2019)
2. Aalvik, H., et al.: Establishing a security champion in agile software teams: a systematic literature review. In: Arai, K. (ed.) Advances in Information and Communication, Cham, pp. 796–810 (2023)
3. McGraw, G., Potter, B.: Software security testing. IEEE Secur. Privacy **2**(5), 81–85 (2004). Number: 5
4. Le, T.H.M., Chen, H., Babar, M.A.: A survey on data-driven soft-ware vulnerability assessment and prioritization. ACM Comput. Surv. **55**(5), 100:1–100:39 (2022)
5. Wysopal, C.: Art of Software Security Testing, The: Identifying Software Security Flaws: Identifying Software Security Flaws, 1st edn., 298 pp. Addison-Wesley Professional, Upper Saddle River (2006)
6. Goues, C.L., Pradel, M., Roychoudhury, A.: Automated program repair. Commun. ACM **62**(12), 56–65 (2019)
7. Li, Y., Wang, S., Nguyen, T.N.: DEAR: a novel deep learning-based approach for automated program repair. In: Proceedings of the 44th International Conference on Software Engineering, New York, July 5, pp. 511–523 (2022)

8. Fu, M., et al.: VulRepair: a t5-based automated software vulnerability repair. In: Proceedings of the 30th ACM Joint European Software Engineering Conference and Symposium on the Foundations of Software Engineering, New York, November 9, pp. 935–947 (2022)

9. Saha, R.K., et al.: Elixir: effective object-oriented program repair. In: 2017 32nd IEEE/ACM International Conference on Automated Software Engineering (ASE), pp. 648–659 (2017)

10. Tian, H., et al.: Evaluating representation learning of code changes for predicting patch correctness in program repair. In: Proceedings of the 35th IEEE/ACM International Conference on Automated Software Engineering, New York, Jan. 27, pp. 981–992 (2021)

11. Zhang, S., et al.: Deep learning based recommender system: a survey and new perspectives. ACM Comput. Surv. **52**(1), 1–38 (2020)

12. Vasic, M., et al.: Neural program repair by jointly learning to localize and repair, Apr. 2 (2019). https://doi.org/10.48550/arXiv.1904.01720. arXiv: 1904.01720[cs, stat]. [Online]. Available: http://arxiv.org/abs/1904. 01720 (visited on 05/31/2023)

13. Schramm, L.: Improving performance of automatic program repair using learned heuristics. In: Proceedings of the 2017 11th Joint Meeting on Foundations of Software Engineering, New York, Aug. 21, pp. 1071–1073 (2017)

14. Mashhadi, E., Hemmati, H.: Applying CodeBERT for automated program repair of java simple bugs. In: 2021 IEEE/ACM 18th International Conference on Mining Software Repositories (MSR), pp. 505–509 (2021)

15. Schuster, M., Paliwal, K.K.: Bidirectional recurrent neural networks. IEEE Trans. Signal Proces. **45**(11), 2673–2681 (1997)

16. Hochreiter, S.: The vanishing gradient problem during learning recurrent neural nets and problem solutions. Int. J. Uncertainty Fuzziness Knowledge Based Syst. **6**(02), 107–116 (1998)

17. Cho, K., et al.: Learning phrase representations using RNN encoder–decoder for statistical machine translation. In: Proceedings of the 2014 Conference on Empirical Methods in Natural Language Processing (EMNLP), Doha, pp. 1724–1734 (2014)

18. Hochreiter, S., Schmidhuber, J.: Long short-term memory. Neural Comput. **9**(8), 1735–1780 (1997)

19. Vaswani, A., et al.: Attention is all you need. Adv. Neural Inf. Proces. Syst. **30**, 5998–6008 (2017)

20. Liu, Y., et al.: A survey of visual transformers. IEEE Trans. Neural Networks Learn. Syst., 1–21 (2023)

21. Devlin, J., et al.: BERT: pre-training of deep bidirectional transformers for language understanding (2018). arXiv preprint. arXiv:1810.04805

22. Radford, A., et al.: Language models are unsupervised multitask learners. OpenAI blog **1**(8), 9 (2019)

23. Dai, Z., et al.: Transformer-XL: attentive language models beyond a fixed-length context (2019). arXiv preprint. arXiv:1901.02860

24. Dwivedi, S.K., Singh, V.: Research and reviews in question answering system. Proc. Technol. **10**, 417–424 (2013)

25. MacCartney, B.: Natural Language Inference. Stanford University, Stanford (2009)

26. Feng, Z., et al.: CodeBERT: a pre-trained model for programming and natural languages (2020). arXiv preprint. arXiv:2002.08155

27. Liu, Y., et al.: RoBERTa: a robustly optimized BERT pretraining approach, Jul. 26, 2019. https://doi.org/10.48550/arXiv.1907.11692. arXiv: 1907.11692[cs]. [Online]. Available: http://arxiv.org/abs/1907.11692 (visited on 11/19/2023)

28. Guo, D., et al.: UniXcoder: unified cross-modal pre-training for code representation (2022). arXiv preprint. arXiv:2203.03850

29. Ma, S., et al.: VuRLE: automatic vulnerability detection and repair by learning from examples. In: Foley, S.N., Gollmann, D., Snekkenes, E. (eds.) Computer Security – ESORICS 2017, vol. 10493, pp. 229–246 (2017)

30. Church, K.W.: Word2vec. Nat. Lang. Eng. **23**(1), 155–162 (2017)

31. Chi, J., et al.: SeqTrans: automatic vulnerability fix via sequence to sequence learning. IEEE Trans. Software Eng. **49**, 564–585 (2020)

32. Tufano, M., et al.: An empirical investigation into learning bug-fixing patches in the wild via neural machine translation. In: 2018 33rd IEEE/ACM International Conference on Automated Software Engineering (ASE), New York, pp. 832–837 (2018)
33. Ponta, S.E., et al.: A manually-curated dataset of fixes to vulnerabilities of open-source software. In: Proceedings of the 16th International Conference on Mining Software Repositories, Montreal, Quebec, pp. 383–387 (2019)
34. Sennrich, R., Haddow, B., Birch, A.: Neural machine translation of rare words with subword units. In: Proceedings of the 54th Annual Meeting of the Association for Computational Linguistics (Volume 1: Long Papers), Berlin, pp. 1715–1725 (2016)
35. Chen, Z., Kommrusch, S., Monperrus, M.: Neural transfer learning for repairing security vulnerabilities in C code. arXiv:2104.08308 [cs] (2022)
36. Chen, Z., Kommrusch, S., Monperrus, M.: Neural transfer learning for repairing security vulnerabilities in C code. IEEE Trans. Software Eng. **49**(1), 147–165 (2023)
37. Guo, J., et al.: A deep look into neural ranking models for information retrieval. Inf. Process. Manage. **57**(6), 102067 (2020)
38. Chen, Z., Kommrusch, S., Tufano, M., Pouchet, L.-N., Poshyvanyk, D., Monperrus, M.: SequenceR: sequence-to-sequence learning for end-to-end program repair. IEEE Trans. Software Eng. **47**(9), 1943–1959 (2021). https://doi.org/10.1109/TSE.2019.2940179
39. Fan, J., et al.: A c/c++ code vulnerability dataset with code changes and cve summaries. In: Proceedings of the 17th International Conference on Mining Software Repositories, Seoul, pp. 508–512 (2020)
40. Bhandari, G., Naseer, A., Moonen, L.: CVEfixes: automated collection of vulnerabilities and their fixes from open-source software. In: Proceedings of the 17th International Conference on Predictive Models and Data Analytics in Software Engineering (2021)
41. Klein, G., et al.: OpenNMT: open-source toolkit for neural machine translation (2017). arXiv preprint. arXiv:1701.02810
42. Luong, T., et al.: Addressing the rare word problem in neural machine translation. In: Proceedings of the 53rd Annual Meeting of the Association for Computational Linguistics and the 7th International Joint Conference on Natural Language Processing, Beijing, pp. 11–19 (2015)
43. Blagec, K., et al.: A global analysis of metrics used for measuring performance in natural language processing (2022). arXiv: 2204.11574
44. Paszke, A., et al.: Pytorch: an imperative style, high-performance deep learn-ing library (2019). arXiv: 1912.01703 [cs.LG]
45. Wolf, T., et al.: Transformers: state-of-the-art natural language processing. In: Proceedings of the 2020 Conference on Empirical Methods in Natural Language Processing: System Demonstrations, pp. 38–45 (2020)
46. Evaluating models. https://cloud.google.com/translate/automl/docs/evaluate. Accessed 06 June 2023
47. Chen, Z., et al.: Sequencer: Sequence-to-sequence learning for end-to-end program repair. IEEE Trans. Software Eng. **47**(09), 1943–1959 (2021)
48. Li, Z., et al.: SySeVR: a framework for using deep learning to detect software vulnerabilities. IEEE Trans. Dependable Secure Comput. **19**, 1–1 (2021)
49. Choi, Y., et al.: Learning sequential and structural information for source code summarization. In: Findings of the Association for Computational Linguistics: ACL-IJCNLP 2021, pp. 2842–2851 (2021)
50. Guo, D., et al.: GraphCodeBERT: pre-training code representations with data flow (2020). arXiv preprint. arXiv:2009.08366

ChatGPT as a Full-Stack Web Developer

Väinö Liukko (iD)**, Anna Knappe** (iD)**, Tatu Anttila, Jyri Hakala, Juulia Ketola, Daniel Lahtinen, Timo Poranen** (iD)**, Topi-Matti Ritala, Manu Setälä, Heikki Hämäläinen, and Pekka Abrahamsson** (iD)

Abstract The arrival of ChatGPT has also generated significant interest in the field of software engineering. Little is empirically known about the capabilities of ChatGPT to actually implement a complete system rather than a few code snippets. This chapter reports the firsthand experiences from a graduate-level student project where a real-life software platform for financial sector was implemented from scratch by using ChatGPT for all possible software engineering tasks. The resulting code was reviewed by a seasoned software engineering professional. The static code analysis was performed by using commercial software. The main conclusions drawn are as follows: (1) these findings demonstrate the potential for ChatGPT to be integrated into the software engineering workflow; (2) it can be used for creating a base for new components and for dividing coding tasks into smaller pieces; (3) noticeable enhancements in GPT-4, compared to GPT-3.5, indicate superior working memory and the ability to continue incomplete responses, thereby leading to more coherent and less repetitive dialogues; and (4) ChatGPT produced code that did not include any major errors but requires efficient prompting to be effective.

Keywords AI assisted · Software development · Software engineering · AI programming · ChatGPT · Large language models · Artificial intelligence · Full-stack application

V. Liukko · A. Knappe · T. Anttila · J. Hakala · J. Ketola · D. Lahtinen · T. Poranen (✉) ·
T.-M. Ritala · P. Abrahamsson
Tampere University, Tampere, Finland
e-mail: vaino.liukko@tuni.fi; anna.knappe@tuni.fi; tatu.anttila@tuni.fi; jyri.hakala@tuni.fi;
juulia.ketola@tuni.fi; daniel.h.lahtinen@tuni.fi; timo.poranen@tuni.fi; topi-matti.ritala@tuni.fi;
pekka.abrahamsson@tuni.fi

M. Setälä · H. Hämäläinen
Solita Ltd., Tampere, Finland
e-mail: manu.setala@solita.fi; heikki.hamalainen@solita.fi

1   Introduction

The introduction of ChatGPT into the landscape of technology has generated a notable amount of disruption, especially within the field of software engineering. However, despite this growing interest, empirical knowledge about its actual capabilities remains limited. This lack of comprehensive understanding is particularly evident when considering the potential of these tools to design and implement holistic systems as opposed to merely generating discrete fragments of code. There exists a significant difference between crafting isolated code snippets and deploying a fully realized software solution, a distinction that is yet to be thoroughly explored in the context of ChatGPT.

This article describes a student software project that was created to explore the use of artificial intelligence (AI) in software development. The main goal of the project was to investigate the effectiveness of ChatGPT in practice.

Overall, this project contributes to the field of AI-assisted software development by providing valuable experience of using ChatGPT as tool in software development. The remainder of this article provides related research in Sect. 2. A detailed description of the project and the research design is in Sect. 3. Results are provided in Sect. 4. Section 5 features a professional evaluation of the software produced. Discussion is found in Sect. 6, and Conclusions are presented in Sect. 7.

2   AI-Assisted Software Development

Artificial intelligence (AI) is a branch of computer science that focuses on creating intelligent machines that can perform tasks that typically require human intelligence, such as understanding natural language, recognizing patterns, making decisions, and solving problems.

One type of AI tool that has gained significant attention in recent years is the large language model (LLM) like OpenAI's GPT-4 [24]. LLM is AI model that is trained on massive amounts of data to generate humanlike text output. GPT-4 uses transformer-style model to predict the content and structure of text based on an input, usually text as well. This can be used in a wide range of natural language processing tasks, such as language translation, text summarization, and answering questions.

ChatGPT has provided a chatbot interface for interacting with OpenAI's GPT-models [4]. This has made the capabilities of LLMs more widely known, which in turn has sparked the research around use cases for this technology. Current research include studies related to prompt patters [36], human-bot collaborative architecting [1], and using ChatGPT for programming numerical methods [16]. Treude [33] has developed a prototype to compare different GPT model solutions, and Dong and others [8] developed a self-collaboration code generation framework. Surameery and Shakor [31] have applied ChatGPT to solve programming bugs. A systematic literature review on using LLMs in software engineering is provided by Hou and others [12].

There are some recent and somewhat similar research approaches that we report in our work. Monteiro and others [21] conducted an experiment where three software developers used ChatGPT to implement a Web-based application using mainstream software architectures and technologies. Waseem and others [35] also investigated the utilization of ChatGPT in the software development process within a student team context.

3 Research Design

In this section, we introduce the project background, project implementation and phases, development environment, development process, documentation, and implemented features.

3.1 Project Background

Solita Ltd. [27] is a large software consultancy company in the Nordic countries. Solita collaborates with universities by inventing exercise topics and supervising student exercises. As part of a university project work course, they challenged the student team to undertake an AI-assisted, large-scale project.

Project topic was chosen from well-defined public procurement requests on the Hilma portal [11], a Web site for procurement in the Finnish public sector. It was agreed in the project that the specifications would not be directly used as input material for AI, but the prompts given to AI were written mostly by the team themselves. However, the number of fields in the user interface was kept the same as in the original request, etc.

The selected project, Valvontatyöpöytö (VTP), is a platform for financial supervision, designed to support the operations of an organization. The intended user group for the VTP is financial professionals, including supervisors, managers, and analysts.

3.2 Project Implementation and Phases

The VTP project [34] was proposed in the end of December 2022. The project was then accepted by a seven member team. The project started at the end of January 2023. The team consists of three masters-level students and four bachelor-level students of computer science or information technology. None of the team members

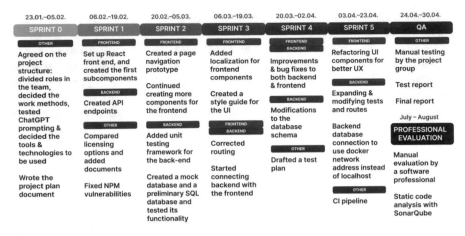

Fig. 1 Project phases and implemented features per sprint

had earlier experience on AI-assisted software development. General overview of the course's practices and schedule is described by Sten and others [30].

Project phases, produced documents, and the features implemented in each sprint are depicted in Fig. 1. Throughout the project, many students were also engaged with other assignments and courses. Given the limited hours that students could allocate each week, 2-week sprints were adopted. The initial sprint, labeled Sprint 0, was designated for project planning and setting up the development environment. This was followed by four 2-week implementation sprints. The final implementation sprint was extended to 3 weeks, concluding the project course with a 1-week QA sprint. The primary goal of the QA sprint was to document the software's state for a course report. The professional evaluation of the code produced by the team was conducted separately during the writing of this article.

3.3 Development Environment

The development environment was built in a step-by-step manner by consulting ChatGPT when making decisions on suitable technologies. The team provided ChatGPT prompts explaining what they were currently trying to accomplish, and it replied with multiple recommendations. The team then selectively picked from the recommendations based on their own preferences and previous experience. The effect of picking technologies with such a process is twofold. Firstly, ChatGPT is more likely to recommend technologies it has knowledge of. Secondly, it makes the teams' efforts in reviewing the generated code easier.

Table 1 lists technologies used in the project with the corresponding selection criteria. As seen in Table 1, there are exceptions on which ChatGPT was not consulted at all. These include using ChatGPT as the sole AI assistant and

Table 1 Technical implementation environment and technology selection criteria

Item	Description	Selection criteria
Language	JavaScript [14]	Recommended by ChatGPT
Language	HTML and CSS [6]	Recommended by ChatGPT
Language	Shell [2]	Developer decided
Containerization	Docker [7]	Customer requirement
Database	MySQL [22]	Recommended by ChatGPT
AI assistant	ChatGPT 3.5 and 4.0 [4]	Customer requirement
Front-end framework	React [25]	Recommended by ChatGPT
Back-end framework	Node.JS [23] and Express [9]	Recommended by ChatGPT
Test framework	Mocha [20] and Chai [3]	Recommended by ChatGPT
Version control system	GitHub [34]	Team decided
Licence	MIT [19]	Recommended by ChatGPT

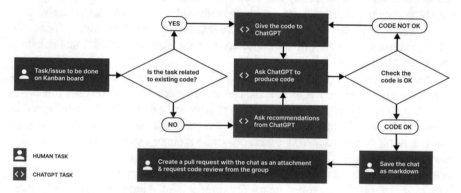

Fig. 2 Daily process of working with ChatGPT

containerization of the produced application, both of which were requirements laid out by the customer. The team decided to use GitHub as their version control system to enable easy collaboration. The only exception in languages used in the project comes from a Bash script used by the backend container to wait for the database to fully initialize before trying to establish a connection.

3.4 Development Process

The team's process of working with ChatGPT is illustrated in Fig. 2. When a task was related to existing code, the assigned team member would provide the relevant code to ChatGPT and request it to generate a solution. If the task was not related to existing code, the team member would first ask the ChatGPT for recommendations before requesting it to produce the code. Once ChatGPT generated the code, the team member would review it for correctness. If the code was deemed satisfactory, the team member would add it to the code base, save the chat session as a Markdown [10] file, and create a pull request with the chat as an attachment. If the code was not acceptable, the team member would provide the problematic code back to ChatGPT and repeat the process, iterating until a satisfactory solution was achieved or asking for a new recommendation for another approach.

In the team's experience with the described workflow, ChatGPT's efficacy varied depending on the nature of the task at hand. While the process appears quite linear and systematic when documented in this manner, it often felt less straightforward in practice, involving considerable trial and error. This experience suggests that a more experienced team might have navigated these challenges more efficiently, potentially avoiding some of the iterative cycles encountered. Challenges arose, for instance, when attempting to convey concepts that were inherently visual or spatial. In such scenarios, the limitations of a text-based interface became evident. Ideas that might be effortlessly communicated through diagrams or images proved cumbersome and, at times, inefficient to describe solely with words. Similarly, tasks that necessitated only minor code adjustments could have been more efficiently addressed manually, rather than submitting the code back to ChatGPT and detailing the required modifications.

The project team logged their weekly working hours according to different categories (Documentation, Requirements, Design, Implementation, Testing, Meetings, Studying, Other, Lectures). In the end, the project had a total of 793 hours logged as shown in Table 2. Throughout the project, the project team met with the customer twice a week to ensure quality assurance and planning were on track. This is the reason why meetings (265 hours, 33%) have such a considerable part in the logged hours. The implementation took 195 hours (25%) and studying 131 hours (17%). The logged time also included university course-related subjects, such as lectures and other studying, which did not relate directly to the implementation of the project.

Table 2 Project's working hours and activities from sprints 0 to QA during time period 23.1.2023–30.4.2023

	S0	S1	S2	S3	S4	S5	QA	Total
Doc.	13.5	0.0	2.0	7.0	5.8	10.8	8.0	47.1(6%)
Req.	8.0	2.0	1.0	1.0	2.0	0.0	0.0	14.0(2%)
Des.	16.0	9.7	7.0	7.5	1.0	0.5	4.0	45.7(6%)
Impl.	0.0	22.2	38.5	37.0	33.6	64.4	0.0	195.7(25%)
Test.	0.0	2.8	10.5	3.5	5.2	8.2	0.5	30.7(4%)
Meet.	39.0	36.2	35.0	44.5	43.2	57.2	10.2	265.3(33%)
Stud.	18.5	35.0	17.2	29.5	16.0	15.0	0.0	131.2(17%)
Other	1.0	2.2	0.5	4.4	7.0	3.1	0.1	18.3(2%)
Lect.	8.5	4.5	2.0	2.2	24.2	4.0	0.0	45.4(6%)
Total	104.5	114.6	113.7	136.6	138.0	163.2	22.8	793.4(100%)

3.5 Documentation

ChatGPT assisted in generating the project's main documentation, which included the project plan (during the Sprint 0), test plan (Sprint 4), test report (QA sprint), and final report (QA Sprint). The course lecturers had provided a structured table of contents for the documents and specific guidelines for each section. ChatGPT elaborated on these guidelines, as they were given to it. Although some content needed adjustments, especially where personal data was concerned, ChatGPT efficiently populated many sections of the reports.

ChatGPT was used, for instance, when drafting the test plan. It provided numerous suggestions, many of which were incorporated into the document, although some were deemed unnecessary for the project's scope. Additionally, certain sections of the test report were generated with the assistance of ChatGPT. This was achieved by inputting lines of code containing tests from the repository and prompting ChatGPT to generate text for the test report, accurately detailing the testing methods employed.

In addition to the main project documents, a style guide for the user interface was created during the Sprint 3. The style guide was crafted using ChatGPT's GPT-3.5 version. The model was prompted to design a color palette, typography, and other visual elements appropriate for an application within the financial sector. This guide was documented as an HTML page with CSS, and it encompassed specific CSS classes designed for select components in the UI component library. With the introduction of ChatGPT's GPT-4 version, the style guide was redeveloped to compare the outputs of the two models. The subsequent version became the primary reference for UI development, with ChatGPT being prompted using relevant sections of the style guide during the development of the UI library.

3.6 Implemented Features

Based on ChatGPT's suggestion, we began by setting up the foundation for our React JavaScript project. Implemented features per sprints are shown in Fig. 1. Following the wireframes in the original procurement requests, we commenced implementing the Inspection Information page shown in Fig. 3. We adopted a component-by-component approach to building the application, and once the first frontend components were completed, we proceeded to develop the backend and database infrastructure.

To better comprehend the application's functionality, we utilized the wireframe images to create a prototype. In our development process, we proceeded to implement a new view for the application, the Inspection Plan page. Additionally, we created localization possibility into the application, allowing for text to be displayed in both Finnish and English. With the assistance of ChatGPT, we created a style guide for the UI and began implementing it into the application.

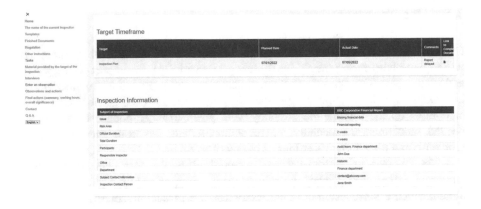

Fig. 3 Inspection information page in VTP

We proceeded to build the correct routing and to integrate the frontend and backend together. Recognizing the need for adjustments to the database schema, we initiated revisions while concurrently addressing application styling and adding several popup forms.

4   Results

In this section we observe ChatGPT discussions, code and lessons learned.

4.1   Discussions with ChatGPT

We stored ChatGPT conversations that were relevant to the project in Markdown format. The resulting Markdown files were included into the description part of pull requests made to the project GitHub repository [34].

The length of the conversation varied significantly based on the magnitude of the changes requested and whether any issues arose. Throughout the project, 60 pull requests were merged into the codebase. Out of these, 53 had ChatGPT conversations attached, with the number of prompts in each ranging from 1 to 129. On average, a pull request required 20 prompts to be merged. A common way to start conversation with ChatGPT was to describe the problem or wanted feature or to paste existing code and ask for needed changes. If the AI model couldn't give a solution directly based on the first prompt, the developer would give more information or clarifications in an iterative manner where the solution was found by fine-tuning the earlier answers.

4.2 Code

The application implements a basic three-tier architecture, where the front-end communicates with the back-end through a REST API. Each tier runs in their own Docker container, and the whole system is managed with Docker Compose.

Table 3 provides a breakdown by type of file and line for the project's code base. File and blank, comment, and code line counts were calculated from the project's repository using cloc [5]. The vast majority of lines shown are a result of bootstrapping a React project to be used as the front-end client. This includes most of the JSON lines that node package manager uses for managing dependencies.

However, the team managed to use ChatGPT to generate all of the code directly related to running the project. This includes containerization (both Dockerfiles, a YAML file), CI pipeline (other YAML file), database initialization clauses (SQL), and the entire RESTful API that makes up the project's back-end, including unit tests for its routes. Furthermore, all React components, their layout, and styling (CSS) were created by ChatGPT based on the teams instructions. The HTML files contain a UI style guide. In total, excluding the JSON files, over 4000 lines of code were generated by ChatGPT.

In general, ChatGPT produces code that appears to be relatively high quality. The code mostly works; it is laid out in a logical manner and has well-named variables that make it easy to understand. Its two biggest pitfalls are consistency and attention to detail. The former shows as stylistic differences in blocks of code produced in separate replies by ChatGPT, which were sometimes incompatible to the point of not functioning. The latter problem was mainly encountered when attempting to fit pieces of the project together as it grew more complex which meant conversations with ChatGPT needed more context to be provided. The team noticed a marked improvement in both areas when using GPT-4 over GPT-3.5.

Table 3 Output of the cloc [5] package based on the project's repository as of 24.4.2023

Language	Files	Blank	Comment	Code
JSON [15]	6	0	0	19145
JavaScript [14]	54	487	68	3622
CSS [6]	14	133	22	697
HTML [13]	3	42	30	357
SQL [29]	1	19	3	185
Bourne Shell [2]	1	12	6	164
Markdown [10]	4	51	0	84
YAML [37]	2	11	0	66
Dockerfile [7]	2	14	3	20
SVG [32]	1	0	0	1
SUM	88	769	132	24341

4.3   Development Team's Observations and Lessons Learned

Incorporating ChatGPT for code generation and problem-solving in programming has been beneficial, though it comes with its own set of limitations. The team has kept a detailed log of their experiences using ChatGPT throughout the project's life cycle. These observations have been organized into several key categories:

- **Limited Contextual Memory**: The model often forgets variable names and user-requested changes and overlooks the impact of changes on other parts of the system.
- **Token Limitation Constraints**: Long responses are sometimes cut short, or essential contextual information cannot be included due to prompt length restrictions, such as a lengthy code file.
- **Overly Broad Responses**: Requests for minor modifications might lead to unnecessary alterations in other code segments.
- **Limited Understanding of Visual Concepts**: The model cannot visualize user interface elements, making it difficult to modify them based on verbal descriptions.
- **Non-deterministic Behavior**: Different outputs can cause compilation issues when integrating code generated by the model.
- **Training Data Limitations**: Some solutions are outdated due to changes in frameworks or libraries since the last model update in 2021.
- **Hallucination**: The model sometimes references non-existent library versions or unpromptedly changes variable names.
- **Impact of Prompt Quality**: The clarity and completeness of the prompt significantly affect the response quality. Precise, context-rich tasks often yield the best results.

Although these issues present themselves differently, they share common underlying causes, such as the model's size, token limit, and contextual memory—its ability to process large inputs and understand textual relationships. Advancements in these areas could mitigate many observed issues. For example, hallucinations could be reduced with more contextual clues in the input, and lengthy responses would not be problematic if they fit within the token limit.

The release of GPT-4 provided practical insights into these technical improvements. Despite GPT-4's slower text generation compared to GPT-3.5-turbo, our team valued its enhanced contextual memory. The benefits were so significant that team members preferred to take breaks rather than revert to the older model when reaching the maximum 3-hour query limit on the new model.

In the realm of software development, ChatGPT has shown a duality of capability. It excels as a starting point for crafting new code components but often requires additional effort to refine and perfect the end product. The model's consistency in updating code, its recall for implementing revisions, and its handling of errors can be unpredictable. Misinterpretations of questions, non-deterministic responses, and the inherent token limits of the answers are challenges the team has navigated.

Nonetheless, by decomposing complex requests into smaller, manageable tasks, articulating clear and detailed descriptions, and employing creative strategies to sidestep token constraints, the team has significantly enhanced the utility of ChatGPT. This approach mirrors the concept of rubber duck debugging," where articulating a problem clearly—even to an inanimate object—can lead to solutions. When interacting with ChatGPT, the clarity of the prompt directly influences the quality of the code generated. This reinforces the principle that sound development practices remain crucial, even when AI is involved in the coding process. Just as with any tool, the proficiency of its use is as important as the tool's inherent capabilities.

5   Evaluation

In this section, we provide a professional evaluation (see, e.g., [26]) of the application and findings from a static code analysis [18]. The evaluation was done by a software professional with over 5-year experience in the modern software development and masters-level academic degree in computer science.

The evaluation criteria were based on software maintainability. For example, consideration was given to the amount and validity of tests created for the application, how input validation was implemented, and the directory structure and file-naming conventions used. The criteria were similar to those used when existing projects are evaluated for maintenance and further development. The time spent on the evaluation was half a workday.

The evaluation is divided into three parts. Initially, it addresses the backend, where the file structure and test coverage are assessed, along with REST handlers, database usage, error handling, and issues related to maintainability. Regarding the frontend, the focus is on the file structure and test coverage, as well as the use of styles and implemented functionalities. For the static analysis part, observations made by the SonarQube product regarding bugs, maintainability, security, test code coverage, and code duplication are discussed.

5.1   *Professional Evaluation of the Backend*

File Structure and Test Coverage

The backend directory structure was very flat. Dividing files into different directories would have made it easier for new developers to understand the codebase. Otherwise, file naming was good and clear.

The backend was implemented as a Node.js Express application, which is a standard choice. The application initialization was done well and clearly followed standard practices. There was some inconsistency in route definition, but this was not harmful from a maintenance perspective.

Functionality-wise, the backend system was significantly more extensive than what was implemented on the user interface side. A clear deficiency was the complete lack of access control implementation.

Test coverage for functionalities was at a fairly good level, at 75%. However, the Plans functionality was not tested at all.

The implementation of tests left something to be desired, complicating further development. Tests were conducted exclusively against the REST API. Some tests mainly verified the API contract to check whether the expected response was returned. However, these did not test whether the desired operation had been implemented correctly.

Some tests also examined functionality, but in these cases, verification was performed by making direct database calls. This created a strong dependency between the tests and the database, leading to fragile tests that could be easily broken by database layer changes.

REST Handlers and Database

In the software, all functionality took place as part of REST handlers. This is a good option for very small applications, but in an application of this scale, a layered architecture with services called in handlers would be a significantly better option, especially from the perspective of not duplicating functionality in handlers.

No input validation was implemented in the handlers, which can be considered a significant deficiency. This allowed, among other things, the entry of arbitrary values from the domain perspective, such as negative week numbers and the like.

In terms of database usage, pagination had not been implemented, which is very likely to cause problems for system operation as data volumes grow. Database queries were simple and were parameterized according to good practice. Transactions were not implemented, but there was little need for them in the functionality. Poor implementation of query execution was exemplified by the /api/drafts/:id/full implementation, where three separate queries were executed unnecessarily, even though a single query could have achieved the same result. Since queries were not made within a transaction, this could potentially lead to inconsistent responses.

Error Handling

Error handling in handlers was implemented so that calls within async functions were wrapped in try-catch structures. The standard practice would be to implement a separate error-handling wrapper in which handler functions would be wrapped. Doing this would make the code clearer to read and avoid situations where an error is not caught, and the response object's send function is not called due to oversight.

Maintainability

From a maintenance perspective, the backend system could be developed further. Initially, time should be spent fixing the most obvious shortcomings in validation, test implementation, and error handling.

Generally speaking, the deficiencies are not insurmountable for ChatGPT. For example, when GPT-4 was asked to add input validation, it added the express-validator library and implemented the validation correctly.

5.2 Professional Evaluation of the Frontend

File Structure and Test Coverage

The user interface was implemented using the React UI library, a common and safe choice. The user interface was partially translated; some components had hard-coded Finnish parts that should be translated.

The file and directory structure was better organized than that of the backend system. However, there was some inconsistency as calls to the backend system were found both in the components and in a separate Service directory. State management between components was handled with callbacks, and there was no single source of truth.

No tests had been implemented for the user interface, leading to buggy functionalities. For example, application forms didn't support error handling or validation, and the system couldn't distinguish between the lack of a response from the backend and missing information.

GPT-4 could produce test templates for components, so this deficiency was not mainly caused by the AI tool used.

Based on manual testing, the appearance was satisfactory from a B2B perspective. The display did not scale correctly for mobile devices, but using such a system on a small mobile device would be atypical.

Styling and Implemented Functionalities

Regarding styles, both individual CSS files corresponding to each component and the styled-components library were used. A more consistent implementation would have been preferable. However, such inconsistency is not uncommon in human-implemented systems. The source code included a style guide, but it was not followed.

Many functions had been implemented without connecting to the backend system. However, in a mock sense, the user interface was suitable for preliminarily demonstrating how it would work and could serve as a basis for further development.

In summary, most of the findings seems to be caused by lack of context or more precise prompts. ChatGPT seems to be, for example, capable of generating validation for routers if prompted to do so. The results could be different if the prompts had been created by more experienced developers. The flat directory structure also could be avoided if the context could include the whole source code of the project.

5.3   Static Code Analysis

The quality of the software was also examined using static analysis tools. Static analysis refers to analyzing software without executing the program. For this purpose, we used the SonarQube product [28], which is widely used in software production. Its users include IBM, Microsoft, and NASA.

The analysis from SonarQube provided observations on reliability (bugs), maintainability (code smells), security (security hotspots), code coverage, and code duplications. The observations for bugs and maintainability are graded as either blocker, critical, major, minor, or info. Security hotspot observations are categorized into high, medium, and low levels.

Regarding bugs, the analysis identified two. A major-level bug was related to a component in the user interface named "Error." While "Error" is not a reserved word per se, it's a distinct identifier that should not be used as a variable name.

A minor-level observation was related to a style guide that had an HTML table without a table description. This omission is an accessibility issue. Since this observation is related to development guidelines, it is not considered as serious as if the observation were in the actual application user interface code.

There were 43 observations related to maintainability. Out of these, 31 are of major level, and 12 are of minor level. A total of 12 major observations were about variables in the code that are redundant, meaning they are assigned a value without being used. 11 major observations related to iteration where the array index is used as the React component's key value. The key value should be stable, which an array index is not. In the following example, instead of the index, some unique identifier of the criterion should be used as the key value.

```
<TableBody>
{criteria.map((criterion, index) => (
<TableRow key={index}>
...
<TableCell>{criterion}</TableCell>
</TableRow>
))}
</TableBody>
```

Other major observations included three where optional chaining in JavaScript was not used, i.e., accessing object properties with the question mark notation. The remaining observations were related to duplicate selectors in CSS code or passing objects through React's context, leading to performance issues.

Minor observations related to unused or duplicated import statements and a few unused variables that SonarQube did not grade as major.

The analysis did not find any vulnerabilities. There were nine security hotspots, with one high-level observation related to a hard-coded database password in a docker file. Two medium observations related to potential recursive copying during docker image creation and two observations about docker images being run as the root user. Minor notes related to enabling CORS and executing NPM commands in a docker file without the ignore-scripts switch, which could lead to accidental execution of shell command scripts.

In terms of duplication, SonarQube estimated that 7.7% of the lines were duplicates. A typical example of duplication is REST API handlers that have very similar try-catch structures. For these, duplication can't be considered a significant problem, as there are still differences in content, for example, in the handler's parameters and the database queries made.

In summary, the static code analysis yielded a relatively small number of issues. Importantly, there were no critical-level findings. Most of the issues, such as removing unused variables, can be easily resolved. The most concerning issue involved the iteration of React components, as this could lead to bugs in the sorting or filtering of component values. This finding is not due to a lack of context or prompting but appears to be caused by actual code generation. This is different from missing features like validation, which can be fixed through better prompts.

5.4 The Summary of Evaluation

The evaluation found that the backend, implemented in Node.js Express, exhibited a flat directory structure that could hinder new developers but was otherwise well-organized. While the backend was more feature-rich compared to the frontend, it lacked critical aspects such as access control and input validation. Test coverage was generally good at 75%, although some areas were not tested. Tests were found to be fragile due to direct database dependency. Error handling and route definitions also had room for improvement, while the system was found to be lacking in layered architecture and transaction management. The frontend, built with React, had a better-organized directory structure but exhibited inconsistencies in backend calls and state management. No UI tests were implemented, leading to bugs and a lack of error handling. The interface was partially localized, and although it did not scale well for mobile, it was deemed satisfactory for B2B use. Inconsistencies in styling were noted, but these are not uncommon in human-coded systems.

Both the frontend and backend could benefit from further refinement, particularly in validation, error handling, and test implementation. However, when tasked with specific improvements such as input validation, GPT-4 was able to perform adequately. The most serious error was found in React implementation and can be only caught by an experienced developer.

Static analysis of the software was performed using SonarQube, a widely recognized tool in the industry. The analysis focused on multiple dimensions including reliability (bugs), maintainability (code smells), and security (security hotspots), as well as code coverage and duplications. Importantly, the analysis did not find any vulnerabilities. Two bugs were identified. The maintainability observations were more numerous, with 43 in total: 31 were major and 12 were minor. Many of these related to redundant variables and unstable key values in React component iteration. Overall, the static analysis highlighted several areas for improvement in code quality and maintainability.

6 Discussion

Our empirical data suggest that the effectiveness of using ChatGPT in developing a software system is significantly influenced by the design of the prompts. A majority of the observed limitations appear to emanate from a lack of context or insufficiently specific prompts, echoing findings from previous literature highlighting the importance of prompt engineering in natural language processing tasks [17, 36]. Monteiro et al. [21] found similarly that developers with strong expertise in specific technologies and frameworks were more effective in guiding ChatGPT for tasks like bug fixing.

The ability of ChatGPT to generate useful and accurate outputs, such as validation logic for routers, underscores its potential utility. However, this raises the question of how much expertise is required in crafting the prompts. More experienced developers might elicit more sophisticated and contextually appropriate responses from ChatGPT, a key factor for companies and researchers contemplating the integration of ChatGPT into their development pipelines.

Our study also highlights several practical implications. The integration of Chat-GPT into the software development workflow revealed key benefits and challenges, offering valuable insights for practitioners. Initially, ChatGPT clearly expedited the initial development stages, reducing the time required for initial project setup and swiftly generating foundational code structures for our React-based project. This acceleration was particularly notable in the creation of boilerplate code and standard features, such as setting up RESTful API routes using Node.js.

However, ChatGPT's limitations became apparent in more complex tasks. One notable issue was its inconsistent handling of complex database interactions, often requiring manual adjustments, particularly with intricate SQL queries and database schema designs. This highlighted the need for human oversight in such areas.

In terms of documentation, ChatGPT's assistance proved to be a double-edged sword. While it efficiently populated many sections of the reports, the generated content sometimes lacked the nuanced understanding necessary for complex technical topics. This is in line with findings of others where AI-assisted documentation can be beneficial but requires careful review and refinement by experienced developers.

Moreover, the team's experience underscores the importance of combining AI assistance with human expertise. This is in line with Monteiro et al. [21] who suggest that inconsistencies in coding standards and idioms necessitate human intervention. ChatGPT can provide a solid starting point for coding tasks, but its output often requires further refinement. For instance, ChatGPT effectively suggested and initiated the structure for the RESTful API in our project, but the team had to extensively refine the code to ensure it met industry standards and aligned with the project's specific requirements.

From the perspective of software production, ChatGPT could potentially be used in the creation of new software. However, it is particularly important for prompt crafting and quality assurance that the production process involves experienced software developers who can identify situations where, for example, necessary validations for inputs are missing from the generated code. In other words, it is not recommended that junior developers solely rely on ChatGPT because they might struggle to ask correct questions or notice missing tests.

Further practical recommendations include integrating ChatGPT with rigorous code reviews, especially when working on complex system integrations. This approach ensures that while the initial development can be accelerated through AI-generated code, the final product maintains the high quality and reliability required in professional software development.

The educational value of using ChatGPT in a development setting should not be underestimated. Particularly for junior developers, the iterative process of refining prompts and interpreting AI-generated code can serve as a valuable learning experience, emphasizing the importance of clear communication and detailed understanding of coding practices and principles.

ChatGPT played a central role in the team's development workflow, taking on tasks that traditionally would have been done manually. While the team made extensive use of prompts to perform most aspects of the process, more time should have been invested in upfront design. Also, although code reviews were conducted, they were not systematically integrated throughout the development cycle. Despite these challenges, the team felt that the quality of the outcomes produced through a ChatGPT-driven workflow was generally good. However, the absence of client feedback and a lack of senior expertise in evaluating work products introduced a pervasive sense of uncertainty within the team.

We argue that while ChatGPT presents a promising tool for augmenting the software development process, it is not a panacea. Its effective use requires a balanced approach, combining the efficiency and speed of AI with the critical oversight and expertise of human developers. As AI technology continues to evolve, its role in software development is likely to expand, but this study clearly demonstrates the necessity of human involvement for ensuring the quality and viability of software products.

7 Conclusions

This chapter presents firsthand experiences of using ChatGPT to develop a full-stack software application. The project, undertaken by a team of master's and bachelor's level students, aimed to develop a financial supervision platform with the aid of ChatGPT. Overall, this study contributes to the growing body of literature on the application of language models in software engineering. This study also provides insights for researchers and practitioners interested in exploring the use of ChatGPT for developing real-world software systems.

Based on the results from this exploratory study, the main conclusions drawn were as follows: (1) these findings demonstrate the potential for ChatGPT to be integrated into the software engineering workflow; (2) it can be used for creating a base for new components and for dividing coding tasks into smaller pieces; (3) noticeable enhancements in GPT-4, compared to GPT-3.5, indicate superior working memory and the ability to continue incomplete responses, thereby leading to more coherent and less repetitive dialogues; and (4) ChatGPT produced code that did not include any major errors but requires efficient prompting to be effective.

References

1. Ahmad, A., Waseem, M., Liang, P., Fehmideh, M., Aktar, M.S., Mikkonen, T.: Towards human-bot collaborative software architecting with ChatGPT (2023). arXiv preprint arXiv:2302.14600
2. Bourne, S.: Bourne shell. https://en.wikipedia.org/wiki/Bourne_shell. Accessed 6 Nov 2023
3. Chai - a BDD / TDD assertion library. https://www.chaijs.com/. Accessed 6 Nov 2023
4. ChatGPT. https://chat.openai.com/ (2023). Accessed 6 April 2023
5. cloc - Count lines of Code. https://github.com/AlDanial/cloc (2023). Accessed 13 April 2023
6. CSS - Cascading Style Sheets. https://www.w3.org/TR/CSS/#css. Accessed 6 Nov 2023
7. Dockerfile - Docker instruction file. https://docs.docker.com/. Accessed 6 Nov 2023
8. Dong, Y., Jiang, X., Jin, Z., Li, G.: Self-collaboration code generation via ChatGPT (2023). arXiv preprint arXiv:2304.07590
9. Express - a back end web application framework. https://expressjs.com/. Accessed 6 Nov 2023
10. Gruber, J.: Markdown - markup language. https://daringfireball.net/projects/markdown/. Accessed 6 Nov 2023
11. Hilma - Public procurement. https://www.hankintailmoitukset.fi/en/ (2023). Accessed 31 March 2023
12. Hou, X., Zhao, Y., Liu, Y., Yang, Z., Wang, K., Li, L., Luo, X., Lo, D., Grundy, J., Wang, H.: Large language models for software engineering: A systematic literature review (2023). arXiv preprint arXiv:2308.10620
13. HTML - HyperText Markup Language. https://html.spec.whatwg.org/. Accessed 6 Nov 2023
14. JavaScript - programming language. https://en.wikipedia.org/wiki/JavaScript. Accessed 6 Nov 2023
15. JSON (JavaScript Object Notation) - a lightweight data-interchange format. https://www.json.org/json-en.html. Accessed 6 Nov 2023
16. Kashefi, A., Mukerji, T.: ChatGPT for programming numerical methods (2023). arXiv preprint arXiv:2303.12093
17. Liu, Y., Du, H., Niyato, D., Kang, J., Cui, S., Shen, X., Zhang, P.: Optimizing mobile-edge AI-generated everything (AIGX) services by prompt engineering: Fundamental, framework, and case study (2023). arXiv preprint arXiv:2309.01065

18. Louridas, P.: Static code analysis. IEEE Softw. **23**(4), 58–61 (2006)
19. MIT Licence - a permissive free software license. https://en.wikipedia.org/wiki/MIT_License. Accessed 6 Nov 2023
20. Mocha - a JavaScript test framework. https://mochajs.org/. Accessed 6 Nov 2023
21. Monteiro, M., Branco, B.C., Silvestre, S., Avelino, G., Valente, M.T.: End-to-end software construction using chatgpt: An experience report (2023). arXiv preprint arXiv:2310.14843
22. MySQL - an open-source relational database management system. https://www.mysql.com/. Accessed 6 Nov 2023
23. Node.js - a cross-platform, open-source server environment. https://nodejs.org/en. Accessed 6 Nov 2023
24. OpenAI: GPT-4 Technical Report (2023). arXiv preprint arXiv:2303.08774
25. React - an open-source front-end JavaScript library. https://react.dev/. Accessed 6 Nov 2023
26. Rosqvist, T., Koskela, M., Harju, H.: Software quality evaluation based on expert judgement. Softw. Qual. J. **11**, 39–55 (2003)
27. Solita Company. https://www.solita.fi/en/company/ (2023). Accessed 29 Sept 2023
28. SonarQube. https://www.sonarsource.com/products/sonarqube/ (2023). Accessed 29 Sept 2023
29. SQL - Structured Query Language. https://en.wikipedia.org/wiki/SQL. Accessed 6 Nov 2023
30. Sten, H., Ahtee, T., Poranen, T.: Evaluation of students' capstone software development projects. In: SEFI Annual Conference, pp. 531–540 (2018)
31. Surameery, N.M.S., Shakor, M.Y.: Use Chat GPT to solve programming bugs. Int. J. Inf. Technol. Comput. Eng. **3**(01), 17–22 (2023). ISSN: 2455-5290
32. SVG - Scalable Vector Graphics. https://www.w3.org/Graphics/SVG/. Accessed 6 Nov 2023
33. Treude, C.: Navigating complexity in software engineering: A prototype for comparing GPT-n solutions (2023). arXiv preprint arXiv:2301.12169
34. VTP - Source code repository for the Valvontatyöpöytä. https://github.com/AI-Makes-IT/VTP (2023). Accessed 29 Sept 2023
35. Waseem, M., Das, T., Ahmad, A., Fehmideh, M., Liang, P., Mikkonen, T.: Using chatgpt throughout the software development life cycle by novice developers (2023). arXiv preprint arXiv:2310.13648
36. White, J., Hays, S., Fu, Q., Spencer-Smith, J., Schmidt, D.C.: ChatGPT prompt patterns for improving code quality, refactoring, requirements elicitation, and software design (2023). arXiv preprint arXiv:2303.07839
37. YAML - a human-readable data serialization language. https://yaml.org/. Accessed 6 Nov 2023

Part IV
Generative AI in Software Engineering Processes

Transforming Software Development with Generative AI: Empirical Insights on Collaboration and Workflow

Rasmus Ulfsnes (iD)**, Nils Brede Moe** (iD)**, Viktoria Stray** (iD)**, and Marianne Skarpen** (iD)

Abstract Generative AI (GenAI) has fundamentally changed how knowledge workers, such as software developers, solve tasks and collaborate to build software products. Introducing innovative tools like ChatGPT and Copilot has created new opportunities to assist and augment software developers across various problems. We conducted an empirical study involving interviews with 13 data scientists, managers, developers, designers, and front-end developers to investigate the usage of GenAI. Our study reveals that ChatGPT signifies a paradigm shift in the workflow of software developers. The technology empowers developers by enabling them to work more efficiently, speed up the learning process, and increase motivation by reducing tedious and repetitive tasks. Moreover, our results indicate a change in teamwork collaboration due to software engineers using GenAI for help instead of asking coworkers, which impacts the learning loop in agile teams.

Keywords Agile software development · Product development · Teamwork

1 Introduction

There is a growing trend among companies to adopt digitalization and engage in digital transformation[36]. This transformation process requires technologies

---

R. Ulfsnes (✉) · N. B. Moe
SINTEF, Trondheim, Norway
e-mail: rasmus.ulfsnes@sintef.no; nils.b.moe@sintef.no

V. Stray
SINTEF, Trondheim, Norway

Department of Informatics, University of Oslo, Oslo, Norway
e-mail: stray@uio.no

M. Skarpen
NTNU, Trondheim, Norway
e-mail: marskarp@stud.ntnu.no

as software, data, and artificial intelligence [5], forcing a shift in the use of strategic frameworks [30], and new ways of developing technology for highly skilled employees with intelligent technology [36].

Technology for assisting developers with writing code, particularly using Integrated Development Environments (IDEs), is not a new concept [17, 26]. The task of autocompletion of code, and generating of test, and various other tasks has been particularly interesting for software, as natural language matches quite well as the software code is hypothesized to be a natural language [16]. Subsuquently, this hypothesis has led to lots of research on artificial intelligence (AI) for software engineering [32, 33]. With the introduction of generative artificial intelligence (GenAI)—a type of artificial intelligence (AI)—both the software development processes and tooling have started to change fast. Further, GenAI can revolutionize software development by automating repetitive tasks, improving code quality, enhancing collaboration, providing data-driven insights, and ultimately accelerating the development life cycle [25, 31]. There is a growing research into how to use Copilot [28] or generative AI systems such as ChatGPT [37] and its capability to automate software engineering tasks [20]. However, good tooling is not enough.

In order for a company to succeed with software product development, well-working teams and good processes are key. Software engineering is a social activity that is focused on close cooperation and collaboration between all team members [21] and across teams in the organization [2]. Therefore, it is important to note that while AI has great potential, it also comes with challenges [1] such as ethical considerations, data privacy concerns, the need for skilled professionals to handle the technology within software teams, and a potential change in the team dynamics. However, research on team dynamics is lacking. In order to understand the effects on team-dynamics, we also need to consider the individual work practices, to grasp the effects on a team level. This chapter explores how are software engineers' work practices transformed and potential impact on the transformation on collaboration.

We have interviewed 13 data scientists, managers, developers, designers, and front-end developers to investigate how they use GenAI technology and how their workday has changed. Finally, we discuss how this technology might affect software development teamwork.

2   Related Work

2.1   Productivity and Work Satisfaction

Competing for talents requires a conscious effort to offer an attractive workplace [24]. Further, the ability to balance the need and nature of the workdays for different team members is directly related to the outcome of the product [34]. For software developers, Meyer et al. [22] outline a framework that describes what makes a good workday. There are three main factors: value creation, efficient use of time, and perception. Value creation is about whether or not the developers feel they are creating something, and the factor has six sub-factors. The second factor, efficient use of time, has two sub-factors, meeting expectations and the ability to work focused. In essence, the assessment of a workday being good or bad is largely influenced by the expectations for the day. For example, if one anticipates a day filled with meetings, the day can be considered good even if most of the time is spent in meetings. However, if one hopes for a day of focused work and the day is filled with meetings, the day is perceived as a bad workday. Coworker interruptions were specifically described as negatively influencing developers' ability to focus or work as planned, although being able to help a coworker was generally considered positive and rewarding. Lastly, perception is about how they perceive their own productivity.

Developer satisfaction and work productivity are related; therefore, they need to be key considerations for software companies [15]. More productive developers may be more satisfied, and more satisfied developers may be more productive. Autonomy, being able to complete tasks, and technical skills all affect productivity. By introducing new technology like GenAI, a team member's productivity may be positively affected. At the same time, work culture and team collaboration are important for job satisfaction. An increased reliance on tools like GenAI may enhance individual productivity while inadvertently reducing inter-team interactions, ultimately affecting long-term job satisfaction and collective productivity. Introducing GenAI in software teams is therefore a balancing act.

2.2 Software Development, Knowledge Work, and Technology

Software engineering requires the input and consolidation of various information to produce code [26]. Furthermore, with the advent of DevOps with its increase in speed of delivering continuously [13] and increased accessibility to third-party libraries and frameworks, the process of software engineering has shifted from being about understanding the computer and the programming language toward understanding how to compose relevant libraries and frameworks, with applicable testing.

Software development encompasses more than just programming and teamwork; it also involves actively seeking knowledge online and in knowledge management systems [12], conducting testing and code reviewing [14], and taking advantage of software such as Integrated Development Environments. IDEs have been a researched topic for quite some time [26] as well as how online resources [8, 18] aid and enhance the development process, both in speed and quality across varying ranges of experience. Through the use of IDEs, software engineers have gotten access to capabilities for refactoring, debugging, source repositories, third-party plugins[26], and auto-completion of code [6]. In addition, developers need to browse through a plethora of different files in existing software solutions in order to get a grasp of how changes to the code need to be implemented [17].

More recently, better autocompletion methodologies and technologies have been introduced to provide more context-relevant suggestions using statistical methods [6], and the naturalness of software [16] is a great target for utilizing natural language processing and generative AI. GitHub Copilot has shown promising effects for assisting developers in writing code and assisting with test writing [4, 25]. Early studies on knowledge work show that generative AI is able to disseminate knowledge previously shown as tacit[7] and dramatically increase both quality and production [10]. Both studies show that the effects are most noticeable for the lower-skilled workers, while higher-skilled workers have a lower increase in production and quality.

2.3 *Teams, Knowledge Sharing, and Performance*

Software product development is done in teams [19]; therefore, the success of software development depends significantly on team performance. Today, the premise is that software teams should be autonomous or self-managed [27]. In their review, Dickinson and McIntyre [11] identified and defined seven core components of teamwork. Using these components and their relationships as a basis, they proposed the teamwork model that is used in this work. The model consists of a learning loop of the following basic teamwork components: communication, team orientation, team leadership, monitoring, feedback, backup, and coordination. Later, Moe et al. [23] used this model to explain agile teamwork. The introduction of GenAI is likely to affect these teamwork components.

3 Research Method and Analysis

This study was conducted in the context of two research programs on software development processes, where several companies introduced generative artificial intelligence (GenAI) in their product development process. GenAI, especially those built on LLMs, is a new phenomenon that has not been previously studied. Due to the uncertain nature of the phenomenon, we chose an exploratory multi-case study [38]. We selected our informants using snowball sampling [3] in Slack asking for subjects that used GenAI for a wide range of activities. As of the tools used, our studies found that ChatGPT and GitHub Copilot were the most common for code and text, while some reported that they used Midjourney and DALL-E 2 for image creation.

Table 1 Data sources

ID	Role	Work experience in years
I1	Developer & Team lead	5
I2	Developer	5
I3	Technical Strategy Consultant & Director	30
I4	Tech Lead & Machine learning engineer	6
I5	Principal Engineer and Enterprise Architect	15
I6	Data Science Manager	6
I7	Developer	10
I8	CTO	25
I9	Director	30
I10	Developer	N/A
I11	Designer	13
I12	Designer	3
I13	Developer	3

3.1 Data Collection and Analysis

We interviewed 13 people, as shown in Table 1. The informant group had a broad range of roles: data scientists, managers, developers, designers, and front-end developers. Based on a literature review, we developed a semi-structured interview guide. Questions included the following: *How do you use GenAI services? Which effects do you get from using them?* The interviews were done by the first, third, fourth, and fifth authors to spread out any subjective biases.

The analysis was divided into two cycles of coding as suggested by Saldana [29], with the third and first author conducting a combination of descriptive and initial coding [9] on the first eight interviews. Then the third and first authors had a discussion about the emerging categories and themes. This led to a revised interview guide. Finally, the last five interviews were conducted.

After the last round of interviews, the fourth author performed a descriptive coding of the remaining interviews. At the same time, the first author performed a second-cycle [29] focused coding of all interviews. Then, the observed themes and categories were merged through mutual workshops and discussions with all authors.

4 What Is Generative AI Used for in Software Development?

Software development consists of a number of activities, ranging across multiple roles in cross-functional teams. When using source repository systems or IDEs, the use case is often clear. However, the use of GenAI takes on a much more individual form. There are currently no standards or norms for how, when, and for what purpose you should apply GenAI to, and employees in software-intensive

Table 2 List of GenAI activities

Activity	Description
Asking for assistance when stuck	When stuck on a particular task, GenAI can help getting out of the slump
Learning	GenAI provide an interactive way of learning new things
Creating a virtual environment for a product	By asking GenAI to provide an simulated/virtual environment to learn and test products
PowerPoint and email writing	GenAI is useful for helping with writing text for email, powerpoint.
Non-technical boilerplate	Providing a boilerplate for how to get started with powerpoint, workshops
Boilerplate code	GenAI can provide boilerplate code that acts as a skeleton for further development
Working with existing code	GenAI are used for refactoring, adding small features, making code more robust, converting code, debugging, writing tests, Search Engine Optimization (SEO)

organizations are using it based on their own preferences. GenAI tools for a wide range of activities. See Table 2 for an overview of such activities.

The type of GenAI activities and utilization depends on individual preferences, the task to be solved, and the user's role in the organization. Developers typically use GenAI when working with the source code, while managers use it for, e.g., organizing workshops or creating content for PowerPoint presentations.

4.1   Asking for Assistance When Stuck

When a person was stuck on a particular problem or did not know how to proceed, ChatGPT was used as an assistant or fellow team member, where interacting with it using chat could help a person solve complex problems or get increased progress. For non-technical problems, this could be a case of writer's block, formulations, or when they are zoning out: *"For me, the main thing is to get unstuck, whether I am struggling with writer's block or formulations, just by interacting with ChatGPT and getting an immediate response is something else."*

This highlights that there is an effect of just having the chat window open and getting feedback without interrupting others. Formulating the problem to ChatGPT made it easier to keep focus on the task, helped on the thought processes, and helped see the problem in a new light. Developers referred to such interaction with ChatGPT as rubber-ducking. The idea of rubber-ducking is to explain the problem one seeks to solve to an inanimate object (e.g., a rubber duck), in an attempt to achieve a deeper understanding of the problem and a potential solution through the process of explaining it to someone (or something) using natural language.

Using GenAI as a sparring partner was both faster than asking human colleagues and also took away the feeling of disturbing them in their work. Further, being able to formulate the question as you would to a *human* felt easier than the alternate Google search, where you need to consider the specific keywords and what results they can give you.

4.2 Learning

GenAI provided more opportunities and avenues for engagement in learning compared to reading books, using Google, or watching videos. One approach was to engage interactively with the chat, assigning a role to the AI like "act as a tester," and then engaging with that persona to learn about testing. They could then ask that persona to explain a particular topic like they were doing testing for the first time.

"And then I continue. And I notice that I learn much faster this way. Because it's like having a personal tutor. Where you can ask yourself questions. And then I always have to double-check."

The same approach was also applied when working on code, when using new features, or when working on areas that the informants were not that knowledgeable about. A data scientist explained how to use the technology to learn more about programming: *"Almost as if I were asking someone much more skilled, like a developer in this case."*

4.3 Virtual Environments

Creating a virtual environment for a product was used to develop software for a trading platform. They engaged with ChatGPT and asked it to simulate that it was a stock exchange. They then provided ChatGPT with information about which stocks could be traded at the exchange and asked it to simulate different trading scenarios. This provided a novel way for the informant to understand the intricacies of a stock exchange. Further, this means that ChatGPT had the context for the particular trading platform the informants were interested in.

And then I said, "now I'm going to make an application out of this in such-and-such language." And so it has the context for everything while I kept asking it further questions. This integrated approach to both understanding a domain also then produced the relevant context that ChatGPT could use to generate relevant code.

4.4 Copywriting

Maybe not surprisingly, ChatGPT was used to assist in copywriting text, especially useful when integrated into the tool the informant was using, getting live feedback; this was particularly useful for persons that were not native or fluent in English or Norwegian. However, some experienced that GenAI was not very useful for email and text writing for two main reasons: there was a significant overhead in engaging sufficiently with ChatGPT to create emails, and the quality did not get better.

"I think I have asked it to write emails, but for me it is just faster to write it myself. The formulation was better though."

4.5 Boilerplating Code and Text

Getting started with a relatively novel coding project in any company requires quite a lot of boilerplate code; this type of code does not add functionality relevant to the business case but is required to get the project up and running with the necessary declarations and structures. Both back-end and front-end developers used ChatGPT to create tailored boilerplate code:

If I have a task, to create a list of tricks with something, and thumbs up and thumbs down on each element, for instance. I often start by describing what I want to ChatGPT. Then, it writes the code for me. GenAI was also used for repetitive or tedious non-technical tasks. For example, managers and architects stated to use ChatGPT to consolidate text used for production of bid to customers. One manager explained, *A bid I would normally have spent a lot of time in writing, I only spent 20 minutes on. Previously I would have spent a lot of time, looking for previous bids, adapting it and merging it. It is terrible to say it out loud [laughing], as this kind of is in someway reducing the need for my work. This type of work is what the company pays me to do.*

Another example is when you are building up technical specifications and technical architectures where the style of the text is quite consistent but the content varies between use cases or getting feedback on emails and getting a head start on the writing of the text.

4.6 Working with Existing Code

This was the most common activity among software developers. GenAI was used on many different tasks, ranging from refactoring or simplifying code, code review, translating code from one programming language to another, and simply explaining the code. Testing was also well suited for GenAI utilization; given its repetitive nature, GenAI was used to create numerous tests for the code. The informants also noted that the generated tests sometimes accounted for scenarios and test cases that they themselves had not thought of.

It was mostly a matter of thinking up all the things that could go wrong and creating unit tests for them. And that's where CoPilot was brilliant, as it came up with things that could go wrong that I had never thought of.

5 How and Why Do We Interact with GenAI?

In the previous section, we described how GenAI is used for a variety of activities. In the studied companies, GenAI was becoming an integrated part of their daily work, and most explained that they used GenAI daily or "all the time."

Among the study participants, we found two styles of interaction: *simple dialogue* and *advanced dialogue extended with prompt engineering*. The interaction style depended on the work context and types of problems to be solved. Table 3 contains an overview of the effects and drawbacks from interacting with GenAI.

5.1 Effects

By spending less time on manual and repetitive tasks, the improved productivity brought more enjoyment, motivation, and fun to the work. The repetitive tasks were

Table 3 Use of GenAI—benefits and challenges

Mode	Benefits	Challenges
Simple	– Asking questions is easier than searching – ChatGPT immediately provides an (almost) usable result – More efficient – More fun – More time to learn – Increased motivation and work satisfaction	– Input cleaning – Lack of tool integration – Lack of information after 2021 – Output needs to be worked on – Culturally biased output
Advanced (simple and prompt engineering)	– Interactive learning – More precise answers – Ability to take on different roles – Pair-prompt engineering – ChatGPT as advisor—rubberducking	– Limited context ability – Less pair-programming – Still requires other people when the complexity increases – Prompt engineering requires competence

seen as menial, and not particularly mentally challenging. Further, as time was freed up, more time could be spent on creative and challenging tasks. Moreover, engaging with the GenAI itself was experienced as fun and increased the motivation to experiment with different applications of the new technology.

Interacting through dialogue with ChatGPT increased engagement. It was experienced as a more "natural" engagement then searching for answers to problems on Google. Having a dialogue with ChatGPT was also described as faster than concocting the necessary string of Google search keywords. Moreover, ChatGPT responds immediately with the, assumed, correct answer to the question while googling often required additional steps, vetting the correct site on the search page, entering the particular page, and analyzing the Web page for the potential answer to the question. One informant was so conscious about speed that they deliberately chose GPT v3.5 over v4 in certain cases (at the time of our data collection, v3.5 was faster than v4), where the precision and quality of the v3.5 answer was assumed to be sufficient.

GenAI's utility also extended beyond quick and precise answers, with informants reporting a freedom in interacting with an artificial tool rather than having to deal with the social considerations involved in asking a team member.

Yeah, so you don't need to be too polite either. You don't have to have the correct phrasing or anything. You can just throw something out, I feel. Then you can get an answer, and if it's not quite right, you can refine the question again.

The threshold of asking ChatGPT was significantly lower than asking another person or in a Slack channel. This threshold for asking colleagues could potentially be high in a busy work environment, as one does not wish to interrupt an already-busy colleague. Further, you get feedback immediately, while it might take a while to get feedback on Slack.

5.2   Challenges

While there are many positive benefits of using GenAI, there are also challenges. The elusiveness of data confidentiality, data policy, and sensitivity meant that everyone was acutely conscious about which data to input into the chat interface. This made the work process somewhat awkward, requiring cleansing and anonymization of the text being sent into ChatGPT. Developers in companies using open-source technology were less lenient in protecting code than those in companies with internal code repositories. Moreover, the general lack of tool integration meant that there was a substantial amount of copy-paste to move text and code between different windows. One developer using Copilot X reported that the integration in the IDE meant that the code could be autocompleted and explained by ChatGPT in a seamless process, which reduced their work immensely: *I think it would have been easier to adopt a GenAI tool if I had used something like Copilot. Because then it would have been, in a way, integrated into the workflow.*

With regard to the output, all informants noted that the content produced by GenAI, regardless of tool, seldom represented a final product and typically required further refinement to be applicable in a real-world context. The general attitude from the interviewees was that they expected the output to be wrong.

Regarding technological development, which is characterized by a rapid pace and an increasing number of available libraries and technology, the cutoff date for ChatGPT's training data in September 2021 represented a significant drawback, where the error rate was annoyingly high.

One architect creating project startup documents experienced that ChatGPT was culturally biased toward how more hierarchical companies would perform activities in a project. This meant that ChatGPT had to be prompted with specific information regarding the methodology and project practices:

You kind of have to trick it into the right context if it's (GenAI) going to be part of agile processes.

5.3 Prompt Engineering

Several interviewees talked about how the quality of their prompt affected the quality of the response and how the use of prompt engineering techniques like contextualizing the problem, using personas, etc. guide and steer the dialogue with ChatGPT. Prompt engineering was applied to all the activities in Table 2. One informant explained asking ChatGPT to create a description of the most critical code reviewer in the world. They then told ChatGPT to act like this description while reviewing the code in a pull request. Another more technical aspect was telling ChatGPT to act like an SQL database to test queries. The effect of using prompt engineering was seen as a matter of precision and quality, thus reducing the time spent on working on modifying the output. One explained the usage of prompt engineering as follows:

It's like putting up fences on the bowling lane and then narrowing it down even more. It can almost only go one way, and that's a strike.

An important prompt engineering technique was assigning different roles to ChatGPT for the same question to get more than one perspective or answer on a problem. One explained:

"I want you to respond like a wealth manager," "I want you to respond like a friend," or "like a so-and-so..." And then you get different answers.

Using prompt engineering while writing code was described as feeling similar to programming with a partner. The flip side was that the developers mentioned that they were doing less pair programming as they were getting the wanted rubber ducking effect from using GenAI.

6   Discussion

One of the notable consequences of integrating GenAI tools into software development tasks is a visible shift in collaborative communication dynamics. Some of the informants appear to have a growing inclination to consult AI-driven solutions for issues and tasks they previously discussed with their human colleagues. This shift can have dramatic effects on the team's ability to perform. According to Liu et al. [19], a team's ability to perform is highly dependent on the knowledge sharing of the team. This implies that reducing knowledge sharing by replacing this with generative should be observed. This opposes the findings by Brynjolfsson et al. [7], with knowledge dissemination between high-skilled and low-skilled workers in customer service. These findings point to a significant difference between work done by teams in software development and individual work in customer service. However, we find that individuals become more efficient and save time, which they spend on more rewarding tasks.

If team members reduce their interactions in favor of focusing on individual tasks, a phenomenon known as an isomorphic team structure may emerge. The advantages of this structure are that it is organizationally simple, allows many tasks to be completed in parallel, and can clearly define and understand task responsibilities. However, the effect of such a structure is that the developers focused on their own modules and often created their own plans and made their own decisions. In addition, problems are seen as personal, individual goals are more important than team goals, and team members become less aware of what others are doing and get less support and help from others [23]. In a good working team, learning is a continuous feedback (see Fig. 1a). By introducing GenAI, this loop will be disrupted or reduced (Fig. 1b), thus reducing teamwork performance[23]. Additionally, this can also contribute to making persons less satisfied as helping others is a key factor for good workdays [22].

This model posits that the incorporation of GenAI in software development may disrupt the established learning loop. Such disruption will subsequently affect individual and team performance in software development. While it is anticipated that GenAI might enhance individual performance by streamlining tasks, there is a concurrent risk of diminishing overall team performance.

However, everything is not dark; as multiple informants noted, they had an increasing amount of knowledge sharing on how to use GenAI in their work and context. Notably, the practice of "pair prompt engineering" has emerged, akin to the concept of pair programming. This approach facilitates knowledge sharing [35] both on-site and when working remotely. This can thus involve a shift in how the programmers program, creating yet another abstraction layer for code production.

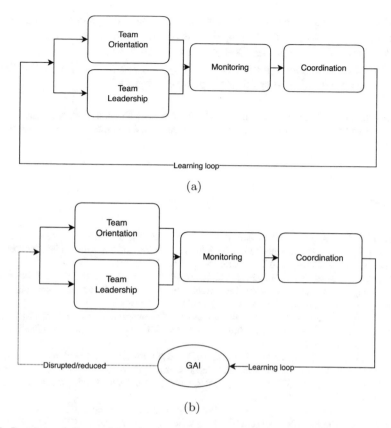

Fig. 1 Regular and disrupted learning loops. (**a**) Regular learning loop. (**b**) Disrupted learning loop

7 Concluding Remarks

In essence, GenAI serves a dual purpose: making everyday tasks more efficient and reigniting creative thinking for leaders and developers. By automating the production of routine code snippets and related tasks, these tools enable programmers to focus on higher-level conceptualization and innovation, resulting in enhanced productivity and code quality. This is similar to findings by Meyer et al. [22], where good workdays are understood as days where they feel productive and are able to work focused. In addition, similar to Brynjolfsson et al.'s findings where there is knowledge dissemination through the GenAI [7], we observe that there are data scientists using GenAI for coding purposes and front-end developers getting assistance in back-end development. Both programmers and leaders acknowledged the potential of generative AI in freeing up valuable time and cognitive resources that could be better allocated to more creative and complex problem-solving tasks.

This is reported to enhance both efficiency and enjoyment. By automating the production of routine code snippets and documentation, these GenAI enabled programmers to focus on higher-level conceptualization and other more complicated tasks, resulting in higher reported productivity. Most informants reported that AI reduced the amount of time developers spent on projects.

Acknowledgments This work was supported by the Research Council of Norway grants 321477 and 309344 and the companies Knowit and Iterate through the research projects Transformit and 10XTeams.

References

1. Bender, E.M., Gebru, T., McMillan-Major, A., Shmitchell, S.: On the dangers of stochastic parrots: Can language models be too big? In: Proceedings of the 2021 ACM Conference on Fairness, Accountability, and Transparency, pp. 610–623 (2021)
2. Berntzen, M., Stray, V., Moe, N.B., Hoda, R.: Responding to change over time: A longitudinal case study on changes in coordination mechanisms in large-scale agile. Empir. Softw. Eng. **28**(5), 114 (2023). https://doi.org/10.1007/s10664-023-10349-0
3. Biernacki, P., Waldorf, D.: Snowball sampling: problems and techniques of chain referral sampling. Sociol. Methods Res. **10**(2), 141–163 (1981). Publisher: Sage Publications Sage CA: Los Angeles, CA
4. Bird, C., Ford, D., Zimmermann, T., Forsgren, N., Kalliamvakou, E., Lowdermilk, T., Gazit, I.: Taking flight with copilot: early insights and opportunities of AI-powered pair-programming tools. Queue **20**(6), 35–57 (2022). https://doi.org/10.1145/3582083. https://dl.acm.org/doi/10.1145/3582083
5. Bosch, J., Olsson, H.H.: Digital for real: a multicase study on the digital transformation of companies in the embedded systems domain. J. Softw. Evol. Process. **33**(5) (2021). https://doi.org/10.1002/smr.2333
6. Bruch, M., Monperrus, M., Mezini, M.: Learning from examples to improve code completion systems. In: Proceedings of the 7th Joint Meeting of the European Software Engineering Conference and the ACM SIGSOFT Symposium on the Foundations of Software Engineering, pp. 213–222 (2009)
7. Brynjolfsson, E., Li, D., Raymond, L.R.: Generative AI at work. Tech. rep., National Bureau of Economic Research (2023)
8. Chatterjee, P., Kong, M., Pollock, L.: Finding help with programming errors: An exploratory study of novice software engineers' focus in stack overflow posts. J. Syst. Softw. **159**, 110454 (2020). Publisher: Elsevier
9. Corbin, J., Strauss, A.: Basics of Qualitative Research: Techniques and Procedures for Developing Grounded Theory. Sage Publications, Thousand Oaks (2014)
10. Dell'Acqua, F., McFowland, E., Mollick, E.R., Lifshitz-Assaf, H., Kellogg, K., Rajendran, S., Krayer, L., Candelon, F., Lakhani, K.R.: Navigating the Jagged Technological Frontier: Field Experimental Evidence of the Effects of AI on Knowledge Worker Productivity and Quality (2023). https://doi.org/10.2139/ssrn.4573321. https://papers.ssrn.com/abstract=4573321
11. Dickinson, T.L., McIntyre, R.M.: A conceptual framework for teamwork measurement. In: Team Performance Assessment and Measurement, pp. 31–56. Psychology Press, London (1997)
12. Dingsøyr, T., Bjørnson, F.O., Shull, F.: What do we know about knowledge management? Practical implications for software engineering. IEEE Softw. **26**(3), 100–103 (2009); Conference Name: IEEE Software. https://doi.org/10.1109/MS.2009.82

13. Fitzgerald, B., Stol, K.J.: Continuous software engineering: a roadmap and agenda. J. Syst. Softw. (2015). http://doi.org/10.1016/j.jss.2015.06.063
14. Florea, R., Stray, V.: A global view on the hard skills and testing tools in software testing. In: 2019 ACM/IEEE 14th International Conference on Global Software Engineering (ICGSE), pp. 143–151. IEEE (2019). https://doi.org/10.1109/ICGSE.2019.00035
15. Forsgren, N., Storey, M.A., Maddila, C., Zimmermann, T., Houck, B., Butler, J.: The SPACE of developer productivity: there's more to it than you think. Queue **19**(1), 20–48 (2021)
16. Hindle, A., Barr, E.T., Gabel, M., Su, Z., Devanbu, P.: On the naturalness of software. Commun. ACM **59**(5), 122–131 (2016); Publisher: ACM New York, NY, USA
17. Kersten, M., Murphy, G.C.: Using task context to improve programmer productivity. In: Proceedings of the 14th ACM SIGSOFT International Symposium on Foundations of Software Engineering, pp. 1–11 (2006)
18. Li, A., Endres, M., Weimer, W.: Debugging with stack overflow: Web search behavior in novice and expert programmers. In: Proceedings of the ACM/IEEE 44th International Conference on Software Engineering: Software Engineering Education and Training, pp. 69–81. ICSE-SEET '22. Association for Computing Machinery, New York (2022). https://doi.org/10.1145/3510456.3514147. https://dl.acm.org/doi/10.1145/3510456.3514147
19. Liu, M.L., Hsieh, M.W., Hsiao, C., Lin, C.P., Yang, C.: Modeling knowledge sharing and team performance in technology industry: the main and moderating effects of happiness. Rev. Manag. Sci. **14**(3), 587–610 (2020). https://doi.org/10.1007/s11846-018-0301-4
20. Melegati, J., Guerra, E.: Dante: A taxonomy for the automation degree of software engineering tasks (2023). arXiv
21. Mens, T., Cataldo, M., Damian, D.: The social developer: the future of software development [Guest Editors' Introduction]. IEEE Softw. **36**(1), 11–14 (2019). Publisher: IEEE
22. Meyer, A.N., Barr, E.T., Bird, C., Zimmermann, T.: Today was a good day: the daily life of software developers. IEEE Trans. Softw. Eng. **47**(5), 863–880 (2019). Publisher: IEEE
23. Moe, N.B., Dingsøyr, T., Dybå, T.: A teamwork model for understanding an agile team: a case study of a Scrum project. Inf. Softw. Technol. **52**(5), 480–491 (2010). Publisher: Elsevier
24. Moe, N.B., Stray, V., Smite, D., Mikalsen, M.: Attractive workplaces: what are engineers looking for? IEEE Softw. pp. 1–8 (2023)
25. Muller, M., Ross, S., Houde, S., Agarwal, M., Martinez, F., Richards, J., Talamadupula, K., Weisz, J.D.: Drinking chai with your (AI) programming partner: A design fiction about generative AI for software engineering. In: HAI-GEN Workshop at IUI 2022: 3rd Workshop on Human-AI Co-Creation with Generative Models (2022). https://hai-gen.github.io/2022/papers/paper-HAIGEN-MullerMichael.pdf
26. Murphy, G., Kersten, M., Findlater, L.: How are Java software developers using the Eclipse IDE? IEEE Softw. **23**(4), 76–83 (2006). Conference Name: IEEE Software. https://doi.org/10.1109/MS.2006.105
27. Ravn, J.E., Moe, N.B., Stray, V., Seim, E.A.: Team autonomy and digital transformation: disruptions and adjustments in a well-established organizational principle. AI & SOCIETY **37**(2), 701–710 (2022)
28. Ross, S.I., Martinez, F., Houde, S., Muller, M., Weisz, J.D.: The programmer's assistant: Conversational interaction with a large language model for software development. In: Proceedings of the 28th International Conference on Intelligent User Interfaces, pp. 491–514 (2023). https://doi.org/10.1145/3581641.3584037
29. Saldaña, J.: The Coding Manual for Qualitative Researchers, 2nd edn. SAGE, Los Angeles, (2013). oCLC: ocn796279115
30. Stray, V., Gundelsby, J.H., Ulfsnes, R., Brede Moe, N.: How agile teams make objectives and key results (OKRs) work. In: Proceedings of the International Conference on Software and System Processes and International Conference on Global Software Engineering, pp. 104–109 (2022)
31. Sun, J., Liao, Q.V., Muller, M., Agarwal, M., Houde, S., Talamadupula, K., Weisz, J.D.: Investigating explainability of generative AI for code through scenario-based design. In: 27th International Conference on Intelligent User Interfaces, pp. 212–228 (2022)

32. Svyatkovskiy, A., Zhao, Y., Fu, S., Sundaresan, N.: Pythia: Ai-assisted code completion system. In: Proceedings of the 25th ACM SIGKDD International Conference on Knowledge Discovery & Data Mining, pp. 2727–2735 (2019)
33. Talamadupula, K.: Applied AI matters: AI4Code: applying artificial intelligence to source code. AI Matt. **7**(1), 18–20 (2021). https://doi.org/10.1145/3465074.3465080. https://dl.acm.org/doi/10.1145/3465074.3465080
34. Tkalich, A., Ulfsnes, R., Moe, N.B.: Toward an agile product management: What do product managers do in agile companies? In: International Conference on Agile Software Development, pp. 168–184. Springer (2022)
35. Tkalich, A., Moe, N.B., Andersen, N.H., Stray, V., Barbala, A.M.: Pair programming practiced in hybrid work. In: Proceedings of the 17th ACM/IEEE International Symposium on Empirical Software Engineering and Measurement (ESEM). Association for Computing Machinery, New York (2023)
36. Ulfsnes, R., Mikalsen, M., Sporsem, T., Hatling, M.: Technology for knowledge work: A relational perspective. In: ECIS 2023 Research-in-Progress Papers (2023). https://aisel.aisnet.org/ecis2023_rip/48
37. White, J., Hays, S., Fu, Q., Spencer-Smith, J., Schmidt, D.C.: Chatgpt prompt patterns for improving code quality, refactoring, requirements elicitation, and software design (2023). arXiv. https://doi.org/10.48550/arxiv.2303.07839
38. Yin, R.K.: Case Study Research and Applications: Design and Methods. Sage, Los Angeles (2018)

How Can Generative AI Enhance Software Management? Is It Better Done than Perfect?

Beatriz Cabrero-Daniel (iD), Yasamin Fazelidehkordi, and Ali Nouri

Abstract Software development teams often deviate from their adopted framework, such as Scrum, and these deviations can sometimes bring consequences with different impact levels if the adaptations are not tailored for the specific teams' needs and circumstances. For instance, agile developers sometimes oversimplify crucial Agile steps, such as estimating needed effort for a specific task or lack of explicit assessment of the criteria for "Definition of Done." This information, though, is useful for subsequent planning activities. We hypothesise that generative AI could be used to help Agile teams conduct a number of software management tasks in a systematic and effective way. A family of experiments to compare the performance of humans and generative AI tools, namely, GPT-models and Bard, will be conducted. The findings from these experiments will serve as a foundation for a discussion on the role of artificial intelligence in software engineering tasks. This discussion will primarily focus on the balance between performance (perfect?) and efficiency (done?) and the importance of human oversight in Agile environments.

Keywords Agile development · Project management · Artificial intelligence · Generative AI · Software development

B. Cabrero-Daniel (✉)
University of Gothenburg, Gothenburg, Sweden
e-mail: beatriz.cabrero-daniel@gu.se

Y. Fazelidehkordi
University of Gothenburg, Gothenburg, Sweden
e-mail: gusfazya@student.gu.se

A. Nouri
Volvo Cars & Chalmers University of Technology, Gothenburg, Sweden
e-mail: ali.nouri@volvocars.com

© The Author(s), under exclusive license to Springer Nature Switzerland AG 2024
A. Nguyen-Duc et al. (eds.), *Generative AI for Effective Software Development*,
https://doi.org/10.1007/978-3-031-55642-5_11

235

1   Introduction

Software development teams often oversimplify crucial Agile steps or deviate from the Scrum framework, which can negatively affect their performance if the adaptations are not tailored for their specific needs and circumstances, e.g., when estimating the effort for a specific task or by not explicitly assessing the criteria for "Definition of Done" [20]. We hypothesize that integrating artificial intelligence (AI) into some tasks (e.g., planning) could lead to a better management of development team resources:

> **Generative AI (GenAI) could help Agile teams conduct software management tasks in a systematic and effective way.**

In order to understand how different GenAI tools perform at different tasks, as compared to humans and what are the nuances in their reasoning, a family of experiments were conducted. Two GenAI tools were used: Bard[1] and GPT-models [15, 21]. The three tools rely on large language models (LLMs) that exhibit general intelligence even when lacking general context of real-world scenarios. These tools have previously exhibited human-level performance on various professional and academic benchmarks [21]. The findings from these experiments will serve as a foundation for a discussion on the capabilities of GenAI tools in software management tasks in Sect. 5. The discussion will primarily focus on the balance between performance and efficiency and the importance of human oversight in AI-assisted Agile settings [9].

2   Background

2.1   Agile and Software Management

Agile: Scrum Framework

Software development methodologies are defined as a set of rules and protocols that are applied in different stages of developing and producing a software product [8]. Agile software development is one of the most popular methodologies that have been used by many software organizations in the past few decades. Among different methodologies of agile processes, scrum is the most popular one used by many companies. Scrum is defined as a practical lightweight method to control the process

---

[1] Visit https://bard.google.com/.

of developing and delivering a software product in a more flexible way [24]. The main advantage of scrum framework is giving the teams flexibility to adapt to the transformations that happen during the development phase of a software that could be due to changes in the project budget, the initial requirements, or the structure of the development team.

Problems in Agile Practices

Many software companies claim scrum as the main framework they use in their workflow. However, according to Mortada et al., due to several reasons, not all development teams are strictly faithful to the scrum guidelines, which results in them applying the scrum practices differently from what is suggested, or they might even not use all of the recommended practices [20]. Mortada et al. discuss several wrong practices in scrum teams including not estimating the time and effort for each user story, not having the correct structure for writing the user stories in the backlog, not having a product backlog, not defining the sprint goal at the beginning of the sprint, and not ending the sprint with demonstrating the desired deliverable [20].

Another challenge for scrum teams could be that developers often do not receive feedback from the right colleagues or stakeholders at the end of the sprint due to not demonstrating the results to the customers [20]. Moreover, risk assessments and understanding priorities of the project are usually done by the business people not developers; however, programmers need the freedom to schedule the riskiest segments of development at first, to reduce the overall risk of the project [3], but then, the question will be how to estimate all these risks? Furthermore, each developer knows how many task points they managed to implement in the last iteration, and as a result, no one signs up for more points than they have in their personal task points budget [13, 19]. Then should AI do that?

2.2 Generative AI

What Is GenAI?

Generative artificial intelligence (GenAI) is a kind of artificial intelligence that can generate different types of content such as pictures, text, audio, and 3D models based on the input they receive. LLMs also known as foundation models relate to self-supervised deep-learning algorithms that are trained based on a wide range of large-scale datasets [4]. Unlike traditional LLMs, new language models (e.g., OpenAI tools such as GPT-3.5) are able to simultaneously process a great amount of data with the help of the transformer neural network technology, which results in them being capable of doing great tasks such as generating texts, writing code scripts, etc. [2]. These models are currently being used in a wide range of contexts and fields such as medical applications, economics, software development, academia (both for research and training purposes), and business.

Why Use GenAI?

The question of whether generative AI is the sole technique to assist developers raises essential considerations about the diverse tools available to support software development. While generative AI offers a powerful approach, it is not the only option, and other methodologies, such as rule-based systems and transparent models, also play significant roles. However, the trade-off between creativity, human oversight, and transparency is a critical factor to consider. Generative AI is renowned for its capacity to produce innovative and diverse solutions, often leveraging large datasets to fuel its creativity.

Benchmarks for GenAI Tasks

Generative AI could be used to solve tasks in many different contexts. The tasks consist of mathematical problems, code generation, giving answers to knowledge-intensive questions such as those in official tests (e.g., US Medical License) [17] or sensitive questions, automating tasks, etc. [6, 26]. In this work, we focus on the application of GenAI in work processes such as scrum practices and team management. More precisely, we will look at these tools:

- GPT-3.5: large language model introduced by OpenAI, which can generate code or natural language text [15].
- GPT-4: previous studies suggest that GPT-4 "is more reliable in performance and safety, however, they are not fine-tuned for specific tasks" [15]. It is a larger model than GPT-3.5, so it takes more time to generate responses [15].
- Bard: previous studies show it solves less problems in benchmarks, compared to GPT-models [12]; some studies connect these results to token limits and capabilities of conversation retention [1].

2.3 Generative AI Affecting Work Processes

While generative AI tools are greatly used by individuals for personal purposes, companies and organizations can leverage these tools to improve their working processes at different stages (e.g., managerial works, interactions with customers) [14]. Managers could use generative AI tools to get recommendations for decision-making, data transformations, and automating the interaction processes with the customers [14]. Organization's data could be used as input to the AI tools for the purposes of creating tables, analyzing statistics, generating models, and monitoring workflows.

Nowadays, most organizations have shifted from traditional working processes like waterfall methods to agility, especially scrum. Nevertheless, not all agile teams follow the scrum guidelines thoroughly, or they sometimes even apply them wrongly [16]. This raises the question of how generative AI can be used as a helping tool that can organize teamwork regarding agile principles to ensure that scrum guidelines are actually followed or they are applied closer to what has been defined in their respective manifestos.

2.4 Ethics and Human Oversight

While LLMs, such as GPT and Bard, can perform great tasks, there are concerns regarding their robustness, transparency, and accuracy [9]. These might urge the need for a human monitoring how they perform in their tasks and ensure that ethical decisions are made [5]. The question then arises of whether it is worth integrating GenAI tools. While training new workers for doing specific tasks costs a lot and takes much time, using AI tools that can perform the same tasks in significantly shorter time and with less costs seems to be a reasonable alternative for companies. However, there are concerns regarding the productivity and performance accuracy of AI-assistant tools compared to humans.

Foundation models, including LLMs, especially those implementing online learning strategies are very sensitive to incorrect, redundant, or unstable data distributions, which can lead to undesired replies or behaviors [5]. Moreover, there are some concerns regarding biases when these models are trained or fine-tuned for very specific purposes, which might make them unable to be creative even when facing new contexts [18]. Another aspect that is concerning both for individuals and companies is privacy of the data they have used to train the model, since these models could be capable of recovering personal or sensitive data that could be used for malicious purposes [18]. Therefore, it is important to be careful when inputting sensitive data to these models. One common work-around for companies is using a local LLM, trained to do specific tasks.

3 Research Method

A number of experiments were designed and conducted following standards for conducting and evaluating research in software engineering. The experiments evaluate the performance of different GenAI tools using a number of Python scripts controlling variables such as the prompting method or the models' temperature, a parameter determining the creativity of the resulting generations.

The goal of these experiments is to answer the following research questions:

- **RQ1** How do GenAI tools perform in software management tasks, compared to humans? Is there any task where GenAI models surpass humans?
- **RQ2** What are the nuances in the reasoning of GenAI tools? Are they model- or prompt-specific? How do models comparatively perform?
- **RQ3** How can GenAI enhance software management tasks? How can GenAI for software management impact human decisions and agency?

Each experiment, described in detail in Sect. 4, focuses on a specific software management task and uses data from different sources:

- **Experiment 1** Human, the second author, and GenAI time estimations for implementing a number of unit tests in C#.
- **Experiment 2** Human and GenAI estimations of team effort needed to complete a set of predefined tasks as compiled in the papers by Gren et al. [10, 11].
- **Experiment 3** List of common Boolean Definition of Done and readiness criteria stated in the white and grey literature.
- **Experiment 4 and 5** Programmatically generated combinations of requirements, tasks, and completed items using scripting in Python.

The experiments allow us to comparatively evaluate the performance of GenAI tools, addressing **RQ1**. The GPT-3.5 is used here as a baseline model, a well-stablished, easy to use, and economic tool. Then, all tasks are replicated using GPT-4 and BARD. The prompts used and generations for all tests in all experiments (a large volume of text files) are provided as supplementary materials. The experiments also allow us to compare GenAI generations with human responses. When both human and LLM solutions were compared, they were both given the same prompts. The differences in the responses are used to address **RQ2**. Finally, a discussion addressing **RQ3** is presented, considering the trade-off between accuracy and increased efficiency in software management tasks.

3.1 Threats to Validity

Everything is very sensitive to **prompt engineering**, which is outside the scope of this work. We used the same prompts for all GenAI tools, not adapting them to the needs of each model and application. To mitigate this a bit, we tested different prompts and reported when significant differences appeared in the results.

The definitions of the tasks might not be using the most precise **terminology** to denote each of the software management tasks. However, the results show that GPT is able to understand the tasks in their context and come up with appropriate responses.

In some of the cases, for instance, when using Bard, it was not possible to generate results programmatically using an API or through scripting language-based strategies. Therefore, some of the experiments compare the result of GPT-models with partial results from Bard, which might bias the comparisons.

The models are **updated periodically** and the task-specific performance levels evolve with time as discussed in [6]. In order to mitigate this challenge, the results from the experiments were gathered in a single run to avoid partial results generated with a specific version of the model.

4 Results

4.1 Time Estimations Versus Actual Elapsed Time

Experiment 1: Unit Test Implementation

The goal of this experiment is to evaluate different two chatbots based on LLMs, ChatGPT, and Bard, in their ability to estimate the time needed to implement a number of unit tests. In this experiment, a human participant, agnostic to the task, and a LLM were given a C# class and some unit tests and were asked, "How many unit tests are missing?" To that question, the human participant replied that 6 unit tests were missing for good coverage. Interestingly, both tools gave very similar answers: "Approximately 5 missing unit tests." While ChatGPT provided a few examples of tests to implement (e.g., "computing the average salary when the team has 0 members"), Bard listed the class method that should be tested (Table 1).

Then, all subjects, human or chatbot, were asked for an estimation of the time needed by the participant to implement the 6 unit tests identified by them. The participant estimated it would take them around 1 hour to implement the tests, Bard estimated 2 or 3 hours, and ChatGPT replied that a junior developer like them would spend between 15 and 30 minutes per test. Then, the participant was asked to implement the missing unit tests, which were checked by a third party for correctness. The participant reported spending 38 minutes, with each unit test taking between 4 and 6 minutes to implement. Overall, all the subjects overestimated the time needed to implement the tests.

Table 1 Summary of experiment 1

Task title	Time estimation for unit tests
GenAI models	ChatGPT, Bard
Ground truth	Second author's implementation of a number of unit tests in C#
Takeaways	LLMs overestimate the time to perform a task even though they perform better if they get information about previous performance

In a second phase of the experiment, new methods, previously unseen by all the subjects, were added to the classes before repeating the aforementioned process. In the second iteration, the human participant reported 5 missing unit tests, while ChatGPT reported 4 test cases, and Bard directly provided the code for 3. All subjects were then asked to estimate the time needed to implement the unit tests, but this time, the information about the work in the first round was given. While the participant estimated it would take them 15 minutes, both ChatGPT and Bard computed the average test time (6.33 seconds) and multiplied by 5 to get an estimation. It is interesting to note that ChatGPT used decimals, while Bard rounded up to 7 minutes, giving a slightly lower estimation (31 vs 35 minutes) as a result. Both chatbots also provided tips and suggestions for the human developer.

The participant finally took approximately 20 minutes to implement the remaining 5 unit tests. This experiment therefore shows that even though LLMs might overestimate the time needed to perform a task, they can provide reasonable suggestions if provided with contextual information. An observation from this experiment is that when asked to implement the 10 identified unit tests, ChatGPT took 21.81 seconds, which raises the question of whether it is worth it to have humans writing unit tests or rather revising the AI generated ones [9].

Experiment 2: GPT Is Biased, But Not as Much as Humans

According to Gren et al., there is a bias by which humans overestimate the time needed to implement a system, given a requirements specification with obsolete or deprecated requirements. This can be seen in the left of Fig. 1, representing the estimations of bachelor students. We replicate here this experiment using OpenAI's `gpt-3.5-turbo` model and the same prompts given to humans, which can be found in [11]. The aggregated results, on the right side of Fig. 1, show that the aforementioned bias cannot be observed in the estimations by GPT-3.5 (Table 2).

However, it is important to note that using different prompts to ask GPT-3.5 to complete Task C (5 requirements, 1 obsolete) leads to significantly different results. The bottom-right plot in Fig. 1 shows the differences between multiple runs of GPT estimations using two different prompts:

1. Your task is to estimate how long (in terms of weeks) it will take to implement the following requirements. `{{list of requirements}}` Please note that R5 should NOT be implemented [10].
2. Your task is to estimate how long (in terms of weeks) it will take to implement the first four requirements (R1–R4) in the following requirement specification: `{{list of requirements}}`

Other alternative prompts, not discussed in this chapter for it would be outside of our scope, were also tested. As a general comment, it is important to note that GPT performed significantly better if the requirement was flagged as obsolete at the beginning of the prompt, not after the `{{list of requirements}}`. A one-way ANOVA test reveals that the means of the groups are statistically

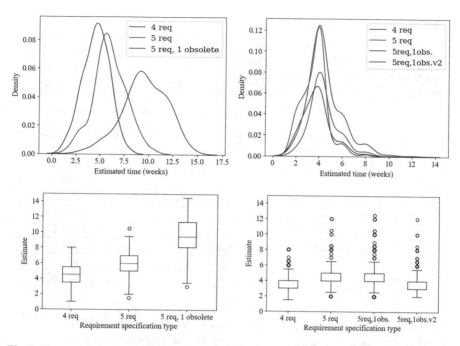

Fig. 1 Humans (left, from [11]) and GPT's estimation (right) of time for specifications with different numbers of requirements and obsolete requirements. Task C was performed with two prompts and obtained significantly different results

Table 2 Summary of experiment 2

Task title	Estimating time in presence of obsolete requirements
GenAI models	OpenAI's gpt-3.5-turbo API
Ground truth	Human and GenAI estimations of team effort needed to complete a set of pre-defined tasks
Takeaways	GPT is biased but not affected by obsolete requirements

significantly different ($p \simeq 10^{-119}$). The one-on-one comparison between the groups was also computed, resulting in a p-value for the pair {5 req, 5 req 1 obsolete} larger than the widely used 5% threshold ($p \simeq 0.93$), which we interpret as the two prompts having equal population means. This can be seen in the right-hand plots in Fig. 1 that represent the GPT estimations for the two cases. The differences between the replies, statistically significant, highlight the importance of good prompt engineering methods to conduct Software Management tasks.

4.2 Experiment 3: Definition of Done

The Definition of Done (DoD) is a formal description of the state of the Increment when it meets the quality measures required for the product [23]. Only when a

Table 3 Summary of experiment 3

Task title	Marking tasks as done based on generic Definition of Done criteria
GenAI models	OpenAI's `gpt-3.5-turbo` API
Ground truth	Percentage of DoD criteria met
Takeaways	The prompt affects GPT's evaluations, no predominant exclusion criteria for DoD was observed

Table 4 Percentage of positive replies for each alternative question. Each prompt was used three times, and done was decided using the "best of three" method discussed in [22]. Each prompt was followed by "Answer only either *Yes* or *No*"

Question	GPT says done
Considering these criteria, is the current status of the task "complete?"	98.83%
Can this work item be presented at the Sprint Review?	99.80%
Can this Product Backlog item be released?	99.76%
Can this work item be considered an Increment already?	82.55%
Is it done?	69.70%
Are we done?	43.84%

Product Backlog item meets the DoD is an Increment born [23]. If a Product Backlog item does not meet the DoD, it cannot be released or even presented at the Sprint Review and should return to the Product Backlog for future consideration instead [23] (Table 3).

Unless the DoD is an organizational standard, each Scrum Team must create a DoD appropriate for the product under development [23]. However, in this experiment, we will assume a generic DoD addressing the 11 important quality properties of software: (i) code is written, (ii) unit tests are written and passing, (iii) integration tests are written and passing, (iv) code was peer reviewed, (v) documentation is updated, (vi) code was refactored (has been improved and optimized and is maintainable), (vii) system testing is done, (viii) security review is done, (ix) acceptance tests are done, (x) feature was delivered, and (xi) feature was installed.

We ran a study using the OpenAI's API for the GPT-3.5 model asking whether an item was done or different combinations of the aforementioned 11 generic criteria as completed. All combinations with any number of elements, where order does not matter, without repetitions (a total of 2046) of the criteria were used. Finally, all the combinations were tested for each of the alternative questions about the state of the increment in Table 4.

We do not have the ground truth for this question or, rather, the human evaluation for which out of the 2046 combinations of criteria correspond to a "done" item for all the questions in Table 4. Strictly speaking, all except one combination (where all criteria are met) should define a "done" item. However, as GPT points out, criteria are interrelated (e.g., passing unit tests assumes the code is written), so the human decision-making process is often more complex than a checklist. The goal of this experiment, though, is only to provide big-numbers-evidence on how different the results can be because of the formulation of the prompt, as reported in the second column of Table 4.

These differences might be explained by the directness of the question formulation and the LLMs' interpretation of the context. For example, the question "Are we done?" is very open-ended, even though the Scrum Guides with the rules for DoD were given as context [23]. GPT might interpret this question to mean if the work day is finished or if the item is meeting the DoD as desired.

The tests were conducted with and without randomizing the order of the criteria and repeated 3 times to reduce the impact of hallucinations in the results. As a result, a total of 6141 queries where sent through API (all responses in Supplementary Materials). Out of all possible combinations of the DoD criteria and prompt question, 87.3% consistently received the same reply (positive or negative). Based on these results, we can state that **changing the prompt changes the GPT's evaluations** even when given the same contextual information (i.e., completed criteria) but the order of the criteria do not. As a final step for this experiment, we computed the frequency of apparitions of criteria in all the prompts. Surprisingly, we could not observe any predominant exclusion criteria (condition *sine qua non*) for DoD according to GPT-3.5. Figure 2b (right) shows that the lack of some tests (unit, integration, and acceptance) and not having released the feature make GPT decide to reply with a "no."

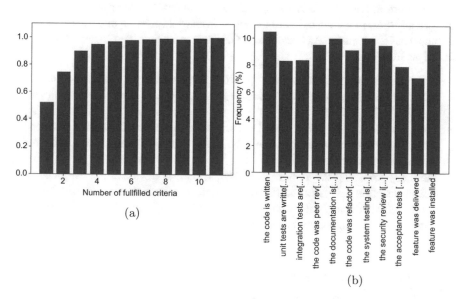

Fig. 2 Results of experiment 3. (**a**) Positive replies with respect to the number of fulfilled criteria. (**b**) Criteria in prompts for work items flagged as not done

4.3 Experiment 4: From Task Titles to Checklists

In this experiment, GPT-3.5 was given a six-item checklist of questions about a system under development:

- Has it been painted black?
- Are all the functionalities tested?
- Does it use distributed computing?
- Does it have a nice alarm sound?
- Is it avoiding collisions?
- Does it minimize its power consumption?

All the combinations of the tasks in Table 6, 63, were listed to generate prompts, randomly selecting tasks from the right column, which complete checklist items, and the left, which do not. As in the previous experiment, each of these combinations was framed as a prompt by attaching the question, "Do these tasks check all the items in the checklist? Write only either yes or no, then (after a full stop) explain why," and sent to GPT using the OpenAI API (Ta) (Table 5).

When asked whether each subset of tasks checked all the items in the checklist or not, GPT was able to correctly map the tasks to the elements in the checklist 85.71% out of a sample of 192 prompt instances, as can be seen in Table 7, one for each combination of the tasks in Table 6. In some of the prompt instances, GPT flagged all items in the checklist as complete even though some tasks were missing. In those cases, the reasoning provided by GPT was analyzed. Three main flaws arose in the justifications:

- **Flaw (1)** A checklist item is "not explicitly mentioned in the completed tasks, but it can be assumed." This assumption represents 60% of the miss-classifications reported in Table 7.
- **Flaw (2)** Because no tasks related to a checklist item "are explicitly mentioned, it cannot be determined if the item is checked," yet GPT states that all the items in the task are complete.
- **Flaw (3)** GPT checks two items based on a single task. For instance, the task description "Tests for collision avoidance implemented and passed" checks the checklist items "Is it avoiding collisions?" and "Are all the functionalities tested?" even though there could be other functionalities.

Table 5 Summary of experiment 4

Task title	From task titles to checklists
GenAI models	OpenAI's gpt-3.5-turbo and gpt-4-0613 API, Bard
Ground truth	six-item checklist of questions and answers about a system under development
Takeaways	GPT-3.5 makes assumptions and attempts to fill the gaps in the provided context, Bard behaves like a rule-based system

Table 6 Set of tasks used to generate lists in experiment 4

Tasks that explicitly check one item in the checklist	Tasks that do not complete any item in the checklist
Tests for collision avoidance implemented and passing	Tests for collision avoidance implemented but it does not pass any
I added a nice sound to the alarm	I added a sound for the alarm
I have painted it black	I have painted it red
I have tested all the functionalities	I have tested some functionalities
The power consumption is fully minimized	The power consumption is monitored
The system now uses distributed computing	The computations are not distributed

Table 7 Percentage of times that GPT checks all the elements in the checklist depending on the percentage of completed items

Completed items (ground truth)	Prompt instances (num. of tests)	GPT says yes / prompt instances
16.66%	6	0%
33.33%	30	0%
50%	60	0%
66.66%	60	14.28%
83.33%	30	61.53%
100% (6 out of 6)	6	100%

This experiment was repeated using OpenAI's `gpt-4-0613` model and with Google's Bard to study whether these assumptions are common across different LLMs. In both cases, the results in Table 7 are improved, reaching 100% accuracy, and none of the items in the checklist are checked if not explicitly addressed by one of the tasks in the provided list. The intuition behind it is that once the mapping between the checklist items and the completed task is done, a task that both GPT and Bard excel at, Bard resembles a rule-based approach, while GPT-3.5 makes assumptions and attempts to fill the gaps in the completed tasks. Section 5 discusses the trade-off between these approaches and highlights the need for a better understanding on how human developers would interact with generative AI tools for the purposes here described.

4.4 Experiment 5: Requirements Met

In this experiment, the LLMs were given a set of requirements for a system followed by a natural language sentence, introduced as written by a developer, which states which functionalities and quality properties are already implemented in the system. Then, the LLM was asked whether the system met the requirements based on that sentence or not. A total of 52 human-written sentences were tested in the scope of this experiment. This application aligns with the strengths of LLMs in understanding and generating text. All the replies were gathered and stored for later analysis. What

Table 8 Summary of experiment 5

Task title	Checking if requirements are met
GenAI models	OpenAI's `gpt-3.5-turbo` and `gpt-4-0613` API, Bard
Ground truth	Set of requirements and matching implemented functionalities, confusion matrix (TP and TN)
Takeaways	GPT models are not acting as a rule-based system, Bard does not warn the user about the dangers

Table 9 Confusion matrix for prompts with different percentages of the "shall" requirements met, that is, with a different sizes of the subset of met requirements

	100% met	Partially met	Total estimation
GPT says met	9	13	22
GPT says not met	3	27	30
Total met	12	40	52

follows is a discussion of the strengths and shortcomings of GPT and Bard in this task (Table 8).

First, the chatbots were given a complete list of ten safety requirements for a system. In order to evaluate whether the LLMs prioritized important requirements, the safety requirements were written using "shall" or "should" to denote mandatory and recommended requirements, respectively. For instance, while "the system shall avoid collisions with a pedestrian," "the system should minimize its power consumption." The cases were divided in two cases, as reported in Table 9. On the one hand, cases where 100% of the requirements are met, i.e., the sentence stated that all of the requirements "shall" requirements were met but some "should" requirements might be missing, and, on the other hand, cases where only some of the "shall" requirements where met. In the first case, GPT-3.5 replied that the requirements were met 75% of the times, and these instances correspond to true positives. However, when the "shall" requirements were partially met according to the statement, GPT-3.5 reported them being met in almost a third of the instances (false positives). Taken together, these results show that GPT-3.5 has an accuracy of 69.23% in this binary classification task.

Then, the explanations for the decisions were analyzed separately. In the case of false positives, that is, implementation descriptions that did not explicitly address all the requirements but that were classified as doing so, GPT often justified its decision using the hierarchy of the requirements. For instance, when the sentence stated that "the system has a functional processor at all times," GPT judged that two requirements were met: (i) "at least one processor shall be functional at all times," and (ii) its parent requirement, "the system shall have redundant processors," even though they were not connected explicitly in the prompt. Highlight dependencies in the requirements are an interesting emerging result that might be helpful to developers performing this task. However, these assumptions might introduce errors in the logic process.

Another surprising behavior was detected during the analysis of the replies by the GPT-3.5 and GPT-4 models. In the replies, GPT models often said that the system was not safe even though all of the safety requirements were met because one or more of the requirements conflicted with the notion of safety, which was not defined in the prompt. For example, "Driving fast can increase the risk of collisions and compromise safety." These results prove that the GPT models are not acting as a rule-based system. Instead, the models understand the context, create a hierarchy and mapping of the requirements, detect conflicts, and are able to come up with sensible and understandable warnings for the user. Interestingly, **Bard did not warn the user about the dangers of speeding, and often stated that speed "is not relevant to safety"** because "speed is not a safety factor in and of itself and a system can be safe at any speed."

5 Discussion

Generative AI tools, including LLMs, demonstrate remarkable abilities across a spectrum of software management tasks. They can automate routine processes, generate code snippets, assist in requirements analysis, and aid in decision-making. The experiments discussed in Sect. 4 look into some of these processes and decisions and serve here as a basis to discuss the trade-off between performance, as compared to humans, and increased productivity in the studied software management tasks.

5.1 Oversight

Independently of their performance, Generative AI tools need appropriate human oversight mechanisms for them to be trustworthy [9]. Generative AI is renowned for its capacity to produce innovative and diverse solutions, often leveraging large datasets to fuel its creativity. Yet, this very attribute may limit the level of human oversight, as AI-generated content can occasionally deviate from users' expectations without them being aware.

> **Takeaway from Experiment 1**
> When given historical context, GenAI tools are better at estimating time to complete a task (in this case, unit test implementation). This can serve as a first estimation in a capacity planning meeting if the tool is provided true information about the increments in the previous sprints.

This result addresses **RQ1**, which questions how GenAI tools perform in software management tasks, compared to humans. Experiment 1 and 2 show that different LLMs can estimate time to complete a task, potentially being useful in capacity planning meetings. This estimate could be used as a reference point, complementing human judgment rather than replacing it entirely.

In the scope of both the EU AI Act [9] and the Scrum Guides [23], it is important to remind the reader that such a GenAI-powered system would need to be used as a suggestion tool for time estimations and appropriate measures should be put in place to avoid unnecessary stress on the employee or foster unfair evaluations the quality of engineer. The tool could be employed at individual, team, or managerial level to ensure that estimations are sensible and complement human judgment without undermining their agency.

5.2 Better than a Human?

However, engineers might feel discomfort when being judged by an AI, particularly in a domain that involves intellectual activities. The introduction of GenAI could potentially create pressure on developers, as its integration might be accompanied by expectations of increased efficiency and accuracy The introduction of GenAI in software management has stirred debates about its suitability, user base, ethical implications, and the potential impacts on developers. The ethical responsibility lies in striking a balance where GenAI aids developers without placing undue stress on them, ensuring a supportive environment that values both human expertise and AI assistance.

One significant observation highlighted in Experiment 2 is that while humans tend to overestimate the time required for project implementation when dealing with obsolete requirements, GPT appears to be free from this bias, indicating its potential utility as an estimation reviewer, addressing **RQ2** on whether there are any tasks where GenAI surpasses humans.

Takeaway from Experiment 2
GPT might be free of some biases that humans have when estimating the effort related to a requirement specification. Therefore, it could be used as an assistant during capacity planning meetings with appropriate human oversight.

Moreover, the results of Experiments 4 and 5 show that by highlighting potential dependencies or conflicts, GPT can also assist in achieving more realistic and achievable project timelines.

5.3 Different Reasoning Strategies

While LLMs exhibit impressive prowess in various tasks, the scope of their effectiveness is not without constraints. The results of Experiment 3, on the other hand, highlight the complexities involved in using language GPT for determining task completion. The more criteria a task fulfils, the more likely GPT is to considered it "done." Once again, this issue might be due to the non-adapted prompt instance. Also, the diversity of the training data can impact its capacity to generate contextually appropriate responses.

Takeaway from Experiment 3
The tested LLMs do not show the capacity to decide which generic criteria are more important for DoD. Instead, the more met criteria, the more likely they are to accept a work item becoming an Increment, independently of which criteria subset is met.

This contrasts with the results in Experiment 4 and 5 where hierarchies arose between the items in the prompt and GPT used a more complex reasoning. The observed nuances in the reasoning of GenAI tools, reported in Sect. 4.3, provide insights to address **RQ2**.

Takeaway from Experiment 4
Different GenAI tools seem to use different approaches to make decisions, some closer to a rule-base system, while others make assumptions and use creative reasoning processes, even when not asked explicitly to do so, sometimes resulting in flawed assumptions.

As aforementioned, the training data significantly impacts the LLM's generations. For instance, in Experiment 5, GPT-3.5 and GPT-4's responses associated speed with risk, even though the requirement itself did not explicitly mention safety. This highlights how the underlying data and training of these models can influence their decision-making, possibly drawing upon instances in their training data where speed correlated with accidents. This is not necessarily bad. The question then arises: how should these AI tools be balanced? This involves ensuring that AI models provide accurate replies while also taking into account the broader context and varied perspectives. In all cases, a tool that clarifies its assumptions could be considered more sensible and would mitigate potential automation bias.

Takeaway from Experiment 5
GenAI tools show the capacity to understand not only implicit hierarchies among requirements but also the general application domain context and warn the user in a transparent way.

It is worth reminding that different models showed not only different performances but also different reasoning stiles. For instance, GPT-4 and Bard appear to diverge from GPT-3.5's approach in Experiments 4 and 5, possibly indicating a progression toward refining AI logic to be more cautious with the assumptions made during the reasoning, in line with the findings in [6]. The discussion then naturally turns to the question of whether simplicity is better or worse. Simpler logic may lead to more **conservative assumptions**, potentially reducing the risk of incorrect judgments based on indirect associations. On the other hand, more complex logic, as seen in GPT-3.5, might lead to misinterpretations of the context and dangerous situations if developers show automation bias.

6 Conclusion

Even though software management strategies using GenAI might not always surpass human performance, they are reasonably able to conduct tasks that are often overlooked by Scrum teams, according to previous studies [20]. However, as presented in Sect. 4, their performance is often sub-par and very sensitive to prompt engineering techniques. Taken together, the results raise the question of whether it is better to have a GenAI tool assist in these tasks even though the results might not be as good as desired? In order to answer this question, there should be careful consideration of the trade-off between traditional approaches and potentially faster, error-prone work.

All in all, integrating GenAI in software management offers distinct advantages related to efficiency, reduced human error, and enhanced productivity. However, the human factor remains crucial, particularly in complex problem-solving, creative tasks, and areas that demand nuanced human judgement. However, the results also highlight the difference between the baseline GenAI models and when software management context is provided. The main takeaway message of the experiments is that **providing context, either in single prompts or in conversations, increases the chance of achieving sensible results**. This further motivates the usage of chain-of-thought strategies to correct and conduct LLM reasoning [25]. For these reasons, ethical concerns should be addressed to avoid potential negative consequences that could emerge from a uninformed or hasty GenAI integration [9].

7 Future Work

GenAI tools' ability to understand and generate text is powerful, but its comprehension lacks the nuanced understanding that would be required to make complex decisions. What follows is a list of examples of tasks that are difficult to automate using AI but that humans would benefit from having AI assistance:

- Understand user needs, and then forge a team; then, we need to estimate the number person, team-weeks, lines of code, function points, or general effort to set expectations of what can be accomplished in the given time frame.
- Preliminary backlog (44% devs without backlog [20]).
- Breakdown of large user stories during or previously to the meeting (56% of devs do not [20]).
- Growth chart in story points [7].
- Suggest lightening the team's methodology, or warn when not sufficient [7].
- Define the sprint goal at the start of the planning meeting, which is something that 82% of developers do not do (neither at start or ever) [20].
- Manage project portfolios, and find stopping points [7].

As AI technologies continue to advance, there is potential for more sophisticated solutions that combine AI-generated content with domain expertise, guiding us toward a more reliable and sensible integration of GenAI within the software management pipeline. Such software management tasks need contextual understanding, domain knowledge, and the ability to weigh different criteria against each other.

To conclude, we want to bring up again the question of whether using GenAI can increase productivity in software management even though there's no guarantee of human-level performance. We therefore need to balance diverse GenAI tools and human intelligence and collaborate with it.

7.1 Balancing GenAIs

Generative AI could be used to work alongside humans, providing them with prior estimations when needed and warning them about potential bias (see Sect. 4.1). How could developers effectively use multiple generative AI tools? Using multiple AI tools can be approached in various ways, each offering its own set of advantages and potential outcomes.

On the one hand, one approach is to employ these tools in parallel to humans and using multiple GenAI tools simultaneously. This setup would allow for the generation of diverse outputs from different AI models, enabling developers to explore a wider range of creative solutions and responses. On the other hand, another strategy involves using these AI tools sequentially, using one first (preferably the better performing one) and then refining the output using the other tool could lead to enhanced results. This could be done in an iterative loop to polish the output over successive iterations. By systematically exploring combinations of fine-tuned and generic LLMs in both content creation and review roles, developers can identify the arrangement that yields the best results for specific tasks. By alternating the roles of content generation and review, GenAI tools and engineers can combine their strengths to collaboratively enhance the final output.

Rule-based systems allow developers to explicitly define rules and conditions, ensuring predictable outcomes. A hybrid approach could also be adopted, dividing tasks into rule-based and creative components. GenAI could be used for the creative aspects, while rule-based systems offer precision in structured tasks where human-defined rules are strict and transparent.

7.2 Collaborate with AI: Tuning, Training, and Feedback

Fine-tuning LLMs for particular tasks holds the promise of enhancing their performance and tailoring their responses to the task's domain. Fine-tuning effectively fine-tunes the model's language generation skills to align with the nuances and expectations of the designated task. However, fine-tuning may lead to overfitting, where the model becomes excessively specialized and may struggle with generating diverse and creative responses even within the domain.

Moreover, fine-tuning demands substantial amounts of task-specific data, which might not always be readily available. For this reason, continuously training models could be a good strategy. Continuously training the GenAI on real-world team-based scenarios could enhance a possible GenAI coworker's understanding over time. The broader question raised is how AI systems strike a balance between making assumptions and ensuring accuracy and how these assumptions and decisions could be seamlessly integrated into different layers of the Agile development workflow.

GenAI could be trained like one more of your colleagues. This is the ultimate collaboration, no? This might hold the potential to revolutionize software management, bridging the gap between automation and human insights.

References

1. Ahmed, I., Kajol, M., Hasan, U., Datta, P.P., Roy, A., Reza, M.R.: Chatgpt vs. bard: A comparative study. UMBC Student Collection (2023)
2. Alberts, I.L., Mercolli, L., Pyka, T., Prenosil, G., Shi, K., Rominger, A., Afshar-Oromieh, A.: Large language models (LLM) and chatgpt: what will the impact on nuclear medicine be? Eur. J. Nuclear Med. Molec. Imag. **50**(6), 1549–1552 (2023)
3. Beck, K.: Extreme Programming Explained: Embrace Change. Addison-Wesley Professional, Boston (2000)
4. Cabrero-Daniel, B., Fazelidehkordi, Y., Ratushniak, O.: Trustworthy "blackbox" Self-Adaptive Systems (2023)

5. Cabrero-Daniel, B., Fazelidehkordi, Y., Ratushniak, O.: Trustworthy "blackbox" Self-adaptive Systems (2023)
6. Chen, L., Zaharia, M., Zou, J.: How is ChatGPT's behavior changing over time? (2023)
7. Cockburn, A.: Agile Software Development (2002)
8. Despa, M.L.: Comparative study on software development methodologies. Database Syst. J. **5**(3), 37–56 (2014)
9. EUR-Lex - 52021PC0206 - EN - EUR-Lex. https://eur-lex.europa.eu/legal-content/EN/TXT/?uri=CELEX:52021PC0206
10. Gren, L., Svensson, R.B., Unterkalmsteiner, M.: Is it possible to disregard obsolete requirements? An initial experiment on a potentially new bias in software effort estimation. In: 2017 IEEE/ACM 10th International Workshop on Cooperative and Human Aspects of Software Engineering (CHASE), pp. 56–61. IEEE (2017)
11. Gren, L., Svensson, R.B.: Is it possible to disregard obsolete requirements? A family of experiments in software effort estimation. Requir. Eng. **26**, 459–480 (2021). https://doi.org/10.1007/S00766-021-00351-7/TABLES/10. https://link.springer.com/article/10.1007/s00766-021-00351-7
12. HANS, F.: ChatGPT vs. bard–which is better at solving coding problems?
13. Jørgensen, M.: Improved measurement of software development effort estimation bias. Inf. Softw. Technol. **157**, 107157 (2023)
14. Korzynski, P., Mazurek, G., Altmann, A., Ejdys, J., Kazlauskaite, R., Paliszkiewicz, J., Wach, K., Ziemba, E.: Generative artificial intelligence as a new context for management theories: Analysis of ChatGPT. Central Eur. Manag. J. **31**(1), 3–11 (2023)
15. Koubaa, A.: Gpt-4 vs. gpt-3.5: A concise showdown (2023)
16. Kuhrmann, M., et al.: What makes agile software development agile? IEEE Trans. Softw. Eng. **48**(9), 3523–3539 (2022). https://doi.org/10.1109/TSE.2021.3099532
17. Lin, J.C., Younessi, D.N., Kurapati, S.S., Tang, O.Y., Scott, I.U.: Comparison of GPT-3.5, GPT-4, and human user performance on a practice ophthalmology written examination. Eye **37**, 1–2 (2023)
18. Lund, B.D., Wang, T.: Chatting about chatgpt: how may ai and GPT impact academia and libraries? Library Hi Tech News **40**(3), 26–29 (2023)
19. Martin, R.C.: Agile Software Development: Principles, Patterns, and Practices. Prentice Hall PTR, Hoboken (2003)
20. Mortada, M., Ayas, H.M., Hebig, R.: Why do software teams deviate from scrum? Reasons and implications. In: Proceedings of the International Conference on Software and System Processes, pp. 71–80. ICSSP '20, Association for Computing Machinery, New York (2020). https://doi.org/10.1145/3379177.3388899.
21. OpenAI: Gpt-4 technical report (2023)
22. Ronanki, K., Cabrero-Daniel, B., Berger, C.: ChatGPT as a tool for user story quality evaluation: Trustworthy out of the box? In: Kruchten, P., Gregory, P. (eds.) Agile Processes in Software Engineering and Extreme Programming – Workshops, pp. 173–181. Springer Nature Switzerland (2022). https://doi.org/10.1007/978-3-031-48550-3_17
23. Schwaber, K., Sutherland, J.: The scrum guide the definitive guide to scrum: The rules of the game (2020). https://scrumguides.org/scrum-guide.html
24. Srivastava, A., Bhardwaj, S., Saraswat, S.: Scrum model for agile methodology. In: 2017 International Conference on Computing, Communication and Automation (ICCCA), pp. 864–869 (2017). https://doi.org/10.1109/CCAA.2017.8229928
25. Wei, J., Wang, X., Schuurmans, D., Bosma, M., Chi, E., Le, Q., Zhou, D.: Chain of thought prompting elicits reasoning in large language models (2022). arXiv preprint arXiv:2201.11903
26. Weisz, J.D., Muller, M., He, J., Houde, S.: Toward general design principles for generative ai applications (2023). arXiv preprint arXiv:2301.05578

Value-Based Adoption of ChatGPT in Agile Software Development: A Survey Study of Nordic Software Experts

Anh Nguyen-Duc and Dron Khanna

Abstract Agile has become popular as a software development paradigm due to its flexibility, iterative process, and customer-centricity. However, managing Agile projects requires effective communication, collaboration, and decision-making. ChatGPT, a large language model, has the potential to enhance these aspects of Agile project management. In this chapter, we conduct a survey study to understand the perception of Agile project managers about adopting ChatGPT in their projects. Based on responses from 73 Agile professions in Nordic countries, we found that (1) in general, the perceived benefits offered by ChatGPT outweigh the perceived complexity required for its setup, (2) Agile professions are positive toward the adoption of ChatGPT on non-technical activities in Agile projects, and (3) administrative tasks involving meetings, emails, and technical writing are seen as the blue ocean, offering significant value with relatively lower setup complexity. We also discuss the limitations of ChatGPT in the Agile project context, such as bias, privacy concerns, and dependency on data quality. Our discussion provides insights into the potential applications of ChatGPT in Agile project management and recommendations for future research.

Keywords Agile software development · Project management · ChatGPT · Generative AI tools · Survey · Questionnaire

1 Introduction

Agile software development places a strong emphasis on collaboration with customers, adaptability, and swift responses to change. Agile software project man-

A. Nguyen-Duc (✉)
Norwegian University of Science and Technology, Trondheim, Norway
e-mail: anhn@ntnu.no

D. Khanna
Free University of Bozen-Bolzano, Bolzano, Italy
e-mail: dron.khanna@unibz.it

agement involves various practices and tools, including daily stand-up meetings, sprint planning, sprint reviews, and retrospectives. Although it has gained popularity recently, contemporary Agile software project management still faces many challenges [11]. These challenges encompass a range of factors, including scaling Agile practices to larger and more complex projects, fostering effective cross-functional teamwork, and ensuring that Agile principles are effectively integrated into organizational culture and structure. On the horizon of technological advancement, we anticipate the emergence of visionary project management tools and practices that will transform how projects are planned, executed, and controlled, potentially addressing some of the existing challenges. One such innovation is the integration of generative AI tools, such as ChatGPT[1](OpenAI) and Google's Bard[2] (Google), into project management workflows. These tools can act as intelligent virtual assistants, reducing the likelihood of human error, optimizing resource allocation, and improving decision-making.

The potential adoption of GenAI tools in engineering activities has been increasingly discussed in the Agile community [12, 23]. Our workshop, titled the "AI-Assisted Agile Software Development Workshop," part of the XP2023 conference, represents one of the pioneering events contributing to this ongoing discourse. The workshop gave participants valuable insights and practical experiences with ChatGPT in concrete Agile project development tasks. However, it's important to note that all the work conducted thus far remains in its early stages, consisting primarily of conceptual ideas and preliminary results.

Moreover, the debate tends to focus on the technical capacity of AI tools in performing tasks rather than on the managerial consideration of adopting AI tools in Agile projects. This motivates us to conduct an empirical study on the perception and intention of adopting ChatGPT among Agile project managers. Understanding how Agile project managers adopt and use technology is essential for implementing AI tools in the current Agile workflow. The results of this research can serve as a valuable resource for software development teams, decision-makers, and organizations considering the adoption of ChatGPT in Agile environments.

In the Nordic regions, the Agile methodology has gained substantial prominence as a popular paradigm for software development across various contexts. It has found application across diverse scenarios, spanning from small to large development teams [4, 9] and various product categories, including Web application, enterprise software and embedded systems [14, 20], and different organizational context [5]. Furthermore, the availability of AI tools such as ChatGPT within the Nordic regions underscores their readiness for technological innovation. These twofold circumstances present the Nordic countries at the forefront of GenAI adoption in a professional Agile project context.

---

[1] https://openai.com/.

[2] https://bard.google.com/.

Our study seeks to tackle the following research question

RQ: How do Nordic project managers perceive the benefits and challenges of adopting GenAI for Agile software management tasks?

Our research aims to offer practical guidance and best practices based on the experiences and opinions of Nordic professionals, along with potential directions for future research. This research contributes to the Agile research and practitioner community by offering valuable insights into the potential of ChatGPT to increase productivity in Agile project management. By conducting a survey study among 73 Agile practitioners in the Nordic region, the research highlights that the perceived benefits of ChatGPT outweigh the complexity of its setup, particularly in non-technical activities, such as administrative tasks.

The remainder of this chapter is structured as follows. The background is described in Sect. 2. Section 3 presents the research approach. Section 4 is our findings. Section 5 contains the discussion, and Sect. 6 concludes the paper.

2 Background

In this section, an examination of previous research on the integration of AI in Agile projects is presented (Sect. 2.1), followed by an introduction to a theoretical framework adopted for empirical exploration (Sect. 2.2).

2.1 AI Adoption in Agile Software Project Management

By the time of this research, empirical studies on the adoption of AI in software project management were in a nascent phase, marked by a scarcity of peer-reviewed empirical literature. The survey by Bera et al., for instance, presented an idea that large language models could replace general tasks under Agile project management in functions such as enhancing contextual information of the project development, working as per Agile guidelines on particular dataset [3]. The study proposes that ChatGPT, as a virtual team member, could provide valuable information, mentor teams, and share the workload. Daun and Brings conducted a study in a student project context, emphasizing the ability of ChatGPT to assist students in Agile software development projects [7]. Dam et al., in their study, describe the importance of AI that can significantly reshape project management tasks [6]. Various uncertainties during project management, such as team dynamics and customer and developer needs, could be replaced with AI assistance tools. Also, AI could be a game-changer for a team for risk prediction, actionable, and decision-making tasks. Moreover, AI could accelerate the productivity and success rate of a project. More recently, Hoda et al. envision an "Agile copilot" concept, in which AI assistants can perform several management activities, including project estimation, user story creations, task breakdown and refinement and test case optimization [12]. Holzmann et al. conducted a Delphi study on 52 project managers to portray the future AI applications in project management [13]. The author presented the list of most crucial project management areas where GenAI can be adopted, i.e., the creation of project schedule, WBS, and task list. Prifti et al. identified the pain points or problems in project management, including safety, privacy, autonomy, data availability, and employment [21]. Then, the paper proposes how AI's assistance can help project managers become more productive and skilled in organizations.

2.2   *Value-Based Acceptance Theory on AI Products*

In fields like information systems, business, and education research, AI products are often treated as new and innovative technology. Consequently, gaining insight into the adoption and the behavioral intentions associated with using AI-based products can be informed by leveraging prior research on the adoption of innovative products by users. Most studies on the use of innovative products are based on theoretical frameworks like the Technology Acceptance Model (TAM) [8], Value-based Acceptance Model (VAM) [17], Theory of Planned Behavior (TPB) [1], and Unified Theory of Acceptance and Use of Technology (UTAUT) [25]. The TAM has been widely used to explain intention to use in various innovative products [2, 10, 19, 24].

Expanding upon the TAM model, Sohn et al. proposed a VAM—Value-based Acceptance—model incorporating a business dimension into the original one, [22]. VAM emphasizes that users of innovative products should be acknowledged not only as technology enthusiasts but also as consumers. As shown in Fig. 1, VAM presents benefits (usefulness and enjoyment) and sacrifice (technicality and perceived fee) as the main factors of perceived value and analyzed intention to use. Additionally, it is based on a cost-benefit paradigm, which reflects the decision-making process where the decision to use is made by comparing the cost of uncertainty in choosing a new technology or product [18]. Therefore, we found

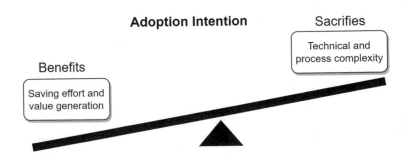

Fig. 1 Value-based acceptance model

VAM as a suitable conceptual framework to explain the adoption of AI products within project management.

In this study, we use the two dimensions of the VAM model—perceived benefits and perceived sacrifice—to study the adoption of ChatGPT. In our case, the help is presented by the perceived generated value in general. The value can be internal—time and effort saved, productivity increased, or external value—customer satisfaction with project performance. The sacrifice is measured by the level of complexity in both technical and process terms. This is the perception of project managers on how complex it is to set up and integrate ChatGPT into their projects, workflows, or organizations.

3   Research Approach

The objective of this 2023 survey was to understand and obtain knowledge of AI assisting project management activities. The study includes two phases: (1) identification of tasks with the possibility of adopting ChatGPT and (2) surveying opinions of Agile professionals about adopting ChatGPT for such tasks. The overview of the research process is shown in Fig. 2.

3.1   Identification of a Possible Task List

The study was initiated in February 2023. A literature review was conducted then; however, only a little was found regarding GenAI and Agile project management. In April 2023, we conducted an informal interview with an Agile project manager in Oslo, Norway. The interviewee started using ChatGPT for professional work, including correcting emails and idea generation. He has provided some ideas on what kind of tasks ChatGPT can apply. During the AI-assisted XP workshop (mentioned in Sect. 1), a focus group was conducted to refine the questions in the context of an Agile project that ChatGPT can assist. Afterward, key focus group members conducted another online meeting to discuss strengths, weaknesses, opportunities, and threats regarding adopting ChatGPT on each task. To simplify the list, we classify the functions into two types: (1) technical activities (including requirement work, software design, coding, testing, and deployment) and managerial activities

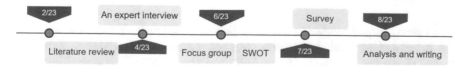

Fig. 2 An overview of the research process

(planning, estimations, control, meetings, communication, etc.). A final list was refined and presented in Table 1.

3.2 Survey Design

Based on the task list (Sect. 3.1), a questionnaire was designed in the first week of August 2023. The purpose of the questionnaire is to gather the opinions of Nordic Agile experts and evaluate the tendency of their perception of ChatGPT adoption in the Agile context. The survey aims to describe a trend of a specific population. We adopted a structured cross-sectional survey process between July 2023 and August 2023.

The survey consists of two main parts. Part 1 is questions about the background and experience of the participants. Part 2 is a list of multiple-choice questions using a 5-point Likert scale. In the Likert scale, two questions were (1) the level of effort saved and generated and (2) the level of complexity to set it up. Five standard choices existed (1 the least to 5 the most) under the two questions. This was done so the participants could opt out if the respondent needed to be more confident or interested in the question. Respondents can also specify freely via text with enhanced responses. Each question is also provided with an opt-out option. The sampling strategy for this study is convenient and localized. Responses are collected from our professional network (ca. 23% of the total number of answers), social media (ca. 15%), and professional recruitment platforms (ca. 62%).

The survey was available from July 15 to August 15. The total number of responses is 115. After filtering out the invalid responses (empty responses, responses with random answers, and responses from people without relevant background or experience), the number of included responses for analysis is 73. The demographic information of the survey respondents, i.e., their locations, knowledge of Agile project, and experience with using ChatGPT or GenAI tools, are shown in Fig. 3. As indicated, a significant proportion of the respondents originate from Norway, which reflects the authors' professional network. Most respondents have experience working or managing Agile projects between 1 and 10 years. The majority of respondents have employed GenAI tools, such as ChatGPT, in both their everyday tasks and professional endeavors.

3.3 Data Analysis

The dataset is preprocessed to remove invalid data points. Descriptive statistics are calculated for each quantitative question. Questions contribute to either the technical or managerial behaviors of Agile project managers. Hence, the Likert data

Table 1 Tasks and reasons for adopting ChatGPT

Category	Tasks	Reasons
Technical activities	User story/requirement generation	Quickly generate user stories or requirements based on input criteria, goals, and constraints
	User story correction/ refinement	Provide detailed suggestions for refining user stories, enhancing their clarity, completeness, and alignment with project objectives
	Requirement estimation and prioritization	Assist in estimating the effort required for each requirement given enough historical data
	Requirement modelling and analysis	Aid in creating visual models or diagrams that represent complex requirements accurately
	Decision support by presenting available technological options	For popular technologies (Web, mobile app, etc.), offer insights into available technological options
	Designing overall architecture against given set of requirements	Assist in designing a coherent architecture that aligns with specified requirements
	Designing detailed architecture of components from the overview ones	Help translate high-level architectural concepts into detailed component designs, ensuring a clear and consistent implementation of the overall architecture
	Providing guidance on software design patterns	Guidance on selecting appropriate design patterns, explaining their advantages and disadvantages, and helping developers make design choices that optimize code structure and maintainability
	Assisting with software performance optimization	Provide suggestions and best practices for optimizing software performance, including code refactoring, resource allocation, and algorithmic improvements, to enhance system efficiency
	Generating code from given libraries	Generating code snippets, functions, or a whole file from input libraries
	Optimizing code against quality attributes	Suggest improvements to enhance quality attributes such as performance, security, and maintainability
	Code summarization and explanation	Provide concise summaries and detailed explanations of code
	Reverse engineering and code refactoring	Recommend code refactoring strategies, rewrite your code to improve code structure and readability
	Converting codebase to different languages or configurations	Help automate the process of translating code from one programming language or configuration to another
	Moving codebase to the cloud	In a given context, questions about cloud or cloud migration can be assisted by ChatGPT
	Automate code analysis and anomaly detection	Automate the code analysis process, identifying anomalies, and suggesting corrective actions
	Automate commit workflow (commit, comment, pull, push request)	Tools like copilot to streamline the code commit workflow by generating commit messages, comments, pull requests, and push requests

(continued)

Table 1 (continued)

Category	Tasks	Reasons
Managerial activities	Preparing for the sprint planning meeting	Analyze documents, generate meeting plan and agenda, keep track of meeting minutes
	Defining sprint goals	Synthesize input from stakeholders and historical data to assist in defining clear and achievable sprint goals
	Selecting product backlog items	Assist in selecting the most appropriate backlog items by considering factors like priority, dependencies, and business value
	Creating a sprint backlog	Automate the process of populating the sprint backlog with selected items, ensuring that it reflects the sprint goals and team capacity
	Facilitating the review meeting	Assist in organizing and structuring the review meeting by generating agendas, tracking progress against sprint goals, and prompting discussions on completed work
	Preparing for the retrospective meeting	Analyze historical data and team feedback to prepare meaningful topics for discussion in the retrospective meeting
	Onboarding new team members	Providing automated onboarding guides and documentation, helping new team members quickly integrate into existing workflows and processes
	Supporting engineers' retention and team health	Analyze team dynamics and recommend strategies to improve team health and retain engineers
	Documenting the review outcome	Help create detailed and standardized documentation of the review outcomes
	Writing or improving formal emails	Help compose well-structured and professionally written formal emails, ensuring clarity, conciseness, and appropriate tone, which can enhance communication effectiveness
	Meeting preparation with agenda, slides, note-taking, etc.	Assist in meeting preparation by generating agendas, creating presentation slides, and even automating note-taking, saving time and ensuring organized and productive meetings
	Stakeholder management with meeting reminders, communication strategy, etc.	Help manage stakeholders by sending meeting reminders, suggesting communication strategies, and providing timely updates, facilitating smooth and efficient interactions
	Assisting technical writing	Support technical writers by generating technical documentation, explanations, and guides, ensuring accuracy, consistency, and accessibility of technical content

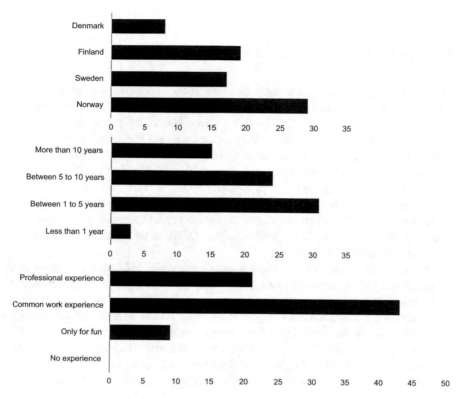

Fig. 3 Demographic of survey participants

are analyzed at the interval measurement scale (mean value). We documented and labelled open-ended questions. We assume that the perception of the benefits and sacrifices when adopting GenAI tools are independent of the respondent's mind. When comparing two separate sets of responses from a Likert question, we ran a two-tailed independent t-test to compare the respondents' perceptions of the benefits and sacrifices. It is a known approach to measure user value as a trade-off between relative quality and relative price or, in our case, between the perceived benefits and perceived complexity. In an interval measurement scale, we calculated the user value below. Technical and managerial tasks are then sorted according to the user value.

$$UserValue = PerceivedBenefit - PerceivedComplexity \qquad (1)$$

4 Results

4.1 Agile Project Technical Tasks

The Agile project managerial task outlines seventeen tasks we asked for in the survey. We calculated their mean value in terms of perceived benefits and complexity. We obtained the maximum perceived benefit for *Code summarization and explanation*, i.e., (3.69). Also, very close to it, we received the *Generating code from given libraries* mean value (3.66). Whereas the minimum perceived benefit for *Requirement modelling and analysis*, i.e., (3.37). Among the seventeen mentioned tasks, we did not find a higher degree of difference concerning the mean values, the maximum and minimum mean value of the perceived benefit, i.e., (3.69 − 3.19 = 0.50). Whereas in terms of the perceived complexity, we observe a more significant difference, i.e., (3.55 − 2.59 = 0.96), some Agile project technical tasks were more challenging to achieve.

The technical tasks with the highest user values are *code summarization and explanation (1.1), generating code from libraries (0.87), user story correction and refinement (0.73), and user story generation (0.7)*. T-test showed a statistical difference in the distribution of respondents' rates on the benefit and complexity of these tasks. The technical tasks with negative user value (perceived complexity more than perceived benefits) are designing overall architecture against a given set of requirements (−0.07), designing the detailed architecture of components from the general ones (−0.17) and requirement modelling and analysis (−0.18).

Proposition 1 *Overall perceived benefits exceed perceived complexity when it comes to the adoption of GenAI in technical tasks.*

We conducted t-tests between the benefits scores and complexity scores to test if they are significantly different from each other. Ten tasks resulted in p-values lower than 0.05, while seven yielded p-values higher than 0.05. These findings indicate that our results are unlikely to be solely attributed to random chance, meaning that for ten tasks, respondents differ in the associated benefits and complexity.

Proposition 2 *Perceived benefits of adopting GenAI are different among technical activities. The adoption of GenAI for code summarization and generation and user story generation and refinement present the best user value.*

Regarding the standard deviation (SD), we obtained a low value for most of the tasks, indicating remarkable agreement among the respondents voting. Also, the reactions and ratings were reasonably uniform, with less disagreement in their perceptions. This also means that we will obtain similar responses if we conduct the same survey questions with the same respondents and under the same conditions.

While the perceived value of the user value has a relatively large range from 1,1 to −0,18, the range of perceived benefits does not vary that much (between 3,75 and 3,34). This shows a significant impact of perceived complexity on realizing the benefits of GenAI among technical activities. In Table 2, tasks related to

Table 2 Technical tasks assisted by GenAI perceived sorted by user value

Tasks	Perceived benefit	Perceived complexity	User value	t-test
(1) Code summarization and explanation	3.69	2.59	1.1	0.00**
(2) Generating code from given libraries	3.66	2.79	0.87	0.00**
(3) User story correction/refinement	3.54	2.81	0.73	0.00**
(4) User story/Requirement Generation	3.55	2.85	0.7	0.00**
(5) Optimizing code against quality attributes	3.59	2.92	0.67	0.00**
(6) Decision support by presenting available technological options	3.56	2.94	0.62	0.00**
(7) Converting codebase to different languages or configurations	3.65	3.13	0.52	0.00**
(8) Providing guidance on software design patterns	3.6	3.11	0.49	0.00**
(9) Assisting with software performance optimization	3.75	3.3	0.45	0.00**
(10) Automate code analysis and anomaly detection	3.69	3.31	0.38	0.00**
(11) Moving codebase to the cloud	3.19	2.88	0.31	0.14
(12) Requirement estimation and prioritization	3.19	3.05	0.14	0.36
(13) Reverse engineering and code refactoring	3.51	3.4	0.11	0.66
(14) Automate commit workflow (commit, comment, pull, push request)	3.29	3.22	0.07	0.71
(15) Designing overall architecture against given set of requirements	3.47	3.54	−0.07	0.75
(16) Designing detailed architecture of components from the overview ones	3.34	3.51	−0.17	0.32
(17) Requirement modelling and analysis	3.37	3.55	−0.18	0.24

** less than 0.01

requirements and coding rank at the higher end, while tasks concerning processes and architecture are positioned at the lower end of the spectrum.

Proposition 3 *The user value for adopting GenAI in architectural and process-related tasks is notably lower when contrasted with coding and requirement tasks.*

4.2 Agile Project Managerial Tasks

The Agile project managerial task outlines thirteen tasks we asked for in the survey. We calculated their mean value in terms of perceived benefits and complexity. We obtained the maximum perceived benefit for *writing or informal emails & assisting technical writing,* i.e., (3.9) and the minimum perceived benefit for *Supporting engineers' retention and team health,* i.e., (2.92). We observed that technical-related tasks have higher benefits than human-factor-related tasks. Among the thirteen mentioned tasks, we found a higher degree of difference concerning the mean values of perceived benefit, i.e., (3.9 − 2.92 = 0.98) around a mean value of 1 compared to the previous section, whereas in terms of the perceived complexity, we observed a more significant difference, i.e., (3.37 − 2.07 = 1.30); some Agile project managerial tasks were more challenging to achieve.

The managerial tasks with the highest user values are *writing or improving formal emails (1.83), assisting technical writing (1.53), preparing meetings with agendas, slides, note-taking (1.07), and documenting review outcomes (0.82).* T-test showed a statistical difference in the distribution of respondents' rates on the benefit and complexity of these tasks.

Proposition 4 *Overall perceived benefits exceed perceived complexity when it comes to the adoption of GenAI in managerial tasks.*

The managerial task with negative user value (perceived complexity more than perceived benefits) is *Supporting engineers' retention and team health (−0.45).* Also, we found out that only one t-test for *Supporting engineers' retention and team health* is 0.05 and does not prove that there is a significant effect. Moreover, only four tasks obtained a t-test value above 0.05; the eight were less than 0.05. This proves that our results are unlikely to have appeared by random chance alone. The first eight task results are primarily solid and well-grounded, stipulating a higher degree of confidence in the observed effect. Regarding the standard deviation (SD), we obtained a low value for almost all thirteen tasks, meaning the responses were tightly clustered around the mean value. The low SD value obtained indicates more remarkable agreement among the participants in voting.

While the perceived value of the user value has a relatively large range from 1,83 to −0,45, the content of perceived benefits does not vary that much (between 3,9 and 2,92). This shows the impact of perceived complexity on realizing the benefits of GenAI among management activities.

Proposition 5 *User values vary significantly among managerial activities. The adoption of GenAI for project communication and documentation presents the best user value.*

Table 3 Managerial tasks assisted by GenAI perceived sorted by user value

Tasks	Perceived benefit	Perceived complexity	User value	t-test
(1) Writing or improving formal emails	3.9	2.07	1.83	0.00**
(2) Assisting technical writing	3.9	2.37	1.53	0.00**
(3) Meeting preparation with agenda, slides, note-taking, etc.	3.46	2.39	1.07	0.00**
(4) Documenting the review outcome	3.4	2.58	0.82	0.00**
(5) Stakeholder management with meeting reminder, communication strategy, etc.	3.34	2.6	0.74	0.00**
(6) Preparing for the sprint planning meeting	3.3	2.64	0.66	0.00**
(7) Creating a sprint backlog	3.44	2.8	0.64	0.00**
(8) Selecting product backlog items	3.22	2.73	0.49	0.00**
(9) Defining sprint goals	3.2	2.85	0.35	0.06
(10) Preparing for the retrospective meeting	3.02	2.76	0.26	0.14
(11) Onboarding new team members	3.05	2.89	0.16	0.36
(12) Facilitating the review meeting	2.95	2.88	0.07	0.69
(13) Supporting engineers' retention and team health	2.92	3.37	−0.45	0.05*

* less than 0.05
** less than 0.01

5 Discussion

In this section, we discussed our observations in connecting to related work regarding benefits (Sect. 5.1) and concerns (Sect. 5.2).

5.1 On the Benefit of Adopting GenAI

Our findings reveal a positive attitude among our respondents when harnessing the capabilities of ChatGPT. Our list of identified managerial and technical tasks (Table 1) covers all tasks of Agile copilot vision from Hoda [12]. When compared to Holzmann's anticipated project management scenarios [13], there is an alignment on 7 out of the 13 managerial tasks, as shown in Table 3. However, notably, the managerial tasks that hold the highest practical value for users are absent from

Holzmann's expected list. Tasks like the creation of project schedules, analyzing implications of missing deadlines, and updating project progress and schedules are notable omissions. This omission could be attributed to the substantial contextual information required for these tasks, and it's possible that our participants needed to fully explore ChatGPT's capabilities to realize this level of functionality.

Bera et al. describe ChatGPT as a virtual team member who could perform the tasks of an Agile coach or scrum master [3]. While our examination of tasks demonstrates ChatGPT's application in various tasks traditionally carried out by humans, the role of ChatGPT currently remains at the assistance level. Mainly all the tasks (see Tables 2 and 3) such as sprint backlogs, online meetings [16], Agile retrospective [15], etc. applied by humans can be assisted by ChatGPT as a virtual assistant rather than a virtual member. It aids in completing discrete tasks but does not entirely automate entire workflows. The reason for this might be that, at the moment, the capacity of ChatGPT, at least the available version, is not yet ready to handle complex decision-making, context understanding, and various interconnected tasks. Another reason can be adopting ChatGPT in sensitive PM tasks, especially when considering confidential or legal concerns in the project.

5.2   Concerns with the Adoption of GenAI

According to Prifti, five concerns of GenAI adoption include safety, privacy, autonomy, data availability, and employment [21]. We clarify these points in the context of Agile project management. While ChatGPT can generate text responses based on input, it may only sometimes grasp the context accurately, potentially resulting in irrelevant or erroneous information. For instance, when a team member provides a vague task description like "Create a new feature for our application," ChatGPT might suggest irrelevant or impractical ideas. In contrast, an experienced team member or project manager can offer more context-aware guidance. Moreover, ChatGPT's effectiveness can be diminished in non-textual communication channels, such as voice or video calls, integral to Agile project management. For instance, during a stand-up meeting, if team members use voice messages, ChatGPT might miss vital information and provide inaccurate feedback. In contrast, face-to-face conversations allow for better task clarification.

ChatGPT's general training data might need to be improved when deep domain knowledge is required, like in software development. For instance, if a team member seeks guidance on Test-Driven Development (TDD), ChatGPT might need more specific knowledge and provide complete or accurate advice. In contrast, an experienced team member or domain expert can offer detailed and precise guidance on TDD.

Data quality and availability for ChatGPT's training have a critical impact on response quality. Biased or incomplete training data can lead to more accurate responses. In Agile project management, unbiased and accurate feedback is crucial.

For example, if ChatGPT's training data leans toward a specific programming language, it might not provide impartial feedback on alternative technologies.

Lastly, ChatGPT utilizes sensitive project data to generate responses. If this data is not adequately secured, it becomes susceptible to cyberattacks and data breaches, posing a significant risk in Agile project management. For instance, a security breach could result in the leakage of sensitive project information. To mitigate this risk, robust security measures are essential, ensuring only authorized personnel can access the system.

6 Conclusions

This research unveils the current practices and perceptions regarding the adoption of ChatGPT in Agile software development. Our survey of 73 software professionals in the Nordic region highlights a range of tasks that can be enhanced with ChatGPT and assesses the perceived value associated with these tasks. The study provides insights into how ChatGPT can improve various aspects of Agile software development based on a value-based approach. **Technical tasks** such as *generation of code, summarizing and explaining the codes*, and **managerial tasks** related to communication and documentation such as *technical content and emails, meeting agendas, note-taking* could lead to better, faster, and efficient software development and delivery process. Moreover, human factor and team dynamics-related tasks such as *onboarding team members and communications strategies* could lead to better collaboration, communication, and decision-making. ChatGPT could potentially reduce the company developers' load by focusing on tasks like *user story generations, corrections and its refinement, automate commit workflow*, and helping team leads in *providing guidance on software design and performance optimization*. However, we are limited in empirically supporting this claim. Future research can further evaluate our task list using objective measurements to gauge the actual value derived from adopting ChatGPT. Longitudinal studies in established settings are needed to gain a deeper understanding of the sustainable benefits, challenges, and lessons learned. These insights will be instrumental in assessing long-term trends and the enduring impact of ChatGPT in Agile software development.

References

1. Ajzen, I.: The theory of planned behavior. Organiz. Behav. Human Decis. Process. **50**(2), 179–211 (1991)
2. Alhashmi, S.F.S., Alshurideh, M., Al Kurdi, B., Salloum, S.A.: A systematic review of the factors affecting the artificial intelligence implementation in the health care sector. In: Hassanien, A.E., Azar, A.T., Gaber, T., Oliva, D., Tolba, F.M. (eds.) Proceedings of the International Conference on Artificial Intelligence and Computer Vision (AICV2020), pp. 37–49. Advances in Intelligent Systems and Computing, Springer International Publishing

3. Bera, P., Wautelet, Y., Poels, G.: On the use of ChatGPT to support agile software development. In: Agil-ISE 2023: 2nd International Workshop on Agile Methods for Information Systems Engineering (Agil-ISE 2023): Short Paper Proceedings of the Second International Workshop on Agile Methods for Information Systems Engineering (Agil-ISE 2023): Co-located with the 35th International Conference on Advanced Information Systems Engineering (CAiSE 2023), vol. 3414, pp. 1–9. CEUR. ISSN: 1613-0073

4. Berntzen, M., Hoda, R., Moe, N.B., Stray, V.: A taxonomy of inter-team coordination mechanisms in large-scale agile. IEEE Trans. Softw. Eng. 49, 699–718. Accepted: 2022-05-05T07:41:26Z Publisher: Institute of Electrical and Electronics Engineers (IEEE)

5. Cico, O., Souza, R., Jaccheri, L., Nguyen Duc, A., Machado, I.: Startups transitioning from early to growth phase - a pilot study of technical debt perception. In: Klotins, E., Wnuk, K. (eds.) Software Business. Lecture Notes in Business Information Processing, pp. 102–117. Springer International Publishing, Cham

6. Dam, H.K., Tran, T., Grundy, J., Ghose, A., Kamei, Y.: Towards effective AI-powered agile project management. In: 2019 IEEE/ACM 41st International Conference on Software Engineering: New Ideas and Emerging Results (ICSE-NIER), pp. 41–44

7. Daun, M., Brings, J.: How ChatGPT will change software engineering education. In: Proceedings of the 2023 Conference on Innovation and Technology in Computer Science Education V. 1, pp. 110–116. ITiCSE. Association for Computing Machinery (2023)

8. Davis, F.D.: Perceived usefulness, perceived ease of use, and user acceptance of information technology. MIS Quarterly 13(3), 319–340. https://doi.org/10.2307/249008. publisher: Management Information Systems Research Center, University of Minnesota

9. Dingsoeyr, T., Falessi, D., Power, K.: Agile development at scale: the next frontier. IEEE Softw. 36(2), 30–38. Conference Name: IEEE Software

10. Gao, L., Bai, X.: A unified perspective on the factors influencing consumer acceptance of internet of things technology. Asia Pacific J. Marketing Logist. 26(2), 211–231 (2014). Publisher: Emerald Group Publishing Limited

11. Hoda, R., Murugesan, L.K.: Multi-level agile project management challenges: a self-organizing team perspective. J. Syst. Softw. 117, 245–257 (2016)

12. Hoda, R., Dam, H., Tantithamthavorn, C., Thongtanunam, P., Storey, M.A.: Augmented agile: human-centered AI-assisted software management. IEEE Softw. 40(4), 106–109. Conference Name: IEEE Software

13. Holzmann, V., Zitter, D., Peshkess, S.: The expectations of project managers from artificial intelligence: a delphi study. Project Manag. J. 53(5), 438–455 (2022)

14. Jabangwe, R., Nguyen-Duc, A.: SIoT framework: Towards an approach for early identification of security requirements for internet-of-things applications. e-Informatica Softw. Eng. J. 14, 77–95 (2020)

15. Khanna, D., Wang, X.: Are your online agile retrospectives psychologically safe? The usage of online tools. In: International Conference on Agile Software Development, pp. 35–51. Springer (2022)

16. Khanna, D., Nguyen-Duc, A., Wang, X.: From mvps to pivots: A hypothesis-driven journey of two software startups. In: Software Business: 9th International Conference, ICSOB 2018, Tallinn, Estonia, June 11–12, 2018, Proceedings 9, pp. 172–186. Springer (2018)

17. Kim, H.W., Chan, H.C., Gupta, S.: Value-based adoption of mobile internet: an empirical investigation. Decision Support Syst. 43(1), 111–126. Publisher: Elsevier Science, Netherlands

18. Lin, T.C., Wu, S., Hsu, J.S.C., Chou, Y.C.: The integration of value-based adoption and expectation–confirmation models: an example of IPTV continuance intention. Decision Support Syst. 54(1), 63–75

19. Min, S., So, K. K. F., Jeong, M.: Consumer adoption of the uber mobile application: Insights from diffusion of innovation theory and technology acceptance model. In: Future of Tourism Marketing. Routledge, p. 14 (2021)

20. Nguyen Duc, A., Khalid, K., Lønnestad, T., Bajwa Shahid, S., Wang, X., Abrahamsson, P.: How do startups develop internet-of-things systems - a multiple exploratory case study. In: 2019 IEEE/ACM International Conference on Software and System Processes (ICSSP), pp. 74–83

21. Prifti, V.: Optimizing project management using artificial intelligence. Eur. J. Formal Sci. Eng. **5**(1), 29–37 (2022)
22. Sohn, K., Kwon, O.: Technology acceptance theories and factors influencing artificial intelligence-based intelligent products. Telemat. Informat. **47**, 101324 (2020)
23. Sravanthi, J., Sobti, R., Semwal, A., Shravan, M., Al-Hilali, A.A., Bader Alazzam, M.: AI-assisted resource allocation in project management. In: 2023 3rd International Conference on Advance Computing and Innovative Technologies in Engineering (ICACITE), pp. 70–74
24. Sukkar, A.A., Hasan, H.: Toward a model for the acceptance of internet banking in developing countries. Inf. Technol. Develop. **11**(4), 381–398 (2005). https://onlinelibrary.wiley.com/doi/pdf/10.1002/itdj.20026
25. Venkatesh, V., Morris, M.G., Davis, G.B., Davis, F.D.: User acceptance of information technology: Toward a unified view. MIS Quarterly **27**(3), 425–478. https://doi.org/10.2307/30036540

Early Results from a Study of GenAI Adoption in a Large Brazilian Company: The Case of Globo

Guilherme Pereira (ID)**, Rafael Prikladnicki** (ID)**, Victoria Jackson** (ID)**, André van der Hoek** (ID)**, Luciane Fortes, and Igor Macaubas**

Abstract Given the nascent and evolving nature of the latest generative AI tools, there is little advice as to how best adopt generative AI tools within software teams or what benefits and concerns can be expected. In this chapter, we share the experiences of Globo, a large media group that has recently begun to adopt OpenAI ChatGPT and GitHub Copilot for software development activities. We describe Globo's adoption approach and provide early insights into potential benefits and concerns in the form of eight initial lessons that are apparent from diaries kept by developers as well as semi-structured interview with them. Among the lessons learned are that the use of generative AI tools drives the adoption of additional developer tools and that developers intentionally use ChatGPT and Copilot in a complementary manner. We hope that sharing these practical experiences will help other software teams in successfully adopting generative AI tools.

Keywords Generative AI · Software teams · Developer tools · Experience report

1 Introduction

Software teams have always adapted their ways of working in response to technological and social advances. From the adoption of agile and lean ways of working, through embracing DevOps practices, to utilizing cloud infrastructure, modern-day engineering teams have accelerated their deliveries to where development cycle times are measured in hours and days with multiple deployments to production

G. Pereira · R. Prikladnicki (✉)
Pontifícia Universidade Católica do Rio Grande do Sul, Porto Alegre, RS, Brazil
e-mail: guilherme.v003@edu.pucrs.br; rafaelp@pucrs.br

V. Jackson · A. van der Hoek
University of California, Irvine, Irvine, CA, USA
e-mail: vfjackso@uci.edu; andre@ics.uci.edu

L. Fortes · I. Macaubas
Globo, Rio de Janeiro, Brazil

per day [12]. Generative AI, as evidenced through tools like OpenAI ChatGPT[1] and GitHub Copilot,[2] is the latest disruption that is expected to have a profound impact on software teams [6]. An often touted key benefit is an increase in developer productivity due to the ability of generative AI tools to speed up development activities, such as coding [14] and testing [9], by automatically generating code. Leveraging this automation requires developers to change the way they work; they spend less time writing code and more time reviewing and understanding code [5].

Yet adopting new ways of working and new tools is challenging for individuals, teams, and companies. It can be time-consuming and expensive to retrain teams to use new tools and to adapt their practices, especially when the tools are immature and still evolving with little practical guidance, all while ensuring that code is still shipped and deadlines are met. Companies thus need to be clear on the benefits before embarking on a potentially lengthy and costly journey of adopting generative AI tools [1].

To help others who are considering embarking on such a journey, we provide this preliminary experience report of Globo, a media group that has recently adopted both OpenAI ChatGPT and GitHub Copilot for software development activities. We share the approach for rolling out the tools and provide early insights into the potential benefits and issues of using generative AI. We defined the following research question: what are the main lessons learned by adopting generative AI for software development at Globo?

The remainder of this chapter is organized as follows: Sect. 2 presents background information, while Sect. 3 introduces the research design. Section 4 presents the eight lessons learned, while Sect. 5 concludes the chapter.

2   Background Information

This section provides a brief overview of the capabilities, benefits, and limitations of GenAI tools used by software developers, with a focus on the two adopted by Globo: OpenAI ChatGPT and GitHub Copilot.

GenAI is artificial intelligence capable of generating text, images, or other media, using generative models [19]. These models learn patterns from input data to generate data with similar characteristics. Recent advances in neural networks have led to a number of GenAI tools. Some are general-purpose conversational agents (e.g., OpenAI ChatGPT, Google Bard[3]), while others are geared toward a specific audience such as developers (GitHub Copilot). In both cases, the models have been trained on input data scoured from many sources on the Internet, including some that

---

[1] https://openai.com/chatgpt.

[2] https://github.com/features/copilot.

[3] https://bard.google.com/.

are software engineering relevant (e.g., code from open-source projects maintained on GitHub).

Within software development, ChatGPT has been shown to assist developers in a variety of common software development activities, including authoring requirements [27], generating architecture [2] and design models [8], fixing defects [24], generating code [20], and seeking help [13].

Research on Copilot notes that it provides developers a perceived productivity boost, enabling them to work faster on repetitive tasks and an ability to focus on more satisfying work [14]. Code generated by Copilot is of low cyclomatic complexity [21] and is of the same complexity and as readable as human-generated code [3]. When given coding problems, Copilot has been shown to generate valid (e.g., compilable, interpretable) code although less than half of the solutions were correct [28]. As well as coding, Copilot can assist with authoring unit tests and identifying defective code [5].

However, it is not all positive news when it comes to using GenAI for software activities. Drawbacks of using GenAI include hallucination, as in when ChatGPT generates code that references libraries or packages that do not exist. This can provide an exploitation entry point for bad actors [16], leading to security risks [25]. Also, code generated by ChatGPT and Copilot can contain vulnerabilities [15]. The code may contain bugs that may not be immediately apparent on initial inspection [18]. In addition to these security and technical issues, there are wider societal concerns such as potential copyright issues [17], the potential for bias [7], and emerging legal issues [23].

Moreover, developers need to change their working practices to derive benefits from GenAI tools. They need to be cognizant of recommended prompt engineering techniques [26], that is, how to best structure and organize their prompts to gain helpful answers. Also, to overcome some of the limitations of GenAI tools such as generating defective or insecure code, engineers need to review and understand the code [20].

3   Research Design

The setting of the study is the Digital Platforms structure within Globo,[4] a large media group based in Latin America. This structure is part of the Digital Hub, which is Globo's Digital Technology division, and has three areas: GloboID (identity provider), Webmedia, and Publishing platform. These areas have approximately 250 people who provide solutions for digital products.

The study particularly concerned a pilot of introducing ChatGPT and Copilot to six teams with over forty employees total in various roles (e.g., developers, UX, DevOps, product owners, managers). A typical team consists of about five

---

[4] https://grupoglobo.globo.com/.

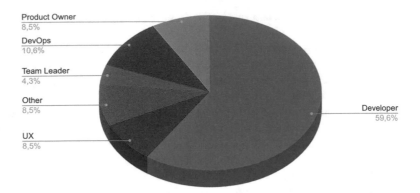

Fig. 1 The participants roles in their respective teams

developers, a UX designer, and a dedicated product owner. Each team is responsible for both the development and deployment of the software it develops. Figure 1 depicts the distribution of participants based on their respective roles within the teams. Developers are predominant. The teams follow agile practices from well-known frameworks such as Scrum and XP, and they also use Kanban. Teams are self-organized and usually run monthly sprints.

Within this software division, it had been agreed with the main executives to evaluate the use of generative AI tools, specifically ChatGPT and GitHub Copilot, in software development tasks. These two tools were chosen mainly for the following reasons:

1. GitHub was already in use by the teams.
2. These two tools appear the most commonly used and talked about when generative AI is brought into software development.

A project was initiated with the goal of rolling out the generative AI tools to the development teams while ensuring that data was captured to evaluate the benefits the AI tools provided. Specifically, the company aimed to assess the impact of using these tools in the software development process to support the decision of whether to invest in the technology more broadly across the organization.

The versions of the tools that were introduced are GitHub Copilot for Business and OpenAI ChatGPT 3.5. The company decided to use the free version of OpenAI's tool due to operational issues.

3.1 Project Approach

A multidisciplinary team was assembled to execute the project. This team consisted of a project manager, representatives from the company's legal department, and researchers from two universities—PUCRS and UCI (one professor and one PhD student each). Legal representatives were also included, as the company had several legal concerns about the use of generative AI. These were mostly about data leakage, code ownership, and code licenses that may govern the code being suggested by the tools.

The academic researchers' involvement in the study primarily consisted of acting as unpaid consultants to the project team. They helped on designing the study, including strategies for data collection and analysis. These also include recommended metrics and qualitative data that would be helpful in assessing the potential benefits of the use of generative AI tools in software activities. The project consisted of three phases planned to be completed in five months from August 2023: Preparatory (1 month), Pilot (1 month), and Rollout (3 months). At the time of writing, the Rollout phase is ongoing.

The first phase was necessary to undertake any preparatory activities required by the pilot and rollout, such as license procurement and agreement on the specific metrics to be used to understand the outcomes of the study. It included meetings with Digital Platforms management to define the study protocol, decide which teams would take part in the study, and choose which of the six teams would do the pilot before all teams participated in the rollout.

The aim of the pilot was to obtain feedback on the use of generative AI tools from a single team, so as to be able to refine and align the study protocol with actual experiences. The outcomes of this phase were presented to both the participants and the management of the company for a final round of feedback.

Globo's management selected the pilot team based on the characteristics and availability of the team. The pilot team subsequently participated in a kickoff event to familiarize its members with the project and establish the essential infrastructure. Team members were instructed to use the tools freely but record experiences and examples of use in a spreadsheet (called a "diary" in the remainder of this chapter). Effectively, the team members were encouraged to experiment with the tools leading to experiential learning.

Participants were encouraged to use the tools freely in any software engineering activity they felt appropriate. Following the lessons learned in the pilot stage, the third phase of the project has now been kicked off with six participating teams. The same instructions were provided to these teams. This third phase is in progress.

3.2   Data Collection

Various of qualitative data was captured both during the pilot and the first few weeks of the broader rollout. Data collected during the pilot consisted of:

- At the start of the pilot, an initial survey[5] (pre-survey) captured the profile of the participants and their expectations and concerns regarding the use of the tools.
- Daily, a free-style document for team members to share their day-to-day experiences with the tools (the "diary"). In this document, participants were encouraged to provide descriptions of tasks and situations in which they utilized the tools.
- Weekly, a 30-minute meeting took place between the researchers and the pilot team to collect participants' experiences of the tools that week. This included discussions on the tasks they were trying to accomplish with the AI tools and whether the tools were helpful.
- At the end of the pilot, a second survey[6] (post-survey) captured participants' perceptions of the tools, including their impact on the development process.

During the rollout phase, the same data was captured as in the pilot phase. However, some adjustments were made in the diary document to collect which AI tool was used for which tasks. We also collected how participants felt about their GenAI experience on that particular day, using a three-point scale: happy, neutral, and sad.

All the members of Team 1 participated in the pilot phase. In the current stage, the initial survey was answered by 47 people distributed among the 6 teams, in the roles shown in Fig. 1.

Due to the increase from one pilot team to six participating teams, in-person debriefs were held every 15 days on a team basis for 30 minutes. We used the following questions to guide the discussion:

- Please share the positive aspects and difficulties of interacting with ChatGPT and Copilot.
- Do you feel more productive?
- Did you identify any security threats or data leaks when you used the tools?
- Do you know and use any prompt engineering techniques?
- How has using Copilot/ChatGPT increased or reduced creativity and innovation in your coding, design, and other tasks?
- Do you think you are saving time?
- If so, what have you done with the time saved?
- How has using Copilot/ChatGPT affected your general attitude toward work, as well as your personal well-being at work?

To date, we have interviewed each team two times. Table 1 indicates the type of application the teams develop. Table 2 contains other relevant information about the teams, the technologies they use, and software development processes and practices adopted.

---

[5] https://forms.gle/pPiF3vCAtahVrjcH9.

[6] https://forms.gle/wwYiCKAg6V314KZKA.

Table 1 Project developed by teams

Team	Application description
T1	Develops a microfrontend platform that standardizes and facilitates the development of user flows in registration, authentication, authorization, and privacy
T2	The team works on the audio and video player for Android platforms. It plays all of Globo's videos and podcasts on all the products that have apps for these platforms
T3	The team handles the delivery of streaming videos on demand from packaging to distribution to users on our CDN
T4	The team develops the authorization application. The systems are responsible for provisioning services to users
T5	The Platform team responsible for digital interactivity in the company's applications, e.g., voting and comments. This is delivered to the end user and also consumed by other products
T6	On-demand image processing system. We work with compression, cropping, resizing, and applying filters

Table 2 Way of working for each team

Team	Number of members	Technologies	Sw Dev process	Roles
T1	8	Go, React, Typescript.	Kanban practices	4 Dev, 2 UX, 2 other
T2	10	Kotlin, Kotlin Multiplatform	Kanban practices	7 Dev, 1 product owner, 1 team leader, 1 Other.
T3	10	Go, Ruby.	Adapted scrum practices	5 Dev, 3 DevOps, 1 product owner, 1 team leader
T4	8	Go, React Typescript	Adapted scrum practices	4 Dev, 1 DevOps, 1 product owner, 1 UX, 1 other.
T5	6	Go, Lua, Python, JavaScript.	Adapted scrum practices	5 Dev, 1 UX.
T6	5	Go, Python, JavaScript.	Scrum practices	3 Dev, 1 DevOps, 1 product owner.

3.3   Data Analysis

Using the diaries and data collected during the meetings, the qualitative data analysis process was conducted in two distinct phases by the researchers, comprising an initial screening phase and a subsequent detailed analysis phase. In both phases, one researcher examined the data to identify insights and look for themes that were subsequently discussed and reviewed with other members of the research team. To help guide the analysis, five dimensions were considered:

Developer Concerns We sought to identify the concerns and reservations expressed by developers concerning the adoption of generative AI tools in their daily workflow.

Positive and Negative Aspects A central aspect of our analysis was the exploration of both positive and negative facets associated with the integration of generative AI tools in software development, allowing for a balanced understanding of their impact.

Tasks Enhanced We explored the specific types of tasks and software development activities where generative AI tools proved to be particularly advantageous, discerning their areas of usefulness.

Productivity Enhancement Lastly, we sought to evaluate the extent to which these tools contributed to overall productivity gains within the software development process.

Usage Across Roles An integral element of the analysis was an examination of how developers and other team members across different roles were leveraging generative AI tools, shedding light on variations in usage patterns.

This analysis resulted in the identification of the initial eight lessons described later.

3.4   Limitations and Threats to Validity

Our study is subject to some threats and limitations. First, the absence of quantitative data, such as bug counts or delivery times, restricts the ability to provide concrete, measurable insights into the impact of these tools on development processes. That is, our study shares perceptions from developers that ultimately may not be true. Complementary or quantitative studies are needed.

Second, the study's focus on a single large company may limit the generalizability of its findings. Lastly, qualitative data collection, particularly through diaries and interviews, introduces the possibility of response bias and subjectivity. While we sought to minimize this risk by comparing developers' perspectives with existing literature and interviewing a number of different teams to see if there was commonality in the perceptions across teams, such risks will always persist.

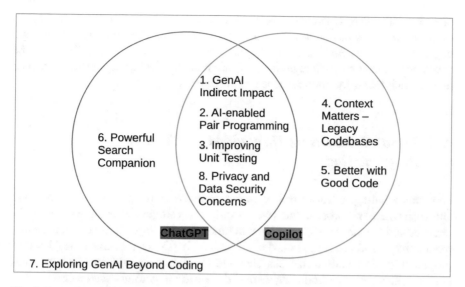

Fig. 2 Lessons learned

4 Eight Lessons

This section presents lessons learned from our ongoing study, until now, based on the teams described in Sect. 3.2. By analyzing the diaries and checkpoint meetings, we have identified eight preliminary lessons about the adoption and usage of GenAI by the developers. The lessons cover a variety of software development activities. Some of the lessons apply to one of the tools only (e.g., Context Matters), whereas others apply to both tools (e.g., Improving Unit Testing). These eight lessons are shown in Fig. 2 and categorized by the applicable tool (ChatGPT and/or Copilot).

4.1 Lesson 1: GenAI's Indirect Impact

At Globo, the influence of GenAI went beyond its primary functions. The development teams increasingly recognized that GenAI indirectly encouraged them to explore tools and practices that enhance code quality and overall project success. Specifically, the Globo developers started using Sonar[7] not just as a post-development auditing tool but especially to collect evidence of the efficiency of GenAI (a requirement of the project). By analyzing the code generated or written with the assistance of GenAI, Sonar provided valuable insights into code quality, identified potential vulnerabilities, and highlighted areas for improvement. The

---

[7] https://www.sonarsource.com/.

developers also used ChatGPT to help using Sonar. A developer mentioned, "*I used ChatGPT to ask a question about how to use Sonar on a monorepo. The answer helped me confirm what I already thought was the way to go* (Team 1, Dev 1)." The developers noted that the integration of Sonar into the development process enabled them to maintain a continuous focus on code quality.

4.2 Lesson 2: Learning Through AI-Enabled Pair Programming

Pair programming, a core practice in Extreme Programming, is a collaborative approach where two programmers work together at a single computer, with one writing code and the other reviewing it in real time. This strategy improves code quality, reduces bugs, and promotes knowledge sharing [10]. With the advent of AI-driven programming companions like ChatGPT and Copilot, pair programming transcends human collaboration, introducing a novel dimension to coding excellence.

In our study, ChatGPT and Copilot were widely used as a pair in coding tasks like code generation and repair. The Globo developers often cited extreme pair programming [4] when describing their interaction with tools. According to them, ChatGPT and Copilot contributed in ways different from pair developers. Copilot was seen more as a smart autocomplete as it analyzes the code in real time, offering suggestions, autocompleting repetitive tasks, and providing context-aware code recommendations. This led to accelerated development: "*Today, in pair programming with our team intern, we used Copilot to accelerate development* (Team 1, Dev 2)" ChatGPT, on the other hand, behaved like another developer as they can direct questions to it and discuss ways to write better code. Developers engaged in a conversation with ChatGPT and sought suggestions, clarifications, and even debugging assistance. Its ability to provide instant code snippets, explanations, and algorithmic insights mirrored the collaborative nature of pair programming. As one developer described, "*We used ChatGPT to pair program, and it gave good answers to our questions* (Team 1, Dev 3)."

One aspect worth mentioning is that the unique synergy between ChatGPT and Copilot is what truly embodies the spirit of pair programming. Developers engaged in conversations with ChatGPT for problem-solving ideas and then implemented those solutions with Copilot's real-time assistance. As one developer noted, "*Copilot helped complete the front-end code, and I asked ChatGPT a few questions about refactoring* (Team 1, Dev 2)." Using them in tandem ensured that the code produced not only was efficient and bug-free but also inculcated a deeper understanding of programming concepts and best practices. The blend of human expertise with AI intelligence resulted in a synergy that not only enhanced code quality but also facilitated a continual learning journey for developers.

4.3 Lesson 3: Improving Unit Testing

Several developers participating in the study highlighted the usefulness of Copilot in implementing unit tests, "*Copilot helped me create unit tests in a more practical way for the code I refactored yesterday* (Team 1, Dev 1)". According to them, the tool often accelerated the development of this class of tests considerably, which seems to stem from Copilot's extensive codebase knowledge. As developers wrote code, Copilot suggested unit test cases, stubs, and mock data. It helped automate the creation of test suites, making it easier to achieve comprehensive test coverage. Globo's experience thus aligns with prior observations (e.g., [6]).

ChatGPT appeared in a somewhat different context. Globo developers used ChatGPT to understand application errors and solve problems in both production and development environments. By describing the problem in plain language, developers engaged in a conversation with ChatGPT to identify potential bug causes. For example, a critical bug in production was solved through the help of ChatGPT: "*ChatGPT helped me quickly answer questions about the (Go) language to solve an implementation* (Team 3, Dev 1)." The developers also felt that bugs were solved quicker because ChatGPT provided richer answers than search engines: "*I felt I got the answer more clearly and quickly than if I'd gone to Google directly* (Team 5, Dev 1)."

Copilot excels in expediting the creation of unit tests, while ChatGPT's benefit lies in diagnosing the root causes of bugs, even in production environments. For example, Copilot helped develop unit tests with method syntax and mock-up objects, while ChatGPT was a suitable alternative to solving doubts about a specific programming language or a specific tool such as cache-control headers. Together, the combination of Copilot and ChatGPT in testing represents a potent synergy in software development.

4.4 Lesson 4: Context Matters—GenAI and Legacy Codebases

Based on the conversation with the teams, we found that Copilot's performance varied significantly depending on the context of the application it is used with. Developers working on legacy code found Copilot was not helpful, while others found it more beneficial with new projects and codebases.

The integration of Copilot into projects featuring legacy code and older technology often presented developers with a unique set of challenges. Copilot's understanding of the context in such cases was less accurate due to outdated conventions, coding practices, and technology stacks. It sometimes struggled to provide relevant suggestions and did not always fully comprehend the intricacies of legacy systems. Adapting Copilot to understand and work effectively with legacy code often required manual adjustments and a deeper contextual understanding by developers. As one developer working on legacy code noted, "*Copilot can't help.*

It doesn't seem to understand code that isn't well-structured (Team 1, Dev 4)."
Interestingly, it appears that ChatGPT copes better with legacy code as the same
developer describes, *"ChatGPT gives pertinent answers to specific questions, even
about legacy technologies* (Team 1, Dev 4)."

According to the Globo developers, Copilot shined in the realm of new projects
and fresh codebases. Its understanding of modern coding conventions, current
technology stacks, and best practices was better. As one developer noted, *"Copilot
is competent to recognize context within the file* (Team 5, Dev 1)," and another noted
its support for modern-day coding practices: *"Copilot looks smart for testing well-
structured code. Good for isolated components* (Team 2, Dev 1)."

Overall, this is an important point for Globo to take forward and explore, given
that some of its codebase contains legacy code. A key outcome, then, is that it could
be beneficial to explore how to make GenAI tools more supportive of legacy code
perhaps by building an internal language model based on its own code base. How
this then balances with knowledge learned from external sources will remain to be
seen.

4.5   Lesson 5: Copilot Is Better with Good Code

While Copilot really helped the teams, it relied on developers crafting high-quality
code to provide better suggestions. The responsibility for the quality of code
suggestions was a shared endeavor that hinged on the developer's expertise. A Globo
developer said that *"Copilot depends on the developer. For example, if you start
writing a method with a proper name, [it] makes better suggestions. Sometimes it
can't even do it* (Team 2, Dev 1)."

Developers had to be mindful of the code they wrote, ensuring it was readable
and maintainabl, and followed established coding standards. Copilot, in turn,
complemented the developer's work by offering suggestions that aligned with the
code's context. Copilot leveraged its understanding of code patterns, best practices,
and programming languages to offer suggestions. However, developers were the
ones who set the foundation by writing code that was well structured, adhered to
best practices, and was clear in its intent. To illustrate this, another developer said,
"Creating a function with a descriptive name will help the Copilot answer (Team 3,
Dev 2)."

4.6   Lesson 6: ChatGPT as a Powerful Search Companion

Some Globo developers turned to ChatGPT as a viable and favored search platform
compared to Google, dedicated software engineering Q&A platforms such as Stack

Overflow,[8] or even documentation. They did this because ChatGPT allowed them to pose their questions in plain language and receive immediate, context-aware responses. The Globo developers felt that this type of interaction significantly reduced the time they spent searching and filtering through search results, making it an attractive choice for developers seeking swift and precise answers. Specifically, the developers noted that ChatGPT helped speed up their work as *ChatGPT helps with technical questions faster than Google* (Team 5, Dev 2) and *AI delivers a more practical summary* (Team 3, Dev 2) in comparison to traditional search engines. Moreover, the developers felt the answers were more *assertive* than Google searches, leading to *accelerated work.*

4.7   Lesson 7: Exploring GenAI's Beyond Coding

While it is clear that GenAI has found its place in coding and testing, there is a widespread lack of awareness regarding its potential in other software development activities, such as software requirements or software design. Most of the Globo reports to date concerned how developers explored several ways of generating code, obtaining debugging support, and expediting the testing process.

However, GenAI has the capability to assist beyond coding, such as in software requirements, from generating user stories and use cases to aiding in requirement analysis and documentation. One of the teams started exploring this, using it to streamline the process by seeking recommendations from ChatGPT and ensuring that requirements are well-defined. One team member mentioned that *"ChatGPT provides good support for writing documentation. I use it a lot for documentation . (Team 4, Dev 1)."* (In this case, they mean requirements documentation, not code comments.)

GenAI can also be a good resource in design activities. It has the capability to assist in creating wireframes, generating design documents, and even automating certain design tasks. By providing design suggestions, aiding in prototype creation, and facilitating iterative design, GenAI can optimize the entire design process. At Globo, some aspects of this were explored. For example, one team member mentioned that *"ChatGPT helped us with a task that required us to build a flow diagram. It helped to elucidate complex flows in blocks of code (Team 4, Dev 2)."*

However, our study so far showed that the use of GenAI beyond coding is underexplored at Globo. The teams have not yet explored GenAI for requirements, design, and even other activities such as software architecture. The examples mentioned above are the only instances of its use for such tasks so far. At the same time, recent literature suggests that this is common at other places too [22].

---

[8] https://stackoverflow.com/.

4.8   Lesson 8: Privacy and Data Security Are Important Concerns

The use of GenAI brings an issue of great concern—privacy. Privacy, especially at the organizational level, is a fundamental right and a critical consideration in the age of AI. The sensitive nature of data, proprietary information, and the potential for data breaches underscore the importance of safeguarding an organization's digital assets. Based on the data collected so far, this concern with privacy limited the use and potential of GenAI in several ways. One of the primary concerns was the integration of third-party code or services, as this introduced a degree of uncertainty. This is illustrated by another quote from the study: "*Gen AI may make us use third-party code that we are not authorized to use, or we will not cite the source* (Team 6, Dev 1)." A second concern was around data leakage: "*There is concern mainly about the leakage of credentials and/or sensitive information that may be contained in the code* (Team 5, Dev 2)." Another developer said, "*ChatGPT needs context. It generates insecurity as more context is needed to get a satisfactory response* (Team 4, Dev 2)." One immediate action was the development of a best practice guide by the legal team at Globo. How best to address these concerns is something to be explored further as Globo continues its adoption of GenAI.

4.9   Discussion

Although the adoption of GenAI is ongoing at Globo, these first eight lessons provide some interesting perspectives for further consideration. One noteworthy perspective is that when examining the lessons holistically, it seems that ChatGPT and Copilot are complements, rather than alternatives. Based on the analysis, they are complements for two reasons: (i) they support somewhat different use cases, and (ii) where they support the same use case, they do so in different ways by playing to each other's strengths. For example, Globo developers are using ChatGPT as a search companion (Lesson 6), because of its natural language user interface and understanding of context. For AI-enabled pair programming (Lesson 2), both ChatGPT and Copilot assisted the developer. A developer first would engage with ChatGPT to explore the problem and solution space and then complete the implementation using Copilot's intelligent autocomplete.

While Globo developers reflected on how GenAI can help them in effective ways to save time (e.g., improving testing (Lesson 3)), they also raised concerns such as the ability of GenAI to support legacy codebases (Lesson 4) and the potential for privacy risks (Lesson 8). These are crucial to address if the potential of GenAI is to be fully realized. As stated earlier, how to do so remains an open question.

The adoption of GenAI tools is also spurring Globo to adopt additional tools such as Sonar for measuring code quality and identifying potential vulnerabilities (Lesson 1). This adoption could potentially assist with some of the potential privacy and security risks noted in Lesson 8, though it is not a complete solution for that. Again, the Globo teams will need to consider the limitations and what can be done further.

Finally, it is somewhat surprising that GenAI has been little explored by Globo developers for non-coding activities such as requirements engineering or design (Lesson 7). It is unclear why this is, perhaps due to a lack of awareness of the potential of GenAI beyond merely code and test generation. Indeed, the broader research literature does not talk about this much [11], nor does the popular literature (e.g., magazines, blogs). At the same time, because of its generative capabilities, one would expect potential benefits precisely for activities such as requirements and design, where creative and broad exploration can matter. Globo's management plans to look at this potential in this regard in detail.

5 Conclusion

In the era of ever-advancing technology and the relentless evolution of software development, ChatGPT and Copilot have emerged as pivotal players, redefining the way developers write code, conduct testing, and seek answers. These AI-powered companions offered novel solutions to age-old challenges, and their presence has already left an indelible mark on the development landscape. Both tools represent a shift in how developers interact with technology and learn and enhance their craft.

Our findings at Globo include that ChatGPT has not only expedited coding tasks but also evolved into a rapid search companion for developers, often outperforming conventional search engines. Developers feel it offers immediate and precise information, reshaping how they access knowledge and insights.

Copilot, on the other hand, has excelled at creating synergy between human expertise and artificial intelligence, empowering Globo developers to write better code faster. Developers have recognized that Copilot's performance is closely intertwined with their own coding practices, and so are cognizant of the importance of writing their own quality code to receive better suggestions.

As GenAI technology continues to evolve, it is okay to say that ChatGPT and Copilot have marked a new era that prioritizes collaboration between humans and artificial intelligence. The future of software development holds exciting potential as we continue to explore the ever-expanding horizons of AI companions like ChatGPT and Copilot. Yet, we must proceed with care. When real production code, and especially legacy code, is involved, new practices must be found to more effectively leverage GenAI tools.

Acknowledgments This work is partially supported by Globo in Brazil. Rafael Prikladnicki is partially supported by CNPq in Brazil. Guilherme Pereira is supported by the Ministry of Science, Technology, and Innovations, with resources from Law No. 8.248, dated October 23, 1991, within the scope of PPI-SOFTEX, coordinated by Softex, and published in the Residência em TIC 02— Aditivo, Official Gazette 01245.012095/2020-56. This material is based upon work supported by the US National Science Foundation under grant CCF-2210812.

Appendix: Surveys

Pre Survey

This qualitative research begins the execution of the study on the use of generative AI tools in software development at Globo. The objective of the questionnaire is to get to know the members of the teams participating in the study. Your feedback and participation are very important to understanding the characteristics, skills, and perspectives of each participant. The data will only be used for research purposes.

1. Team
2. Age

   (a) 18–25 years old
   (b) 26–35 years old
   (c) 36–45 years old
   (d) 46–55 years
   (e) Above 56 years old

3. Gender
4. Experience in software development

   (a) 1–3 years
   (b) 4–7 years
   (c) 8+ years

5. Certifications in software development
6. Programming languages you've worked with

   (a) Python
   (b) Java
   (c) JavaScript
   (d) C++
   (e) W#
   (f) Ruby
   (g) Go
   (h) Others

7. How long have you worked at the company?

   (a) 1–3 years
   (b) 4–7 years
   (c) 8+ years

8. What is your role on the team?

   (a) Coordinator
   (b) Developer
   (c) DevOps

    (d) Product Owner

    (e) UX

    (f) Other

9. Do you have experience with artificial intelligence (AI) techniques?

    (a) No experience

    (b) Theoretical experiment, without application to real projects

    (c) Application in real projects

10. Have you used generative AI tools (e.g., ChatGPT, GitHub Copilot)?

    (a) Never used

    (b) Yes, but not for real projects

    (c) Yes, even in real projects

11. Do you believe that using generative AI technologies can speed up the software development process?

    (a) Yes

    (b) No

12. Do you believe that the use of generative AI technologies can influence the adoption of best development practices?

    (a) Yes

    (b) No

13. Do you expect the use of generative AI technologies to affect collaboration and communication between development team members? How?

14. In your opinion, does the use of these tools have an impact on creativity in the software development process? How?

15. Do you have any concerns about using these technologies in professional software development?

Post-survey

This qualitative research finalizes the execution of the study on the use of generative AI tools in software development at Globo. The objective of the questionnaire is to understand the perceptions of the experiment participants, after a period of using generative AI tools. Your feedback and participation are very important to understanding the characteristics, skills, and perspectives of each participant. The data will only be used for research purposes.

1. Team

2. Do you find generative AI tools useful for software development? Why?

3. What benefits (not limited to code) have you seen from using generative AI tools?

4. What negative aspects (not limited to code) have been observed in the use of generative AI tools?
5. Do you believe that generative AI tools have facilitated or accelerated the software development process? Why?
6. Have you noticed any differences in code quality when using generative AI tools? In what aspects?
7. Regarding codes written by you without the support of the AI tool, what differences do you notice?
8. Have generative AI tools helped you avoid common mistakes or identify problems in the code? In what way?
9. Do you think generative AI tools have promoted greater knowledge sharing among team members?
10. Describe difficulties or limitations you have encountered when using generative AI tools.
11. Based on your experience during the experiment, what do you think could be improved in generative AI tools?

References

1. Agrawal, K.P.: Towards adoption of generative ai in organizational settings. J. Comput. Inf. Syst. **0**(0), 1–16 (2023). https://doi.org/10.1080/08874417.2023.2240744
2. Ahmad, A., Waseem, M., Liang, P., Fahmideh, M., Aktar, M.S., Mikkonen, T.: Towards human-bot collaborative software architecting with ChatGPT. In: Proceedings of the 27th International Conference on Evaluation and Assessment in Software Engineering. pp. 279–285. EASE '23, Association for Computing Machinery (2023). https://doi.org/10.1145/3593434.3593468. https://dl.acm.org/doi/10.1145/3593434.3593468
3. Al Madi, N.: How readable is model-generated code? Examining readability and visual inspection of GitHub Copilot. In: Proceedings of the 37th IEEE/ACM International Conference on Automated Software Engineering, ASE '22, pp. 1–5. Association for Computing Machinery (2023). https://doi.org/10.1145/3551349.3560438. https://dl.acm.org/doi/10.1145/3551349.3560438
4. Beck, K.: Extreme Programming Explained: Embrace Change. An Alan R. Apt Book Series. Addison-Wesley, Boston (2000). https://books.google.com.br/books?id=G8EL4H4vf7UC
5. Bird, C., Ford, D., Zimmermann, T., Forsgren, N., Kalliamvakou, E., Lowdermilk, T., Gazit, I.: Taking flight with copilot: early insights and opportunities of AI-powered pair-programming tools. Queue **20**(6), 10:35–10:57 (2023). https://doi.org/10.1145/3582083. https://dl.acm.org/doi/10.1145/3582083
6. Ebert, C., Louridas, P.: Generative AI for software practitioners. IEEE Softw. **40**(4), 30–38 (2023). https://doi.org/10.1109/MS.2023.3265877
7. Ernst, N.A., Bavota, G.: AI-driven development is here: should you worry? IEEE Softw. **39**(2), 106–110 (2022). https://doi.org/10.1109/MS.2021.3133805
8. Fill, H.G., Fettke, P., Köpke, J.: Conceptual modeling and large language models: impressions from first experiments With ChatGPT. Enterprise Modell. Inf. Syst. Architec. **18**, 1–15 (2023). https://doi.org/10.18417/emisa.18.3. https://folia.unifr.ch/global/documents/324646
9. Guilherme, V., Vincenzi, A.: An initial investigation of ChatGPT unit test generation capability. In: Proceedings of the 8th Brazilian Symposium on Systematic and Automated Software Testing. SAST '23, pp. 15–24. Association for Computing Machinery, New York (2023). https://doi.org/10.1145/3624032.3624035

10. Hannay, J.E., Dybå, T., Arisholm, E., Sjøberg, D.I.: The effectiveness of pair programming: A meta-analysis. Information and software technology. Inf. Softw. Technol. **51**(7), 1110–1122 (2009)
11. Hou, X., Zhao, Y., Liu, Y., Yang, Z., Wang, K., Li, L., Luo, X., Lo, D., Grundy, J., Wang, H.: Large language models for software engineering: A systematic literature review (2024) (arXiv:2308.10620). arXiv. https://doi.org/10.48550/arXiv.2308.10620
12. Humble, J., Kim, G.: Accelerate: The science of lean software and devops: Building and scaling high performing technology organizations. IT Revolution (2018)
13. Kabir, S., Udo-Imeh, D.N., Kou, B., Zhang, T.: Who answers it better? An in-depth analysis of ChatGPT and stack overflow answers to Software Engineering Questions (2023). https://doi.org/10.48550/arXiv.2308.02312. http://arxiv.org/abs/2308.02312
14. Kalliamvakou, E.: Research: Quantifying GitHub Copilot's impact on developer productivity and happiness (2022). https://github.blog/2022-09-07-research-quantifying-github-copilots-impact-on-developer-productivity-and-happiness/
15. Khoury, R., Avila, A.R., Brunelle, J., Camara, B.M.: How secure is code generated by ChatGPT? (2023). https://doi.org/10.48550/arXiv.2304.09655. http://arxiv.org/abs/2304.09655
16. Lanyado, B.: Can you trust ChatGPT's package recommendations? (2023). https://vulcan.io/blog/ai-hallucinations-package-risk/
17. Lucchi, N.: ChatGPT: a case study on copyright challenges for generative artificial intelligence systems. Eur. J. Risk Regul., 1–23 (2023). https://doi.org/10.1017/err.2023.59
18. Moradi Dakhel, A., Majdinasab, V., Nikanjam, A., Khomh, F., Desmarais, M.C., Jiang, Z.M.J.: GitHub copilot AI pair programmer: asset or Liability? J. Syst. Softw. **203**, 111734 (2023). https://doi.org/10.1016/j.jss.2023.111734. https://www.sciencedirect.com/science/article/pii/S0164121223001292
19. Murgia, M.: Generative AI exists because of the transformer (2023). https://ig.ft.com/generative-ai/
20. Nascimento, N., Alencar, P., Cowan, D.: Comparing Software Developers with ChatGPT: An Empirical Investigation (2023). arXiv preprint arXiv.2305.11837. https://doi.org/10.48550/arXiv.2305.11837. http://arxiv.org/abs/2305.11837
21. Nguyen, N., Nadi, S.: An empirical evaluation of GitHub copilot's code suggestions. In: Proceedings of the 19th International Conference on Mining Software Repositories, MSR '22, pp. 1–5. Association for Computing Machinery (2022). https://doi.org/10.1145/3524842.3528470. https://dl.acm.org/doi/10.1145/3524842.3528470
22. Ozkaya, I.: Can architecture knowledge guide software development with generative ai? IEEE Softw. **40**(05), 4–8 (2023). https://doi.org/10.1109/MS.2023.3306641
23. Ray, S.: Samsung Bans ChatGPT Among Employees After Sensitive Code Leak (2023). https://www.forbes.com/sites/siladityaray/2023/05/02/samsung-bans-chatgpt-and-other-chatbots-for-employees-after-sensitive-code-leak/
24. Sobania, D., Briesch, M., Hanna, C., Petke, J.: An Analysis of the Automatic Bug Fixing Performance of ChatGPT (2023). https://doi.org/10.48550/arXiv.2301.08653. http://arxiv.org/abs/2301.08653
25. Tal, L.: Can machines dream of secure code? From AI hallucinations to software vulnerabilities (2023). https://snyk.io/blog/ai-hallucinations/
26. White, J., Fu, Q., Hays, S., Sandborn, M., Olea, C., Gilbert, H., Elnashar, A., Spencer-Smith, J., Schmidt, D.C.: A Prompt Pattern Catalog to Enhance Prompt Engineering with ChatGPT (2023). https://doi.org/10.48550/arXiv.2302.11382. http://arxiv.org/abs/2302.11382
27. White, J., Hays, S., Fu, Q., Spencer-Smith, J., Schmidt, D.C.: ChatGPT Prompt Patterns for Improving Code Quality, Refactoring, Requirements Elicitation, and Software Design (2023). https://doi.org/10.48550/arXiv.2303.07839. http://arxiv.org/abs/2303.07839
28. Yetistiren, B., Ozsoy, I., Tuzun, E.: Assessing the quality of GitHub copilot's code generation. In: Proceedings of the 18th International Conference on Predictive Models and Data Analytics in Software Engineering. PROMISE 2022. pp. 62–71. Association for Computing Machinery (2022). https://doi.org/10.1145/3558489.3559072. https://dl.acm.org/doi/10.1145/3558489.3559072

Part V
Future Directions and Education

Generating Explanations for AI-Powered Delay Prediction in Software Projects

Shunichiro Tomura ⓘ and Hoa Khanh Dam ⓘ

Abstract A project failure can be attributed to complex negative factors that can deviate project progress from the original schedules, and one of the root causes can be a delay. Hence, the early detection of a delay sign can be a critical component for the success of a project. One approach that contributes to solving the problem can be the development of prediction models, and machine learning methods can be a promising approach due to the recent success in other areas. Therefore, we introduce an AI-based novel approach using an explainable graph neural network that elucidates the causes of a delay without compromising its prediction performance. Three experimental results demonstrate that (1) our model can predict the delay with 4% higher accuracy on average, (2) our model returns a stable result by providing a similar prediction performance with a similar explanation when the same prediction tasks are given, and (3) the generated explanations can provide actual reasons for the delay prediction given that the optimal threshold is used. These points can provide a more supportive delay prediction system to users, reducing the failure of projects in terms of time control.

Keywords Explainable AI · Graph neural network · Software project · Delay · Prediction

1 Introduction

Generative artificial intelligence (AI) has recently achieved remarkable performance in automatically generating content (e.g., text and images) and supporting decision-making processes. Generative AI models were built on highly complex algorithms with billions of parameters, which resulted in significant performance improvements. However, those complexities provide further difficulty in understanding why and how those AI models generate their output, either in the form of content or

S. Tomura · H. K. Dam (✉)
Decision Systems Lab, University of Wollongong, Wollongong, NSW, Australia
e-mail: hoa@uow.edu.au

© The Author(s), under exclusive license to Springer Nature Switzerland AG 2024
A. Nguyen-Duc et al. (eds.), *Generative AI for Effective Software Development*,
https://doi.org/10.1007/978-3-031-55642-5_14

predictions. Hence, there is a need to empower AI models with explanations. In this chapter, we will explore the application of explainable AI in the context of software project management.

Managing software projects is highly challenging due to many uncertainties arising from various sources. A study conducted by McKinsey and the University of Oxford on 5,400 large-scale IT projects revealed that software projects often run 66% exceeding the budget and 33% overtime [22]. For another instance, the well-known Standish Group's CHAOS report found that 82% of software projects were delayed [12], indicating that delay can be one of the common issues in software projects.

A project requires the completion of a (large) number of tasks. Each task often has a planned deadline, and the project team needs to complete as many tasks in time as possible to avoid adverse impact on the overall progress of the project. This time management issue can be more complex as software is increasing in both size and complexity. Hence, one important form of automated project management support is the capability to predict, at any given stage project, which ongoing tasks (among hundreds to thousands of them) are at risk of being delayed. Foreseeing those delay risks would empower project managers and team leads to assess the risks and deploy prudent measures to mitigate them, reducing the chance of their project getting delayed.

A number of machine learning-based techniques (e.g., [5, 7, 8]) have recently been proposed to predict delays in resolving software issues. Those approaches leverage the historical project data to extract past patterns of delayed issues and their features. These data and features are then used to train a machine learning model to predict if an ongoing issue (or tasks) will be delayed. However, those proposed models either do not integrate attribute dependency or provide explainable prediction results.

As an alternative approach, recent breakthroughs brought by a deep learning class of graph neural networks (GNNs) in different domain applications allow us to explore the use of GNNs in delay prediction. Task dependencies are common in software projects, and they form a graph of tasks, a suitable input for GNNs. Thus, the first contribution of this chapter is introducing a novel use of a graph convolutional network [20] for task delay prediction.

GNNs are however considered as "black-box" models, making it difficult for project managers and team leads to understand them and interpret their predictions. Hence, our second contribution is a method for generating explanations for delay prediction models. We extend the Integrated Gradients approach [32] with node clustering and outlier analysis to generate explanations for our model's predictions. The detection of delay possibility in the early stage with explanation can provide an opportunity to eliminate the delay risk at a lower cost while using our method at the later stage can shrink the delay period by identifying the causes. Our research can provide an example indicating the significance of interpretability for generative AI.

Our method is evaluated by (1) a performance comparison with the pre-proposed methods and (2) an investigation of the *stability* and *fidelity* of the model explanations. These evaluation aspects answer **three research questions**:

1. **Does our method improve the delay prediction accuracy in software projects?**
   Our model achieved on average 68% precision, 84% recall, and 74% F-measure, which are higher than the state-of-the-art results [6].
2. **Does our method provide similar explanations for similar tasks that have the same prediction outcome?**
   This question addresses the *stability* of our model's explanations. High stability means that small variations (which do not change the prediction) in the tasks and their dependencies do not change the explanation substantially. Our model achieved at least 91% stability for the prediction and at least 77% stability for the explanation on average, demonstrating the high stability of our approach.
3. **Do the explanations demonstrate the model's actual reasons for predicting if tasks are delayed or not?**
   This question addresses the *fidelity* of our model's explanations. An explanation with high fidelity should contain components that truly influence the model's decision for its prediction. Our model achieved at least 75%–87% fidelity in two different experiments, demonstrating high fidelity.

2   Motivating Example

A project typically requires a (large) number of tasks to be completed. Each task has a planned due date, which in practice can be set in one of the following ways, (1) explicitly giving it a due date or (2) allocating it to a release, and the release's deadline is implicitly considered as the task's due date. Tasks that are completed after their planned due date are considered as *delayed tasks*—as opposed to *non-delayed tasks*, which were completed in time. Project tasks are often characterized by a set of attributes such as task priority, type, assignee, title, and description This information can be extracted to form a set of features or risk factors such as task type, percentage of delayed issues that the assignee is involved with, the assignee's workload, task priority, and changing of priority. Previous work [7, 8] have used those features to develop a model for predicting task delays.

A task may also depend on other tasks. Figure 1 illustrates an example of task dependencies in the Spring project.[1] Task SGF-314 is related to tasks SGF-263, SGF-270, SGF-309, SGF-331, and SGF-333 by either explicitly specifying in the tasks' record or implicitly inferring from the tasks' information such as assigned to the same developer, sharing the same attributes and similar in the details. The approach proposed in [6] identifies those task relationships and uses them to build a networked classifier for predicting task delays. This approach has demonstrated an improvement in predictive performance and, to the best of our knowledge, is currently state of the art in predicting task delays.

---

[1] https://spring.io/projects

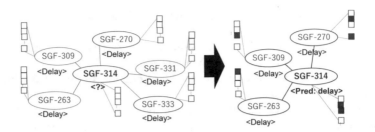

Fig. 1 Dependencies of SGF-314. The square boxes are attributes corresponding to each task. The goal is to correctly predict the delay probability of SGF-314 with an explanation. The red-colored nodes, edges, and attributes are highlighted as explanatory components for the prediction

Task dependencies form a graph of tasks where each node represents a task and an edge represents a dependency between two tasks. Task nodes, edges, and task attributes are considered as **components** of the graph. Predicting if a task will be delayed or not can be seen as a node classification problem. We need to predict a label (delayed or non-delayed) of an unlabelled node that is connected to some labelled nodes. Graph neural networks (GNNs) have generated breakthroughs in node classification across different domains. Thus, there is an opportunity to leverage graph neural networks here, which is the first focus of this chapter. We investigate if the use of a graph neural network would improve the predictive performance of delay prediction.

The second focus of our work is proposing a method that can generate explanations. The right-hand side of Fig. 1 illustrates an example of such an explanation. Task SGF-314 is predicted to be delayed, and an explanation is provided in terms of a small subset of features and dependent tasks, which are likely to contribute to the delay. Those are the red-colored nodes, edges, and attributes in Fig. 1.

3   Related Work and Research Questions

3.1   Delay in Projects and Delay Prediction

Delay is one of the common negative phenomena in projects [33]. According to a survey [12], about half of the projects experienced a delay, and more than 10% of them were delayed above 200% from their initial plans. Numerous reasons such as cost, unit integration [10], and unexpected events can induce a delay, but human-related factors can be one notable cause [18]. For example, the work in [11] found that 97% of successful projects were led by well-experienced project managers. However, such people may not be available all the time. Workers without adequate project management skills may need to take charge of projects if appropriate ones are not vacant [23]. Their poor management skills may impair the quality of time management. An aid is essential for such cases to achieve delay prevention.

Automated support can be one of the approaches that can be offered to accomplish a delay prediction [4]. Machine learning-based support can help project teams prevent a delay beforehand so that the project can be completed within the proposed time frame. Several machine learning-based methods [5, 7, 8] can forecast a delay in a project. However, these methods do not make use of dependencies between task nodes. A task delay cannot be precisely predicted without the utilization of task dependencies since a delay on one task may impact other tasks. The impact of task dependencies has been analyzed and emphasized in the work of [25]. We believe that using task dependencies and modelling them as a graph can improve accurate delay prediction. This leads to our first research question:

RQ1. Does our graph-based method improve the delay prediction accuracy in software projects?

3.2 Explainability Evaluation

Most of the work on explainable artificial intelligence (e.g., [3, 14, 19, 28, 31]) has focused on four main evaluation criteria for explainability.

Accuracy evaluates the degree of negative effects that reduce the performance of predictions itself. The addition of an explainable algorithm should not hurt the prediction accuracy as a trade-off. This metric is the most commonly used evaluation metric due to its simplicity for the measurement. A range of techniques (e.g., [17, 21, 29, 35, 40]) use accuracy for validating the robustness of their approaches.

Consistency examines the replicability of the same explanations under different models. Explanations are accounted as inconsistent if generated explanations are dissimilar by models, although both input and the corresponding output are the same. Model-agnostic methods (e.g., [1, 26, 37, 38]) tend to achieve this criterion.

Fidelity specifies that the components in an explanation should actually explain the prediction. If the chosen components' values are manipulated, then the prediction should be altered likewise. The importance of this concept is emphasized in [15], which proposes several aspects that make the fidelity-based experimental tests more reliable. Several research results (e.g., [15, 16, 30, 34, 37, 39]) utilize the essence of fidelity to validate their methods.

Lastly, *stability* monitors the insusceptibility of explanation to the modification of non-explanatory components. If the prediction is perturbed by manipulating non-explanatory components, then the explanation does not fully elucidate the prediction. A range of works (e.g., [2, 13, 27, 41]) have used stability as a metric for assessing explainability.

Our approach is model agnostic; thus, it does not affect the prediction accuracy. In addition, this approach assures consistency since explanations are not impacted by the model structure, i.e., our approach is not tied to any specific prediction model. Thus, we focus on the fidelity and stability of our approach, which leads to our two research questions:

RQ2. Does our method provide similar explanations for similar tasks that have the same prediction outcome?

RQ3. Do the explanations demonstrate the model's actual reasons for predicting if tasks are delayed or not?

4 Proposed Approach

The entire mechanism of our approach is demonstrated in this section. Figure 2 shows the brief flow of our approach, which consists of five steps.

4.1 Delay Prediction

We represent the task network of a project as a graph. A graph is composed of nodes, also called vertices, and edges. If one node has a dependency on another node, then an edge is created between them. Nodes and edges can be denoted as $X = \{x_1, x_2, \ldots, x_i\}$ and $E = \{e_{11}, e_{12}, \ldots, e_{ij}\}$, respectively. The dependencies among nodes are stored in an adjacency matrix A. If two nodes form an edge, then the value of the corresponding element in the matrix is one. Zero would be allocated otherwise. A graph is then expressed as $G = \{X, E, A\}$.

To predict if a given task will be delayed, we construct a graph that captures the dependencies between this task and other tasks in the project. The graph is then input to a Graph Convolution Network (GCN) model adopted from [20]:

$$Z = f_{out}(\hat{A}, \ f_h(Conv(\hat{A}, X W^{(0)}))) W^{(1)} \tag{1}$$

where I is an identity matrix, $\hat{A}$ is rewritten as $A + I$ ($\hat{A}$ shows the task edges between connected task nodes and itself), and W is a weight matrix demonstrating weights conjoining two layers.

Our GCN model assumes one hidden layer, and hence $W^{(0)}$ is the weights matrix connecting the input layer with the hidden layer. Similarly, $W^{(1)}$ is the weight matrix between the hidden layer and the output layer. f_h is the activate function in the hidden layer. f_{out} is the activate function for the output layer correspondingly. $Conv$ convolutes the graph to elicit patterns and clues for the prediction.

4.2 Delay Component Calculation

The calculation of the delay contribution level in each component (neighbor task nodes, edges, and task attributes) reveals candidate components heavily influencing

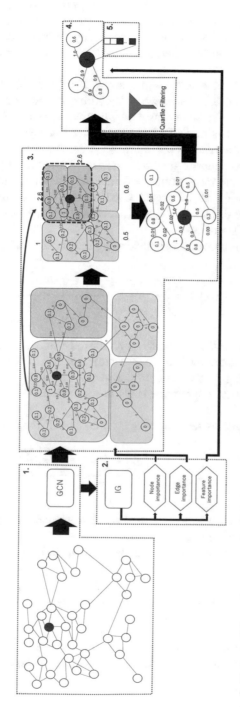

Fig. 2 The overall flow of our approach: (1) Delay prediction. (2) Component importance calculation. (3) Base subgraph extraction. (4) Irrelevant task nodes filtering. (5) Delay-explaining attributes identification

the delay probability. We adopt Integrated Gradients [32], a method that calculates the importance level of each component in a quantitative manner by measuring a change (gradient) in a delay probability caused by adding a component. The importance level of a component is then computed by the summation of all integrals from the gradient.

We adopt Integrated Gradients for two reasons. Firstly, despite the simplicity, precise importance calculation is achieved. According to the study in [31], the performance of Integrated Gradients was the highest next to Class Activation Map (CAM) [42]. Since CAM is available only when the last layer of a network is a global pool, Integrated Gradients are more versatile. Another research [2] also demonstrated that model-agnostic methods such as Integrated Gradients tended to accomplish a higher and more stable performance. Secondly, model structures do not limit the capability of Integrated Gradients as long as the models are differentiable. GCNs are differentiable, and therefore Integrated Gradients can be utilized to explain GCN's prediction.

We compute the importance of a task node using Integrated Gradients as follows:

$$IG(x_i) \approx \sum_{j=1}^{a} \left(x_{ij} - x'_{ij} \right) * \sum_{k=1}^{m} \frac{\partial F\left(x'_{ij} + \frac{k}{m} * \left(x_{ij} - x'_{ij}\right)\right)}{\partial x_{ij}} * \frac{1}{m} \tag{2}$$

where x_i is a task node in the graph, x_{ij} is an attribute in x_i, x'_{ij} is the baseline feature value for x_{ij}, a is the total number of attributes in each task node, and m indicates the total number of divisions for calculating the integral via quadrature. The summation of attribute importance leads to the importance of the task node itself.

Similarly, the importance of task edges can be measured in the following method:

$$IG(e_{io}) \approx \left(e_{io} - e'_{io}\right) * \sum_{k=1}^{m} \frac{\partial F\left(e'_{io} + \frac{k}{m} * \left(e_{io} - e'_{io}\right)\right)}{\partial e_{io}} * \frac{1}{m} \tag{3}$$

where e_{io} shows the task edge between x_i and x_o. This calculates the gradient values between with and without the target task edge.

Furthermore, attribute importance is calculated by the following equation:

$$IG(T_t) \approx \sum_{i=1}^{n} \left(x_{it} - x'_{it} \right) * \sum_{k=1}^{m} \frac{\partial F\left(x'_{it} + \frac{k}{m} * \left(x_{it} - x'_{it}\right)\right)}{\partial x_{it}} * \frac{1}{m} \tag{4}$$

n is the total number of nodes in the graph. The importance of the attribute T_t is acquired from the summation of the attribute T_t importance in each node.

These three Integrated Gradients specify the importance level of each component, which is used to extract the explanatory components that actually contribute to a prediction outcome.

4.3 Explanatory Delay Subgraph Extraction

By leveraging the importance level calculated in the previous process, a subgraph representing a base explanation is extracted from the input graph using modularity-based node clustering [9], which is described below:

$$Q = \frac{1}{2m} \sum_{io} \left[A_{io} - \gamma \frac{k_i k_o}{2m} \right] \delta(c_i, c_o) \tag{5}$$

m is the number of edges. This is multiplied by 2 because an edge is built as the integration of two edges from respective task nodes (edges from task nodes x_i and x_o). A is an adjacency matrix indicating the connection between task nodes x_i and x_o; k_i and k_o are the number of edges from x_i and x_o, respectively; and $\delta(c_i, c_o)$ signals whether the selected task nodes belong to the same community as a binary form. γ is used for adjusting the community granularity. Initially, the value is set as one, and as the value decreases, more communities containing a fewer number of task nodes are created [24]. The goal is to embrace task nodes, which can significantly change the modularity value Q by including them in a community.

The node clustering repeats twice for different purposes. The first clustering identifies the community holding the target node. The second clustering partitions the selected community into smaller communities. The communities whose important levels are equal to or higher than the target task node's community are encompassed as a segment of the final subgraph. The importance of each community can be estimated as below:

$$imp(com_s) = \sum_{i=1}^{n'} imp(x_i) \tag{6}$$

where x_i denotes a task node in the community s and n' is the total number of task nodes included in s. Through this clustering, the rough selection of task nodes and edges is achieved.

4.4 Irrelevant Task Nodes Filtering

While the node clustering can filter the majority of irrelevant task nodes, the subgraph may still contain fewer explanatory task nodes due to the community-wise selection. There is a possibility that the subgraph includes non-explanatory task nodes. In addition, if the clustering extracts task nodes from a large and complex graph, the size of the subgraph remains vast. Such a subgraph does not allow users to intuitively distinguish influential task nodes for the prediction. Hence, further filtering is conducted by using a simple filtering approach from the percentile-based method [36] described as follows:

$$filtered(x_{i*}) = \begin{cases} 0 & abs(imp(x_{i*})) > \tau \\ 1 & else \end{cases} \tag{7}$$

where x_{i*} is a task node in the subgraph and τ is the threshold based on the percentile of all task nodes' importance values in the extracted subgraph. For example, $Q3$, $Q3 + (Q3 - Q1)$ or $Q3 + (Q3 - Q1) * 1.5$ can be used as the threshold. After the task node selection, all the task edges between non-target task nodes are removed. Task edges that directly connect the target task node with others are the ones that actually influence the prediction at a high level. Within the remaining task edges, the quantile filtering is conducted in a similar way with Eq. (7). Task edges that are higher than the edge threshold remain in the subgraph.

4.5 Delay-Explaining Attributes Identification

After identifying the final subgraph, each feature attribute's importance is calculated from Eq. (4). They are ranked in the order of the importance level as below:

$$rank(T_t) = desc(abs(imp(T_t))) \tag{8}$$

The attributes that reach the highest rank are the most influential attributes for the prediction, and as the rank lowers, the influential level also drops. This information is tied to the delay explaining attribute analysis, which checks whether observed attribute values in the target node exceed corresponding attribute thresholds. If an attribute value is higher than the attribute threshold in the absolute value expression, then it is treated as an outlied attribute value. Such a task attribute is selected as one factor, which may increase the delay probability. If there is an attribute that is ranked as the most influential attribute and the value is higher than the threshold, then the attribute is regarded as a factor explaining the delay.

Attribute thresholds are computed from the quantile values from feature attributes in all non-delay task nodes. The quantile for the attribute T_t is calculated from the attribute T_t's value from all non-delay nodes. Equation (7) is used for checking each target task node's attribute. If zero is measured, then the attribute value is determined as a delay factor.

5 Evaluation

5.1 Experimental Design

In this section, we conduct several experiments to measure the ability of our approach. The initial step for the evaluation is the selection of experiment datasets. The datasets from [6] are used for the experiments. These datasets contain actual tasks from five open-source projects; Apache, Duraspace, JBoss, Moodle, and Spring. All the projects utilize JIRA, which allows us to manage the entire project flow and store the events and attributes regarding the projects. Each of the projects consists of a list of tasks with fifteen feature attributes and task edges connecting two task nodes. Each task node is labelled with either delayed or non-delayed.

Task edges can be classified into two types. Explicit edges are the ones that are initially recognized by actual task managers. Implicit edges are proposed by [6], which introduces seven different edge attributes based on the same task creator. In our experiments, both edge types are employed.

The datasets were randomly split into train and test sets in a way that the ratio of non-delay and delay becomes the same in both sets. For each dataset, the task data was divided into two with a ratio of 7:3. The number of train and test task nodes per label in each project is shown in Table 1. JBoss has the largest records at 5,969, followed by Moodle, Duraspace, Spring, and Apache. While the proportion of delay against non-delay varies in each dataset, all the datasets' labels are imbalanced. Therefore, an oversampling approach is adopted to the delayed tasks in training data so that the ratio of non-delay and delay becomes 1:1. A further refinement in the resampling method may improve the model performance, which is a part of our future improvement.

Our GCN model is structured with one hidden layer and a dense layer at the end. The number of neurons in the hidden layer is 500. A weight regularizer is introduced to prevent overfitting by using L2 with a rate of 0.01. The activate functions for the hidden and output layers are ReLU and Sigmoid, respectively. Nadam is used for the optimizer. The learning rate is set as 0.001 for Spring, Duraspace, JBoss, and Moodle, whereas 0.01 is adopted for Apache in order to optimize the model performance. Since there are only two labels, binary cross entropy is used to compute the loss. The number of epochs is set as 500. Each training dataset and

Table 1 The number of issues per label in each project

	Non delay			Delay		
	Train	Test	Total	Train	Test	Total
Apache	276	118	394	71	31	102
Duraspace	671	288	959	110	47	157
JBoss	4,179	1,790	5,969	1,569	672	2,241
Moodle	902	385	1,287	109	47	156
Spring	361	156	517	54	23	77

the corresponding graph are separately used, and therefore five GCN models are constructed in total.

The evaluation consists of four different experiments. The first experiment compares the performance of our method with the state of the art in issue delay prediction [6]. The second experiment is designed to investigate the stability of the generated explanations and predictions. The last two experiments validate the fidelity of our generated explanations.

5.2 Experimental Results

Performance Comparison

This experiment answers our first research question:

RQ1. Does our method improve the delay prediction accuracy in software projects?

Method We compare the performance of our method with the best method (Stacked Graphical Learning) for issue delay prediction proposed in [6]. The performance is measured by precision, recall, F-measure, and AUC from delayed data. To reach a stable conclusion, we ran the experiment 30 times and computed the average results.

Result The precision, recall, and F-measure of our approach are 68%, 84%, and 74%, respectively, on average, which outperforms those of Stacked Learning (see Fig. 3). Our model outperforms the others in all the datasets except Moodle. Although the average AUC of Stacked Learning is higher than that of our approach, the gap is subtle. Therefore, our approach is capable of predicting a delay with higher performance without compromising its prediction performance.

JBoss performance produced by our approach records the highest at 83%, which is 20% higher than the Stacked Learning approach proposed in [6]. This can be due to two reasons. Firstly, the size of the JBoss data is noticeably larger than the other projects. Our approach may have been able to obtain a sufficient amount of data, which could contribute to refining the prediction competence. Secondly, the total number of delayed issues in JBoss is not considerably fewer than the non-delay issues compared to the other datasets. A sufficient amount of information to enhance the delay prediction ability may have been provided to the model. Thus, the performance can be superior to the other methods if a large amount of less imbalanced data is available. Further validation is required as a part of future research as well.

Stability Check

This experiment answers our second question:

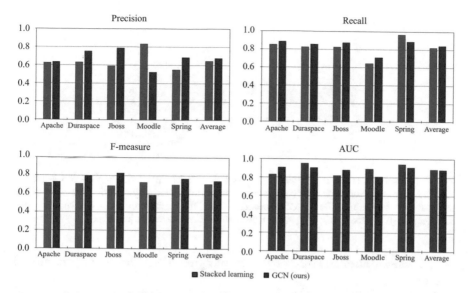

Fig. 3 Comparison of performance (the performance of Stacked Learning is adopted from [6])

RQ2. Does our method provide similar explanations for similar tasks that have the same prediction outcome?

Method This experiment consists of two rounds. After computing delay probability and generating an explanation graph in the first round, all the task nodes that are directly linked to the target task node are chosen. Among the selected task nodes, all the attributes of the task nodes that are excluded from the explanation graph are manipulated with small values. The manipulation values are calculated by following this equation: $min((T_t) + 1) * 0.001$ where T_t is an attribute value and min is the minimum function which returns the minimum value of the attribute from all the task nodes in the dataset. For example, if the attribute's minimum value is 0, then 0.001 is returned as the manipulation value. This manipulated dataset is used for the second round. If both the prediction and explanation are similar to the first round's, then our model is stable against trivial changes, and unstable otherwise. The summary of the experiment is illustrated in Fig. 4. This experiment was run 30 times by selecting different delayed test task nodes in every dataset with three different thresholds: $Q3$, $Q3 + (Q3 - Q1)$, and $Q3 + (Q3 - Q1) * 1.5$.

In order to measure the stability, four metrics are applied. Prediction stability measures the matching rate of predictions between the first and second rounds. The higher the value becomes, the more stable the model prediction is against irrelevant values. Therefore, we expect to observe a higher prediction stability value. We also performed the Wilcoxon signed-rank test to statistically validate the delay probability changes. The raw predictions are expressed from zero to one, and as the value becomes closer to one, the likelihood of delay increases. Prior to the experiment, we propose two hypotheses.

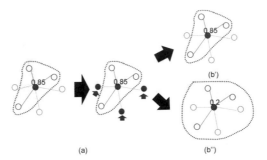

Fig. 4 The red dot is the target delay node, and the dotted line is the explanation graph for the prediction. (**a**) Non-explanatory components are manipulated with small values (**b'**). If the explanation is stable, then the raw delay probability and the explanation should be similar to the first round's. (**b''**) Otherwise, the prediction and explanation would not be stable

- H_0: there are no differences between the raw predictions from the first and second rounds.
- H_1: there are differences between the raw predictions from the first and second rounds.

If we fail to reject the null hypothesis H_0, then in practical terms, we can assume that the predictions in the two rounds are the same. We use Cohen's effect size to statistically measure the value difference between the first and second rounds. The value in this experiment is expected to be small. Explanation stability is the metric that indicates the similarity level of explanations between the two rounds. This metric is calculated as below:

$$E_{stability} = \frac{sum\left(nodes'_{first} + nodes'_{second}\right)}{sum\left(nodes_{first} + nodes_{second}\right)} \tag{9}$$

where $nodes_{first}$ and $nodes_{second}$ represent each task node in the first and second explanation graphs, respectively. The denominator denotes the total task nodes in the first and second explanation graphs. The numerator represents the total task nodes selected in both rounds. This metric ranges from 0 to 1. As the value becomes closer to 1, a higher similarity is demonstrated.

The result of this experiment is shown in Table 2. $\tau 1$, $\tau 2$, and $\tau 3$ are the threshold 1, 2, and 3, respectively. $\tau 0$ is when no threshold is set, which is used for the total edges. *, **, and *** show that the p-value is smaller than the significance level at 0.05, 0.01, and 0.001, respectively. P stability, E stability, and T edges denote prediction stability, explanation stability, and total edges, respectively.

Result Prediction stability higher than 90% is observed in most of the cases in all the projects regardless of the thresholds. The high prediction stability values show that there is no difference in the predictions before and after the manipulation. The predictions are insusceptible to the minor and unimportant changes. This high

Table 2 Stability test results

	P stability			p-value			Effect size			E stability			T edges
	$\tau 1$	$\tau 2$	$\tau 3$	$\tau 1$	$\tau 2$	$\tau 3$	$\tau 1$	$\tau 2$	$\tau 3$	$\tau 1$	$\tau 2$	$\tau 3$	$\tau 0$
Apache	0.93	0.97	1.00	0.98	0.78	0.50	−0.08	−0.10	−0.42	0.75	0.79	0.79	47
Duraspace	0.90	0.87	0.93	0.69	0.84	0.93	−0.02	−0.10	−0.01	0.82	0.85	0.94	89
JBoss	0.93	0.90	0.80	0.77	0.87	0.86	0.12	0.09	−0.12	0.70	0.61	0.59	380
Moodle	0.80	0.93	0.90	0.58	0.63	0.49	0.12	−0.10	−0.07	0.73	0.78	0.79	144
Spring	0.97	1.00	0.97	0.35	0.22	0.77	−0.06	0.06	0.02	0.86	0.88	0.89	85
Average	0.91	0.93	0.92	0.67	0.67	0.70	0.01	0.00	−0.12	0.77	0.78	0.80	149

prediction stability is also confirmed by the Wilcoxon test and effect sizes. All the p-values computed from the raw probabilities from each of the two rounds are by far higher than any of the significance levels. The effect size values in all the cases are close to zero. Hence, we fail to reject the null hypothesis, which meets our expectation (high stability).

The stability also needs to be confirmed from the explanation side as well via the explanation stability metric. Explanation stability is achieved at least 77% on average in all the different thresholds. Similar explanations are returned to the same task nodes. One noticeable tendency is that the stability value increases as the threshold becomes higher except for JBoss. The average stability value shifts from 80% to 85% when the threshold changes from $\tau 1$ to $\tau 3$ excluding JBoss. Therefore, the threshold needs to be adjusted based on the expected stability level. The threshold adjustment can be conducted by considering it in the aspect of fidelity as well (which is extended in the discussion section). JBoss shows a different tendency with rather low performance because of the large average total task edges at 380. This might raise the difficulty of precisely generating similar explanations to the model.

Fidelity Check

Fidelity check consists of two experiments, which correspond to answering our last question:

RQ3. Do the explanations demonstrate the model's actual reasons for predicting if tasks are delayed or not?
(a) Non-explanatory delay components removal test

Method This experiment is decomposed into two rounds (see Fig. 5). The first round predicts the raw delay probability of a delayed test task node, followed by identifying explanatory task nodes and edges. All irrelevant edges connected to the target node are eliminated by updating the adjacent matrix in the manipulation process. The second round predicts the raw delay probability of the same test task node again, but the updated adjacent matrix is used. After both rounds, we compare

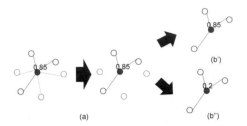

Fig. 5 (**a**) After the first round, the task edges of non-explanatory components connected to the target task node are removed. (**b'**) If the explanation satisfies fidelity, then the removal does not change the prediction. (**b"**) If the prediction significantly changes, then our method does not satisfy fidelity

Table 3 Non-explanatory components removal test result

	Fidelity			p-value			E size		
	$\tau 1$	$\tau 2$	$\tau 3$	$\tau 1$	$\tau 2$	$\tau 3$	$\tau 1$	$\tau 2$	$\tau 3$
Apache	0.91	0.87	0.91	0.24	0.34	0.11	−0.07	−0.09	0.04
Duraspace	0.93	0.87	0.93	0.93	0.44	0.32	0.02	0.01	0.17
JBoss	0.90	0.90	0.93	0.96	0.54	0.88	−0.07	−0.02	−0.15
Moodle	0.97	0.93	0.93	0.27	0.28	0.36	−0.09	−0.09	0.02
Spring	0.93	0.80	0.93	0.94	0.12	0.81	−0.12	−0.11	0.03
Average	0.93	0.87	0.93	0.67	0.34	0.50	−0.06	−0.06	0.02

the first and second prediction results. If the manipulation does not change the result, then the explanation entails high fidelity. The prediction consistency shows that the components of the explanation graph are the actual factors influencing the result. Similar to the previous experiments, this experiment was also run 30 times by randomly selecting delayed tasks in test data. To check the effect of the threshold for node and edge filtering, we also used three different thresholds: $Q3$, $Q3 + (Q3 − Q1)$, and $Q3 + (Q3 − Q1) * 1.5$.

In this experiment, the fidelity performance is measured by three metrics. Fidelity assesses the similarity percentage of predictions between the first and second rounds. Fidelity ranges from 0 to 1 where it is high if the value is close to 1 and vice versa. This is averaged by the number of test data points (ran 30 times) in each project. p-value from the Wilcoxon signed-rank test indicates the statistical difference between the first and second raw predictions. The null and alternative hypotheses are the same as in the previous experiment. Since we assume that the removal of non-explanatory components does not change the prediction, we expect to fail to reject the null hypothesis. Similarly, we expect the effect size to become small.

The result is shown in Table 3. All the variables and symbols denote the same meaning as the previous experiment.

Result More than 90% of fidelity is achieved in the majority of the cases. The removal of non-explanatory components did not affect the predictions in all datasets. This high fidelity is statistically confirmed by the Wilcoxon test result and effect size as well. All the p-values are larger than all the significance levels even if the lowest threshold ($\tau 1$) is selected. Hence, we failed to reject H_0 in all the cases. The effect size from all the cases is close to zero as well. The results from this experiment allow us to conclude that our method is capable of correctly including explanatory components inside the explanation graph. However, it does not provide sufficient evidence to demonstrate the high fidelity since the actual influence level of the explanatory components is not tested. Therefore, we conducted another experiment that checked the effect of these components.

(b) Explanatory delay components manipulation test

Method This is also a two-round experiment (see Fig. 6). The first round predicts the raw delay probability of a delayed test task node and extracts explanatory task nodes and edges. The attributes in the selected task nodes are manipulated if the values are above the corresponding attribute threshold. Their values are adjusted to become just below the threshold value. In addition, if these selected task nodes' labels are delayed, then their labels are changed into non-delay. After removing all the delay factors, the model predicts the delay probability for the same target task nodes by using the manipulated data. We compare the raw delay probability from the first round to the second round. If the explanatory task nodes in the subgraph actually affect the prediction, then the raw probability should become closer to zero in the second round. This is because all the factors explaining the delay are eliminated. Otherwise, the explanation would not satisfy the fidelity.

Three metrics are used in this experiment. The change rate is the rate of the number of cases whose raw delay prediction dropped between both rounds. A higher value shows that more cases observed probability drops. p-value from the Wilcoxon signed-rank test is another metric that statistically demonstrates the raw probability difference between the two rounds. The null and alternative hypotheses are identical to the previous experiment. The significant difference is that we expect p-values

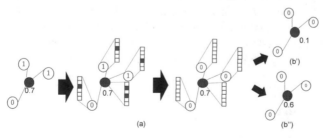

Fig. 6 (a) All delay factors are removed from the subgraph. (b') If the explanation satisfies fidelity, then the raw probability becomes lower than the first round. (b") If not, then the probability does not change

Table 4 Explanatory components manipulation test result

	Change rate			p-value			Effect size		
	$\tau 1$	$\tau 2$	$\tau 3$	$\tau 1$	$\tau 2$	$\tau 3$	$\tau 1$	$\tau 2$	$\tau 3$
Apache	0.63	0.57	0.63	0.00***	0.39	0.36	0.37	0.12	0.11
Duraspace	0.75	0.52	0.50	0.00***	0.10*	0.26	0.18	0.11	−0.04
JBoss	0.83	0.47	0.73	0.00***	0.91	0.01**	0.77	−0.13	0.15
Moodle	0.8	0.53	0.53	0.10	0.25	0.53	0.64	0.50	0.25
Spring	0.83	0.5	0.57	0.00***	0.18	0.18	0.53	0.30	0.11
Average	0.75	0.52	0.50	0.02*	0.35	0.27	0.50	0.18	0.12

to become smaller than a significance level, which leads to the rejection of the null hypothesis. This proves that manipulating selected components alters the raw probability, and thus they are actually important for the prediction. The expectation of effect size is also opposite to the previous experiments. Since the values from the first and second should be significantly different, the effect size needs to be large. Table 4 shows the results of this experiment. $\tau 1$, $\tau 2$, and $\tau 3$ are the same thresholds 1, 2, and 3 as in the previous experiments. The marks *, **, and *** also denote the same significance levels.

Results The change rate demonstrates significant negative values at the lowest threshold with 75% on average. However, if the threshold is too high, substantial delay probability reduction cannot be observed by the rate significantly becoming small at 50%. This is because a number of explanatory components are also filtered. They can be influential to the delay although they are not encompassed in the subgraph. The target nodes still receive delay influences from these components, and the raw delay probability remains at a similar level as a consequence.

The p-values and effect sizes capture this tendency as well. At $\tau 1$, almost all the projects are able to reject the null hypothesis at the level of 0.05 as the maximum significant level. However, as the threshold increases, all the projects except Duraspace and JBoss cannot reject the null hypothesis at any significance level. The effect size in $\tau 1$ is 0.5, but as the threshold becomes higher, the value becomes closer to zero. Therefore, the selection of the optimal threshold is also important in the view of fidelity so that the null hypothesis is rejected. These two experiment results show that by selecting the optimal threshold, our method can satisfy fidelity. Our method includes truly explanatory components in the generated explanation, and they are influential to the predictions.

6   Conclusions

In this paper, we proposed a new method that is capable of more accurate delay prediction and generating explanations for the prediction. The experiment results demonstrate that our approach achieved 68% precision, 84% recall, and 74% F-measure on average. In addition, the explanations generated from our model also achieved high stability and fidelity, indicating the effectiveness of our approach.

7 Data Availability

All the code and data used in this chapter are available at https://zenodo.org/record/6999325#.YvxsjHZBxyw. The datasets were obtained from [6] and published at https://github.com/morakotch/datasets/tree/master/delayed%20issues/ASE2015.

References

1. Alvarez-Melis, D., Jaakkola, T.S.: A causal framework for explaining the predictions of black-box sequence-to-sequence models. arXiv:1707.01943 (2017)
2. Alvarez-Melis, D., Jaakkola, T.S.: Towards robust interpretability with self-explaining neural networks. arXiv:1806.07538 (2018)
3. Ancona, M., Ceolini, E., Öztireli, C., Gross, M.: Towards better understanding of gradient-based attribution methods for deep neural networks. arXiv:1711.06104 (2018)
4. Brynjolfsson, E., Mitchell, T.: What can machine learning do? Workforce implications. Science **358**, 1530–1534 (2017)
5. Choetkiertikul, M., Dam, H.K., Ghose, A.: Threshold-based prediction of schedule overrun in software projects. In: Proceedings of the ASWEC 2015 24th Australasian Software Engineering Conference, pp. 81–85 (2015)
6. Choetkiertikul, M., Dam, H.K., Tran, T., Ghose, A.: Predicting delays in software projects using networked classification. In: 2015 30th IEEE/ACM International Conference on Automated Software Engineering (ASE) (2015)
7. Choetkiertikul, M., Dam, H.K., Trany, T., Ghose, A.: Characterization and prediction of issue-related risks in software projects. In: 2015 IEEE/ACM 12th Working Conference on Mining Software Repositories, pp. 280–291 (2015)
8. Choetkiertikul, M., Dam, H.K., Tran, T., Ghose, A.: Predicting the delay of issues with due dates in software projects. Empirical Software Eng. **22**(3), 1223–1263 (2017)
9. Clauset, A., Newman, M.E.J., Moore, C.: Finding community structure in very large networks. arXiv:cond-mat/0408187 (2004)
10. da Costa, D.A., McIntosh, S., Kulesza, U., Hassan, A.E., Abebe, S.L.: An empirical study of the integration time of fixed issues. Empirical Software Eng. **23**(1), 1–50 (2018)
11. Frese, R.: Project success and failure: What is success, what is failure, and how can you improve your odds for success? (2003). Retrieved from http://www.umsl.edu/~sauterv/analysis/6840_f03_papers/frese/
12. Group, T.S.: The CHAOS Report. The Standish Group International, Inc., Boston (2015)
13. Guidotti, R., Ruggieri, S.: On the stability of interpretable models. In: 2019 International Joint Conference on Neural Networks (IJCNN) (2019)
14. Hooker, S., Erhan, D., Kindermans, P.J., Kim, B.: A benchmark for interpretability methods in deep neural networks. arXiv:1806.10758 (2019)
15. Jacovi, A., Goldberg, Y.: Towards faithfully interpretable NLP systems: how should we define and evaluate faithfulness? arXiv:2004.03685 (2020)
16. Ji, C., Wang, R., Wu, H.: Perturb more, trap more: understanding behaviors of graph neural networks. Neurocomputing **493**(7), 59–75 (2022)
17. Kapishnikov, A., Bolukbasi, T., Viégas, F., Terry, M.: XRAI: better attributions through regions. arXiv:1906.02825 (2019)

18. Khan, K., Zafar, A., Alnuem, M., Khan, H.: Investigation of time delay factors in global software development. World Acad. Sci. Eng. Technol. Open Science Index 63, International Journal of Computer and Information Engineering **6**(3), 318–326 (2012)
19. Kindermans, P.J., Schütt, K., Müller, K.R., Dähne, S.: Investigating the influence of noise and distractors on the interpretation of neural networks. arXiv:1611.07270 (2016)
20. Kipf, T.N., Welling, M.: Semi-supervised classification with graph convolutional networks. arXiv:1609.02907 (2016)
21. Lin, C., Sun, G.J., Bulusu, K.C., Dry, J.R., Hernandez, M.: Graph neural networks including sparse interpretability. arXiv:2007.00119 (2020)
22. Michael, B., Blumberg, S., Laartz, J.: Delivering large-scale IT projects on time, on budget, and on value. Technical report (2012)
23. Munns, A.K., Bjeirmi, B.F.: The role of project management in achieving project success. Int. J. Project Manage. **14**, 81–87 (1996)
24. Newman, M.E.J.: Community detection in networks: modularity optimization and maximum likelihood are equivalent. arXiv:1606.02319 (2016)
25. Nguyen, T.H.D., Adams, B., Hassan, A.E.: Studying the impact of dependency network measures on software quality. 2010 IEEE International Conference on Software Maintenance, 1–10 (2010). https://doi.org/10.1109/ICSM.2010.5609560
26. Plumb, G., Molitor, D., Talwalkar, A.: Model agnostic supervised local explanations. arXiv:1807.02910 (2019)
27. Plumb, G., Al-Shedivat, M., Cabrera, A.A., Perer, A., Xing, E., Talwalkar, A.: Regularizing black-box models for improved interpretability. arXiv:1902.06787 (2020)
28. Pope, P.E., Kolouri, S., Rostami, M., Martin, C.E., Hoffmann, H.: Explainability methods for graph convolutional neural networks. In: Proceedings/CVPR, IEEE Computer Society Conference on Computer Vision and Pattern Recognition (2019)
29. Rathee, M., Zhang, Z., Funke, T., Khosla, M., Anand, A.: Learnt sparsification for interpretable graph neural networks. arXiv:2106.12920 (2021)
30. Ribeiro, M.T., Singh, S., Guestrin, C.: "why should i trust you" explaining the predictions of any classifier. arXiv:1602.04938 (2016)
31. Sanchez-Lengeling, B., Wei, J., Lee, B., Reif, E., Wang, P., Qian, W., McCloskey, K., Colwell, L., Wiltschko, A.: Evaluating attribution for graph neural networks. Advances in Neural Information Processing Systems 33 (NeurIPS 2020) (2020)
32. Sundararajan, M., Taly, A., Yan, Q.: Axiomatic attribution for deep networks. In: Proceedings of the 34th International Conference on Machine Learning (2017)
33. van Genuchten, M.: Why is software late? An empirical study of reasons for delay in software development. IEEE Trans. Software Eng. **17**(6), 582–590 (1991)
34. Velmurugan, M., Ouyang, C., Moreira, C., Sindhgatta, R.: Developing a fidelity evaluation approach for interpretable machine learning. arXiv:2106.08492 (2021)
35. Vu, M.N., Thai, M.T.: PGM-explainer: probabilistic graphical model explanations for graph neural networks. arXiv:2010.05788 (2020)
36. Walfish, S.: A review of statistical outlier methods. Pharm. Technol. **30**(11), 82 (2006)
37. Ying, R., Bourgeois, D., You, J., Zitnik, M., Leskovec, J.: GNN explainer: a tool for post-hoc explanation of graph neural networks. Preprint. arXiv:1903.03894 (2019)
38. Ying, R., Bourgeois, D., You, J., Zitnik, M., Leskovec, J.: GNNExplainer: generating explanations for graph neural networks. In: Advances in Neural Information Processing Systems (2019)
39. Yuan, H., Yu, H., Gui, S., Ji, S.: Explainability in graph neural networks: a taxonomic survey. Preprint. arXiv:2012.15445 (2021)
40. Zhang, J., Lin, Z., Brandt, J., Shen, X., Sclaroff, S.: Top-down neural attention by excitation backprop. In: European Conference on Computer Vision (2016)
41. Zheng, S., Song, Y., Leung, T., Goodfellow, I.: Improving the robustness of deep neural networks via stability training. arXiv:1604.04326 (2016)
42. Zhou, B., Khosla, A., Lapedriza, A., Oliva, A., Torralba, A.: Learning deep features for discriminative localization. arXiv:1512.04150 (2015)

Classifying User Intent for Effective Prompt Engineering: A Case of a Chatbot for Startup Teams

Seyedmoein Mohsenimofidi, Akshy Sripad Raghavendra Prasad, Aida Zahid, Usman Rafiq, Xiaofeng Wang, and Mohammad Idris Attal

Abstract Prompt engineering plays a pivotal role in effective interaction with large language models (LLMs), including ChatGPT. Understanding user intent behind interactions with LLMs is an important part of prompt construction to elicit relevant and meaningful responses from them. Existing literature sheds little light on this aspect of prompt engineering. Our study seeks to address this knowledge gap. Using the example of building a chatbot for startup teams to obtain better responses from ChatGPT, we demonstrate a feasible way of classifying user intent automatically using ChatGPT itself. Our study contributes to a rapidly increasing body of knowledge of prompt engineering for LLMs. Even though the application domain of our approach is startups, it can be adapted to support effective prompt engineering in various other application domains as well.

Keywords Large language models · ChatGPT · Prompt engineering · User intent · Digital assistant · Startups

1 Introduction

Prompt engineering is a technique used to design and formulate effective prompts to get optimal answers from large language models (LLMs), a prime example of which is ChatGPT. The nuanced art of crafting prompts plays a crucial role in fine-tuning LLMs for specific tasks to improve their performance in specific domains [3].

A key facet of prompt construction, often underexplored in existing literature, is understanding the intent behind a user's query to an LLM, which is integral to establishing meaningful and contextually relevant interactions with it. User intent encapsulates the underlying motivation, purpose, or desired outcome behind a user's query [11]. By delving into the intricacies of user intent, prompt engineers can

S. Mohsenimofidi · A. S. R. Prasad · A. Zahid · U. Rafiq · X. Wang (✉) · M. I. Attal
Free University of Bozen-Bolzano, Bolzano, Italy
e-mail: seyedmoein.mohsenimofidi@unibz.it; akshySripad.raghavendraprasad@unibz.it;
aida.zahid@unibz.it; urafiq@unibz.it; xiaofeng.wang@unibz.it; mohammadidris.attal@unibz.it

© The Author(s), under exclusive license to Springer Nature Switzerland AG 2024
A. Nguyen-Duc et al. (eds.), *Generative AI for Effective Software Development*,
https://doi.org/10.1007/978-3-031-55642-5_15

gain the ability to tailor prompts that align with the user's expectations, eliciting responses that transcend mere linguistic accuracy to encompass contextual relevance and coherence.

Despite the central role user intent plays in shaping effective prompts, the existing literature on prompt engineering sheds little light on this essential component. The complexity and nuances involved in deciphering and categorizing user intent can be attributed to ambiguous queries, diverse language usage, and varied communication styles [4]. The scarcity of studies on user intent within the context of prompt engineering underscores a knowledge gap that needs to be tackled to harness the full potential of LLMs.

Our study aspires to address this gap and contribute to effective prompt engineering for LLMs. The research question that guides our research is:
How to identify the intent of a user's query as part of prompt engineering for LLMs using ChatGPT?

Utilizing a practical example centered around the development of a chatbot tailored for startup teams seeking improved responses from ChatGPT, we illuminate a feasible approach to classifying user intent automatically using ChatGPT itself. The chatbot we developed, called DAS (Digital Assistant for Startups), intends to automate the prompt engineering process for startup teams so that they can benefit from improved interactions with LLMs. User intent classification is one key component of DAS. Through this specific application scenario, we demonstrate how user intent can be classified as part of prompt construction, thus contributing to the evolving field of prompt engineering for LLMs. Our study also presents practical implications for the effective utilization of prompt engineering in the context of startups.

2 Prompt Engineering and User Intent

A prompt is a query or input that is submitted to an LLM such as ChatGPT to guide its output generation. A prompt can be a combination of many forms such as a question, a statement, or a keyword, and such forms can be used to customize the output and interactions with LLMs. With the usage of a prompt, the users will have the facility to specify the context and constraints for the generated output, and such a facility will allow them to produce more structured and refined responses [10].

Prompt engineering refers to the engineering process of designing and implementing a prompt that will help in the customization of the desired output from an AI Large language model such as ChatGPT. Essentially, prompt engineering is the process of learning how to effectively interact with AI in a manner that produces the desired outcome by letting it do what is needed [5].

There are suggested principles of prompting to get the result related to a prompt that would be accurate and relevant to the context [1], including *Choose your words precisely*, *Define your prompt with focus and purpose*, *Try to be concise and specific*, *Try to provide context*, and *Try to ask for more*.

These principles are also reflected in prompt patterns [10]. Prompt patterns are reusable solutions to the raised problems while interacting with LLMs. The concept and inspiration behind prompt patterns are derived from software patterns. Just as software patterns offer a structured method to address challenges in software development, prompt patterns offer a systematic approach to customize the output and interaction with LLMs. The main motivation behind prompt patterns is that such patterns can be used to enhance the discipline of prompt engineering. These patterns can be grouped into five categories: input semantics, output customization, prompt improvement, error identification, interaction, and context control. What remains unclear is how to decide which specific pattern is the most appropriate one to be applied to a user's query.

A comprehensive guide of prompt engineering for ChatGPT [5] indicates a way to address this concern. The guide covers various aspects of prompt engineering for ChatGPT, including its fundamentals, effective techniques, best practices, and advanced strategies. Leveraging System 1 and System 2 questions is introduced as one technique for effective prompt crafting. According to the author, understanding the difference between System 1 and System 2 questions can improve the quality of ChatGPT's responses. System 1 questions typically require quick, intuitive, or pattern-recognition-based answers, while System 2 questions involve more deliberate, analytical, or complex problem-solving. Tailoring prompts to the type of question being asked will allow one to optimize the interaction and maximize the usefulness of the generated output. The guide does not suggest any specific classification of user questions, but it does emphasize the importance of understanding user intent, that is, the user's purpose of interacting with ChatGPT. It helps craft a prompt that aligns with the user's expectations.

However, as far as the authors are aware of, there is a scarcity of studies on user intent within the context of prompt engineering for LLMs. Our study intends to fill this knowledge gap.

3 The Context of the Study

The study presented in this chapter is part of a research project to develop a chatbot for startups. Our eventual goal is to help startup teams benefit from LLMs by reducing the efforts required from them to learn prompt engineering. Figure 1 shows the architecture and process of the chatbot.

As shown in Fig. 1, the chatbot is composed of two parts: a prompt book and a prompt engine. The prompt engine is the intermediary between the user and an LLM, engineering the original query from a user to effective prompts using the prompt book. In this way, the user can have natural and intuitive interactions with ChatGPT without learning how to do prompt engineering. By controlling the flow of information and processing user queries, the chatbot streamlines the interaction process and improves the user experience with an LLM.

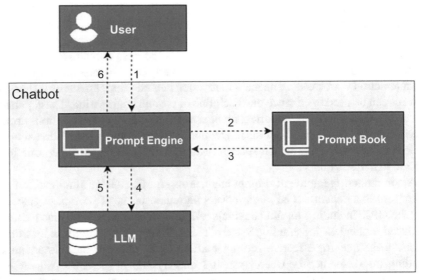

1. Asks a question related to startup domain.

2. Consults the prompt book to decide the user intent and the prompt pattern(s) to apply.

3. Applicable prompt patterns and prompt template selected.

4. Prompt-engineered user's query sent to LLM to get the response.

5. Response from LLM sent back to the prompt engine.

6. Refined response sent back to the use.

Fig. 1 The architecture of the chatbot based on an LLM

In the center of the chatbot is what we called the "prompt book." The inspiration for designing the prompt book originates from the exploration of prompt patterns proposed in the paper [10]. The prompt book is composed of three parts: (1) a set of prompt patterns and the corresponding templates for generating prompts; (2) the list of user intent types that can be used to classify a user's query; and (3) the matching between the types of user intent and the prompt patterns.

In our previous work [9], we evaluated the prompt patterns suggested in [10] to understand their applicability and how to adapt them in the context of startups. The selected and adapted prompt patterns can be found online.[1] In this chapter, we focus on the second element of the prompt book and the list of user intent types that can be used to classify the queries from a startup team.

---

[1] https://figshare.com/s/feef2d27953be1188093

4   The Research Process

To answer the research question posed in Sect. 1, which is necessary in order to implement Step 2 described in Fig. 1, we need to define the types of user intent relevant in the startup domain and to implement it as part of the chatbot's functionality. Figure 2 depicted the research process we employed to achieve the goal.

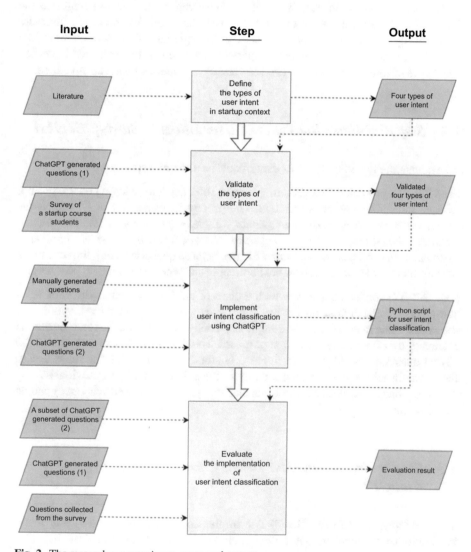

Fig. 2 The research process: input, steps, and output

4.1 Step 1: Define the Types of User Intent in Startup Context

Since the chatbot was meant for supporting startup teams, our first attempt was using the core pillars of startups defined in [6]: product, team, finance, and market. However, we came to the realization quickly that this classification scheme is irrelevant to our need to choose appropriate prompt patterns. Instead the purpose, or the user intent, behind an asked question seems to be more relevant in choosing which prompt pattern to use. We need a classification scheme to categorize the intent of a startup team when they interact with an LLM. We reviewed literature purposefully to find the ways to classify the queries of startup teams when interacting with mentors or domain experts. As a result of this step, we identified four types of intent that could be used to classify the queries from startup teams.

4.2 Step 2: Validate the Types of User Intent in Startup Context

To evaluate the identified types of user intent, we took two sub-steps:

Step 2.1 We prompted ChatGPT to generate 100 questions using a generic prompt without indicating any types of intent. The prompt is: *please act as an knowledge expert in the domain of startups, and could you please provide me with 100 common questions that startup teams ask to startup mentors, investors, other entrepreneurs or to themselves?* Then, we classified manually these questions using the four types of user intent, to see whether they are applicable and whether any new type emerges.

Step 2.2 We conducted a survey with a class of graduate students who attended a startup course at a Finnish university. The survey was conducted at the beginning of the course. The questionnaire is completely anonymous. It includes two questions related to user intent: (1) "For what purposes would you like to use a chatbot?" (2) "What questions would you like to ask a chatbot?" By analyzing the responses to these two questions, we validated the types of user intent identified previously.
The 100 ChatGPT-generated questions and the questionnaire and responses can be found online.[2]

4.3 Step 3: Implement User Intent Classification Using ChatGPT

We used OpenAI's API for ChatGPT to implement the classification of user intent in an automatic manner so that it will become part of the chatbot functionality. This

---

[2] https://figshare.com/s/feef2d27953be1188093

option can also keep the stack of technology required to implement the chatbot to a minimum. The recent studies on prompt engineering and intent classification using ChatGPT suggested that synthetic data generated by ChatGPT can be used, and few-shot prompting can achieve relatively good results when real data is scarce [2, 7, 8]. Therefore, we generated 4 questions per user intent type manually and then prompted ChatGPT to generate additional 26 questions per user intent type. In total, we prepared 120 questions. These 120 questions are used in the Python script for user intent classification. The 120 questions, the prompts used to generate 104 of them, and the Python script are shared online.[3]

4.4   Step 4: Evaluate the Implementation of User Intent Classification

To evaluate whether the Python script works, we used three data-sets:

Data-Set 1: A Subset of 120 Examples Used in the Python Script We selected 28 questions from the 120 examples used in the Python script, 7 per user intent type selected randomly. The Python script was run on these 28 questions to classify them again. The script was run 5 times to see whether the results are consistent across these rounds.

Data-Set 2: The 100 Questions Generated by ChatGPT in Step 2.1 We ran the Python script on these 100 questions 5 times as well.

Data-Set 3: Questions Collected from the Survey These are the questions provided by the students from the startup course. We first classified them manually using the types of user intent and then ran the Python script on these questions 5 times, similar to what was done on the other two data-sets.

All the data used and generated in this step are shared in the same online repository.[4]

5   Results

5.1   The Types of User Intent and Validation

Four types of user intent are included in the prompt book: *seeking information, seeking advice, brainstorming,* and *reflecting on own experience*. Their definitions are provided in Table 1.

---

[3] https://figshare.com/s/feef2d27953be1188093
[4] https://figshare.com/s/feef2d27953be1188093

Table 1 The types of user intent in the startup context

User intent	Definition
Seeking information	Seeking information in the startup context involves the act of acquiring factual information related to startups and the startup ecosystem or startup experience of other people. The accuracy and trustworthiness of the answers matter most for these types of questions. Typically, questions with such intent are asked in third-person or in an impersonal manner
Seeking advice	Seeking advice in the startup context refers to the process of seeking and acquiring guidance and advice from experienced individuals such as entrepreneurs or experts in the fields. Taking into consideration the specifics of a startup team and making the reasoning explicit can help produce advice that suits better the team. Typically, questions with such intent are asked in first-person manner
Brainstorming	Brainstorming in the startup context refers to the process of creative thinking to obtain good ideas related to the development of a startup, e.g., having multiple options of the business models of a startup idea. Questions with such intent typically require divergent thinking. These questions are typically asked in first-person manner
Reflecting on own experience	Reflecting on own experience in the startup context refers to the process of analyzing a startup team's own past experiences in order to learn from them to enhance future actions and decision-making. Questions with such intent are always asked in first-person manner

The result of manually classifying the 100 ChatGPT generated questions shows that all questions can be categorized using the types defined in Table 1. The majority (57) are classified under *seeking advice*, 35 under *seeking information*, and 8 are *brainstorming* questions. None of these questions is of reflective intention.

The result from the conducted survey shows somehow different patterns. We received 49 responses from the survey with the Finnish graduate students at the beginning of their startup course in October 2023. These students came from different faculties including IT, business and management, and finance. The class has a good balance of gender and nationality, and most of them are in their 20s to early 30s. Figure 3 shows the levels of their knowledge of startups at the beginning of the course, from 1 (very little) to 9 (very knowledgeable).

As shown in Fig. 3, the majority of the class believe that they already have certain levels of startup knowledge, with a few of them (8) considering themselves knowledgeable or very knowledgeable on the topic. The median self-assessed startup knowledge level of the respondents is 4.0. The mean score is approximately 4.57. Therefore, the collective self-assessed knowledge level is below the midpoint on the scale used in the survey.

Figure 4 shows their attitudes toward using a chatbot to support their startup-building processes, which are mostly positive, with 51% of the respondents answering "Yes" and 46.9% saying "Maybe." Interestingly, for the respondents

How do you evaluate your own startup related knowledge?

49 responses

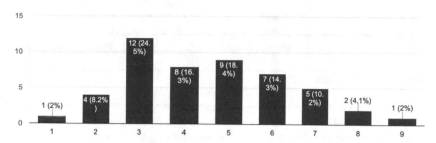

Fig. 3 Startup related knowledge of the respondents

Would you use a chatbot to support your startup building process?

49 responses

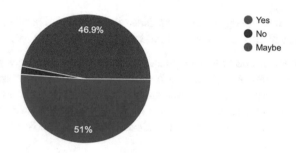

Fig. 4 Intention of using chatbot

who answered "Yes," their mean startup knowledge level is approximately 4.96, higher than that of the "Maybe" group (approximately 4.26). This suggests that the students who are more open to using a chatbot for startup support ("Yes") tend to rate their startup knowledge slightly higher than those who are uncertain ("Maybe"). However, the difference in the levels of self-assessed startup knowledge between the two groups ("Yes" vs. "Maybe") is not statistically significant, according to the independent t-test (approximately 1.35 with p-value of about 0.183, higher than the common threshold of 0.05).

Regarding the evaluation of the types of user intent, 47 responses were received to the first evaluation question, *For what purposes would you like to use a chatbot?*, which is a multiple-choice one based on the four types of user intent as defined in Table 1. As shown in Fig. 5, among the four types of user intent, *brainstorming* is the most frequently chosen type, followed by *seeking information* and *seeking advice*. *Reflecting on own experience* is less often in comparison to the other types but still considered relevant by some respondents.

47 responses

Fig. 5 Intent validation

The other evaluation question in the survey is an open-ended question: *What questions would you like to ask a chatbot?* Twenty-nine responses were received. The following are some exemplar questions provided by the students:

- Seeking information: *Tell me about the recent start-ups on my field of work. Which companies are currently already on the market doing this idea?*
- Seeking advice: *How good is my idea? Is my idea feasible in current enterprise situation?*
- Brainstorming: *Give me 10 ideas for a business model for a business operating in xxxx xxxx.... Give me some startup ideas related to...(industry)*

We classified these responses manually. Six responses are either not questions or too short and generic to be classified. Among the remaining 23 responses, 9 are classified under *seeking advice*, 8 *brainstorming*, and 6 *seeking information*. Similar to the result of the 100 ChatGPT-generated questions, no question is of the intent of *reflecting on own experience* even though it is considered relevant by some respondents.

5.2   Evaluation of the User Intent Classification Using ChatGPT

As described in Step 4 in Sect. 3, we used three datasets to evaluate the implementation of user intent classification using ChatGPT. Dataset 1 is the reuse of the examples, to make sure the classification implementation work technically. It is not surprising that ChatGPT classifies the questions in Dataset 1 most correctly (except 1 out of 28 questions) and consistently across 5 runs.

Dataset 2 and Dataset 3 are used to evaluate how well ChatGPT classifies new questions using the 120 examples provided. Dataset 2 contains synthetic questions generated by ChatGPT, and Dataset 3 contains real questions collected from the survey. Table 2 shows the agreement levels (Cohen's Kappa) between the manual classification and those from ChatGPT, as well as between various rounds of ChatGPT classifications. The results from both Dataset 2 and Dataset 3 are reported in the same table.

Table 2 Agreement levels of various classification rounds

		Manual classification	ChatGPT classification				
			1st run	2nd run	3rd run	4th run	5th run
Manual classification		–	0.479	0.536	0.471	0.67	0.536
ChatGPT classification	1st run	0.261	–	0.801	0.865	0.802	0.801
	2nd run	0.272	0.767	–	0.796	0.867	1
	3rd run	0.215	0.725	0.728	–	0.799	0.796
	4th run	0.167	0.732	0.867	0.746	–	0.867
	5th run	0.174	0.711	0.715	0.811	0.768	–

Note: gray cells contain Cohen's kappa values from Dataset 2 ($n = 100$); white cells contain Cohen's kappa values from Dataset 3 ($n = 23$); all values have p-value lower than 0.05

As shown in Table 1, ChatGPT performed better on the real questions collected from the survey than on the synthetic questions generated by itself. The agreement levels between the manual classification of the real questions and ChatGPT classifications range from 0.47 to 0.67, indicating moderate to substantial agreement. The agreement levels between various rounds of ChatGPT classification range from 0.711 to 1, indicating substantial to almost perfect agreement. This indicates that ChatGPT performs consistently across the runs.

6 Concluding Remarks

In this chapter, we focused on the classification of user intent, one important facet of a nuanced process of crafting effective prompts for ChatGPT. The presented work is part of the design process of a chatbot to support the startup teams. The defined types of user intent are a key element of the prompt book that underpins the implementation of the chatbot. We evaluated the defined user intent types using both synthetic startup questions generated by ChatGPT and a survey of the graduate students attending a startup course at a Finnish university. Additionally, we demonstrated how to automate the classification of user intent using ChatGPT itself and evaluated the effectiveness of reliability of the classification results.

The primary contribution of this research lies in the approach we described to identify user intent behind the interactions with LLMs, which is a critical aspect often overlooked in prompt engineering for LLMs. The development of the chatbot stands as an illustration of this approach, offering startup teams an intuitive and efficient method to engage with LLMs without requiring extensive knowledge in prompt engineering. Through the example of developing the prompt book that underpins the chatbot, we demonstrated how user intent can be defined and implemented.

Our findings indicate that the classification of user intent into four categories— seeking information, seeking advice, reflecting on own experience, and brainstorming—provides a good framework for selecting appropriate prompt patterns to formulate effective prompts to interact with ChatGPT. We have also shown that it is possible to effectively classify user queries using ChatGPT.

6.1   Limitations of the Study

There are several limitations in our study. Firstly, it primarily focused on the startup environment, which may not fully represent the diverse range of scenarios where LLMs like ChatGPT are applied. However, we do believe that the methodology and insights gained from this study can be adapted to various other domains where LLMs are utilized. Future work could explore the application of this user intent classification framework in different sectors, such as education, healthcare, or customer service.

Another limitation of our study is that the evaluation of the user intent categories used a small sample of students in one course in one university, which limits the generalizability of the evaluation results to the general population of startup teams. Therefore, a larger sample of startup teams would provide more valid evaluation results.

We also recognized the inherent challenges in training LLMs to accurately interpret and respond to nuanced human queries, a task that often requires continuous refinement and adaptation. There is a significant opportunity to refine the classification model by incorporating more dynamic and context-aware algorithms, potentially integrating advanced natural language processing techniques.

Lastly, the study focused on a specific LLM, which is ChatGPT, and this may limit the generalizability of the findings to other LLMs. The research also relied heavily on the accuracy and reliability of ChatGPT, which, although state of the art, is not devoid of potential biases or errors.

6.2   Future Work

We are in the process of implementing the complete chatbot based on the research presented in this chapter and in our previous work [9]. We planned two steps of evaluation that allow us to evaluate the chatbot, including the results presented in this chapter, in a more systematic manner: (1) small-scale evaluation with several startup teams and (2) large-scale quantitative evaluation through the implemented chatbot.

In the small-scale evaluation, we will sit side by side with the selected startup teams and administrate their interactions with ChatGPT, first using standard Chat-GPT without specific prompting, and then we guide the startup teams to use our chatbot. We will collect all the data generated in the process, including the questions asked, the user intent classifications, the generated prompts, and the responses from both standard ChatGPT and from our chatbot. We will use the generated data to validate the content in the prompt book, including the user intent classification. We envision that the classification of user intent as well as the templates of the selected prompt patterns will be modified, extended, and improved after the small-scale evaluation.

For the large-scale evaluation, we will make the chatbot accessible freely for startup teams to use. With their permission, we will collect relevant data for research purposes. Both prompt book and the usability of the chatbot will be evaluated and improved using the data from a larger sample of startup teams.

Acknowledgments We would like to express our sincere thanks for the support we received from the students who are involved in our research both at our university and from the University of Jyväskylä, Finland.

References

1. Atlas, S.: ChatGPT for higher education and professional development: a guide to conversational AI (2023). Independently published
2. Bouzaki, A.G.: Enhancing intent classification via zero-shot and few-shot ChatGPT prompting engineering: generating training data or directly detecting intents. Master thesis. NATIONAL AND KAPODISTRIAN UNIVERSITY OF ATHENS (2023)
3. Clavié, B., Ciceu, A., Naylor, F., Soulié, G., Brightwell, T.: Large language models in the workplace: a case study on prompt engineering for job type classification. Preprint. arXiv:2303.07142 (2023)
4. Dhole, K.D.: Resolving intent ambiguities by retrieving discriminative clarifying questions. Preprint. arXiv:2008.07559 (2020)
5. Ekin, S.: Prompt Engineering for ChatGPT: A Quick Guide to Techniques, Tips, and Best Practices. Preprint (May 2023). https://doi.org/10.36227/techrxiv.22683919.v2, https://www.techrxiv.org/doi/full/10.36227/techrxiv.22683919.v2
6. Giardino, C., Bajwa, S.S., Wang, X., Abrahamsson, P.: Key challenges in early-stage software startups. In: Agile Processes in Software Engineering and Extreme Programming: 16th International Conference, XP 2015, Helsinki, May 25–29, 2015, Proceedings 16, pp. 52–63. Springer, Berlin (2015)
7. Tang, R., Han, X., Jiang, X., Hu, X.: Does synthetic data generation of LLMs help clinical text mining? Preprint. arXiv:2303.04360 (2023)
8. Ubani, S., Polat, S.O., Nielsen, R.: ZeroShotDataAug: generating and augmenting training data with ChatGPT. Preprint. arXiv:2304.14334 (2023)
9. Wang, X., Idris, M.A., Rafiq, U., Hubner, S.: Turning large language models into AI assistants for startups using prompt patterns. In: International Conference on Agile Software Development, pp. 22–26. Springer International Publishing, Cham (2023)
10. White, J., Fu, Q., Hays, S., Sandborn, M., Olea, C., Gilbert, H., Elnashar, A., Spencer-Smith, J., Schmidt, D.C.: A prompt pattern catalog to enhance prompt engineering with ChatGPT. Preprint. arXiv:2302.11382 (2023)
11. Zhang, J., Bui, T., Yoon, S., Chen, X., Liu, Z., Xia, C., Tran, Q.H., Chang, W., Yu, P.: Few-shot intent detection via contrastive pre-training and fine-tuning. In: Moens, M.F., Huang, X., Specia, L., Yih, S.W.t. (eds.) Proceedings of the 2021 Conference on Empirical Methods in Natural Language Processing, pp. 1906–1912. Association for Computational Linguistics, Online and Punta Cana (2021). https://doi.org/10.18653/v1/2021.emnlp-main.144, https://aclanthology.org/2021.emnlp-main.144

Toward Guiding Students: Exploring Effective Approaches for Utilizing AI Tools in Programming Courses

Mika Saari, Petri Rantanen, Mikko Nurminen, Terhi Kilamo, Kari Systä, and Pekka Abrahamsson

Abstract This study explores the role of artificial intelligence (AI) in higher education, with a focus on the teaching of programming. Despite the growing use of AI in education, both students and teachers often struggle to understand its role and implications. To address this gap, we conducted surveys on two different university programming courses to assess the experiences and perspectives of over 200 students on the use of AI in programming education. Combined, these findings underscored the need for guidance on how students should use AI tools. Furthermore, the findings suggest that AI is becoming increasingly integrated into university education, especially in programming courses. Responding to this need, we extend the contribution of the study by introducing a set of best practices for AI tool usage in programming courses. Overall, the study highlights the need for greater awareness and understanding of AI in university teaching and the fact that teachers have an important role to play in providing guidance to students on the responsible use of AI tools.

Keywords Programming education · Programming course · Artificial intelligence · AI · Curriculum development

1 Introduction

AI-assisted teaching and learning, e.g., the use of conversational style language models like ChatGPT,[1] has the potential to revolutionize the way programming courses are taught. With artificial intelligence (AI), students can receive tailored, personalized, and interactive support, receive immediate feedback, and have access

[1] https://chat.openai.com

M. Saari (✉) · P. Rantanen · M. Nurminen · T. Kilamo · K. Systä · P. Abrahamsson
Tampere University, Tampere, Finland
e-mail: mika.saari@tuni.fi

© The Author(s), under exclusive license to Springer Nature Switzerland AG 2024
A. Nguyen-Duc et al. (eds.), *Generative AI for Effective Software Development*,
https://doi.org/10.1007/978-3-031-55642-5_16

to a virtual tutor 24/7. AI can also analyze the students' performance and provide suggestions for improvement, making the learning experience more efficient and effective. Additionally, AI can automate tedious tasks such as grading code, freeing up instructors to focus on more important tasks such as providing meaningful feedback and engaging in interactive discussions. The role of AI-assisted learning in higher education (HE) can be viewed both from the perspective of the learner and the teachers.

This study is an extension of our earlier study [14], which focused on the students' point of view, based on a survey of BSc-level programming students. In that paper, it was investigated how much students already use AI to support their learning of programming and for what purposes. The survey incorporated both multiple-choice items and open-ended questions to gather data. Responses to the open-ended questions were systematically categorized using relevant keywords. The results were presented as percentage distributions and in the form of bar charts [14].

In this study, we used additional data from another programming course. The collected data consists of students' written feedback of how they use AI tools when they program the exercises related to the course.

Based on the collected data, this chapter presents best practices for teachers on how to guide students in the use of AI. Thus, the following research question was formulated:

RQ: What are the best practices for including AI in programming courses?

The rest of the chapter is structured as follows: Sect. 2 clarifies the research environment, including recent AI-related studies. Section 3 focuses on the research methodologies, context, and data collection and analysis methods and also discusses the findings of the surveys. Section 4 contains the proposed best practices and a discussion of them. Also, the threats to validity and possible future research items are discussed. Finally, Sect. 5 summarizes the research in relation to the research question.

2 Background and Motivation

In the context of this research, the keyword "programming course" was used for identification by conducting a search of relevant studies in the IEEE Xplore database, resulting in a total of 16 publications. Three of these studies, namely, [2, 5, 17], emphasized the role of instructional guidance during the learning process.

Question and answer sites, such as Stack Overflow, are often used for finding help on programming-related tasks. How students use Stack Overflow was studied in detail by Robinson [13]. Traditionally, search engines have been used to seek further assistance for programming tasks. However, a new trend is emerging where people are turning to AI-based solutions. These solutions may take the form of virtual assistants or chatbots, such as Siri, Alexa, or Google Assistant [8]. The increasing popularity of AI-assisted learning, utilizing chatbots as a means of providing personalized and interactive educational experiences, can be seen by taking a look at the recent publications in the IEEE Xplore database.[2] For example, using the keywords "chatbot" and "education" on April 12, 2023, yielded 251 results, 79% (198) of which were published in the last three years.

In the evolving domain of engineering education, the integration of machine learning (ML) and AI is becoming increasingly prevalent. A recent practice paper [6] underscores this trend, emphasizing not only the pedagogical implications but also the profound impact on engineering education research methodologies. Critically, the study delves into the ethical challenges posed by generative AI technologies. It highlights the necessity for a comprehensive framework addressing the responsible use of AI while also engaging with the current literature to offer insights into the potential challenges and opportunities AI introduces in both educational and research contexts.

In a study conducted at the Department of Mechanical Engineering of the Universitat Politécnica de Catalunya, an examination was made of the potential of ChatGPT, which is based on the GPT-3 AI model, as a teaching tool in mechanical engineering education. The study introduced a four-level pyramid structure, indicating how ChatGPT can be used in various pedagogical functions: (1) information retrieval and understanding, (2) application and analysis, (3) synthesis and evaluation, and (4) creation and innovation. Although ChatGPT is not yet capable of addressing specific mechanical engineering problems, it has the potential to assist in certain tasks, especially in generating code in various programming languages. The study also emphasized the responsible use of technology, promoting critical engagement while also considering the technology's limitations and student feedback [12].

Since the introduction of ChatGPT in November 2022, there has been a rapid shift in AI usage, with the previously used solutions (e.g., chatbots, question-and-answer sites) being superseded by AI-enhanced versions. Based on our earlier study [14], the majority of students enrolled on programming courses have either started to use ChatGPT or at least have tried it, and similar findings were discovered by Puig-Ortiz et al. [12] for mechanical engineering courses, although perhaps not all courses have been properly prepared for this sudden change. Various universities quickly published guidance[3] for use of AI tools, but it is unknown how many of these guidelines are actually based on scientific studies, especially when considering the rather brief timeframe between the introduction of ChatGPT and the publication of the guidelines. Judging from a survey [16] made by the United Nations Educational, Scientific and Cultural Organization (UNESCO), it also seems that most schools and universities lack formal guidelines on AI usage altogether.

---

[2] https://ieeexplore.ieee.org/Xplore

[3] For   example,   https://www.tuni.fi/en/students-guide/handbook/uni/studying-0/academic-integrity-students/use-ai-based-applications   https://www.ed.ac.uk/bayes/ai-guidance-for-staff-and-students https://oue.fas.harvard.edu/ai-guidance

Further, a look at peer-reviewed scientific publications shows that no research—at least publicly—seems to exist that would attempt to formulate or back up the quickly formed guidelines published by universities. As of September 2023, searching works published since 2022—assuming that there should have been a definitive need to publish updates to any previous guidelines since the wide-scale adoption of GPT-based AI tools—by using terms such as "AI best practices education" and "AI guidelines education" returns hundreds of results in Google Scholar.[4] Rigorously going through all these results would be quite time-consuming, but at a quick glance, the vast majority of the results seem to examine either the ethical or technical aspects of using AI in education (e.g., [9, 10]). A large number of studies also seem to be opinion papers, white papers, or other non-peer-reviewed publications, perhaps reflecting the rapid increase in AI usage and the relative novelty of the topic. A search using the same terms on IEEE Xplore[5] produces 62 results, with similar focus, although the work of [3] also emphasizes the need for guidelines while mainly discussing the wider aspects of forming policies for AI adoption in education. AI is a powerful tool for programming [1]. Perhaps that's why the use of AI in programming education is also an interesting research topic in Arxiv[6] [4, 7, 11, 15, 18]. In any case, studies conducting surveys on students—i.e., collecting the students' points of view—appear to be virtually non-existent, possibly because of the limited time available (since the publication of ChatGPT) for conducting such research.

Thus, in this study, we will map the challenges faced by students in using AI and utilize the collected data to formulate a list of clear and simple guidelines, which could be applied in incorporating the use of AI in programming courses.

3   Methodology: Utilizing Surveys to Establish Operational Guidelines

The process of our research is illustrated in Fig. 1. In our previous study [14], we performed a survey (*Round 1*, in Fig. 1), for students on a basic university programming course and analyzed its results. The key findings of the earlier study are included as one of the starting points for this study. We supplemented these findings by executing another survey in a mobile programming course, which is generally targeted to students who are further advanced in their studies as compared to the basic course. A total of 223 students answered the surveys. The details of the first survey are presented in [14], and the second is discussed in-depth in the following subsections.

---

[4] https://scholar.google.com/

[5] https://ieeexplore.ieee.org

[6] https://arxiv.org/

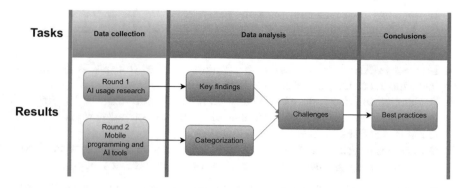

Fig. 1 Process used in seeking best practices: flow of the tasks undertaken and their results

The results of the second survey were analyzed and categorized in an attempt to find common issues, concerns, and comments reported by the students. The help of the ChatGPT tool was used in formulating the categories, with the authors of this work fine-tuning the results. The process of creating the categories is explained in more detail in Sect. 3.2.

The key findings of the first survey, as well as the categorizations produced from the second survey, were further analyzed to detect the challenges related to the use of AI in programming courses, with the reasoning being that whatever problems the students faced should be taken into consideration when formulating any guidelines for the use of AI.

Finally, based on the identified challenges, best practices (guidelines) were crafted, including suggestions given by the students participating in the surveys, and complemented by the insight of the authors. The first and fourth authors of this chapter worked as teachers on the programming course of the first survey, the first and second authors on the mobile programming course of the second survey, and with the others having long experience in teaching in general. Thus, the mix of student feedback enriched by views from the teachers should provide a comprehensive view on designing the best practice guidelines.

3.1 Data Collection and Analysis: First Round—AI Usage Research

The research investigated student usage of AI tools, specifically in the context of programming courses. Two questions were central: one multiple-choice question gauging the frequency of AI use and an open-ended question examining motivations for using or not using AI. These findings are presented in the original study [14], in which about 200 students responded to the survey.

In our study [14] evaluating students' perspectives on AI, several key findings emerged. These insights provide an overview of the students' attitudes toward the integration of AI tools in their learning process:

A **Interest in AI:** There is interest in AI among newer students, suggesting its inclusion in curricula could be beneficial.
B **Resistance to AI:** While AI is largely seen as a helpful tool for learning and coding tasks, some students resist its use, either for unspecified reasons or a belief that it makes tasks too easy.
C **Difficulties in using AI:** Initial difficulties with AI tools could result in discontinuation, hinting at a need for more introductory guidance or support.

Implications from the First Round The findings suggest that while a majority of students are open to utilizing AI tools in their academic pursuits, there is a need for more structured introduction and guidance, especially to overcome initial obstacles.

3.2 Data Collection and Analysis: Second Round—Mobile Programming and AI Tools

This section introduces the data collection and analyses from the Mobile Programming course. A noteworthy aspect of this course was the use of AI tools. Students had the opportunity to use tools such as OpenAI's ChatGPT and GitHub Copilot[7] for programming tasks. In the following paragraphs, we will scrutinize the data collected in this course and highlight the results and insights obtained from the integration of AI tools.

Course Overview The university introduced a programming course on Mobile Programming, corresponding to 5 ECTS (European Credit Transfer and Accumulation System) points. The main objective of this course was practical programming skills with a particular focus on mobile development. The course was optional in several study programs.

Course Details The course included a comprehensive set of 18 programming exercises that were designed to offer students a deep dive into the complexities and nuances of mobile programming. The chosen environment for these exercises was Android, necessitating the use of the Java programming language.

Integration of AI Tools In a unique approach, the course allowed, and even encouraged, the utilization of AI tools to aid in the problem-solving process. Specifically, students had the option to use ChatGPT, a conversational AI developed by OpenAI, and GitHub Copilot, an AI-based programming tool that integrates with common programming Integrated Development Environments (IDEs).

---

[7] https://github.com/features/copilot

Student Documentation and Reflection Alongside their programming assignments, students were required to maintain a diary. This diary was meant to document the advantages they experienced while solving the exercises and the challenges or issues they faced. In the diary, AI tools were mentioned specifically in cases where they were utilized, detailing the assistance received and any challenges or insights encountered.

Data Collection and Analysis Upon the conclusion of the course, the students' experiences regarding the AI tools were compiled. In total, 99 students were registered on the course. Out of these, 22 passed successfully. Feedback was requested from the students, resulting in a total of 31 feedback submissions. It should be noted that not all students provided feedback; while some chose not to comment, others submitted more than one feedback entry. To ensure privacy, all data was anonymized prior to further processing. This collected data, termed "AI tools usage experiences," underwent a twofold analysis:

1. **Automated Categorization by ChatGPT:** Initially, the AI tools usage experiences were fed to ChatGPT for categorization. The aim was for AI to identify common themes, patterns, and sentiments across the student feedback.
2. **Manual Evaluation by Research Group:** After the categorization by ChatGPT, the list was then thoroughly reviewed by the first, second, and third authors of this chapter. The group aimed to validate, refine, and contextualize the insights compiled by the AI.

To verify the ChatGPT results, the automated categorization was performed several times with different AI prompts. An iterative approach to prompting the AI also played an important role. The best result for ensuring accuracy was given by the prompt where categorization was requested along with the division of the feedback into categories.

The prompt for ChatGPT: *The mobile programming course is a study opportunity offered to students. The aim of the course is to learn the basics of Android programming, available features (cloud services and authentication), and special features brought by phones (map, positioning, sensors offered by the device). You are doing research on the AI tools used to support studying in the course. The goal is to find out, based on student feedback, how students should be guided in the use of AI. Below is the feedback. Categorize the feedback into a sufficient number of categories.*

In this, the equivalency of category and feedback was also checked by the additional prompt *In addition, number the feedback in the list according to the categories.*

Final Category List Based on both the AI-assisted and human evaluations, a consolidated category list was derived, as presented below:

D **General utilization of AI:** This category includes feedback that mentions the use of AI in general for coding and learning support.

General utilization of AI usually means that students use AI tools. For this, the typical feedback items were as follows: "ChatGPT's intelligence and ability to understand a wide range of questions and requests helped me figure out how to replace Copilot's features in my own way," and "AI-based assistants like ChatGPT can provide equally valuable advice and guidance when it comes to solving problems and developing programming skills." Here, AI tools are seen as a virtual assistant to whom you can direct questions related to the topic. The number of feedback items in this category was three.

E **Specific use cases:** This category contains feedback that mentions specific use cases of AI, including feedback referencing distinct applications of AI. Feedback examples such as "I particularly utilized ChatGPT for assistance with writing labor-intensive yet relatively clear code" include code troubleshooting, setting permissions, using sensors, constructing strings, and creating varied code samples. The number of feedback items in this category was four.

F **Successes:** This feedback focuses on solutions and tips provided by AI that were helpful to the students.

This feedback category highlights the effective solutions and advice given by AI that proved beneficial for learners. Here are two example comments by students: "ChatGPT also helped me debug my code," and "ChatGPT not only facilitated my progress and augmented my knowledge, but I also inquired not just about direct solutions but about the underlying theory behind the topics." The number of feedback items in this category was five.

G **Problems and challenges:** This category includes feedback in which students highlight challenges they faced when using AI, such as incorrect code, deprecated code, broken code, and compatibility issues with new libraries.

The problems and challenges segment gathers feedback from students pointing out the obstacles they encountered when leveraging AI. Some of these challenges include faulty code, outdated code, malfunctioning code, and incompatibility with recent libraries. Here are some associated remarks: "I noticed that documentation was often better at resolving situations in problem cases than AI." The overall number of feedback items in this category was 3.

H **Comparisons to other resources:** This feedback compares the use of AI to other sources, such as Google, Stack Overflow[8] search results, and official documentation such as the Android Developer site.[9]

As mentioned in one piece of feedback, "I observed that in problematic scenarios, documentation often outperformed AI in providing solutions." The number of feedback items in this category was two.

I **Criticism and suggestions:** In this category, students suggest that the use of AI should be better guided and that students should be critical of the answers provided by AI.

---

[8] https://stackoverflow.com/

[9] https://developer.android.com/

Within the criticism and suggestions section, learners advocate for more structured guidance when employing AI and emphasize the importance of being discerning about the solutions provided by AI. To examine some specific feedback: "ChatGPT isn't some magical tool as one might assume; often, I had to resort to entirely different solutions because ChatGPT couldn't grasp the situation." "ChatGPT wasn't always able to offer fully functional code examples." "While ChatGPT was generally useful, it surprisingly delivered erroneous code in its responses." The number of feedback items in this category was two.

In feedback analysis regarding AI utilization, students predominantly use tools like ChatGPT for programming guidance. While these AI tools are valued for their assistance in programming, there are areas for improvement. For optimal results, they should be used alongside traditional resources.

3.3   Challenges of AI in Teaching Programming Courses

While generative AI tools like ChatGPT offer a revolutionary approach to facilitating IT education, they are not without limitations. The feedback collected in this study shows that, although ChatGPT serves as an instrumental aid in learning and problem-solving, the current technologies do not fully meet user expectations. Students have pointed out various challenges they faced when integrating the tool into their learning process. The following list delves deeper into these drawbacks and the inherent constraints of using tools like ChatGPT in an educational setting, highlighting the importance of balanced reliance on AI tools and traditional learning resources. The list is taken from student experiences in both programming courses (first round [14] and second round).

1. **Not a magic solution:** It is essential to understand that the tool is not a silver bullet. It has its limitations, and there were moments when it was unable to assist students or offer the desired solutions.
2. **Erroneous outputs:** AI tools occasionally provided incorrect or non-functional code. This means students had to spend extra time debugging or searching for alternate solutions.
3. **Deprecated solutions:** AI tools sometimes offered solutions or code snippets that are deprecated, meaning they are outdated or no longer recommended for use. Using deprecated solutions can lead to inefficiencies or conflicts in modern coding environments.
4. **Limited knowledge of recent developments:** As technology and programming languages evolve rapidly, AI's knowledge might lag behind the most recent advancements or best practices. Some students pointed out that, e.g., ChatGPT lacked information about the latest developments, affecting its ability to provide the best or most relevant answers.
5. **Misdirection and wasted time:** There were instances where the AI tool led students to an incorrect path. This misdirection not only affected the student's

immediate task but also resulted in wasted time and effort trying to rectify the issue.

6. **Complexity handling:** Some students noted that while ChatGPT was good for basic queries or general guidance, it struggled with intricate problems, especially those related to integrating libraries or specific system configurations.

7. **Gap in understanding context:** AI models do not possess an inherent understanding of context. There were situations where the tool was unable to recognize missing methods in a class or provide solutions based on the broader project context, which a human tutor might be able to grasp.

8. **Missing guides:** Basic usage guides for commonly used tools were usually missing.

The compilation presented above was generated by leveraging feedback obtained from students. The primary objective was to pinpoint specific problematic areas. Following the identification of these issues, appropriate solutions can be explored. In this context, we will discuss further the elements instrumental in the identification of these problem areas.

It has to be accepted that these are not magic tools and solutions to every problem. While AI has its merits, there were times when it failed to aid students or provide the answers they were seeking. The feedback raises several overall issues: there is a need to integrate more AI-critical thinking into the education process. This would help students in refining the code generated by AI, noticing its mistakes, and understanding its limitations. Also, many have reported bugs in ChatGPT. In addition, some believe that, at present, AI's role and effectiveness in education are rather overhyped.

AI tools, at times, offered incorrect or unusable code. As technology and programming languages are evolving rapidly, AI's knowledge might not always keep pace with the most recent advancements or best practices. Some students, for instance, pointed out that tools like ChatGPT lacked information about the latest developments. This limitation affected the AI's capability to deliver the best or most pertinent solutions. Consequently, students found themselves investing extra time in debugging or seeking alternative methods. Moreover, there were instances when the AI suggested deprecated code. Furthermore, there were occasions where the AI tool inadvertently led students down the wrong path. This misdirection not only impacted the student's immediate task but also led to unnecessary time and effort spent trying to rectify the problem.

Some students observed that while ChatGPT is effective for straightforward questions or general advice, it has difficulties with complex issues, particularly when it comes to integrating libraries or dealing with specific system setups. A notable gap in understanding context was evident, as AI models do not possess an inherent understanding of context. There were situations where the tool could not recognize missing methods in a class or provide solutions based on the broader project context, which a human tutor might be able to grasp. Additionally, ChatGPT was not able to provide completely functional code examples.

The last challenge on the list does not only refer to AI tools. Basic guides for frequently used tools are often absent. It appears that many courses, regardless of the university or school, use similar tools. It is inefficient to teach the usage of the same tools in every course. This is similar to the instruction of other common tools, such as version control systems (e.g., git) or various IDEs. Moreover, the teaching of these tools might not always be comprehensive. It might be expected that students learn about these essential tools on their own. When dealing with AI, there is an increased risk that students might misuse the tools unless proper guidance is provided. However, dedicated research on this topic is required before this assumption can be confirmed.

4 Discussion

In this section, conclusions are presented, namely, the best practices, to tackle the challenges previously mentioned. The challenges are based on our earlier study and the material studied here as shown in Fig. 1.

Initially, the results and observations from our earlier publication [14] were utilized. These observations were based on feedback given by students on whether they use AI as an aid in their studies. The survey touched lightly upon how AI tools were used.

Additional data from the Mobile Programming course was incorporated into the source material because there was a desire to determine concretely how students used AI tools. In this context, students were encouraged to use AI, but, in turn, more detailed documentation was required from them on how the tools were used.

4.1 Best Practices for Including AI in a Programming Course

In the academic world, there is growing interest in combining AI with traditional teaching methods. Considering the empirical findings described earlier, it is important to create a framework that facilitates the use of AI tools in educational contexts, especially in the coding field. Consequently, based on the aforementioned data (Fig. 2.), we present a set of methodically constructed guidelines. The purpose of these guidelines is to create an approach for students to incorporate AI tools into their learning endeavors.

I. **Introduction to the use of AI:** Offer preliminary training or a demo on how AI tools, such as ChatGPT, can be utilized during coding and learning.
II. **Sharing best practices:** Create guidelines or a guide that includes best practices for utilizing AI during coding.

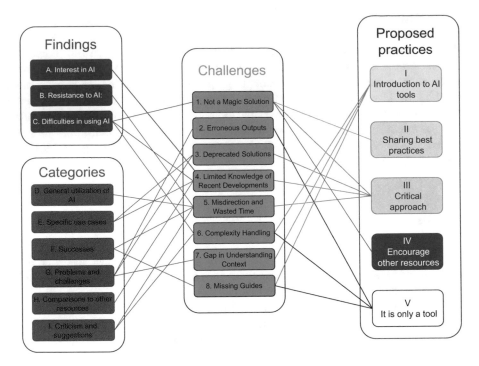

Fig. 2 Relations between findings, challenges, and guidelines

III. **Critical approach:** Emphasize that the code produced by AI is not always
flawless and that students should always test and check the code before
deploying it.
IV. **Encourage use of other resources:** Although AI is a useful tool, students
should also be encouraged to use other resources, such as official documentation, when they face challenges.
V. **It is only a tool:** Students should remember that AI is specifically a tool and
the main purpose of studying (courses) is not to learn how to use a particular
tool but to understand the core content of the course.

In the listing above, the numbering does not indicate the order of importance, and
the numbers are only for referencing purposes.

The utilization of AI tools has become paramount for enhancing productivity
in both programming and educational contexts. An introductory training module
clarifies the fundamental principles and functionalities of visible AI instruments,
including but not limited to ChatGPT, Copilot, Bing Chat, and Bard. Emphasis is
placed on finding out the prerequisites for engagement with these technologies.
Concurrently, students familiarize ourselves with the instructions that define their
essential use cases. As an integral part of this curriculum, insights are provided into
AI tools to improve learning outcomes and hands-on experiences.

Sharing Best Practices Construct a guide that incorporates best practices for integrating AI into coding. Students should begin with AI at the start of the course. It should start with simple AI examples and a demo, such as creating a "Hello World" program in Java. As skills develop, the difficulty level should be increased progressively. Questions should be encouraged with examples, like explaining the differences between Integer and int.

It is essential to understand that the code generated by AI is far from perfect. Students will always have to verify and test it before use. Students need to analyze the code because the code might contain errors and need to be comprehended and checked. Additionally, AI can sometimes produce entirely incorrect results, akin to hallucinations.

While AI is a valuable asset, it is essential for students to diversify their sources of information. This is because relying solely on AI as an information source is not advisable for the reasons mentioned above. Besides, programming language documentation can serve as an excellent alternative, and discussion forums or programming communities, like Stack Overflow, provide invaluable insights and knowledge.

Students have to recognize that AI is just one tool among many. The primary goal of undertaking courses is not merely to become proficient with a specific tool but to grasp the fundamental concepts of the subject.

4.2 Threats to Validity

In researching the best practices for including artificial intelligence in programming courses, several threats to the study's validity must be acknowledged. The generalizability of the outcomes depends on various factors, including the diverse profiles of students. The groups of students mentioned in this study had completed at least two programming courses (basic and advanced level).

Differences in familiarity with AI tools and individual learning styles can impact the applicability of findings. The self-study method was quite common in both groups. However, both student groups studied in the spring of 2023, so the AI tools were new to them. Additionally, the rapid evolution of technology also presents a challenge. As AI tools and technologies continue to develop, findings based on their current state may become outdated or less relevant.

Internal factors also pose threats to validity. The effectiveness of AI in programming courses may greatly depend on the instructor's proficiency with these tools. The ability of instructors to integrate AI effectively into their curriculum could significantly influence the outcomes. In both these groups, the instructor encouraged the use of AI tools. However, it is important to note that the AI tools and their usage were new to the instructor as well.

Finally, the way in which data is interpreted, such as student feedback and performance metrics, can influence the conclusions drawn. Given the dynamic nature of AI tools and educational methods, the replicability of the study's findings in different contexts or at different times might yield diverse results. Acknowledging these threats to validity is essential for understanding the limitations of the study, and under which conditions, the identified best practices for including AI in programming courses may be most effective.

4.3 Future Research

While this research has laid the foundation for understanding the effective incorporation of AI tools in programming education, there are still several directions to consider for future studies. One of the foremost extensions to this research would be to implement the proposed guidelines in real-world courses. This would provide empirical evidence on the efficacy, practicality, and potential areas of refinement for the guidelines. Practical trials would offer insights into any unforeseen challenges that students or educators might encounter. Also, some of the results obtained in the current study may reflect the specific processes and practices of Tampere University. To ascertain the universality of the findings and to comprehend possible variations in different educational settings, it would be beneficial to gather comparative data from other universities or educational institutions.

Furthermore, as the scope of this study was limited to the domain of programming education, it would be worthwhile to explore how these guidelines could be extrapolated to other fields. Given their generalized nature, there is a theoretical basis for believing that similar guidelines could be effective in diverse educational disciplines. However, empirical investigations would be necessary to determine their actual efficacy and whether potential modifications would be required for different subjects.

5 Summary

This research studied the significance of AI within higher education, emphasizing its application in studies in programming and software engineering. We performed a survey, encompassing feedback from over 200 students to find out the common AI-related challenges faced by students in programming courses. Based on the survey data, we found out that while the adoption of AI tools in education is increasing, there exists a marked lack of understanding among educators and students about its functionalities and potential repercussions. A repeated theme from the findings is the evident demand for structured guidelines on usage of AI tools. In response, this study introduced a set of guidelines aimed at helping both students and teachers alike to overcome the common pitfalls of incorporating AI in programming courses. These guidelines highlight the need to share recognized best practices among students and teachers and to encourage critical thinking toward data produced by

AI. Furthermore, one should always keep in mind that AI is—in essence—a tool, with its own limitations and possibilities, and not a silver bullet that can solve every problem in existence. And, as with any tool, it is important to learn how to use it properly.

References

1. Becker, B.A., Denny, P., Finnie-Ansley, J., Luxton-Reilly, A., Prather, J., Santos, E.A.: Programming Is Hard - Or at Least It Used to Be, vol. 1, pp. 500–506. ACM, New York (2023). https://doi.org/10.1145/3545945.3569759, https://dl.acm.org/doi/10.1145/3545945.3569759
2. Carreira, G., Silva, L., Mendes, A.J., Oliveira, H.G.: Pyo, a Chatbot Assistant for Introductory Programming Students, pp. 1–6. IEEE, Piscataway (2022). https://doi.org/10.1109/SIIE56031.2022.9982349, https://ieeexplore.ieee.org/document/9982349/
3. Chan, C.K.Y.: A comprehensive AI policy education framework for university teaching and learning. Int. J. Educ. Technol. Higher Educ. **20**(1), 38 (2023). https://doi.org/10.1186/s41239-023-00408-3
4. Denny, P., Leinonen, J., Prather, J., Luxton-Reilly, A., Amarouche, T., Becker, B.A., Reeves, B.N.: Promptly: using prompt problems to teach learners how to effectively utilize AI code generators (2023). http://arxiv.org/abs/2307.16364
5. Ismail, M., Ade-Ibijola, A.: Lecturer's Apprentice: A Chatbot for Assisting Novice Programmers, pp. 1–8. IEEE, Piscataway (2019). https://doi.org/10.1109/IMITEC45504.2019.9015857, https://ieeexplore.ieee.org/document/9015857/
6. Johri, A., Lindsay, E., Qadir, J.: Ethical concerns and responsible use of generative artificial intelligence in engineering education. In: Proceedings of the SEFI 2023 51st Annual Conference, 11.-14.9 2023, Dublin (2023)
7. Kiesler, N., Schiffner, D.: Large language models in introductory programming education: ChatGPT's performance and implications for assessments (2023). http://arxiv.org/abs/2308.08572
8. Luger, E., Sellen, A.: Like Having a Really Bad PA, pp. 5286–5297. ACM, New York (2016). https://doi.org/10.1145/2858036.2858288, https://dl.acm.org/doi/10.1145/2858036.2858288
9. Mhlanga, D.: Open AI in education, the responsible and ethical use of ChatGPT towards lifelong learning. SSRN Electron. J. (2023). https://doi.org/10.2139/ssrn.4354422, https://www.ssrn.com/abstract=4354422
10. Nguyen, A., Ngo, H.N., Hong, Y., Dang, B., Nguyen, B.P.T.: Ethical principles for artificial intelligence in education. Educ. Inf. Technol. **28**, 4221–4241 (2023). https://doi.org/10.1007/s10639-022-11316-w, https://link.springer.com/10.1007/s10639-022-11316-w
11. Pankiewicz, M., Baker, R.S.: Large language models (GPT) for automating feedback on programming assignments (2023). http://arxiv.org/abs/2307.00150
12. Puig-Ortiz, J., Pá mies-Vilá, R., Jordi Nebot, L.: Exploring the application of ChatGPT in mechanical engineering education. In: Proceedings of the SEFI 2023 51st Annual Conference, 11.-14.9 2023, Dublin (2023)
13. Robinson, D.: How Do Students Use Stack Overflow? (2017). https://stackoverflow.blog/2017/02/15/how-do-students-use-stack-overflow/. Last accessed 29 Mar 2023
14. Saari, M., Rantanen, P., Nurminen, M., Kilamo, T., Systä, K., Abrahamsson, P.: Survey of AI tool usage in programming course: early observations. In: Agile Processes in Software Engineering and Extreme Programming – Workshops. Springer, Cham (2024)
15. Savelka, J., Agarwal, A., Bogart, C., Song, Y., Sakr, M.: Can generative pre-trained transformers (GPT) pass assessments in higher education programming courses? (2023). https://doi.org/10.1145/3587102.3588792, http://arxiv.org/abs/2303.09325

16. UNESCO survey: Less than 10 on AI, https://www.unesco.org/en/articles/unesco-survey-less-10-schools-and-universities-have-formal-guidance-ai. Accessed 29 Sep 2023
17. Verleger, M., Pembridge, J.: A Pilot Study Integrating an AI-driven Chatbot in an Introductory Programming Course, pp. 1–4. IEEE, Piscataway (2018). https://doi.org/10.1109/FIE.2018.8659282, https://ieeexplore.ieee.org/document/8659282/
18. Zastudil, C., Rogalska, M., Kapp, C., Vaughn, J., MacNeil, S.: Generative AI in computing education: perspectives of students and instructors (2023). http://arxiv.org/abs/2308.04309

Printed in the United States
by Baker & Taylor Publisher Services